# Puttin' On

## Din

**THE JUNIOR LEAGUE OF DEKALB COUNTY, GEORGIA**

*20th Anniversary Edition*

**The Junior League of DeKalb County** is an organization of women committed to promoting voluntarism, developing the potential of women and improving communities through the effective action and leadership of trained volunteers. Its purpose is exclusively educational and charitable.

**Affiliated with the Association of Junior Leagues International**, the Junior League of DeKalb County reaches out to women of all races, religions and national origins who demonstrate an interest in and commitment to voluntarism.

The cover design has been donated to the Junior League of DeKalb County by a former League member, Ellen Cavendish Phillips. Ellen graduated with a degree in Art and Biology from Agnes Scott College in Decatur, Ga. After college, Ellen taught art classes and continued to paint and exhibit her own work. Ellen has received innumerable awards and honors, including a commission from the DeKalb Chamber of Commerce to paint a portrait of Hank Aaron commemorating the 25th anniversary of his historic home run. Continuing in the League tradition, Ellen remains very active in her community.

The scene depicted by Ellen Phillips is of the Junior League of DeKalb's headquarters, The Mary Gay House. The house was once the home of a Southern heroine and author, Mary Ann Harris Gay. Her firsthand accounts of the Civil War are chronicled in her book, *Life in Dixie During the War*. They include her dangerous journey through enemy lines to deliver Northern newspapers borrowed from Yankee occupationists and uniforms to the Confederates. The house was built around 1820 and placed on the National Register of Historic Places in 1975. The house is available for rent for special occasions.

*Puttin' on the Peachtree. Dining in. Atlanta Style.*
The Junior League of DeKalb County, Georgia, Inc.

| | | | | | |
|---|---|---|---|---|---|
| 1st edition | Sept. 1979 | 20,000 | 5th edition | Jun. 1986 | 20,000 |
| 2nd edition | Dec. 1980 | 20,000 | 6th edition | May 1991 | 15,000 |
| 3rd edition | Apr. 1982 | 20,000 | 7th edition | Jan. 1999 | 15,000 |
| 4th edition | Mar. 1984 | 20,000 | | | |

ISBN 0-9618508-2-5

Printed in the USA by

WIMMER
The Wimmer Companies
Memphis
1-800-548-2537

# Table of Contents

# Original Cookbook Committee
# 1979

**Chair**
Elise Griffin

**Co-Chair**
Barrie Aycock

**Committee**

Joan Adams
Molly Ahlquist
Susan Barton
Emy Blair
Billie Bothwell
Phyllis Kennedy

Terry Morris
Susan Morley
Jane Nardone
Sandra Pritchett
Julia Ray
Sallie Smith

The success of this cookbook is credited to the support of many dedicated volunteers who have given of their expertise and enthusiasm. To name all these would be impossible. Thus in special mention, we list below the cookbook chairs in order as they have served since the original printing of *Puttin' on the Peachtree* in 1979:

Elise Griffin
Barrie Aycock
Winnie Goodman
Connie Panter
Sandy Jernigan
Terri Goldstein
Marge Carter
Chris Kendrick
Pattie Tuggle
Sally Maloof
Lynne Lock

Susan Roberson
Kathy Mulling
Barbara Williams
Betsy Menneg
Carolyn Yelton
Caroline Miller
Renee Swaim
Cathie Jones
Laurie McDowell
Sandra Smith
Montie Stone

# History of the
# Junior League of DeKalb County

Every purchase of *Puttin' on the Peachtree* helps the Junior League of DeKalb improve lives, especially for women and children, locally and nationally. Our organization, which started in 1934 with only 16 members, now includes 500 volunteer members contributing 40,000 hours of service annually.

Since its founding, JLD has taken a project-oriented approach to solving the problems of the day. The first project, the Children's Milk Fund, led the way to organizing medical, dental and hearing clinics in the 1940s. The 1950s saw the development of a Children's Emergency Shelter and a hospital for DeKalb County. Historic preservation was a prominent project area in the 1960s and 1970s. In the last two decades, the women of JLD have unflinchingly taken on the sensitive issues of rape and domestic violence.

Today, the Junior League of DeKalb is a strong voice of leadership throughout the state. Through time, money and advocacy, we work to:

- Prevent and lessen the effects of violence against women and children through the establishment of the DeKalb Rape Crisis Center and the International Women's House and support of the DeKalb Children's Emergency Shelter.
- Improve educational and recreational opportunities for children, most recently by awarding Mini-grants to schoolteachers annually.
- Encourage the arts and historic preservation. In addition to our affiliation with the DeKalb Historical Society, JLD has restored the Mary Gay House and helped establish Callanwolde Fine Arts Center and the Spruill Arts Center.
- Aid organizations promoting health care by our current and past volunteer involvement with Egleston Children's Hospital, Scottish Rite Children's Medical Center, Senior Connections and Wesley Woods Geriatric Center. A past project included establishing the DeKalb General Hospital Auxiliary.

With such a rich history of service, our future is limitless. Our members are committed to helping others with enthusiasm and innovative ideas. The Junior League of DeKalb County will continue to be on the forefront, meeting the needs of our communities.

In addition to the rewards of great dining, we hope you will enjoy knowing that you have become a participant in our success. We could not do it without your support.

**Thank you—and bon appétit!**

# Introduction

Our forebearers brought to this country a knowledge of sensible, life-sustaining food. They combined that knowledge with the bounty from the Georgia soil and called it "Southern Cooking".

The native Indians added appreciation of the gifts of woods and waters.

Country folks taught us that good food shared with good friends is reason enough for a celebration.

Shy mountain women proved to us that food speaks clearly of love when the tongue cannot.

City sophisticates helped us find creative expression in cooking for the sheer fun of it.

As Atlanta grew from country crossroad beginnings to become the major city of the New South, people from every corner of the world came to share the spirit of this always new city. Each individual brings a totally unique culinary heritage, whether an exotic ingredient from some faraway place or simply "the way Mama always did it." Formerly foreign words, curry and cumin, pita and pasta, stir-fry and strudel, have become common kitchen vocabulary. We still call it Southern Cooking because the basic Southern components of freshness, abundance and hospitality are always present!

We invite people into our homes to mark special occasions or we simply share the warm companionship of time and food together. Whatever our reasons for entertaining, food shared with friends must be our best; cooked with love, served with style.

Wherever you cook, there's a phrase for it:
In the city, it's puttin' on the ritz.
In the country, it's puttin' on the dog.
In some places in between, it's puttin' on your best bib and
    tucker.
In Atlanta, it's PUTTIN' ON THE PEACHTREE!
It speaks of entertaining people you care about and doing it
    well.
It's Dining In. Atlanta Style.

# Menus for all Occasions

No matter what the occasion, every meal can be cause for puttin' on the peachtree. Whether you are preparing an elegant dinner, an outdoor barbeque or a dish for the family reunion, the following menu suggestions will make the event special as well as delicious!

# Exceptionally Elegant

In Atlanta, Georgia, where gracious parties and meals have not gone by the wayside, style is almost as important as taste. The perfect menu can turn an ordinary evening into a gala affair.

### New Year's Eve Cocktail Buffet

Caviar and Artichokes     p. 6
Quiche Hors D'oeuvres     p. 13
Veggies with Vegetable Party Dip     p. 13
Stuffed Mushrooms     p. 18
Baked Cheese Sandwiches     p. 28
Shrimp Arnaud     p. 25
Ham Biscuits with Mustard Spread     p. 19
Cranberry Nut Muffins     p. 247
Cheese Marmalade Tarts     p. 8

### Dinner Club

Kir     p. 34
Artichoke Mixed Salad     p. 190
Tournedos in Puff Pastry     p. 93
Crunchy Asparagus     p. 152
Mushroom Stuffed Tomatoes     p. 176
Devonshire Cream     p. 264

### Concert in the Park

Dill Weed Dip for Veggies     p. 12
Bleu Cheese Slaw     p. 200
Baked Ham     p. 118
Chilled Lemon Broccoli     p. 159
Baps     p. 234
Sangria     p. 32
Pecan Tassies     p. 302
Chocolate Macaroons     p. 300

# All-Star Southern

In keeping with our Southern heritage, great meals need to include lots of fresh veggies, enjoyed out-of-doors before the big game or as the main event. Some of y'all may not know that we Southerners take football and barbeque as seriously as our food.

### A Winning Tailgate Party

### Get Your Vegetables

### Simply Southern Supper

# Just Like Family

Family is the core of Southern culture, and nothing brings the family closer together than the dinner table. After all, who better to enjoy your home cookin' than those you love the most?

### Lazy Summer Supper

Vegetable Party Dip with French Bread    p. 13
Summer Pasta    p. 72
Darvish Salad    p. 194
"The" Strawberry Pie    p. 296

### Autumn Celebration

Pork Tenderloin Lorraine    p. 113
Easter Potato Casserole    p. 171
"Skinny" Green Beans    p. 155
Apple Cream Pie    p. 294

### For Mom on Mother's Day

Banana Bites    p. 4
Grilled Ham Slice    p. 116
The Potato    p. 170
Sliced Tomatoes
Cottage Coconut Pie    p. 292

### Dad's Backyard  Picnic

Charcoaled Flank Steak    p. 96
Onion Pie    p. 166
Hot Bean Salad    p. 193
Beer Bread    p. 235
Peach Custard Pie    p. 293

### Treats (No Tricks) for Grownups

Chips & Guacamole Dip    p. 12
Homestyle "Boursin" and Crackers    p. 5
Asparagus Bites    p. 3
Emergency Tuna Pate    p. 15
Hot Dogs Creole    p. 118
Pumpkin Cheesecake    p. 283
Hot Spiced Wine    p. 33

# Wedding Weekend

Although the actual wedding ceremony may only last a few minutes, the events last several days and include many meals. The guests from near and far come to see the nuptials, and the food can often be the center of the celebration.

### Showered with Compliments

Fresh fruit with Dip for Fruit     p. 12
Mystery Canapes     p. 15
Shrimp Mold     p. 27
Baked Cheese Sandwiches     p. 28
Ethel Mincey's Punch     p. 31
Chinese Almond Cakes     p. 314
Pineapple Torte     p. 270

### Ladies Luncheon

Hot Cheese Puffs     p. 9
Crunchy Pea Salad     p. 198
Crab Stuffed Chicken     p. 124
Tomato Lemon Aspic     p. 185
Sour Cream Rolls     p. 233
Bourbon Slush     p. 29
Sherman Strikes Again     p. 271

### The Rehearsal Dinner

Raspberry Apéritif     p. 34
Party Casserole     p. 129
Herb Rice Blend     p. 65
Six Vegetable Medley     p. 179
Chocolate Mousse     p. 281
Irish Coffee     p. 30

### Brunch for a Bunch

Sacramento Fruit Bowl     p. 183
Sausage Quiche     p. 58
Blintz Casserole     p. 59
Monterey Fondue Casserole     p. 59
German Butterkuchen     p. 248

The reprint committee would like to thank Susan Barton, Fran Scott, and Carroll Ball for providing the menus.

# Guidelines for Healthy Eating

Your favorite recipes can be modified to make them more nutritious or lower in fat by reducing or substituting ingredients that are more acceptable. Test new ways to decrease the amount of fat, calories, sugar and salt in your recipes. Remember that recipes are only guidelines, not rules, for preparing food. Don't be afraid to experiment.

**The Food Pyramid.** The USDA recommends that Americans eat healthier by using their suggestions for daily servings of the following:

6–11 Servings of grain
3–5 servings of vegetables        2–4 servings of fruit
2–3 servings of dairy products
2–3 servings of meat, fish, eggs, nuts
using sparing amounts of fats, oils and sweets

**Calories.** To maintain your ideal weight you can estimate the number of calories allowed daily. Simply multiply your ideal weight (be realistic) by 13 if you are moderately active and by 15 if you are very active.

**Fat.** Only 30 percent of your total daily calories should come from fat. If you take your daily calorie intake, drop the last digit and then divide by 3, and you will have the recommended fat allowance.

**Sodium and Cholesterol.** The Recommended Daily Dietary Allowances (for healthy adults over 25) are no more than 2,400 mg sodium (this equals about $\frac{1}{2}$ to $1\frac{1}{2}$ teaspoons of salt) and no more than 300 mg cholesterol.

# Substitutions

- 2 egg whites or egg substitute = 1 whole egg
- Use graham cracker or chocolate cookie crumb crusts in recipes that call for a higher fat pastry dough crust.
- Instead of chocolate chips or nuts, use raisins.
- Instead of ground beef, use ground round or LEAN ground turkey.
- Use $\frac{1}{2}$ prune or banana puree for butter or margarine in baking and cooking.
- Use corn oil, canola oil and peanut oil. To substitute liquid oil for solid fats, use about $\frac{1}{4}$ less than called for in the recipe.
- To decrease the amount of sodium in your foods, use low sodium or unsalted ingredients in your recipes.
- Reduce sugar by $\frac{1}{4}$ to $\frac{1}{3}$ in baked goods. Substitute flour for the omitted sugar. Adding cardamon, cinnamon, nutmeg or vanilla to your recipes will enhance the impression of sweetness.
- To increase fiber, choose whole grain for part of your ingredients instead of highly refined products using whole wheat flour, oatmeal and whole cornmeal. Whole wheat flour can be substituted for up to $\frac{1}{2}$ of all purpose flour.
- Use plain lowfat or nonfat yogurt instead of sour cream. You can also substitute buttermilk or blended lowfat cottage cheese.
- Use skim milk or 1% milk instead of whole milk or half and half. For extra richness, try evaporated skim milk.

# Cooking Techniques

- Cooking methods: Bake, broil, poach, microwave or steam foods instead of frying.
- Seasoning: Use herbs, juices, and vinegar instead of fats for flavoring.
- Saute in water, juice, broth, or use nonstick vegetable spray.
- Make soups, sauces and gravies ahead of time, refrigerate and skim the hardened fat off the top before reheating.
- Thicken sauces, gravies, stews and soups with pureed vegetables. Try cooked winter squash, potatoes, dried beans and peas, carrots and cauliflower.

# Healthy Shopping

- Choose skim milk, low fat cheeses, low fat versions of sour cream and mayonnaise.
- Choose leaner cuts of meat (like tenderloin, top round or flank steak) instead of fatty, marbled varieties (like rib roast, T-bone and ground chuck).
- Choose more dark green and dark yellow vegetables.
- Fresh or frozen vegetables have less added salt than canned.

Sources:   USDA
National Institutes of Health
American Heart Association
American Diabetes Association

## Almond Bacon Cheese Spread

½ cup diced almonds
4 strips bacon, crisply cooked
   and crumbled
2 cups grated American
   cheese, packed
4 Tablespoons chopped green
   onion
1 cup mayonnaise
½ teaspoon salt

Mix ingredients thoroughly. Chill to enhance flavors in a covered container. May be prepared the day before serving. 2½ cups

JoAnn P. Whitehead (Mrs. Harry C.)

## Antipasto Spread
Serve this as a first course

½ cup butter
12 ounces tomato paste
5 ounces cocktail onions
   and juice
4 ounces sliced canned
   mushrooms, drained
14 ounces tuna, drained
1 chopped dill pickle
8 ounces shrimp, cooked
   and chopped
6 ounces green olives with
   pimientos, sliced
¼ cup dry red wine (Burgundy
   or Bordeaux)
¼ cup beer
1 Tablespoon sugar
Dash crushed basil
Dash paprika
14 ounces cherry peppers,
   seeds removed, chopped

Melt butter. Combine all ingredients and chill several hours. May be served with wheat crackers, melba toast, or as first course on a lettuce bed.

Susan M. Morley

# Asparagus Bites

1 (8 ounce) package cream
   cheese, softened
4 ounces blue cheese,
   crumbled
1 egg, well beaten
1 can asparagus spears,
   drained
Thin sliced white bread
2 sticks butter or margarine,
   melted

Mix cream cheese with blue cheese and add egg. Count number of asparagus spears in can; count out same number of slices of bread. Trim crusts from bread. Roll trimmed bread as thin as possible with rolling pin. Spread each slice of bread with cheese and egg mixture. Place asparagus spear on each bread slice and roll up. Cut each rolled slice into thirds. Dip each roll into melted butter. Place close together in shallow baking pan. May be frozen at this stage. Bake at 400° for 15-20 minutes if not frozen. Bake 30 minutes or until browned if frozen. 8-10 servings

**Ruth D. Hardy (Mrs. Wallace E.)**

# Artichoke Spread

1 can artichoke hearts (6-8 in
   can—not marinated)
1 cup mayonnaise
1 cup grated Parmesan cheese
Dash garlic powder

Drain artichoke hearts well; chop. Mix with mayonnaise, cheese and garlic powder. Bake in an oven-proof casserole at 350° for 25 to 30 minutes. Serve with crackers. Ingredients may be mixed ahead and baked later but not frozen.

**Joan M. Adams (Mrs. John P., Jr.)**

## HINT

If substituting fresh herbs for dried, use 3 or 4 times as much. Add herbs at same time as salt and pepper to meats, vegetables, sauces, and soups. In long-cooking foods, such as stews, add herbs during last half hour of cooking time.

# Hot Stuffed Avocado

3 large or 4 small avocadoes, peeled
Lemon juice to coat
6-8 Tablespoons vinegar or lemon juice
6-8 cloves garlic
2 Tablespoons butter
2 Tablespoons flour
1 cup light cream
1 Tablespoon grated onion
¼ teaspoon celery salt
Salt and pepper to taste
2 cups cooked Alaskan crab, shrimp, lobster or chicken
½ cup grated sharp cheddar cheese

Roll outside of peeled avocado in lemon juice to preserve color. Cut avocados in half. Remove pits and place 1 Tablespoon vinegar or lemon juice and clove of garlic in each half. Let stand 30 minutes. Meanwhile, melt butter and blend in flour. Add cream and stir over heat until thickened. Add grated onion, spices and meat. Pour vinegar and garlic from avocado and fill with meat mixture. Sprinkle with cheese and place in baking dish filled with ½-inch of water. Bake 15 minutes at 350°. 6 servings

**Cookbook Committee**

# Banana Bites

Cut bananas into 1 inch lengths. Dip in thawed lemonade concentrate (undiluted). Roll in fine flake toasted coconut. Serve on toothpicks.

Variation: Omit lemonade and roll slices in wheat germ, coating well. Freeze. Serve frozen on toothpicks.

**Agnes Siebert (Mrs. "Sam")**

# Beer Cheese Dip

½-1 cup beer, boiled and cooled
3 (6 ounce) rolls Kraft nippy cheese
1¼ ounces Roquefort cheese
2 Tablespoons butter
1 medium onion
2 cloves garlic
1 teaspoon Worcestershire sauce
½ teaspoon Tabasco
1 loaf Rye bread (round)

Put all ingredients into a blender (add beer carefully so as not to let mixture be too runny). Blend until smooth. Hollow out a loaf of Rye bread; cut the hollowed out portions into cubes. Cubes may be toasted in oven if desired. Pour dip into Rye loaf. Dip cubes into loaf.
10-12 servings

**Judy Scheidt (Mrs. Kenneth A.)**

## Homestyle "Boursin"

8 ounces whipped butter,
  softened
16 ounces cream cheese,
  softened
2 cloves garlic, mashed or
  pressed
½ teaspoon oregano
¼ teaspoon basil
¼ teaspoon dill weed
¼ teaspoon marjoram
¼ teaspoon black pepper
¼ teaspoon thyme

Mix all ingredients thoroughly
in electric mixer. Refrigerate
overnight to blend flavors. Serve
at room temperature with assorted
mild crackers. Keeps well and
can be frozen.

**Tippi Lassiter**

## Marinated Broccoli
Beautiful served in a crystal bowl

1 cup cider vinegar
1 Tablespoon sugar
1 Tablespoon dill weed
1 Tablespoon MSG
1 teaspoon salt
1 teaspoon pepper
1 teaspoon garlic salt
1½ cups vegetable oil
3 bunches broccoli, broken
  into flowerettes

Combine ingredients and
marinate for 24 hours. 12 servings

**Pat W. Engel (Mrs. John D.)**

## Clara's Crab

2 (6-ounce) packages frozen
  crabmeat, thawed and
  drained
3 hard boiled eggs, chopped
Juice of ½ lemon
1 teaspoon Worcestershire
  sauce
2 green onions, white and
  green parts, chopped
¾ cup (or more) mayonnaise
Salt, and cayenne pepper
  to taste

Break up crabmeat and add
seasonings. Toss lightly with
mayonnaise. Serve with crackers,
or stuffed in tomatoes for a
delightful cold appetizer. 2 cups

**Nancy Wactor (Mrs. William R.)**

# Caponata
### (Italian Eggplant Relish)

2 medium eggplants (about 2 pounds)
Salt
½ cup olive oil
1 medium onion, finely chopped
2 large stalks celery, thinly sliced
½ cup wine vinegar
½ cup tomato purée
1 Tablespoon sugar
½ cup capers
6 large green olives, sliced or about 2 Tablespoons sliced salad olives
Salt and pepper to taste

Cut off ends of eggplant. Cut unpeeled eggplant into ¾ inch cubes. Place in a colander. Sprinkle with salt and let eggplant remain for about 20 minutes until much of the liquid has been drawn from them. In a non-stick pan, heat olive oil and brown eggplant cubes lightly. Place in a colander over a bowl to drain. Cook onion and celery in remaining oil in pan over low heat until soft, not brown. Pour wine vinegar over onions and celery and let steam covered a few minutes until liquid evaporates. Return eggplant to pan and combine with onion and celery. Blend sugar, and tomato purée into the eggplant mixture. Add capers, olives, pepper and salt to taste. Let relish heat through. May be frozen. Serve cool as an antipasto, appetizer or main course accompaniment.

**Mrs. August J. Nardone**

# Caviar and Artichokes
### Elegant appetizer for a small dinner party

1 can marinated artichoke hearts, drained
4 hard boiled eggs
4 green onions
1 small jar black caviar
Mayonnaise

Finely chop artichokes, eggs and onions in separate bowls. In small bowl (1 quart or less) layer in following order: ½ of eggs, artichokes, caviar, onions and mayonnaise. Repeat layer. Chill. Unmold and serve with crackers. Must be prepared the day before serving to allow flavors to blend. 8 servings

**Jane G. Skelton (Mrs. Douglas)**

# Cha Gio
## Vietnamese Spring Roll

1 package spring roll skins
  from Oriental grocery store;
  soak in water before use
1½ pounds ground pork
½ pound shrimp, peeled and
  deveined
1 small bundle bean threads
  (cellophane noodles)
1 raw egg
1 bunch green onions
4 cloves garlic
6-8 mushrooms (dried or fresh)
2 carrots, shredded
2 teaspoons fish sauce or soy
  sauce
Peanut or vegetable oil
SAUCE:
Fish sauce or soy sauce to
  taste
Water
Sugar

Finely dice all vegetables except carrots, which have been shredded. Soak noodles until they expand. Mix ingredients together. Place 2 Tablespoons of the mixture on each skin, turn ends up and roll. Fry in vegetable oil until crisp. Dip in sauce to serve.

Sauce: Blend fish sauce or soy sauce, with water and sugar to taste.

**Sharon Samford**

# Champignon Schnitte

2 Tablespoons butter
1 pound fresh mushrooms,
  sliced
2 medium onions, chopped
Salt to taste
1-2 loaves cocktail size rye
  or pumpernickel bread
1 (12-ounce) package grated
  Swiss cheese
1 cup grated Parmesan cheese

Melt butter in large frying pan. Add mushrooms and onion. Cook until onions are soft and mushrooms are beginning to turn brown. Add salt. Remove from heat. Spread mixture on slice of bread using 1 Tablespoon per slice. Arrange in baking pan. Sprinkle Swiss cheese liberally over slices; then sprinkle with Parmesan cheese. Broil until cheese melts and lightly browns. Remove and serve immediately. May be frozen. Thaw and broil.
40 pieces

**Camille T. Allen (Mrs. Julian D.)**

## Cheese Marmalade Tarts

1 (4-ounce) jar Old English
  Cheddar Cheese
1 cup plus 2 Tablespoons
  sifted flour
1 stick margarine
2 Tablespoons cold water
Orange marmalade

Cut margarine and cheese into flour as for pastry. Mix with water and shape into a ball, or place margarine, cheese and flour in food processor and process for 10 seconds; add water and process until a ball is formed. Put in wax paper and refrigerate overnight. Roll dough and cut into 3-inch circles on a floured board (the rim of a can works well for this). Put approximately ½ teaspoon marmalade onto center of each circle and fold over. Dampen edges with water to seal and press down with tines of a fork. Prick a few holes in the top. Bake at 375° for 10 minutes. May be prepared ahead or frozen. Wonderful to pass at cocktail party. 20 servings

**Linda D. Bobo (Mrs. W. Earl)**

## Curried Cheese Ball with Fresh Pears

3 fresh Anjou, Boxc or Comice
  pears
1 (8-ounce) package cream
  cheese, softened
2 Tablespoons powdered sugar
½ teaspoon curry powder
⅓ cup flaked coconut
⅓ cup chopped pecans
Maraschino cherry for garnish

Refrigerate pears. Combine cream cheese, sugar, curry powder, coconut, and half of the pecans. Mix with hands, or in a food processor, process for 15 seconds or until smooth. Wrap in plastic wrap and refrigerate until firm. Press remaining pecans on cheese ball and garnish with a maraschino cherry. To serve, core and slice pears into wedges; use cheese as a spread for wedges; serve as an appetizer or dessert. 8 servings

**JoAnn P. Whitehead (Mrs. Harry C.)**

# Hot Cheese Puffs
An easy cocktail party food

2 egg whites
½ teaspoon baking powder
¼ teaspoon salt
¼ teaspoon paprika
½ cup sharp grated Cheddar
  cheese
Toast rounds, sautéed on
  one side in butter
Bacon, cooked, drained and
  crumbled

Beat egg whites until stiff. Beat in baking powder, salt and paprika. Fold in cheese. Heap onto toast rounds, dry side down. Broil 4 or 5 minutes until brown. Sprinkle with bacon.

Mrs. Ellis H. Taylor

# Hot Crab and Cheese Crackers

1 (6½-ounce) can crab, drained
  and checked for shells
1 Tablespoon minced onion
1 cup shredded sharp Cheddar
  cheese
1-2 Tablespoons mayonnaise
Paprika
Melba toast rounds

Mix all ingredients. When ready to serve, spread on melba toast rounds, sprinkle with paprika and broil until bubbly. 6-8 servings

Pat W. Engel (Mrs. John D.)

# Crab Meat Hot Dip

3 (8 ounce) packages
  Philadelphia cream cheese
2 (6½ ounce) cans crab meat
  and juice, checked for
  shells
2 cloves garlic, crushed
½ cup mayonnaise
2 teaspoons prepared mustard
½ cup sherry
1 teaspoon onion juice
Lawry's seasoned salt

Heat all ingredients together in a double boiler until well blended and cheese is melted. Refrigerate. Reheat before serving. Serve in a chafing dish or fondue pot. Serve with plain crackers, not salted crackers or chips. 20 servings

Beverly Bibent (Mrs. Maury J.)
Cincinnati, Ohio

# Chicken Bites with Sauce
Unusual and delicious

3 whole chicken breasts, boned
Small amount of butter or
  margarine
1 cup sour cream
½ cup mayonnaise
¼ cup chili sauce
2 Tablespoons horseradish
1 Tablespoon Worcestershire
  sauce
2 Tablespoons lemon juice
¼ teaspoon Tabasco
1 teaspoon curry powder
2 Tablespoons chutney,
  finely minced
4 Tablespoons capers
2 Tablespoons chopped parsley

Cut chicken breasts into bite sized pieces and place in a pan with a small amount of butter or margarine. Cover with a sheet of wax paper and place in a 400° oven for 6-8 minutes. They are done if they spring back when pressed with a finger. Combine chicken with all other ingredients. Refrigerate several hours or overnight. To serve, pile in the center of a serving dish surrounded by lettuce leaves. Sprinkle with additional parsley and capers. Serve with toothpicks. 6 servings

**Robbin A. Churchill (Mrs. John S.)**
*Jacksonville, Florida*

# Chicken Liver Pâté

½ pound chicken livers
1 teaspoon salt
Pinch cayenne pepper
1 stick butter
¼ teaspoon nutmeg
1 teaspoon dry mustard
⅛ teaspoon ground cloves
2 Tablespoons finely minced
  onions
1 large clove garlic, crushed

Barely cover chicken livers with water and bring to a boil. Reduce heat, cover and simmer 15 to 20 minutes. Drain and put in blender or food processor. Mix with remaining ingredients. Blend well. Pack in crock or jar and refrigerate at least 24 hours before serving. Pâté may be frozen at this point. Serve with crackers or French bread.

**Lynn H. Barnes**

HINT ■■■■■■■■■■■■■■■■■■■■■■■■■■■■

To mince parsley easily, bunch the leafy tops together and cut with scissors into a measuring cup. Then to mince finer, put scissors in the cup and snip away.

# Deviled Clams

¼ pound butter
3 medium onions, chopped
2 green bell peppers, chopped
2 (6½ ounce) cans minced
    clams and juice
1 teaspoon curry powder
Dry bread crumbs
4 slices bacon

Sauté onions and peppers in butter in covered pan until tender. Add clams, juice and curry powder. Stir in enough bread crumbs to thicken. Place in individual baking shells. Top with ½ slice bacon. Pour small amount of water in pan around shells to keep shells from becoming too hot. Bake at 400° until bacon is crisp, about 20 minutes. May be prepared in advance and baked when ready to serve. 6 servings

**Mr. H. Malcolm Teare**

# Curry Dip

½ cup mayonnaise
1 cup sour cream
2 Tablespoons lemon juice
1 teaspoon curry powder
½ teaspoon paprika
2 Tablespoons minced parsley
½ teaspoon tarragon
2 Tablespoons grated onion
2 teaspoons prepared mustard
1 Tablespoon minced chives
Dash Tabasco
Dash salt and pepper

Combine all ingredients in a quart size covered container. Refrigerate at least 24 hours before serving. Will keep for several days in the refrigerator. Serve with carrots, celery, cucumbers, mushrooms, yellow squash or cauliflower. 1 quart

**Nancy W. Jones (Mrs. Edmund W.)**

# Cheese-Ground Beef Dip

½ pound ground beef
½ pound Velveeta cheese
½ pound sharp Cheddar
    cheese
1 roll garlic cheese
1 egg
1 cup green chilies and
    tomatoes, chopped
Tabasco to taste

Brown and drain ground beef. Melt cheeses in top of double boiler. Add all other ingredients. Serve hot with Dorito chips.

**Mrs. Gary Hays**

# Dip for Fruit

1 cup sour cream
1 Tablespoon gelatin
¼ cup sugar
½ teaspoon vanilla
1 cup heavy cream, whipped
Bite size pieces of fruit

In bowl of double boiler over hot water, mix sour cream, gelatin and sugar until gelatin dissolves and sugar melts. Stir in vanilla. Cool mixture. Fold in whipped cream. Refrigerate until ready to use.

**Sidney Murphey (Mrs. William)**

# Guacamole Dip
Delicious in sandwiches
or as a dip with corn chips or fresh vegetables

2 very ripe avocados
½ cup sour cream
Juice of 1 lime
1 clove garlic, crushed
Salt and freshly ground pepper
   to taste
3 Tablespoons Jalapeno relish

Scoop out avocado meat. Mash in a non-metal bowl with remaining ingredients. It should be a very rough puree. Cover closely with plastic wrap and refrigerate until ready to use.

**Susan L. Kreitzman**
*"In Good Taste" School of Cookery*

# Dill Weed Dip

1 cup sour cream
⅓ cup mayonnaise
1 Tablespoon shredded green
   onion
1 Tablespoon dried parsley
1 teaspoon dill weed
1 teaspoon Beau Monde
   seasoning

Combine ingredients and chill. Serve with chips or vegetables.

**Pat Brasher**
*San Antonio, Texas*

**MICROWAVE HINT** ■■■■■■■■■■■■

To separate slices of cold bacon easily, heat package for a few seconds.

# Raw Spinach Dip

1 package chopped frozen
   spinach
½ cup dehydrated parsley
   flakes
½ cup chopped green onions
2 Tablespoons Salad Supreme
½ Tablespoon dill seed
1 cup mayonnaise

Thaw spinach and squeeze in cheesecloth. Combine spinach with rest of the ingredients. Refrigerate at least 3 hours; may be prepared 1 or 2 days in advance. Serving suggestions: Serve as a dip with corn chips, fill hollowed-out cherry tomatoes with dip, or place a dollop of dip on a thick slice of tomato and heat.

# Vegetable Party Dip

1 cup mayonnaise
1 teaspoon tarragon vinegar
1 teaspoon horseradish
⅛ teaspoon black pepper
1½ teaspoon curry powder

Mix all ingredients together until smooth. Refrigerate one hour before using. Serve with crisp vegetables. 1 cup

**Nancy Kirby (Mrs. Jeff D., III)**

# Quiche Hors D'oeuvres

2 pie shells
Melted butter
2 large onions, thinly sliced
1 (6-ounce) can sliced
   mushrooms
1 pound grated Swiss cheese
2 Tablespoons flour
3 eggs
1¼ cups milk
1 teaspoon salt
½ teaspoon pepper
Dash nutmeg

Prick pie shells. Cook 10 minutes at 375°. Cook the onions until tender in melted butter and divide between the shells. Divide the mushrooms between the shells. Toss grated cheese with flour and sprinkle over each pie. Mix eggs, milk, salt, pepper and nutmeg. Pour over ingredients in pie shells. Bake at 400° for 20 minutes, then at 300° for 25 minutes. Let stand until cool. Cut in small wedges or squares and serve immediately. Can be frozen. 4 dozen

**Julia W. Ray (Mrs. Frederick C.)**

# Escargots a la Bourguignonne

3 dozen canned snails
3 dozen shells
½ pound butter
3 Tablespoons finely chopped
    parsley
2 Tablespoons finely chopped
    shallots
1 clove garlic, crushed
¼ teaspoon salt
Freshly ground black pepper
French bread

Wash and drain snails. Wash, drain and dry shells. In small mixing bowl, cream butter until soft using a wooden spoon. Add parsley, shallots, garlic, salt and pepper. Mix well. Insert a snail in each shell, pushing it as far as it will go with finger. Fill shell with butter mixture. Place snails in special snail dishes or in flat baking dish with open ends up. Place any leftover butter mixture around snails. Bake at 425° for 10 minutes until hot and bubbly. Serve at once with French bread and white wine. Butter mixture may be made in advance and stuffed into shells just before baking. 6 servings

**Kimpy Edge (Mrs. J. Dexter)**

# Escargots
Serve in shells, in mushroom caps, or on toast rounds

2 dozen snails, drained
2 cups boiling water
2-3 beef bouillon cubes
½ stick butter
1 teaspoon diced onion flakes
2 teaspoons parsley flakes
½ teaspoon liquid garlic or
    1 clove garlic, crushed
Salt and pepper to taste

Boil snails in bouillon for 2 minutes. (This step really adds a good flavor.) Drain. Melt butter and add rest of ingredients. Place 1 snail in each shell and cover with butter mixture. Heat in 350° oven until butter sizzles. Serve with warm crusty French bread. May be prepared early in day and refrigerated until ready to cook. 4 servings

**Dr. Paul Conner**

---

**MICROWAVE HINT** ══════════════

Melba toast for canapes—Cut thin slices of stale bread into decorative shapes and arrange on a paper towel; cook 2 minutes, let stand 5 minutes.

# Eggplant Caviar

2 Tablespoons olive oil
1 small-medium eggplant,
  peeled and diced
1 large green pepper, chopped
  (about ¾ cup)
2 medium onions, chopped
  (1 cup)
2 Tablespoons tomato paste
1 teaspoon sugar
1½ teaspoons salt
¼-½ teaspoon freshly ground
  black pepper
1 Tablespoon lemon juice

Heat oil; add eggplant, green pepper and onions and sauté 20 minutes stirring frequently. Mix in other ingredients except lemon juice and cook 10 minutes over low heat. Remove from heat and add lemon juice. Blend well. This was a recipe from a friend in Florida. Even those who don't care for eggplant or green pepper have raved about this when used as a cold dip with crackers.

Beth Benefield (Mrs. Phillip)

# Emergency Tuna Pâté

1 (8-ounce) package cream
  cheese
2 Tablespoons chili sauce
2 Tablespoons chopped
  parsley or 3 Tablespoons
  dried
1 teaspoon minced onion
½ teaspoon bottled hot
  pepper sauce
2 (6½-ounce) cans tuna, drained

Blend cream cheese, chili sauce, parsley, onion and pepper sauce until smooth. Add tuna gradually until all is thoroughly blended. Pack in a 4-cup bowl as a mold. Chill at least 3 hours. Unmold on lettuce and serve with crisp, sesame crackers.
8-10 servings

Tippi Lassiter (Mrs. Robert)

# Mystery Canapés

½ cup chopped raw almonds
½ cup mayonnaise
2 Tablespoons catsup
1 cup finely chopped celery
1 cup finely chopped onion
½ teaspoon curry powder
Pinch salt
½ cup pitted chopped dates
Triscuits

Mix all ingredients together and spread on Triscuits. Bake in a 400° oven 1-2 minutes. Mixture will keep in refrigerator up to 2 weeks. 4 cups

Susan N. Barton (Mrs. David L.)

# Fried Gyoza
"Pot Stickers"

5 ounces cabbage, chopped
6 ounces ground pork or beef
   (or combination of both)
2 Tablespoons Japanese soy
   sauce
1 Tablespoon sesame oil
1 teaspoon Mirin (Japanese
   rice wine) or sherry
1 green onion, minced
1 teaspoon grated ginger
1 dried black mushroom,
   soaked in 2 Tablespoons
   water
2-3 Tablespoons peanut oil
¼ cup hot water
1 small package Gyoza skins
   (available at Oriental food
   stores)
DUNKING SAUCE:
¼ cup Japanese soy sauce
1 teaspoon rice wine vinegar
Dash Rayu or sesame oil

Cook cabbage in a small amount of boiling salted water until tender. Squeeze out all liquid and mince fine. Chop mushroom. Mix soy sauce, sesame oil, Mirin, pork, green onion, ginger, mushroom and cabbage. Refrigerate for 1 hour or more. Place a scant teaspoon of mixture on each gyoza skin. Moisten edges with cornstarch and water, fold over and seal. Crimp edges with a fork. Cover bottom of a large non-stick skillet (electric is good) with oil. Brown the gyoza over medium heat (350°) turning frequently. Add ¼ cup water to skillet, cover and steam on low heat 7 minutes. Stir often to prevent sticking. Remove cover, raise heat and cook for 2 minutes until crisp. Place sauce on table in small, individual bowls. Gyoza may be prepared in advance or frozen. Lay them in a single layer on a greased cookie sheet, and cover with greased paper. Thaw before cooking. "Pot Stickers" are usually served as a first course. They are also excellent as an appetizer.
Suggestion: Egg Drop Soup and "Pot Stickers", followed by Beef with Oyster Sauce a crisp green vegetable and hot Chinese tea.

**Cookbook Committee**

# Curried Meatballs

1 pound lean ground beef
2-3 teaspoons curry powder
Salt and pepper to taste
1 cup herb stuffing mix
¼ cup butter

Mix all ingredients well and shape into walnut size balls. Sauté in skillet in butter or cook in microwave. Serve warm from chafing dish or freeze and reheat.
6-8 servings

**Joan King (Mrs. Lewis)**

# Mushroom Tarts
### An hors d'oeuvre, or an entrée with soup or salad

25 thin slices bread
½ stick butter
½ pound fresh mushrooms, chopped
3 Tablespoons chopped green onion
1½ Tablespoons flour
1 cup heavy cream
½ teaspoon salt
Juice of ½ lemon
1½ Tablespoons chopped parsley
1 Tablespoon chives
⅛ teaspoon cayenne
Parmesan cheese

Tart shell: Grease muffin tins using butter. Cut circles out of bread centers using a 4-inch glass. Press gently into tins and bake for 10 minutes at 375°. Shells can be frozen at this point.
25 servings

Filling: Sauté chopped mushrooms and green onions in remaining butter for 20 minutes. Add flour to thicken. Add cream, slowly stirring over heat until bubbles form. Remove from heat and add remaining ingredients except Parmesan cheese. Place tarts on a cookie sheet; fill to top and sprinkle with Parmesan cheese. Cook for 10 minutes at 375°. Filling may be frozen and reheated on stove, or tarts and filling can be frozen already made up.

**Martha K. Randolph (Mrs. William H., IV)**

---

HINT

To cut fresh bread, heat the serrated knife.

# Pickled Mushrooms

Fresh mushrooms
Salt
Marinating solution in these
    proportions:
    ½ cup olive oil
    2 cloves garlic, crushed
    4 Tablespoons white wine
        vinegar
    2 teaspoons grated onion

Trim and wash mushrooms. Measure and place into saucepan with ½ teaspoon salt for every cup of mushrooms. Add no water but simmer them, covered, for 15 minutes. Drain. Mix mushrooms into marinating solution and place into covered container. If you do not have enough oil mixture to cover, make some more. Mushrooms must be covered. Let them age for 3-5 days before using. They will keep for months in refrigerator, if oil layer is on top. Serve with toothpicks on bed of lettuce or parsley. Also can be coarsely chopped, mixed with a little oil sauce and served hot or cold with steaks or hamburgers. Hint: Use a narrow jar to keep for a period of time. Oil layer is thicker in narrow jar.

**Emy E. Blair (Mrs. H. Duane)**

# Stuffed Mushrooms

24 large fresh mushrooms
⅓ cup melted butter or
    margarine
1 (8 ounce) can minced clams,
    drained
3 Tablespoons sliced green
    onion
1 Tablespoon chopped parsley
¼ teaspoon salt
⅛ teaspoon pepper
⅛ teaspoon garlic powder
¾ cup mayonnaise
½ teaspoon prepared mustard

Clean mushrooms with a damp cloth; remove stems, leaving caps intact. Set mushroom caps aside. Chop mushroom stems; sauté in butter 10 minutes. Add clams, onion, parsley, salt, pepper and garlic powder; sauté 5 minutes. Stuff mushroom caps with clam mixture. Place in a lightly greased baking dish; chill. Combine mayonnaise and mustard; top each mushroom cap with mayonnaise mixture. Bake at 350° for 10-15 minutes. 6-8 servings

**Billie E. Bothwell (Mrs. Eugene L., Jr.)**

# Ham Biscuits with Mustard Spread
A big hit at cocktail parties

Biscuits
Swiss cheese
Ham
SPREAD:
2 sticks butter, softened
2 Tablespoons poppy seed
2 small onions or 1 large onion
5 heaping teaspoons prepared
   mustard

Blend spread ingredients in blender until smooth. Refrigerate at least 24 hours. Split biscuits, spread with mixture and top with Swiss cheese and thin sliced ham. Seal in foil and bake at 350° until cheese melts, about 5 minutes. For microwave heat 20 small biscuits covered with paper towel for 1 minute. To freeze, make biscuits and spread them ahead of time. Freeze and reheat as needed. Variation: put mix on lengthwise split French bread. Add ham and cheese and take on a picnic.

**Mrs. J. W. Mullen**

# Baked Oysters Beach House

2 Tablespoons butter
¼ cup chopped green onions
⅛ cup chopped white onions
½ cup sliced fresh mushrooms
⅛ cup diced, peeled tomatoes
½ cup flour
2 cups milk, heated
1 cup fish stock
1 cup white wine
1 teaspoon Worcestershire
   sauce
1 touch Tabasco sauce
2 bay leaves
1 touch finely chopped garlic
Salt and white pepper
2 egg yolks
½ cup cream
36 Long Island oysters on
   the half shell
Hollandaise Sauce (see Index)
Parmesan cheese
Bread crumbs

Melt butter in saucepan, add chopped green and white onions and sliced mushrooms; sauté for about 3 minutes. Add tomatoes and mix well. Stir in flour. Add heated milk, fish stock and white wine, bring to a boil and stir until thick and creamy. Add other seasonings. Mix the egg yolk and cream together and stir into the sauce bringing to another boil. Remove from heat and cool. Remove oysters from shells. Spoon some sauce into empty shells and put oysters on top of the sauce. Bake at 350° for approximately 3-4 minutes. Remove from oven; cover with Hollandaise Sauce and sprinkle with Parmesan cheese and bread crumbs. Broil until browned to perfection. Serve with lemon wedges and Worcestershire sauce. Bon Appetit! 6 servings

**The Abbey Restaurant**
*Atlanta, Georgia*

# Oysters Lafitte

4 Tablespoons butter
1 cup chopped cooked shrimp
2 cups chopped mushrooms
¼ cup chopped green onion
¼ cup snipped parsley
1 clove garlic, minced
2 dozen fresh oysters
½ teaspoon salt
Dash cayenne
1 cup light cream
¼ cup flour
½ cup dry white wine
24 oyster shells or 8 coquille
    shells
Rock salt
⅓ cup fine bread crumbs
2 Tablespoons butter
⅛ teaspoon paprika

Melt butter; add shrimp, mushrooms, onion, parsley and garlic. Cook 1 minute. Drain oysters and set aside; reserve liquid and add enough water to make ¾ cup. Add liquid, salt and cayenne to shrimp mixture; bring to simmer for 1 minute. Combine cream and flour and add to mixture. Stir in wine. Cook until thickened. Arrange oyster shells in shallow pan on bed of rock salt. Place 1 oyster in each oyster shell or 3 oysters in each coquille shell. Spoon sauce over oysters. Combine bread crumbs and butter and sprinkle over oysters. Sprinkle paprika on top and bake at 450° for 10-12 minutes. May be prepared in advance and refrigerated until baking time. Serve as a first course with a spinach salad and a light wine such as Vouvray or a chenin blanc. 6 servings

**Susan M. Morley**

# What's This?

4 dozen oysters, washed
    and drained
1 cup chili sauce
2 Tablespoons Worcestershire
    sauce
2 Tablespoons chopped
    green pepper
12 slices uncooked bacon,
    chopped and cooked until
    half done
1 cup grated Parmesan cheese

Place oysters in a saucepan and heat. Drain again. Put oysters in casserole dish and cover with sauces and pepper. Bake in oven at 350° until oysters puff, about 20 minutes, and until pepper is soft. Remove from oven and sprinkle with bacon and cheese. Return to oven and cook 10 more minutes or until bacon is done. Serve hot with crackers. May be prepared the day before serving or may be frozen.

**Carolyn S. Brooks (Mrs. John L.)**

## Peppers and Anchovies

8 sweet peppers
20 flat anchovy filets
Salt, ground pepper and
    oregano
3 Tablespoons capers
4 cloves garlic, peeled and
    crushed
Olive oil

Broil peppers until skins swell and are charred on all sides. Peel while still hot. Cut peppers into strips 1½-2 inches wide and remove pulp, core and seeds. Pat dry with towel. Choose a shallow dish (for 4-5 layers). Arrange layer of pepper on bottom, lay 4-5 anchovies over them and a touch of salt, plenty of pepper, and a pinch of oregano; repeat the layers. Add olive oil to top layer. Refrigerate at least 4 hours but bring to room temperature just before serving. Note: If refrigerated for more than 24 hours, remove garlic. 4-6 servings

**Decie Nygaard (Mrs. W.F.)**

## Fresh Stuffed Pepper Strips

1 8-ounce package cream
    cheese, softened
6 ounces blue cheese
¼ cup chopped parsley
¼ cup chopped chives
1 large pimiento, chopped
Salt and pepper to taste
2 Tablespoons soft butter
3 green peppers

Combine cream cheese, blue cheese, parsley, chives, pimiento, butter, salt and pepper. Mix until smooth. Cut peppers in half lengthwise and clean out. Cut in half lengthwise again; fill strips with cheese mixture and chill until firm. Cut in half lengthwise again and serve on relish tray or fresh vegetable platter. 24 servings

**Judy L. O'Shea (Mrs. Timothy)**

## Ripe Olive Pâté

1 medium onion, chopped
1 stick butter
1 cup chopped ripe olives
3 Tablespoons cream cheese
Dash thyme
Black pepper (few turns of
    grinder)

Cook onions in butter until soft. Place in blender or food processor. Add other ingredients and blend until smooth. Transfer to a small, greased mold and chill until firm. Serve with thin slices of French bread or on unsalted crackers. 1 cup

**Emy E. Blair (Mrs. H. Duane)**

## Liver Pâté

1 (1-ounce) package unflavored
    gelatin
1 (10-ounce) can consommé,
    undiluted
1 large (4-ounce) can Liverwurst
1 (8-ounce) package cream
    cheese
1 Tablespoon Worcestershire
    sauce
3 Tablespoons rum
1 Tablespoon lemon juice

Moisten gelatin with a little water. Add to consommé and heat until dissolved. Barely cover bottom of 4-6 cup mold with consommé mixture. Refrigerate until set. Put remaining ingredients in blender. Blend. Pour over set gelatin. Chill until set. Unmold when ready to serve.
8-12 servings

**Kenney K. Linton (Mrs. Sidney E.)**

## Hot Beef Spread

1 package dried beef, chopped
1 (8-ounce) package cream
    cheese, softened
2 teaspoons minced onion
½ teaspoon garlic salt
¼ teaspoon pepper
½ pint sour cream
2 Tablespoons butter, melted
½ teaspoon salt
½ cup chopped pecans

Mix first six ingredients together and spread in a lightly greased 9-inch pie pan or casserole dish. Top with a mixture of melted butter, salt and pecans. Bake at 325° for 20 minutes. Serve warm from a fancy pie server or from chafing dish with plain crackers.

**Ann T. McCrory (Mrs. Charles O.)**

# Sausage Strudel

1 pound sweet Italian sausage
1 pound mushrooms (duxelles)
1 (8-ounce) package cream
   cheese, cut in small pieces
Chopped shallots (optional)
¼ cup butter
1 package frozen strudel or
   filo dough
Melted butter
Dried bread crumbs

Remove sausage from casing; scramble and brown. Drain off all fat. For duxelles: chop mushrooms very fine; sauté in ¼ cup butter slowly until all liquid has evaporated. Add shallots if desired. Prepare strudel dough according to package directions. Use 2 sheets to a strudel roll, each one buttered and bread crumbed. Recipe makes 2 rolls. (Work quickly with filo dough as it dries out very fast). Spread sausage, mushrooms and pieces of cream cheese over two-thirds of the length of the strudel dough. Roll up with empty strudel end on the top. Bake at 350° until lightly browned, about 35 minutes. Cut with sharp knife, 8 pieces per roll for hors d'oeuvres, or 4 per roll for luncheon. May be frozen. Prepare as for cooking and then freeze. May take a few minutes longer to brown from frozen state. This is a spicy dish and goes well with green salad. If used as luncheon main dish, treat as you would any Italian food. It does need a plate and fork when served as an appetizer.

**Karen Consolini**
*New York City*

HINT

To keep parsley fresh longer, leave a little moisture on it after washing, and store in a closed jar in the refrigerator.

## Salmon Sour Cream Spread

**SALMON:**
**16 ounces chilled poached**
   **salmon, flaked, boned and**
   **skinned**
**¼ cup mayonnaise**
**2 Tablespoons lemon juice**
**¼ teaspoon garlic salt**
**¼ teaspoon dried dill weed**
**¼ teaspoon Worcestershire**
   **sauce**
**⅛ teaspoon cayenne**
**SPREAD:**
**1 cup sour cream**
**½ cup finely chopped zucchini**
**2 Tablespoons thinly sliced**
   **green onion**
**2 Tablespoons drained capers**

Drain salmon; combine with mayonnaise, lemon juice, garlic salt, dill weed, Worcestershire sauce and cayenne. Place in serving dish. Combine sour cream, zucchini, green onion and capers. Place in adjacent serving dish. Chill until ready to serve. To serve, spread salmon mix on crisp bread or water wafer; top with sour cream spread.

Yield; 1¾ cups salmon mixture
       1¼ cups sour cream
       spread

**Susan M. Morley**

## Scallops Seviche

**26 ounces scallops**
**6½ whole limes**
**6 ounces fresh chopped onion**
**6 ounces chopped green**
   **pepper**
**2 sprigs parsley, chopped**
**1 Tablespoon oil**
**2 teaspoons salt**
**2 teaspoons pepper**

Allow scallops to reach room temperature. Squeeze juice from limes over scallops and allow scallops to marinate for at least 2 hours in lime juice. Drain juice from scallops and add chopped onion, pepper, parsley and oil. Season with salt and pepper. May be used also as an entrée.

**The Peasant Restaurants**
*Atlanta, Georgia*

## Shrimp Alliade

**1 pound peeled cooked shrimp**
**12-14 walnuts, finely chopped**
**3 cloves garlic, crushed**
**¾ cup oil**
**1 Tablespoon lemon juice**
**½ teaspoon salt**
**2 Tablespoons chopped**
   **fresh parsley**

Blend all ingredients and chill several hours before serving. This may be served on lettuce cups as a first course or used as an appetizer. If serving on lettuce cups, drain oil. 8 servings

**Elise M. Griffin**

# Cold Curried Shrimp

4 Tablespoons butter
1 clove garlic, crushed
¼ cup apple, minced
¼ cup onion, minced
2 Tablespoons flour
1 cup stewed tomatoes
2 teaspoons curry powder
Salt and pepper to taste
Mayonnaise
1 Tablespoon lemon juice
2 pounds shrimp, cooked
 and peeled
Thinly sliced cucumbers for
 garnish
Slivered almonds for garnish

Sauté garlic, apple and onion in butter until onion is golden. Remove garlic. Stir in flour and add tomatoes, curry powder, salt and pepper. Bring sauce to a boil and strain it through a fine sieve. Cool. Measure the sauce and add an equal amount of mayonnaise and the lemon juice. Fold in shrimp and chill for 3 hours. Serve on a glass plate garnished with a ring of cucumber slices and sprinkled with almonds.

This amount of sauce is enough for 4 pounds of shrimp.
6 servings

**Pamela T. Marcus**

# Shrimp Arnaud

6 Tablespoons olive oil
2 Tablespoons wine or
 tarragon vinegar
4 Tablespoons Zatarain's
 Creole mustard
½ teaspoon salt
½ teaspoon white pepper
2 Tablespoons finely chopped
 celery
2 Tablespoons finely chopped
 onion
2 Tablespoons finely chopped
 parsley
Horseradish to taste (optional)
Cooked and peeled shrimp

Mix ingredients and blend well. Marinate cooked and peeled shrimp several hours or overnight in prepared sauce. Add horseradish if desired. Three recipes will make enough sauce for 5 pounds of shrimp.

**Josephine C. Fleming (Mrs. Tom)**

## Shrimp Toast or "Kogi Chunkol"
This is a delicious Phillipino delicacy

5 ounces water chestnuts, drained
1 pound raw shrimp
¼ cup chopped green onion tops
2 teaspoons salt
1 teaspoon sugar
1 egg, beaten
15 slices very thin white bread
Breadcrumbs

Purée water chestnuts, shrimp and onions. Add salt, sugar and egg. Spread paste on one side of each bread slice. Sprinkle with crumbs. Cut each slice into 4 triangles. Heat 1 inch of oil to "hot" (not smoking) and fry each triangle, shrimp side down, then brown on other side, (approximately 2 minutes on each side). Drain. May be frozen before serving; defrost, reheat at 400° for 5 minutes. Yield: 60

**Susan Morley**

## Shrimp Spread

2 cups finely diced shrimp, cooked and deveined
½ cup softened butter
2 Tablespoons lemon juice
1 teaspoon salt
¼ teaspoon paprika
1 teaspoon Worcestershire sauce
½ teaspoon prepared mustard

Mix all ingredients by hand until well blended. Place in small shallow bowl with butter spreader; serve with crackers, toast rounds or bread squares. May be frozen. 2 cups

**Josephine D. Weekes (Mrs. John W.)**

## Shrimp Romanoff
From Armando's Restaurant in Acapulco, Mexico

1 cup mayonnaise
¼ cup catsup
4 teaspoons white wine
¾ teaspoon Maggi liquid seasoning
2 pounds shrimp, cooked and shelled

Place all ingredients in bowl and blend until smooth. Refrigerate. When ready to serve, arrange boiled shrimp (which have been refrigerated) on lettuce on individual plates and spoon sauce liberally over shrimp. Sauce may be prepared several days ahead and refrigerated. 8 servings

**Marceline T. May (Mrs. Earle B., Jr.)**

# Shrimp Mold

1 pound cooked shrimp
2 cups mayonnaise
1 small onion, grated
Juice of one lemon
2 Tablespoons horseradish
2 envelopes unflavored gelatin
½ cup water
Few drops of red food coloring
  to make mixture light pink

Sprinkle gelatin in water and place in double boiler to dissolve. Cool. Combine with remaining ingredients. Pour into mold. Chill. Serve with crackers. Should be prepared the day before serving for best results.

**Ann T. McCrory (Mrs. Charles O.)**

# Shrimp Ernie
### From the Olde College Inn in Houston, Texas

2 pounds raw jumbo shrimp,
  shelled and deveined
1 pint salad oil
1 teaspoon salt
1 clove garlic, minced
4 Tablespoons catsup
1 teaspoon paprika

Marinate shrimp in the remaining ingredients overnight. When ready to serve, place shrimp in shallow pan and pour some sauce over (do not cover shrimp). Broil 3-5 minutes each side. Serve from chafing dish as appetizer. 16-20 Shrimp

**Elise M. Griffin**

# Toasted Finger Rolls

1 sliced loaf fresh bread
1 can mushroom soup
1 pound bacon

Remove crust from bread and spread with undiluted soup. Do not use a heavy coat of soup. Roll bread from corner to corner and wrap a piece of bacon (usually half a slice) around each roll, holding in place with a toothpick. Place rolls on ungreased cookie sheet and bake at 325° until golden brown, about 35 minutes. Serve with soup or salad or use as an appetizer. May be frozen. 8 servings

**Beth M. Johnston (Mrs. J. Gibson)**

## Zucchini and Carrot Appetizer
Easy to prepare when done in a food processor
Wonderful for calorie counters

1 medium zucchini
2 Tablespoons oil
1½ teaspoons wine vinegar
   or lemon juice
Dash salt
Dash freshly ground pepper
Mixed herbs (optional)
2 medium carrots

Install medium slicer and feed zucchini into tube. Remove sliced zucchini and set aside. Put oil, vinegar or lemon juice, salt, pepper and mixed herbs in work bowl. Peel carrots and cut them into 2½-inch diagonal lengths. Lay flat in feed tube and shred. Toss carrots lightly with dressing. Mound shredded carrots on sliced zucchini and chill. 6 servings

**Martha H. Whitehead (Mrs. Richard)**

## Baked Cheese Sandwiches

2 cups grated sharp cheese
¼ cup butter
¼ cup mayonnaise
¼ cup minced onions
¼ cup chopped pimentos
Dash of tabasco sauce
12 slices sandwich bread
with crust removed

Combine first six ingredients. Spread mixture on one side of bread slices. Roll tightly and place close together on greased baking sheet. Bake at 350° for 10 minutes. Serve hot. Serve with salad for lunch or as a finger food.
Serves 12

**Linda Hightower (Mrs. Charles R.)**

**MICROWAVE HINT** ■■■■■■■■■■■■■■■■■■■■■■

Dry fresh herbs between 2 layers of paper towel or napkin until they can be crumbled.

## Bourbon Slush

2 regular size tea bags
1 cup boiling water
½ cup sugar
3½ cups water
1 (6 ounce) can frozen orange
    juice concentrate, thawed
½ cup bourbon
1 (6 ounce) can frozen
    lemonade concentrate,
    thawed

Steep tea bags in boiling water 2 to 3 minutes; remove tea bags. Stir in sugar. Add remaining ingredients; mix until sugar is dissolved. Pour into freezer trays; freeze until firm. Remove from freezer about 10 minutes before serving. Spoon into cocktail glasses; garnish with lemon wedges if desired. Keep unused portions in freezer. 1½ quarts

**Beverly W. Bibent (Mrs. Maury J.)**
*Cincinnati, Ohio*

## Strawberry Daiquiri
For strawberry lovers!

1 pound package frozen
    sweetened strawberries
4 ounces light rum
4 ounces (Arrow) strawberry
    liqueur
1 capful lemon juice
    concentrate
Enough ice to fill blender

Put all ingredients in blender. Add ice and blend at high speed. This can be frozen for future use. 4 servings

**Sue C. Smith (Mrs. Douglass C.)**

## Instant Hot Chocolate
Very creamy
Kids love having this available

1 one pound box Nestle's Quik
1 (8-quart) package non-fat dry
    milk
1 (7-ounce) jar powdered
    non-dairy creamer
⅔ cup sifted confectioners
    sugar

Mix all ingredients together and store in jars. To serve, fill cup halfway with mixture and add hot water.

**Kimpy Edge (Mrs. J. Dexter, Jr.)**

HINT

For large parties, use washing machine to store ice, cool beer, etc.

# Café Glacé
### (Iced Coffee)

¾ cup sugar
1½ cups milk
1 teaspoon vanilla extract
1½ cups cold coffee
¾ cup heavy cream
Unsweetened whipped cream

Combine sugar and milk in a saucepan and bring to a boil, stirring until sugar is dissolved. Remove from heat; add vanilla extract and let stand until cold. Combine milk mixture, coffee and cream, mixing well; then pour into a metal pan. Freeze until hard. Put in blender or food processor and process until mushy. (Thawing slightly will make this process simpler.) Pour into tall glasses. Top with spirals of whipped cream. Serve immediately.
4-6 servings

**Lynn H. Barnes**

# Mexican Mocha

¼ cup cocoa
3 Tablespoons sugar
¹⁄₁₆ teaspoon salt
⅓ cup water
3 cups milk
2 Tablespoons kahlua
Whipped cream, flavored with
   dash kahlua

In a saucepan, mix together cocoa, sugar, salt and water. Bring almost to a boil and simmer gently 2 minutes, stirring constantly. Add the milk and immediately lower heat. Keep over low heat, stirring gently until heated through. Take off heat and stir in kahlua. Serve in 4 cups or mugs topped with whipped cream. 4 servings

**Sandra R. Pritchett (Mrs. Edwin P.)**

# Irish Coffee

1½ teaspoons sugar
3 Tablespoons hot coffee
¼ cup Irish whiskey
Hot coffee
3 Tablespoons whipped cream
Nutmeg

Place silver spoon in Irish coffee glass or stemmed glass to absorb heat. Add sugar and 3 Tablespoons hot coffee to glass and stir. Add whiskey and fill glass to within 1 inch of top with hot coffee. Float whipped cream on coffee; sprinkle with nutmeg.
1 serving

**Jeanine C. Andrews (Mrs. Edward B.)**

# Kahlua
Serve as an after dinner liqueur
or over vanilla ice cream with whipped cream, nuts
and shaved chocolate

2 rounded Tablespoons instant
  coffee
1 cup water
3 cups white sugar
1 vanilla bean, finely chopped
1 fifth vodka

Boil coffee, water and sugar. Stir until completely dissolved. Cool completely. Add finely chopped vanilla bean. Add vodka. Cork in airtight vessel. Store in a cool place for 30 days.

**Joy K. Tyler (Mrs. John P.)**


# Lime Cooler
Delicious at a springtime luncheon

2 (6-ounce) cans frozen
  limeade, partially thawed
4 cups water
½ cup lemon juice
1 quart chilled ginger ale or
  club soda
1½ cups Vodka (optional)
Pineapple slices or mint sprigs

Place limeade and water in blender and blend at medium speed until frothy. Stir in lemon juice. Transfer into container and chill at least one hour. When ready to serve, add soda and vodka and shake. Garnish each glass with a mint sprig or a twisted pineapple ring
12 8 ounce servings

**Decie Nygaard (Mrs. W. F.)**


# Ethel Mincey's Punch
A sweet punch especially good in summer

1 gallon water
5 pounds sugar
3 large cans pineapple juice
1 large bottle lemon juice
3 Tablespoons or 2 small
  bottles almond flavoring
2 quart bottles ginger ale

Mix all ingredients except ginger ale which is added just before serving. Fill punch bowl about half full of crushed ice. This will serve 50 (5-ounce) cups.
50 servings

**Claire W. Johnson (Mrs. A. Sidney)**


**HINT**

Freeze crystal clear ice block for punch bowl by using a mold and distilled water. Add strawberries, flowers or greenery if desired.

# Bees Knees

1 ounce lemon juice
1 ounce honey
1 jigger gin
1 teaspoon cherry juice
Ginger ale

Mix equal parts (1 ounce each) of lemon juice and honey. Shake well. Chill. Add one jigger of gin and one teaspoon of cherry juice to above mixture. Stir well, add ginger ale and crushed ice to fill a 10 or 12 ounce glass. 1 serving

**Margaret Westbrook (Mrs. William L.)**

# Bola
A German punch

2 bottles white wine (Chablis or sauterne)
1 bottle champagne
1 pint strawberries, cleaned and hulled

Marinate strawberries in white wine all day. Add champagne just before serving. 20 servings

**Jerry P. Connor (Mrs. Paul)**

# Sangria

2 peaches or nectarines, sliced
½ pint fresh strawberries, hulled
2 Tablespoons sugar
2 Tablespoons brandy
2 Tablespoons orange flavored liqueur
1 bottle (⅘ quart) rose wine
Mint sprigs if desired

Place peaches, strawberries, sugar, brandy and liqueur in pitcher or bowl. Let stand at room temperature 30 minutes. Stir in wine. Refrigerate covered at least 4 hours. Garnish with mint sprigs. 4 servings

# White Sangria

1 large orange, thinly sliced and seeded
1 large lemon, thinly sliced and seeded
1 large lime, thinly sliced and seeded
1 cup Triple Sec or Grand Marnier
½ cup sugar
2 fifths dry white wine, chilled
1 quart club soda, chilled

At least eight hours before serving, mix fruit and Triple Sec in a plastic bag or container. Refrigerate until serving. Before serving, mix fruit and sugar in punch bowl or large pitcher. Add wine and club soda. Do not add ice. 20 servings

**Lynn H. Barnes**

# Hot Cranberry Cheer

1½ quarts cranberry juice
2 quarts unsweetened apple
    juice
½ cup dark brown sugar
½ teaspoon salt
4 cinnamon sticks
1½ teaspoons cloves

Put juices, sugar and salt in coffee pot. Put cinnamon sticks and cloves in top of coffee maker. Juices will brew through spices as beverage perks. Note: All ingredients can be heated slowly in large pot and simmered about 2 hours. 8-10 servings

# Wassail
### For holiday cheer!

½ gallon apple cider (8 cups)
4 cups cranberry juice
1 (6-ounce) can frozen
    lemonade concentrate
1 (6-ounce) can frozen orange
    juice concentrate
4 sticks cinnamon
1½ teaspoons whole cloves
1½ teaspoons whole allspice

Simmer all ingredients for 1-2 hours. Cinnamon, cloves and all-spice can be tied in a cheese-cloth bag and removed before serving or the wassail should be strained before serving. Serve hot in mugs. Dark rum or bourbon may be added before serving or pitchers of rum and bourbon could be passed to be added individually.

Wassail can be made 2 or 3 days in advance, stored in refrigerator and heated before serving. 14 servings

**Myrick L. King (Mrs. David L.G., Jr.)**

# Hot Spiced Wine

½ cup sugar
1 cup water
10 cloves
3 cinnamon sticks
¼ teaspoon allspice
1 orange, sliced
1 lemon, sliced
1 (46-ounce) can pineapple
    juice
1 fifth Burgundy

Combine all ingredients except Burgundy in a pot on the stove or a crock pot (3½ quart size or larger). Cover and heat for at least 1 hour, slowly as in a crock pot. Fifteen minutes before serving, add Burgundy. Heat slowly and serve in mugs or other heat proof cups. 12 servings

**Barbara R. Schuyler (Mrs. Lambert, Jr.)**

# Raspberry Apéritif

1 (10-ounce) package frozen
   raspberries
3 ounces orange liqueur
1 bottle champagne, chilled

Purée and strain raspberries, saving juice, discarding seeds. Chill until very cold. Add liqueur and chilled champagne. Serve in chilled, stemmed glasses. For punch, add 1 bottle ginger ale. 4-6 servings

# Kir or Chablis Cassis

A French apéritif to substitute for the
"before dinner cocktail"

1 Fifth of California Chablis
2 ounces creme de cassis
   (black currant liqueur)
Lemon peel

From a fifth bottle of California Chablis, remove 1 or 2 ounces of the wine and add 2 ounces of creme de cassis to the bottle. A corkscrew of lemon peel can be added to the bottle or small strip of lemon peel can be added to each glass. Shake the bottle gently and chill. Serve "straight up" or "on the rocks". This can also be served from a punch bowl for a crowd.

**Sarah Looper (Mrs. Joseph W.)**

# Purée of Asparagus Soup

1½-2 pounds asparagus or
   3 (15-ounce) cans
   asparagus spears
¼ cup butter
½ cup chopped onion
4 cups chicken broth
⅛ teaspoon nutmeg
Salt and pepper, to taste
Sour cream for garnish
Chopped toasted almonds
   (optional)
Chopped shrimp (optional)

If fresh asparagus is used, cut off upper half and cut into ½-inch pieces. Melt butter in large skillet or Dutch oven; add onions and cook 3 minutes. Add asparagus and cook 1 minute. Add 2 cups broth and seasonings. Cover and simmer until tender. Put in blender until smooth. Chill several hours. Add rest of chilled broth. Mix well and serve in chilled bowls topped with a Tablespoon of sour cream. Garnish with chopped toasted almonds or chopped shrimp, if desired. Variation: For an excellent cold dip, add a carton of sour cream to chilled asparagus purée and omit last 2 cups broth. Serve with raw vegetables. 4-6 servings

**Sallie B. Smith (Mrs. Tommy W.)**

# Cauliflower Ham Chowder

2 cups cauliflower, sliced
1¾ cups chicken broth, or
   1 (13-ounce) can
1 cup light cream
1 can cream of potato soup
¼ cup water
2 Tablespoons cornstarch
¼ teaspoon white pepper
2 cups ham, cooked and diced
Parsley for garnish

Cook cauliflower in chicken broth in large covered saucepan until almost tender—about 10 minutes. Do not drain. In a mixing bowl, gradually stir cream into potato soup. Blend water, cornstarch and pepper; stir into potato mixture. Pour over cauliflower and cook, stirring often, until thick and bubbly. Stir in ham; simmer over low heat for 10 minutes. Garnish with parsley. 4-6 servings

**Barbara Ender (Mrs. Steven)**

## Cream of Broccoli Soup

1 small onion, thinly sliced
1 green onion (white portion
   only) thinly sliced
1 small stalk celery, sliced
   (no leaves)
1 Tablespoon butter
½ cup water
2 teaspoons salt
Dash cayenne pepper
2 Tablespoons uncooked rice
2 cups chicken broth
2 cups cooked broccoli,
   coarsely cut (do not salt
   broccoli while cooking;
   reserve cooking liquid)
½ cup cream or milk

Place onion, green onion, celery, butter and water in 2-quart saucepan; simmer slowly for about 2 minutes over medium heat. Add salt, cayenne, rice and 1 cup broth, and simmer for 15 minutes. DO NOT BOIL. Pour broth-onion mixture into blender or food processor. Blend until liquified. Return to saucepan. Put cooked broccoli and remaining cup of broth in blender or food processor a little at a time, cover and blend until broccoli is liquified. If mixture becomes too thick to flow, add broccoli cooking liquid to thin. Add broccoli to onion mixture in saucepan. Add cream or milk. Heat (DO NOT BOIL) and serve. May be prepared up to 2 days in advance. 4 servings

**Billie E. Bothwell (Mrs. Eugene L., Jr.)**

## Shrimp Chowder

4 large onions, peeled and
   sliced
¼ cup margarine
1 cup boiling water
6 medium potatoes, pared
   and cubed
1 Tablespoon salt
½ teaspoon seasoned pepper
1½ quarts milk
2 cups (½ pound) grated
   sharp Cheddar cheese
2 pounds raw shrimp, shelled
   and deveined
3 Tablespoons snipped parsley
   for garnish

Melt margarine in heavy Dutch oven; sauté onion slices until tender. Add boiling water, potatoes, salt and seasoned pepper. Simmer covered for 20 minutes until potatoes are tender. Do not drain. Meanwhile, heat milk with cheese in saucepan over a very low temperature until cheese has melted and milk is hot. Do not boil. Add shrimp to potatoes and cook until they turn pink—about 3 minutes. Add hot milk and cheese mixture. Heat, but do not boil. Sprinkle with parsley before serving. 8 servings

**Pat Adams (Mrs. P. H.)**

## New England Style Clam Chowder

I researched from 20 to 30 recipes for clam chowder, none
of which contained all of the following, but every ingredient
below was in at least one. Most did not have green onions,
garlic, pimiento, chicken broth, parsley or bacon.
I think they add a great deal.

2 slices bacon
3 Tablespoons butter
1 cup chopped onion,
  (½ regular and ½ green
  onions)
1 cup chopped celery, heart
  and leaves
1 cup chopped carrots
½ cup chopped green pepper
1 clove garlic, chopped
3 Tablespoons flour
3 cups hot chicken stock, or 3
  heaping teaspoons instant
  bouillon dissolved in 3
  cups hot water
1½ cups potatoes, cubed
1 teaspoon salt
¼ teaspoon white pepper
1 (10 ounce) can whole baby
  clams and juice
2 Tablespoons butter
2 Tablespoons flour
2 cups half and half
1 whole pimiento, chopped
3 Tablespoons fresh parsley
  (or 1 teaspoon dried)

Chop and fry bacon. Add 3
Tablespoons butter to bacon and
grease; add onions, carrots,
celery, garlic and green pepper;
saute a few minutes. Add 3 Tablespoons flour, stir awhile (this will
become very dry), and slowly add
hot chicken stock. Cook about 10
minutes; add salt, pepper,
potatoes, clams and juice. Cook
10 minutes. In another pot or
double boiler, make a roux with 2
Tablespoons butter and 2 Tablespoons flour. Add 2 cups half
and half to make a fairly thick
cream sauce. Blend in pimiento
and parsley. Bring almost to boil;
let cool. Combine both mixtures
and store overnight in refrigerator.
Before serving heat almost to
boiling. If too thick, add a little
half and half to thin.

**Frank B. Roberts**

# Billy's Seafood Chowder

4 large onions, chopped (2)
5 large potatoes, diced (2)
2 sticks butter (1)
2 pounds filleted trout
　(¾ pound)
4 pounds cooked, peeled
　shrimp (1½ pounds)
4 pints oysters and juice
　(1½ pints)
4 (8-ounce) bottles clam
　juice (2)
2 pints crabmeat (1)
Salt and pepper to taste
4 quarts half and half (1)
6 quarts milk (2; add more later
　if too thick)

**The numbers to the side in parentheses make less than 2 gallons.**

In large skillet saute onions in one stick butter until clear; add more butter and cook fish until tender. In very large pot, boil potatoes gently until tender but not mushy. Drain. To potatoes add sautéed mixture, oysters, crabmeat, clam juice, cream and milk. Heat slowly on lowest heat until boiling point, (do not let boil) stirring frequently, with wooden spoon. This takes at least 1 hour. This chowder will keep 4-5 days in refrigerator. Reheat on lowest heat and stir frequently. If sticking occurs, change to another pot. It is best made in a large quantity but, since this is very expensive, use the numbers to the side for 1 meal. 4 gallons

**Freddie Fleming (Mrs. William T.)**

# Clam Bisque
Can be doubled easily

1 (7-ounce) can minced clams
2 cups milk
½ teaspoon dill weed
½ teaspoon Beau Monde
　seasoning
1 Tablespoon butter
2½ teaspoons cornstarch
1 Tablespoon cold water

Drain clams, reserving juice. Mix clam juice, milk and dill weed in heavy saucepan. Heat on medium until boiling, add clams, Beau Monde seasoning, butter, and simmer 5 minutes. Mix cornstarch and water, stir into hot bisque, keep warm. Sprinkle with dill weed for garnish when serving. 2-3 servings

**Winnie R. Goodman (Mrs. James)**

## Chicken Soup With Meatballs
This interesting soup freezes beautifully

1 (2 pound) stewing chicken
4 cups water
2½ teaspoons salt
Freshly ground black pepper
¼ teaspoon basil
1 bay leaf
¼ teaspoon mace
1 clove garlic, crushed
½ pound white onions, sliced; or pearl onions
5 small carrots, sliced
1 Tablespoon chopped parsley
1 Tablespoon chopped celery leaves
MEATBALLS:
1 cup ground pork
1 egg
1 slice white bread, crumbled
2½ Tablespoons flour
½ teaspoon salt
Freshly ground black pepper

Simmer chicken 1½ hours in water, salt, pepper, basil, bay leaf, mace and garlic. Remove chicken. Strain broth and skim fat. Bring broth to boil and add onions, carrots, parsley and celery. Simmer gently 10 minutes.
Meatballs: Mix ingredients to form meatballs ¾ inch in diameter. Add to soup and simmer 35 minutes. Meanwhile, skin and bone chicken, returning meat, cut in bite-sized pieces, to soup.
4-6 servings

**Joan Roes (Mrs. Hans)**

## Chicken Velvet Soup
Divinely smooth and rich!

6 Tablespoons butter
6 Tablespoons flour
½ cup milk
½ cup light cream
3 cups chicken broth
1 cup finely chopped cooked chicken
Dash pepper

Melt butter in saucepan. Blend in flour, stirring. Remove from heat and add liquid ingredients. Return to heat and cook, stirring constantly, until mixture thickens and comes to a boil; reduce heat. Stir in chicken and pepper. Return to boiling and serve immediately.
5 servings

**Pamela T. Marcus**

## Green Pea and Crabmeat Soup

1 Tablespoon butter
1 small onion, minced
1 can green pea soup
1 can beef consommé
1 can white crabmeat
1 (3 ounce) can sliced
    mushrooms
⅔ soup can water
⅓ cup sherry
Salt and pepper to taste

Sauté onion in butter. Put onion and remaining ingredients into a saucepan and cook over medium heat for 5-10 minutes. Serve hot. May be prepared the day before serving.

**Myrick L. King (Mrs. David L.G., Jr.)**

## Hangover Soup

3 cans tomatoes, chopped
    drained
1 cup chopped celery
1 large cucumber, chopped
1 green pepper, chopped
1 large onion, chopped
3 cloves garlic, crushed
2 large (46 ounce) cans V-8 juice
½ cup olive oil
½ cup vinegar
1 teaspoon basil
1 teaspoon curry powder
Salt and pepper, to taste
Worcestershire sauce, to taste

Mix ingredients together and taste to adjust seasonings. Keep refrigerated and serve cold. Note: Recipe may be halved.

**Jennifer W. Clements (Mrs. Harold A.)**

HINT

Too much salt in the soup—add a pinch of brown sugar.

# Lentil Soup
### Good hearty winter soup

1 pound dried lentils, washed
¼ cup oil
3 cups diced ham
½ pound Polish sausage cut
   in ½ inch slices
2 large onions, chopped
1 clove garlic, crushed
2 cups celery with leaves,
   chopped
1 tomato, peeled and chopped
3 quarts water
½ teaspoon Tabasco sauce
1½ teaspoons salt
1 (10-ounce) package frozen
   chopped spinach, thawed

Soak lentils in water to cover overnight. Heat oil in large soup kettle and sauté ham, sausage, onion and garlic. Add celery, tomato, lentils, water, tabasco and salt. Simmer for 2 hours until lentils are tender. Add spinach and cook for 10 minutes. This soup freezes very well. Serve with a fruit salad and toasted English muffins with cheese. 4 quarts

**Mrs. Elsie B. Manry**
*Tampa, Florida*

# Navy Bean Soup

1 pound navy beans
1 ham bone with lots of ham,
   fat trimmed off
1 medium onion, chopped
2 ribs celery with leaves,
   chopped
1 bay leaf
1 carrot, finely chopped
3 cups chicken bouillon
8 slices bacon, fried and
   chopped
1 teaspoon seasoned salt
1 teaspoon salt (start with less)
1 potato, peeled and cut into
   ¼ inch cubes
½ cup catsup

Soak beans overnight, or bring to boil for 2 minutes and set aside for 1 hour, covered. Return to heat, add ham bone, onion, celery, carrot, bay leaf and chicken bouillon. Simmer, covered, until beans are done. You may have to add some water. Take out ham bone, trim off all meat, and chop. Purée ½ of soup in blender or food processor and return to pot; add the remaining ingredients and simmer for another 15 minutes. Let cool and refrigerate overnight. If soup is too thick after refrigeration, add milk to thin after reheating. May be frozen.
8 servings

**Frank B. Roberts**

## Fresh Mushroom Soup

1 pound mushrooms
6 Tablespoons butter
2 cups finely chopped onion
½ teaspoon sugar
¼ cup flour
1 cup water
1¾ cup chicken broth
1 cup dry vermouth
1 teaspoon salt
⅛-¼ teaspoon pepper

Slice ⅓ of the mushrooms and finely chop the rest. Melt butter in a large saucepan. Add onions and sugar; sauté over medium heat, stirring frequently until golden— about 15 minutes. Add sliced and chopped mushrooms and sauté for 5 minutes. Stir in flour until smooth; cook for 2 minutes, stirring constantly. Pour in water and stir until smooth. Add remaining ingredients and heat to boiling, stirring constantly. Reduce heat and simmer uncovered for 10 minutes. May be prepared in advance to this point. Cover; refrigerate. To reheat, heat to boiling, cover and simmer 10 minutes. 6 servings

**Carolyn B. Hoose (Mrs. Kenneth A., Jr.)**

## Brennan's Creole Onion Soup

8 medium onions, chopped
1½ cups butter
1¼ cups all-purpose flour
10 cans beef stock or 12 cups homemade beef stock
1 Tablespoon salt
½ teaspoon cayenne pepper
2 Tablespoons cream
1 egg yolk
Buttered croûtons
Parmesan cheese

Melt butter in a large soup pot; add onions and lower heat. Cook until onions are clear. Do not brown. Add flour and cook 10 minutes, stirring. Add salt and cayenne pepper. Blend in beef stock (always stirring) and bring to a full boil. Reduce heat and cook slowly for 20 minutes. Remove from heat. Beat cream and egg yolk together. Add a little hot soup to mixture, blend, then pour back into soup. If soup becomes too thick, add a little more water. To serve: pour into bowls, add croutons and sprinkle with Parmesan cheese. This soup makes a great meal served with a spinach salad and hot French bread. 12 servings or 6 luncheon servings

**Nancy Kirby (Mrs. Jeff D., III)**

# Ertwen Soup
(Pronounced "Air-twin")
A hearty Dutch split pea soup

**1 (16 ounce) package split peas**
**3 quarts water**
**2 pounds pork neck bones**
**or ribs**
**1½ teaspoons salt**
**3 leeks, thinly sliced or 2**
**medium yellow onions,**
**sliced**
**1 stalk celery, chopped**
**3 large potatoes, cubed**
**Leafy tops from 1 bunch celery**
**2 Polish sausages, or ham, or**
**frankfurters**

Soak peas in water overnight. Drain and put in water with pork and salt. Simmer over low heat 3 hours. Add leeks, celery, potatoes and celery tops; simmer over low heat another 30 minutes, stirring often. Slice sausage into bite-size rings and add to soup. Simmer 10 minutes more. Serve with buttered pumpernickel bagels. 3 quarts

**Joan Roes (Mrs. Hans)**

# Steak Soup

**Leftover steak (1 pound**
**approximately)**
**2 cups cold water**
**2 beef bouillon cubes**
**1 large onion, thinly sliced**
**1 cup sour cream**

Cut leftover steak in small cubes; cut away any fat or bones. Cover meat with cold water, add bouillon cubes and onion and cook over low heat for 30-45 minutes. Put in blender or food processor and process until smooth. Return to pan, add sour cream and heat.

**Winnie R. Goodman (Mrs. James E.)**

---

**HINT**

To remove excess grease from soups and gravys, drop in several ice cubes; the grease will cling to the cubes and can be removed easily.

# Garden Tomato Soup
The wine and spices make this soup especially tasty

6 shallots or green onions,
  peeled and sliced
1½ ounces butter
1 heaping Tablespoon flour
4 pints canned consommé or
  meat stock
1½ cups white wine
12-13 large ripe tomatoes,
  chopped
1 heaping teaspoon thyme
½ teaspoon rosemary
Sour cream or cream for
  garnish

Sauté shallots in butter until soft—about 5 minutes. Stir in flour and cook 2 minutes. Add stock, wine, tomatoes and seasonings. Cover and simmer 1 hour. Remove from heat. Process in blender or food processor until smooth. Strain through sieve or cheesecloth. Return to pan and reheat. Garnish with sour cream and serve immediately. This freezes beautifully and doubles easily. 6 servings

**Vivian deKok (Mrs. Peter)**

# Tomato and Mushroom Soup

4 Tablespoons butter, melted
1 onion, chopped
1 cup fresh sliced mushrooms
  or 1 (4-6-ounce) can sliced
  mushrooms
1 (11-ounce) can cream of
  mushroom soup
1 Tablespoon tomato paste
1 (11 ounce) can beef
  consommé
1 (6-ounce) can Snap-E-Tom
  Tomato Cocktail juice
1 (16-ounce) can whole
  tomatoes in thick purée,
  cut up
½ cup heavy cream
2-3 Tablespoons parsley

Sauté onion in melted butter until transparent. Add sliced mushrooms to onions and sauté another minute. Add mushroom soup, tomato paste, consommé, tomato juice and tomatoes. Bring to boil and cook for a few minutes. Up to this point, the soup can be made the night before. Before serving, add cream and parsley. Add salt if needed. 8 servings

**Myrick L. King (Mrs. David L. G., Jr.)**

# Country French Vegetable Soup

The turnip is the secret ingredient that makes this
vegetarian soup so special

1 stick butter
1½-2 cups sliced onion
1 cup sliced carrots
1 cup sliced turnips
1 cup sliced celery
1 cup sliced potatoes
1 teaspoon salt
4 cups water
1 cup heavy cream

GARNISH:
2 Tablespoons butter
1 small turnip, diced
1 carrot, diced
1 stalk celery, diced

Melt 1 stick butter in deep, heavy pot. In food processor with slicing disk or by hand, slice one vegetable at a time. Place sliced vegetables and salt in pot. Stir in butter. Cover tightly and stew over low heat for 20 minutes. In food processor with steel knife or by hand, chop the cooked vegetables and return to pot. Add water and bring to a boil. Simmer for 20 minutes. With steel knife or by hand, finely dice vegetables for garnish. Melt 2 Tablespoons butter in a saucepan. Add chopped vegetables and brown lightly. Add to soup. Add cream, adjust the seasonings and serve either hot or cold. The vegetables may be varied in quantity and type—using what is available. However onions and the turnip are a necessary part of this soup.

**Cookbook Committee**

# Vegetable Soup with Ground Beef

1 pound lean ground beef
1 cup chopped onion
1 clove garlic, minced
1 (15 ounce) can kidney beans
1 cup sliced carrots
1 cup sliced celery
¼ cup uncooked rice
2 (16 ounce) cans stewed
    tomatoes
3½ cups water
5 beef bouillon cubes
1 Tablespoon chopped parsley
1 teaspoon salt
¼ teaspoon basil
⅛ teaspoon pepper
1 cup frozen or fresh green
    beans

Cook beef in skillet with onion and garlic until browned. Drain off fat. Combine all ingredients except beans (if they are frozen), and place in a soup pot or crock pot. Cover and cook on low heat 2-3 hours on range or 8 hours in crock pot. Add frozen beans during last hour of cooking. Note: If crisper vegetables are desired, cook meat, spices and liquid ingredients adding vegetables toward the end of the cooking time. 8 servings

**Pamela T. Marcus**

## Consommé with Sour Cream
An elegant change of pace for hot weather entertaining

2 cans consommé madrilène
1 cup sour cream
1 Tablespoon lemon juice
2 Tablespoons chives
Lemon twists for garnish

Beat all ingredients except lemon twists with a rotary beater to blend. Chill, covered, 3 hours. Garnish each cup of soup with a lemon twist. 4 servings

**Cookbook Committee**

## Chilled Cucumber Yogurt Soup

3-4 cucumbers
4 cups chicken stock
2 Tablespoons minced scallion
½ cup chopped celery
½ teaspoon dried dillweed
½ teaspoon dried mint leaves
1 teaspoon grated lemon rind
2 cups plain yogurt
Minced parsley

Peel cucumbers, cut into halves and remove seeds. Dice enough to make 3 cups. Bring chicken stock to a boil, add cucumbers, scallion, celery, dillweed and mint. Simmer for 10 minutes. Cool: mix in a blender or food processor until smooth. Stir in lemon rind and yogurt. Chill for 3-4 hours. Sprinkle each serving with parsley. 6 servings

**Cookbook Committee**

## Carrot Vichyssoise
This beautifully colored soup is from the
Four Seasons Restaurant in New York

3 cups chicken stock
2 cups peeled, diced boiling
    potatoes
1¼ cups sliced carrots
1 leek, sliced (white part only)
1 cup cream
1 teaspoon salt
Dash of white pepper
Dash of nutmeg
Shredded raw carrot for
    garnish

Place stock, potatoes, carrots and leek in a saucepan, bring to a boil and simmer until vegetables are tender, about 25 minutes. In a food processor or blender, purée mixture, half at a time. Pour into a bowl and add cream and seasonings. Chill. Serve cold. Garnish with shredded carrot. 4 servings

**Jane S. Boyd (Mrs. Benjamin)**

## Chilled Strawberry Soup

2 quarts ripe strawberries
Juice of 1 lemon
3 cups water
¾-1 cup sugar
2 Tablespoons minute tapioca
1 cup sweet white wine

Clean and crush strawberries; add lemon juice. Cover with water; add sugar and tapioca. Boil over medium heat 15 minutes. Remove from heat and add wine. Chill thoroughly and serve very cold as a first course. 6-8 servings

## Cold Peach Soup

4 large ripe peaches
2 cups dry white wine
1 cup water
3 Tablespoons sugar
¼ teaspoon cinnamon
¼ teaspoon curry powder
3 cloves
Sour cream for garnish
Orange slices for garnish

Drop peaches in boiling water for 1 minute. Peel and halve. Purée in blender or food processor. Put purée in enamel saucepan, add wine, water, sugar and spices. Bring to a boil and simmer 10 minutes, stirring. Remove cloves and chill at least 4 hours. Serve in chilled bowls with a thin slice of orange and a dollop of sour cream.

For use as a dessert soup, 1 pint of heavy cream may be added immediately before serving, eliminating the sour cream.
4 servings

# Basic Principles of Egg Cooking

Use a moderate to low temperature with exact timing. When eggs are cooked at too high a temperature or for too long at a low temperature, egg whites shrink and become tough or rubbery, yolks become toughened and their surface may turn grey-green.

Eggs separate better when cold, but beat better at room temperature. Remove from refrigerator about 30 minutes before heating.

One large egg equals approximately 3 tablespoons.

If any of the yolk or any fat gets into egg whites, the white will not beat.

A large egg has about 80 calories, 60 of which come from the yolk.

Contrary to popular opinion, shell color does not affect egg quality or nutritive value. Shell color is determined by the breed of the laying hen. Brown and white eggs are equally good.

Break egg shell by a sharp tap at center with knife blade. Press thumbs into cracks, turning crack down. Pull apart and let egg drop into a bowl. To separate let each half of shell serve as a cup and rock yolk from cup to cup while white pours out.

Cream of tartar added to egg whites increases the stability of meringue. A test to see if meringue has been beaten enough is to rub a little of the meringue between the thumb and forefinger. If you can feel any grains of sugar, the meringue has not been beaten enough. Continue to beat until no grains of sugar can be felt.

When topping a pie with meringue, put meringue on while the filling is still hot and bake at 375°F until the meringue is a light golden brown. This reduces the amount of liquid that collects between the meringue and filling. Spread meringue all the way to the pie crust and make sure the filling is completely sealed to prevent the meringue from shrinking.

When combining beaten egg whites with other heavier mixtures handle carefully so that the air beaten into the whites is not lost. It is best to pour the heavier mixture onto the beaten egg whites. Fold just until there are no streaks remaining in the mixture. Don't stir as this will force air out of the whites.

Never attempt to cook an egg still in the shell in the microwave. Rapid heat applied by the microwave will expand the air inside the egg shell and possibly cause it to explode.

In cooking eggs by microwave, always remember that they continue to cook after they have been removed from the oven. For this reason it is best to remove them while still underdone.

### Soft-Cooked Eggs

Put eggs in saucepan and add enough tap water to come at least 1 inch above eggs. Cover; bring rapidly just to boiling. Turn off heat; if necessary, remove pan from burner to prevent further boiling. Let stand in the hot water 1-4 minutes, depending on desired degree of doneness. Cool eggs promptly in cold water for several seconds to prevent further cooking and to make them easier to handle.

To serve: Break shell through middle with a knife. With a teaspoon, scoop egg out of each half shell into individual serving dish. If egg cup is used, slice off large end of egg with knife and eat from shell.

### Hard-Cooked Eggs

Put eggs in saucepan and add enough tap water to come at least 1 inch above eggs. Cover; bring rapidly just to boiling. Turn off heat; if necessary, remove pan from burner to prevent further boiling. Let stand in the hot water 15 minutes for large eggs—adjust time up or down by approximately 3 minutes for each size larger or smaller. Cool immediately and thoroughly in cold water. To remove shell: crackle it by tapping gently all over. Roll egg between hands to loosen shell; then peel, starting at large end. Hold egg under running cold water or dip in bowl of water to help ease off the shell.

### Poached Eggs

Lightly oil a sauce pan. Add enough water* to make 2 inches deep. Heat to boiling. Reduce heat to hold temperature at simmering. Break eggs, one at a time, into sauce dish; then slip each egg into water, holding dish close to water's surface. Simmer 3-5 minutes, depending on degree of doneness desired. When done, remove eggs with slotted pancake turner or spoon; drain on paper towel and trim edges, if desired.

*Milk or broth may be used instead of water.

### Baked (Shirred) Eggs

Break and slip 2 eggs into greased individual shallow baking dish or ramekin. Add 1 tablespoon of milk or light cream, if desired. Season with salt and pepper. Bake in preheated 325°F. oven 12-18 minutes or until desired degree of doneness. Serve in baking dish. Makes 1 serving.

# Eggs Sardou

6 large artichokes
1 cup creamed spinach
6 eggs
Hollandaise Sauce
CREAMED SPINACH:
1 package chopped spinach,
    cooked to package
    directions and drained
2 Tablespoons butter, melted
2 Tablespoons flour
1 cup milk
HOLLANDAISE SAUCE:
2 sticks butter
3 egg yolks
Juice of 1 lemon, strained
Salt, pepper and cayenne,
    to taste

Prepare creamed spinach by making a cream sauce with the butter, flour and milk and adding spinach. Boil artichokes in salted water, drain and remove choke and leaves. Fill hearts with creamed spinach. Poach eggs and place 1 on each artichoke heart on top of spinach. Cover with Hollandaise sauce, made as follows: In double boiler, gradually add melted butter to egg yolks and lemon juice, stirring constantly until thick. Season to taste and serve over eggs.

This very rich dish is an excellent brunch or luncheon dish.
4-6 servings

# Eggs Hussarde

4 large thin ham slices, grilled
4 Holland Rusks
4 slices grilled tomato
4 soft poached eggs
Marchand de vin sauce
    (see Index)
Hollandaise sauce (see Eggs
    Sardou)
Paprika

Lay a slice of ham across each Holland Rusk and cover with ¼ cup Marchand de vin sauce. Lay slices of tomato on the sauce and place poached eggs on tomato slices. Top with ¼ cup Hollandaise sauce and garnish with a sprinkling of paprika.
4 servings

# Scrambled, Chipped Eggs
Excellent breakfast recipe for anything from
a brunch to a camping trip

3 Tablespoons butter
¼ cup finely chopped green
    onion tops
9 eggs
1 cup cottage cheese
4 ounces shredded dried beef
    (1½ cups)
Salt and pepper to taste

Melt butter in skillet; sauté green onions. Beat eggs with cottage cheese and add to skillet with beef. Cook over low heat until scrambled, stirring constantly. Season to taste. 6 servings

**Phyllis K. Kennedy (Mrs. Crawford M.)**

## Egg Foo Yung and Special Sauce
### A wonderful light supper

½ **pound cooked, chopped**
   **shrimp**
**8 eggs, slightly beaten**
½ **cup chopped green onions**
**1 teaspoon sugar**
**2 teaspoons soy sauce**
**1½ teaspoons salt**
**4 Tablespoons oil**
**SAUCE:**
**1 beef bouillon cube**
**2 Tablespoons soy sauce**
**1 cup water**
½ **teaspoon pepper**
**1 Tablespoon cornstarch mixed**
   **with 1 Tablespoon water**

Mix shrimp together with eggs, green onions, sugar, soy sauce, and salt. Drop by tablespoons in hot oil and fry as for pancakes. Turn when brown. Keep warm and serve with special sauce.

Sauce: Mix all ingredients together and heat to thicken and blend flavors.

**Linda Cohen (Mrs. Larry)**

## Greybowy Tort
### (Mushroom Omelet Pie)

½ **pound mushrooms, sliced**
½ **medium onion, chopped**
½ **cup butter, melted**
**4 eggs**
**1 Tablespoon flour**
**Salt and pepper, to taste**
**2 Tablespoons grated**
   **Parmesan or Romano**
   **cheese**

Sauté mushrooms and onion in butter until golden. Beat eggs, flour, salt and pepper together. Pour this mixture into 2 small buttered skillets and cook until set. Put 1 omelet on a warmed platter; cover with mushrooms and onions. Sprinkle with salt and pepper. Cover with second omelet and sprinkle with grated cheese. Serve with fried potatoes and champagne. 2 servings

**Susan M. Morley**

**HINT**

    Egg yolks will beat better and will combine with hot mixture more easily if you add 1 teaspoon water before beating.

## Poached Eggs in Red Wine Sauce

1 egg per person
3 Tablespoons butter
1 small clove garlic
1 white onion, chopped
2 Tablespoons chopped celery
1 small bay leaf
Salt and pepper, to taste
Dash thyme
2 cups dry red wine
½ English muffin per person
1 teaspoon flour creamed with
   2 teaspoons butter

In a heavy saucepan, melt butter, add garlic for a minute, then remove. Add onion and celery and sauté until tender. Add bay leaf, thyme, salt, pepper and wine. Simmer 10 minutes. While sauce is simmering, butter and toast ½ English muffin per person. Keep warm. Slip 1 egg per person into the simmering sauce and poach for 3 minutes or until white is set. Carefully remove and place on muffin halves and keep warm. Strain sauce into another saucepan; whisk in flour and butter mixture, cook until thickened and spoon over eggs.

**Cookbook Committee**

## Oven Omelet
A good, fast and easy breakfast dish for company

8 eggs
1 cup milk
1 (3 ounce) package thin sliced
   corned beef or ham
Cooked bacon or mushrooms
1 cup shredded Cheddar
   cheese or mozzarella
   cheese
1 Tablespoon minced onion

Preheat oven to 350°. Beat eggs and milk. Tear beef or bacon; chop ham or mushrooms and put into egg mixture. Stir in cheese and onion. Pour into a greased 11½ x 7½ x 1½ inch or 8 x 8 x 2 inch baking dish. Bake uncovered 40-45 minutes or until omelet is set and top is golden brown. 4 servings

**Lucy C. White (Mrs. Richard A.)**

## Dan's Eggs

8 slices bacon, chopped
2 slices white bread, cubed
8 eggs
½ cup milk
½ teaspoon salt
Dash pepper

Fry bacon in large skillet until crisp. Remove and drain. Reserve half of drippings for later use. Add bread cubes to remaining grease and cook until crisp and brown. Remove cubes. Wipe skillet to remove overcooked crumbs. Combine eggs, milk, salt and pepper. Beat well. Cook egg mixture in reserved bacon drippings until nearly set. Stir in cooked bacon and bread cubes. Recipe may be expanded many times when cooking for a crowd. 4 servings

## Brunch Egg Casserole

2 cups plain croûtons
1 cup shredded Cheddar
    cheese
4 eggs, slightly beaten
2 cups milk
½ teaspoon salt
½ teaspoon prepared mustard
⅛ teaspoon onion powder
Dash pepper
4 slices bacon, cooked and
    crumbled

In bottom of 10 x 6 x 1¾-inch baking dish, combine croûtons and cheese. Combine eggs, milk, salt, mustard, onion powder and pepper. Mix until blended. Pour into baking dish. Sprinkle bacon on top and bake at 325° for 50 minutes or until eggs are set. Garnish with bacon curls, if desired. May be prepared the night before serving except for bacon. Perfect for overnight company breakfast, and brunch. 6 servings

**Carolyn S. Brooks (Mrs. John L.)**

HINT ■■■■■■■■■■■■■■■■■■■■■■■■■■■■■■■■■

If some of the egg yolk falls into the whites when separating them, remove it with a bit of shell or by touching it with a cloth moistened in cold water.

## Artichoke Quiche
Outstanding for a luncheon or with cocktails

2 6 oz. jars marinated
    artichokes, drained and
    chopped
8 saltine crackers, crushed
½ pound cheddar cheese,
    grated
4 eggs
1 bunch green onions, finely
    chopped
3 Tablespoons butter
Salt and pepper to taste
Tabasco sauce

Mix artichokes, crackers and cheese together. Sauté onions in butter and add to mixture. Grease 8 x 10-inch baking dish or 9-inch pie pan. Pat artichoke mixture in place. Beat eggs well, season with salt, pepper and Tabasco sauce and pour over top. Bake at 350° for 35 minutes. Cut into small squares for serving. Can be frozen after cooking and allowed to thaw to room temperature, then heated for 20 minutes at 350°. For use as an appetizer, individual quiches may be made in muffin tins.
Serves 8 as appetizer or 4 for an entrée

**Phyllis K. Kennedy (Mrs. Crawford M., Jr.)**

## Crab and Shrimp Quiche

1 (9 inch) deep dish pastry
    shell, unbaked
8 ounces Swiss cheese, diced
2 Tablespoons flour
1 cup milk
3 eggs, beaten
½ teaspoon salt
⅛ teaspoon pepper
Dash ground nutmeg
1 (6 ounce) package Wakefield
    frozen crabmeat and
    shrimp, thawed

Prick bottom and sides of pastry shell with fork; bake at 425° for 6-8 minutes. Set aside. Combine cheese and flour; set aside. Combine milk, eggs, salt, pepper and nutmeg; mix well. Stir in crab and shrimp, and cheese-flour mixture. Pour into pie shell; bake at 350° for 50-60 minutes. Cool slightly before serving. Hint: May be frozen. Bake 40 minutes; wrap tightly in foil and freeze. To serve, thaw quiche and bake 15 to 20 minutes at 350°. 6 servings

**Mrs. Nell Johnson**

## Zucchini Eggplant Quiche

½ pound zucchini, thinly sliced
   diagonally (about 2 small
   zucchini)
½ pound eggplant, diced in ½
   inch cubes (about ½ small
   eggplant)
1 green onion, sliced
1 medium clove garlic, minced
¼ cup melted butter
½ cup peeled and chopped
   tomatoes
½ cup chopped green pepper
½ teaspoon salt
⅛ teaspoon pepper
¼ teaspoon basil
¼ teaspoon thyme
1 (9 inch) pastry shell, partially
   baked
3 eggs
½ cup heavy cream
½ cup Parmesan cheese

Sauté zucchini, eggplant, onion and garlic in butter. Stir in tomatoes, green pepper and spices. Cook over low heat 10-15 minutes until vegetables are tender and liquid evaporated. Spread mixture evenly in pie shell. Beat eggs and cream until mixed, but not frothy. Pour into shell. Sprinkle with Parmesan cheese. Bake in 375° oven 30-35 minutes until set.

Martha H. Whitehead (Mrs. Richard)

## Seafood Quiche

2 pie shells, unbaked
6 ounces frozen or canned
   crabmeat
1½ cups frozen or canned
   tiny shrimp
1 (8 ounce) package Swiss
   cheese, chopped
½ cup chopped celery
½ cup chopped scallions or
   onions
1 cup mayonnaise
2 Tablespoons flour
¾ cup dry white wine
4 eggs, slightly beaten

Thaw crabmeat and shrimp; combine with cheese, onions and celery. Arrange in pie shells. In a food processor or small bowl, mix mayonnaise, flour, wine and eggs. Pour over mixture in pie shells. Bake in a 350° oven for 35-45 minutes, or until silver knife inserted in center comes out clean. May be frozen before cooking; then cook 50-55 minutes at 350°. For a luncheon main dish, each pie will serve 4-6 people. For appetizers, cut each pie into 12 pieces. 2 quiches

Betty Jo Ridley (Mrs. William E.)

## Sausage Quiche

1 pie shell, baked
½ pound hot sausage
2 Tablespoons chopped onions
2 eggs, beaten
¾ cup sour cream
1-2 cups grated Swiss cheese
Salt and pepper to taste
¼ teaspoon nutmeg
½ cup grated Cheddar cheese

Cook and drain sausage; in same skillet, brown onions. In a bowl, mix eggs, sour cream and grated Swiss cheese. Add sausage, onion, salt, pepper and nutmeg. Pour into pie shell. Top with grated Cheddar cheese. Bake at 350° for 30 minutes. Freezes well. 6-8 servings

**Mrs. T.L. McDougald**

## Artichoke Cheese Soufflé

⅔ pound mushrooms,
  chopped
2 Tablespoons butter
½ cup sherry
1 cup heavy cream
1 teaspoon salt
Pepper to taste
4 cooked artichoke bottoms
6 Tablespoons butter
⅓ cup flour
1⅓ cup scalded milk
¾ teaspoon salt
Pepper
Dash nutmeg
3 egg yolks
1½ cups grated sharp cheese
4 egg whites

Sauté chopped mushrooms in 2 Tablespoons butter. Add sherry. Cook for 10 minutes until evaporated. Add cream, salt and pepper. Cook 4-5 minutes until thick. Arrange artichoke bottoms on bottom of an 8-inch buttered and floured souffle dish. Mound mushroom mixture over artichokes. Melt 6 Tablespoons butter in a saucepan. Add flour. Cook for 2 minutes. Add scalded milk, ¾ teaspoon salt, pepper and nutmeg. Cook until thick. Transfer to a large bowl. Cool for 5 minutes. Stir in egg yolks and grated cheese. Beat egg whites with a pinch of salt until stiff. Fold into cheese mixture and gently pour over artichoke-mushroom layers. Bake at 400° for 40 minutes. Serve immediately. 6 servings

**Patricia Ritchie**

# Blintz Casserole
Absolutely divine!
Treat your football fans with this for brunch

**FILLING:**
2 pounds ricotta cheese
2 eggs
¼ cup sugar
⅛ teaspoon salt
1 lemon, juiced or ¼ cup
   lemon juice
8 ounces cream cheese,
   softened
**BATTER:**
½ pound margarine, melted
½ cup sugar
2 eggs
1 cup sifted flour
3 teaspoons baking powder
⅛ teaspoon salt
¼ cup milk
1 teaspoon vanilla

Place all ingredients for filling in mixer and blend well. Set aside. Mix batter ingredients by hand and spoon ½ of batter into a greased 9 x 13 x 2-inch pan. Top this with filling; spreading, not mixing. Spread remaining batter over filling. Bake at 300° for 1½ hours. Serve with fresh fruit and grilled Canadian bacon. 12 servings

**Terry C. Morris (Mrs. Douglas)**

# Monterey Fondue Casserole

12 slices (or less) stale French
   bread
Soft butter
1 (12-16 ounce) can whole
   kernel corn
2 small cans green chilies,
   seeded and cut in strips
2 cups grated Monterey Jack
   cheese or 1 cup grated
   Monterey Jack and 1 cup
   grated Cheddar cheese
3 cups milk or cream
4 eggs
1 teaspoon salt
Dash Tabasco sauce
Pitted black olives (optional)

The day before serving, spread bread with butter and slice in half; arrange half the slices in bottom of a 3-quart or larger baking dish. Cover with half of corn; arrange half of seeded chili strips over this. Sprinkle half of grated cheese over all. Repeat layers. Combine milk, eggs, salt and Tabasco sauce and pour over casserole, adding more milk if necessary, to reach level of bottom of cheese (depending on shape of dish used). Garnish with pitted black olives if desired. Cover with foil or plastic wrap and refrigerate overnight. Bake uncovered at 350° 40-45 minutes or until puffy and brown. 8 servings

**Joan McMahan (Mrs. James P.)**

# Cheese Soufflé Crêpes

¼ cup butter
¼ scant cup flour
¾ cup milk
½ teaspoon salt
¼ teaspoon Worcestershire
   sauce
¼ teaspoon dry mustard
Dash cayenne
1 cup shredded Cheddar or
   Swiss cheese
4 eggs, separated
Butter
12 crêpes (see Index)
2 cups shredded Cheddar
   cheese

Melt butter and stir in flour. Cook 3 minutes, stirring. Stir in milk and seasonings, stirring until thick. Blend in 1 cup cheese and stir. Remove from heat. Beat in yolks one at a time and fold in stiffly beaten egg whites. Spoon ¼ cup mixture in center of each crêpe. Fold sides in. Place in buttered 9 x 13-inch baking dish and brush with melted butter. Bake at 350° 8-10 minutes. Sprinkle liberally with 2 cups grated cheese and bake 5 minutes more. Crêpes may be assembled 1-2 hours ahead and refrigerated, then reheated. Complement with grilled or sliced tomatoes and bacon curls. 6 servings

**Gail Nichols (Mrs. Robert)**
*Young Harris, Georgia*

# Cheese Sandwich Pie

1 egg
¾ cup flour
½ teaspoon salt
⅛ teaspoon pepper
1 cup milk
1 cup (4 ounces) shredded
   cheese (Cheddar, Swiss,
   Muenster, etc. Can use 1
   kind or combination)
Ham (optional)
Bacon (optional)
Onions (optional)
Mushrooms (optional)

In small bowl, combine egg, flour, salt, pepper and milk and any optional ingredients. Mix with rotary beater until blended; stir in half of cheese. Pour into well greased pie pan. Bake at 425° for 30 minutes. Pour on remaining cheese. Return to oven about 2 minutes. Serve as an appetizer or a main dish for lunch or a Sunday night supper. 6-8 servings

**Ann Mallard (Mrs. William)**

## Saucy Cheese Soufflé

1 cup milk
3 Tablespoons Quick Tapioca
1 cup grated mild Cheddar
   cheese
3 egg yolks, beaten
½ teaspoon salt
3 egg whites, stiffly beaten
SAUCE: Serves 8
¼ cup butter
¼ cup flour
½ teaspoon salt
¼ teaspoon dry mustard
1 pint milk, scalded
1¼ cups grated mild Cheddar
   cheese
8 slices bacon, crisply cooked

Cook milk and tapioca until thick. Remove from heat. Add grated Cheddar cheese and stir until melted. Stir in egg yolks and salt. Fold in stiffly beaten egg whites. Pour into a well greased square casserole. Place casserole in pan of hot water and bake at 350° for 1 hour. Top should be brown when taken from oven. Cut into squares and place on plates. Pour a generous Tablespoon of Cheese sauce over soufflé and top with 1 or 2 slices of crisp bacon. 4 servings

Cheese Sauce: Melt butter. Add flour, salt and dry mustard. Add milk gradually. Stir constantly until thick. Fold in mild Cheddar cheese. Keep hot in double boiler.

Soufflé does not need to be served immediately as it does not fall quickly.

**Sherril H. Williams (Mrs. Wheat, Jr.)**

## Cottage Cheese Pancakes
For a special Sunday night supper

1 cup heavy cream
4 eggs
½ cup flour (may need more)
¼ teaspoon salt
¼ cup oil
½ cup milk
½ teaspoon vanilla
8 ounces cottage cheese

Place all ingredients except cottage cheese in blender. Mix well. Fold in cottage cheese. Do not blend lumps out. Heat frying pan and fry as you would any pancake. Try them with pork links rolled inside, with blueberries over the top or with any fruit sauce spooned over the pancakes. 4 servings

**Cookbook Committee**

## Roquefort Soufflé
### An excellent appetizer

3 Tablespoons butter
¼ cup flour
½ teaspoon salt
Dash pepper
1½ cups milk
6 ounces Roquefort cheese,
   crumbled
6 egg yolks
6 egg whites

Melt butter. Blend in flour, salt and pepper. Stir in milk and bring to boil, stirring constantly. Cook 5 minutes. Add Roquefort cheese. Add egg yolks, one at a time, beating hard after each addition. Cool. Recipe may be prepared in advance to this point. Beat egg whites until stiff, but not dry. Add about ⅓ of whites to cheese mixture, blending well. Then very gently fold in remaining whites. Turn into buttered and floured 2-quart soufflé dish and bake in a 375° oven for 30-40 minutes. 4 servings

**Emy E. Blair (Mrs. H. Duane)**

## Garlic Cheese Grits

5 cups boiling water
1 teaspoon salt
1 cup grits
1 roll garlic cheese, cut up
1 stick margarine
3 egg whites, stiffly beaten

Stir grits into boiling, salted water and simmer slowly for 25 minutes stirring often. Remove from heat and add cheese and margarine. Cover and let sit until cool. May be prepared ahead to this point. Fold in egg whites; put in greased casserole and bake for 25 minutes at 350°. 8 servings

**Lee Shelnut (Mrs. M.T.)**

## Bulgur-Nut Pilaf

1 cup bulgur (cracked wheat)
3 Tablespoons butter
2 cups beef or chicken broth
2 medium carrots, shredded
½ to ¾ teaspoon salt
½ cup chopped walnuts,
   pecans or almonds

In large ovenproof skillet or flameproof casserole, sauté bulgur in butter about 5 minutes to brown lightly, stirring occasionally. Stir in broth, carrots and salt; bring to boil. Cover and bake in 350° oven for 25 minutes or until broth is absorbed, stirring occasionally. Stir in walnuts. Good with lamb or poultry. 4-6 servings

# Barley and Mushrooms

4 Tablespoons butter
1 large onion, minced
¼ pound mushrooms, sliced
1 cup barley
4 chicken bouillon cubes or
envelopes
1 teaspoon salt
3 cups water

In large skillet over medium heat, melt butter and sauté onions and mushrooms until tender, stirring occasionally, for about 5 minutes. Remove from skillet. In same skillet, in remaining butter, lightly brown barley, stirring constantly. Stir in bouillon granules or bouillon cubes, onions, mushrooms and water. Heat to boiling. Reduce heat to low. Cover and simmer 35-40 minutes until tender, stirring occasionally until barley is tender and all liquid is absorbed. 8-12 servings

**Pat Adams (Mrs. P.H.)**

# Cheese and Rice Casserole

¼ pound butter or margarine
1 large onion, chopped
1¾ cups uncooked rice
2 cans consommé
1 cup blanched, slivered
almonds
1 small can mushrooms,
drained
¾ pound grated Cheddar
cheese

Sauté onion in butter. Mix all ingredients together in a 9 x 13-inch casserole. Bake uncovered 1 hour and 15 minutes at 300°. Stir occasionally. May be prepared for baking early in day. 10-12 servings

# Fruited Rice Curry

Prepared in advance and kept in an airtight container this makes a very nice gift at holiday time

1 cup long grain rice
2 teaspoons curry powder
2 beef bouillon cubes
¼ cup chopped mixed dried
fruits
¼ cup blanched slivered
almonds
1 Tablespoon instant minced
onion
½ teaspoon salt
2 Tablespoons light raisins

Combine all ingredients. Package in an airtight container.
To prepare Rice Curry: Combine rice mix with 2½ cups water and 2 Tablespoons butter or margarine in saucepan. Cover tightly. Bring to a boil; reduce heat. Simmer for 20 minutes. Do not lift cover. 4 cups

**Lucia H. Sizemore (Mrs. Thomas A., III)**

# Fried Rice

4 strips bacon
1 bunch green onions,
   chopped or 1 large onion,
   chopped
2 eggs, well beaten
2-3 cups cooked, day-old rice,
   cooled
¼ cup Japanese soy sauce
   or more, as desired
OPTIONAL:
Water chestnuts, sliced
Bamboo shoots
Mushrooms, sliced and
   sautéed
Leftover pork, chicken or
   shrimp, chopped

Cook bacon in a large skillet or wok until crisp. Drain on paper towels and crumble, leaving bacon grease in pan. Sauté onions in grease over medium heat until translucent. Add eggs. Scramble until thoroughly cooked and eggs can be broken into very tiny bits. Add rice; stir to combine. Add bacon, water chestnuts, bamboo shoots, mushrooms and chopped pork, chicken or shrimp, as desired. Sprinkle in soy sauce to taste and stir over low heat until mixture is thoroughly combined and warm.

# Exotic Rice

1 can beef consommé
1 can onion soup
1 (8 ounce) can water
   chestnuts, drained and
   sliced
1 (3 ounce) can sliced Broiled
   in Butter mushrooms,
   drained
1 cup uncooked rice
½ teaspoon salt
½ stick butter

Put first 6 ingredients together in a 1½-quart casserole and mix well. Dot with butter. Cover and cook in a 325° oven for 1 hour and 45 minutes. 6-8 servings

**Alice C. Shinall (Mrs. Robert P.)**

# Green Rice with Cheese

⅓ cup melted butter
2 Tablespoons chopped onion
2 eggs, beaten
2 cups milk
1 cup minute rice, uncooked
½ pound Cheddar cheese,
   grated
½ (10 ounce) package frozen
   spinach, thawed
½ teaspoon salt
¼ teaspoon garlic salt

Brown onions in melted butter. Mix remaining ingredients together. Add onions. Mix well. Place in ungreased baking dish. Bake 1 hour at 325°. May be frozen before baking. 6-8 servings

**Diane J. Pitts**

# Green Rice

2 cups uncooked rice
⅔ cup finely chopped green
  peppers
1 cup sliced green onions
⅓ cup chopped parsley
¼ cup olive oil
1½ Tablespoons
  Worcestershire sauce
1 teaspoon salt
¼ teaspoon cayenne pepper
1 quart beef broth

Preheat oven to 350°. Grease
2-quart casserole. Combine all
ingredients. Pour into casserole.
Cover and bake for 45 minutes.
After cooking, toss rice and serve.
May be prepared in advance.
12 servings

Dunja S. Awbrey (Mrs. James J.)

# Herb Rice Blend

A perfect mixture of uncooked rice and assorted dried herbs,
that makes a nice holiday remembrance

1 cup uncooked rice
2 beef bouillon cubes
½ teaspoon salt
½ teaspoon rosemary
½ teaspoon marjoram leaves
½ teaspoon thyme leaves
1 teaspoon dried green onion
  flakes

Mix all ingredients. Put in a
plastic bag or container. Attach
these cooking directions to the
package: Combine rice mixture, 2
cups cold water and 1 Tablespoon
butter in heavy saucepan. Cook
over high heat. When mixture
boils, reduce heat to medium-low.
Stir once with fork. Cover tightly
and simmer 12-14 minutes, or until
all liquid is absorbed.

# Wild Rice Paprika

2 cups wild rice, cooked
2 eggs
½ cup salad oil
1 medium onion, chopped
1 cup fresh chopped parsley
1½ cups grated Cheddar
  cheese
1 cup milk
1½ teaspoons salt
2 teaspoons paprika

Cook wild rice according to
directions on box. Beat eggs; add
oil slowly, then onion and parsley.
Put in cheese, cooked rice, milk
and salt. Add paprika and mix well.
Sprinkle top of casserole
generously with paprika. Bake for
45 minutes at 350°. 12 servings

**Marijo Culwell**

# Indian Pilaf with Carrots and Raisins

¼ cup sugar
2 Tablespoons water
3 cups hot chicken bouillon
1¼ cups diced, pared carrots
2 tablespoons raisins
3 Tablespoons butter
1½ cups uncooked long-grain
    rice
½ teaspoon salt
¼ teaspoon ground cardamon
¼ teaspoon ground cinnamon
¼ teaspoon ground nutmeg

Mix sugar and water in medium size saucepan. Heat to boiling; reduce heat; simmer uncovered until golden; remove from heat. Add bouillon, stirring until sugar is dissolved. Return to heat; cook 2-3 minutes; reserve. Sauté carrots and raisins in butter in 2 quart saucepan, covered, 10 minutes. Add rice to carrot mixture; stir until coated with butter. Stir in reserved bouillon mixture and remaining ingredients. Heat to boiling; reduce heat. Simmer covered until bouillon is absorbed, 25-30 minutes. Transfer to serving dish. Sprinkle with freshly grated nutmeg, if desired. 6-8 servings

**Cookbook Committee**

# Sausage and Wild Rice Casserole

1 pound bulk sausage
2 medium onions, chopped
2 (3 ounce) cans mushrooms,
    drained (whole, button or
    sliced)
2 cups wild rice, washed
¼ cup flour
½ cup heavy cream
2½ cups chicken broth
1 teaspoon MSG
Pinch oregano
Pinch thyme
Pinch marjoram
1 teaspoon salt
⅛ teaspoon pepper
½ cup toasted slivered
    almonds

Sauté sausage; drain on paper towels. Sauté onions in fat left in pan. Add mushrooms and cooked sausage. Meanwhile cook 2 cups thoroughly washed wild rice according to directions on box. Drain. Mix flour with heavy cream until smooth. Add condensed chicken broth and cook until thickened. Add seasonings and toss well. Pour into greased 9 x 13-inch casserole. Bake 25-30 minutes at 350°. Sprinkle with toasted almonds when ready to serve. Freezes beautifully and can serve a crowd. Hint: To soften the cost, use ½ wild rice and ½ white; cook separately; white rice cooks more quickly than wild rice and must not be cooked in the same pot. 10-12 servings

**Decie Nygaard (Mrs. W.F.)**

## Spiced Brown Rice
What a surprise this dish is!
Especially good with pork

1 cup thinly sliced onion
⅓ cup chopped pitted prunes
2 Tablespoons melted butter
2 Tablespoons sugar
1 teaspoon ground cinnamon
¼ teaspoon ground cloves
⅛ teaspoon curry powder
1 cup washed and uncooked
    brown rice
3 cups chicken bouillon
¼ cup pine nuts
2 teaspoons melted butter
Salt and pepper, to taste
Sliced spiced peaches for
    garnish

Sauté onion and prunes in 2 Tablespoons melted butter in heavy 3-quart ovenproof saucepan over medium heat, stirring constantly for 3 minutes. Reduce heat; add sugar; simmer covered until onion is very soft and sugar is caramelized, about 10 minutes. Preheat oven to 350°. Add cinnamon, cloves and curry powder to onion mixture; cook 1 minute. Stir in rice; cook until hot and well coated with sugar. Add bouillon. Heat to boiling; remove from heat; cover and place in center of oven. Bake until rice is tender and liquid is absorbed, about 1 hour. Sauté pine nuts in 2 Tablespoons melted butter in small skillet, stirring constantly, until golden, about 3 minutes. When rice is cooked, add pine nuts, tossing with 2 forks to fluff rice. Add salt and pepper. Transfer to serving dish; garnish with sliced spiced peaches, if desired. May be prepared in advance and reheated in oven or microwave oven. 6 servings

## Rice Stuffing with Grapes

1 (6-ounce) package long grain
    and wild rice
2½ cups water
1 Tablespoon butter
1 teaspoon chicken seasoned
    stock base
1 cup sliced mushrooms
1 cup chopped celery
1 cup halved green grapes
1 (2-ounce) jar chopped
    pimientos, drained

Combine rice, water, butter and stock base in saucepan; bring to boil. Cover tightly and cook over low heat for 15 minutes. Remove from heat; stir in remaining ingredients. Mixture will be moist. Makes enough stuffing for a 10 pound goose. Or serve as a side dish with any wild game, grilled shrimp or scallops. 6-8 servings

**Dorothy W. Smith (Mrs. William P., III)**

# Syrian Rice

Small amount (approximately
   6-8 pieces) spaghetti,
   broken into 1-inch pieces
1 small onion, minced
3-4 Tablespoons olive oil
2½ cups water
2 bouillon cubes (chicken
   or beef)
1 teaspoon salt
½ teaspoon MSG
⅛ teaspoon garlic powder
1 cup uncooked long grain rice

In saucepan soak onion and spaghetti in olive oil for about 5 minutes. Simmer until onions are soft and spaghetti is lightly browned; then add water, all seasonings and bring to a boil. Slowly stir in rice; mix well. Bring to a rolling boil, cover, reduce heat to low and cook until all water is absorbed. Do not stir. Note: The recipe does not call for it, but I wash rice once in cold water before cooking. 8 servings

Constance D. Wilson (Mrs. Alexander E., Jr.)

# Rice Pilaf

2 cups uncooked rice
⅔ cup butter
4 cups chicken stock
¾ cup chopped celery
¾ cup shredded carrots
¾ cup chopped parsley
½ cup chopped green onion
1 cup chopped pecans
Salt to taste

Sauté rice in butter until lightly browned. Add stock and place in a casserole. Bake covered at 350° for 30 minutes. Add celery, carrots, parsley, green onions, pecans and salt. Return to oven for 30 minutes. Excellent with chicken, ham or roasts. 6-8 servings

Elise M. Griffin

# Parsleyed Rice
A new way with rice—delicious!

1 egg, beaten
1 cup milk
1 cup chopped fresh parsley
1 onion, minced
2 cups cooked rice
½ cup grated sharp cheese
2 Tablespoons butter
Salt and pepper

Combine all ingredients and pour into a buttered baking dish. Bake uncovered at 350° for 30 minutes. 8 servings

JoAnn P. Whitehead (Mrs. Harry C.)

## Fettuccine with Zucchini and Mushrooms

½ pound mushrooms, trimmed
  and thinly sliced
1½ sticks butter
1¼ pounds zucchini, scrubbed
  and cut into julienne strips
1 cup heavy cream
7 quarts water
2 Tablespoons salt
1 Tablespoon olive oil
1 pound fettuccine
¾ cup freshly grated
  Parmesan cheese
½ cup chopped parsley
Salt and pepper to taste

In a large deep skillet, sauté mushrooms in ½ stick melted butter over moderately high heat for 2 minutes. Add zucchini, heavy cream and 1 stick butter cut into bits. Bring liquid to a boil and simmer mixture for 3 minutes. Bring 7 quarts water to boil in a large kettle; add 2 Tablespoons salt and olive oil. Add fettuccine and boil until al dente. Drain pasta in a large colander; add it to skillet with grated Parmesan cheese and parsley. Toss mixture, lifting the pasta and combining well. Transfer mixture to a heated platter and serve with additional Parmesan cheese, salt and pepper. 6 servings

**Joe Nardone**

## Fettuccine Milano

1 pound mild Italian sausage
3 cups fresh sliced
  mushrooms
2 cloves garlic, minced
1 large green pepper, seeded
  and cut in chunks
1 cup chopped green onion
1 cup chopped parsley
1 teaspoon crumbled sweet
  basil
½ teaspoon crumbled oregano
¼ teaspoon crumbled rosemary
½ cup olive oil
½ cup melted butter
1 pound hot, cooked fettuccine
  or linguine noodles
Grated Parmesan cheese

Remove sausage from casings. Crumble and brown. Remove from pan and drain. Sauté mushrooms, garlic, green pepper, onion, parsley and seasonings in olive oil and butter until green pepper is soft. Remove from heat. Stir in sausage. Toss with hot fettuccine. Sprinkle generously with Parmesan cheese. Serve with crusty Italian bread. 6 servings

**Alicia LaRocco**

# Noodle Kugel

This is a "sweet starch" and can be used in place
of potatoes or rice

8 ounces cottage cheese (do
    not use "low fat" or
    "dry curd")
1 (1 pound 4 ounce) can
    crushed pineapple with
    juice
12 ounces flat noodles, cooked
4 eggs, beaten
½ cup margarine, melted
½ cup pre-mixed sugar and
    cinnamon
½ pint sour cream
½ cup raisins (optional)

Mix all ingredients and fold
in beaten eggs. Sprinkle with
extra sugar and cinnamon. Bake
in 9 x 13-inch pan at 350° for
1 hour or until knife comes out
clean.

**Mrs. Harvey Cook**

# Paglia E Fieno Papalina

(Straw and Hay)

4-6 Tablespoons butter
1 clove garlic
1 pound fresh mushrooms,
    sliced
Salt
½ pound Prosciutto, minced
    (Canadian bacon may be
    used if necessary)
1 cup light cream
8 ounces egg noodles
8 ounces green spinach
    noodles
¼ cup grated Parmesan
    cheese

Heat half of the butter in deep
frying pan; add garlic clove, sauté
until brown. Remove garlic and
add sliced mushrooms. Sprinkle
lightly with salt and sauté for 10
minutes.

In another pan, melt rest of
butter and fry prosciutto until
browned. Heat cream; keep all the
above warm.

In 2 separate pots of boiling,
salted water, cook both noodles
until tender. Drain. Combine on a
heated serving platter; toss
together with mushrooms,
prosciutto, cream and grated
cheese. Serve immediately.
6 servings

# Baked Manicotti

**PASTA DOUGH:**
**1 cup flour**
**1 cup water**
**¼ teaspoon salt**
**4 eggs**
**FILLING:**
**2 eggs**
**1½ pounds ricotta cheese**
**½ pound mozzarella cheese, cubed, grated or in slivers**
**½ cup grated Parmesan cheese**
**1-2 Tablespoons parsley flakes**
**½ teaspoon salt**
**SAUCE:**
**3-4 cups of your favorite marinara or spaghetti meat sauce**

To make pasta stir flour, water and salt in a bowl until smooth. Beat in eggs 1 at a time. Put about 3 Tablespoons of batter in hot, greased 5-6 inch skillet. Cook until firm but not brown to form a crêpe the size of pan. Turn and cook lightly on the other side. Stack crêpes on a plate with waxed paper between each crêpe until ready to fill. Can be frozen at this point for future use. Combine all filling ingredients. Spread a little of the marinara or meat sauce on the bottom of a 13 x 9 x 1½-inch oblong baking dish. Place about 2-3 Tablespoons cheese mixture on each crêpe. Gently roll pasta around cheese mixture and place each manicotti seam side down in a single layer in the baking dish. Top with additional marinara or meat sauce. Sprinkle with grated cheese. Bake manicotti about 20 minutes or more at 375° until the filling is set and the sauce bubbles. Serve with additional sauce and grated cheese. 6 servings

**Mrs. August J. Nardone**

# Dunbar Macaroni
Serve with a cold meat at an informal dinner

**1 (32-ounce) can tomatoes, mashed**
**Salt and pepper to taste**
**1 medium onion, chopped**
**2 Tablespoons sugar**
**1 (8-ounce) package macaroni, cooked and drained**
**¼ cup margarine**
**1 can mushroom soup**
**1 can chicken broth**
**1 pound sharp Cheddar cheese, grated**

Combine tomatoes, salt, pepper, onion and sugar. Cook gently. Add to macaroni. Combine margarine, soups and cheese; add to tomato-macaroni mixture. Cook in an uncovered casserole at 400° for 25-30 minutes. Allow to stand 5-10 minutes before serving. May be prepared in advance. 12 servings

**Ann T. McCrory (Mrs. Charles O.)**

## Linguine with Artichokes

¼ cup olive oil
½ stick butter
1 teaspoon flour
1 cup chicken broth
1 garlic clove, crushed
1 Tablespoon lemon juice
2 teaspoons parsley flakes
½ teaspoon salt
⅛ teaspoon pepper
1 can artichoke hearts,
    drained and halved
2 Tablespoons Parmesan
    cheese
1-2 teaspoons capers, drained
1 pound linguine
6 quarts water
2 Tablespoons olive oil
1 Tablespoon Parmesan
    cheese
1 Tablespoon softened butter
¼ teaspoon salt

In a large, heavy saucepan, heat ¼ cup olive oil over medium low heat. Add ½ stick butter and melt it; add flour. Cook mixture, stirring for 3 minutes. Stir in chicken broth. Increase heat to moderately high and cook 1 minute. Add crushed garlic clove, lemon juice, parsley flakes, the ½ teaspoon salt and pepper. Cook over moderate/low heat stirring for 5 minutes. Add artichokes, 2 Tablespoons Parmesan cheese and capers. Cook sauce covered, basting artichokes with sauce several times, for 8 minutes. Cook linguine in water approximately 10 minutes or until tender. Drain. In the linguine kettle, combine 2 Tablespoons olive oil, 1 Table-spoon Parmesan cheese, softened butter and ¼ teaspoon salt. Return drained linguine to kettle and toss with cheese mixture. Pour artichoke mixture over pasta, toss and serve on a heated platter with extra Parmesan cheese to sprinkle on top. Sauce may be prepared in advance. 6 servings

**Joe Nardone**

## Summer Pasta

4 fresh tomatoes, peeled,
    seeded and chopped
1 pound mozzarella cheese,
    diced
¼ cup fresh minced basil or
    2 Tablespoons dry basil
1-2 cloves garlic, crushed
1 cup olive oil
Salt and pepper to taste
1 pound spaghetti, cooked
Grated Parmesan cheese

Combine all ingredients except the spaghetti. Let stand at room temperature. Toss with 1 pound hot cooked spaghetti. Serve immediately with grated Parmesan cheese. 4-6 servings

**Carol Olsen (Mrs. Donald)**

# Fish and Shellfish

## Rainbow Trout with Mushroom Herb Stuffing

6 pan-dressed rainbow trout
1½ teaspoon salt
4 cups soft bread cubes
½ cup butter
1 cup sliced fresh mushrooms
½ cup sliced green onions (or more)
½ teaspoon salt
½ cup chopped parsley
1 (2-ounce) jar chopped pimientos
1½ Tablespoons lemon juice
½ teaspoon thyme (or more)
2 Tablespoons butter, melted

Sprinkle 1½ teaspoons salt evenly over inside and outside of fish. Sauté bread crumbs in butter until lightly browned, stirring frequently. Add mushrooms and onions, and cook until mushrooms are tender. Add ½ teaspoon salt, parsley, pimientos, lemon juice and thyme, and toss lightly. Stuff fish with dressing, and arrange in a well-oiled baking pan. Brush with melted butter. Bake at 350° for 25-30 minutes, or until fish flakes easily with a fork. 6 servings

**Cookbook Committee**

## Foil Baked Fish For Grill

3 pounds fish fillet, ½ inch thick (any firm-flesh fish)
5 slices bacon, minced
1 large green pepper, minced
1 large red pepper, minced
1 large onion, minced
1 cup sour cream
1 teaspoon salt
¼ teaspoon pepper
¼ teaspoon paprika
¼ cup butter, melted
Aluminum foil

Cut fish into serving pieces. Cook bacon just enough to render fat; remove and drain. Sauté peppers and onions in bacon fat until soft. Stir in sour cream and add bacon. Sprinkle fish with salt, pepper and paprika. Grease a large sheet of aluminum foil with butter. Spread some of the sour cream mixture on the foil, and top with the fish. Spread remaining sauce on top. Bring foil up over fish, and seal ends tightly. Grill 20-25 minutes almost directly on coals. 6 servings

**Cookbook Committee**

---

HINT

Put lemon on fish after cooking, never before, to keep from getting mushy.

## Grilled Red Snapper

6 snapper fillets (or similar
   fish)
Salt and pepper to taste
1-2 cloves garlic, minced
2-3 lemons, very thinly sliced
½ cup butter
Hickory chips, soaked in water

Season fillets with salt and pepper. In a saucepan, melt butter, add garlic and cook 1-2 minutes. Arrange half the lemon slices in a shallow baking dish, add fish in a single layer and put remaining lemon slices on top. Pour butter over fish. Add hickory chips to slow coals, place dish on heavy-duty foil atop grill and close hood (make a tent with foil if you do not have a covered grill). Cook until fish flakes easily with a fork, 15-20 minutes. Baste occasionally with butter. 6 servings

**Barrie C. Aycock (Mrs. Robert R.)**

## Shrimp Rolled Fillets
Simple to prepare but elegant enough for
your most important guests

¼ cup butter
1 clove garlic, minced
1 small onion, minced
¼ cup minced green pepper
12 large shrimp, cooked,
   shelled and deveined
¼ cup day old bread crumbs
1 Tablespoon parsley
½ teaspoon salt
⅛ teaspoon pepper
4 fillets of sole or flounder
   (1¼ pounds)
BLENDER HOLLANDAISE:
½ cup butter
3 egg yolks
2 Tablespoons lemon juice
Dash cayenne pepper
½ teaspoon salt

Melt 2 Tablespoons butter in a skillet. Sauté garlic, onion and pepper until soft. Dice 8 shrimp and add to sautéed mixture with bread crumbs, parsley, salt and pepper. Remove from heat. Spread 2 Tablespoons of shrimp mixture onto boned side of each fillet, and roll up, lengthwise. Refrigerate on a cookie sheet until ready to bake. Melt the remaining 2 Tablespoons butter. Arrange the fillets in a 10 x 6-inch baking dish, and brush with melted butter. Bake at 350° for 25-30 minutes, or until fish flakes easily with a fork. Pour Hollandaise sauce over fish and garnish with remaining shrimp. 4 servings

Hollandaise: Heat butter until bubbling. Put rest of ingredients in blender and mix on low speed. With motor running, pour bubbling butter into blender in a slow, steady stream; blending until sauce thickens.

**Elise M. Griffin**

# Hill's Broiled Red Snapper
Outstandingly simple and delicious

4 red snapper fillets
Salad oil
½ cup butter, melted
Juice of ½ lemon
¼ cup Worcestershire sauce
Lemon slices (for garnish)
¼ cup chopped parsley (for garnish)

Line a baking pan with aluminum foil and oil lightly. Place fillets on foil, skin side down. Brush top sides of fillets with oil. Place 4 inches below broiler heat and cook 15-20 minutes or until fish flakes easily with a fork. Meanwhile make a heated sauce of the butter, lemon and Worcestershire sauce. Place fillets on serving plate and pour hot sauce over. Garnish with parsley and lemon slices. Serve immediately. 4 servings

# Scalloped Haddock

2 pounds Haddock
1 can cream of mushroom soup
1 (5.33 fluid ounce) can evaporated milk
½ cup sherry
1 teaspoon Worcestershire sauce
Liquid from 1 (3 ounce) can sliced mushrooms
2-3 Tablespoons butter
¼ cup diced onions
½ cup finely chopped green pepper
1 cup finely chopped celery
4 Tablespoons flour
½ cup mayonnaise
½ pound cooked shrimp, cut in bite sized pieces
½ cup thinly sliced water chestnuts
1 can sliced mushrooms (from which liquid was drained earlier)
Salt to taste
Buttered breadcrumbs
Paprika

Rinse Haddock quickly under cold water, remove all bones and place in a single layer in a baking dish. Heat cream of mushroom soup, evaporated milk, sherry, Worcestershire sauce and liquid from mushrooms. Pour over fish. Bake 15 minutes at 400°. While fish is baking, sauté onions, green pepper and celery in butter. Add flour, stir until well blended. Add liquid in which fish was cooked. (Set fish aside.) Add mayonnaise, shrimp, water chestnuts, mushrooms and salt. Add more sherry, if desired. Break fish into pieces. Add very carefully to the sauce. Pour in casserole (about 3-quart). Top with buttered bread-crumbs and paprika. Bake 20-30 minutes at 400°. Freezes well. 8-10 servings

**Virginia P. Rick (Mrs. James, III)**

## Flounder with Cheese Sauce

1½ pounds flounder fillets
¼ cup evaporated milk
¼ cup milk, approximate
¾ teaspoon salt
2 Tablespoons margarine
2 Tablespoons flour
¼ cup diced Cheddar cheese
2 Tablespoons sherry, or to
   taste

Arrange fish fillets in single layer in baking dish. Salt and barely cover with milk. Bake at 400° for 5-10 minutes, until fish flakes easily with a fork. In the meantime, mix margarine and flour in saucepan over low heat. Remove from heat and add cheese. When fish is done, lift out of pan carefully. Set aside. Add liquid from fish to cheese mixture. Heat until cheese is melted and mixture is bubbly. Add sherry to taste. Put fish back in baking dish. Pour cheese mixture over fish. Brown under broiler just before serving. 4 servings

**Virginia P. Rick (Mrs. James, III)**

## Salmon Loaf with Dill Sauce

SALMON LOAF:
2 Tablespoons salad oil
¾ cup finely chopped celery
½ cup chopped onion
1 (7¾ ounce) can salmon
1 egg, slightly beaten
1 (5.3 ounce) can evaporated
   milk
1 cup fine bread crumbs
1 teaspoon salt
¼ teaspoon pepper
DILL SAUCE:
½ cup mayonnaise
¼ cup sour cream
1 Tablespoon lemon juice
1 Tablespoon milk
2 teaspoons dill weed
½ teaspoon sugar
½ teaspoon salt

Prepare at least 1½ hours before serving. Put oil in 2-quart saucepan. Sauté celery and onion over medium heat, about 10 minutes, until tender. Remove from heat; add salmon and salmon liquid, milk, breadcrumbs, salt and pepper. Mix until smooth. Grease 6 x 3½-inch loaf pan and spoon mixture into pan. Bake at 350° for 50 minutes. Remove loaf from pan. Serve either hot or cold with Dill Sauce. 4 servings
   Dill Sauce: Combine all ingredients and refrigerate.

**Susan M. Morley**

# Frog Legs

4 pairs frog legs, cleaned
   and skinned
1 small onion, sliced
2 cloves garlic, mashed in 1
   Tablespoon salt
1 cup white vinegar (or more)
1 lemon, sliced
BATTER:
1 cup flour
1 egg
1 teaspoon salt
1 teaspoon black pepper
¼ teaspoon cayenne pepper
½ cup milk

Place frog legs on a flat dish or pan and cover with vinegar. Sprinkle onions and garlic salt over top. Marinate for 2 hours. Drain. Boil in salted water with lemon for 20 minutes. Remove and drain.

Mix all batter ingredients together. Dip frog legs in batter and fry quickly in hot fat.
4 servings

**Terry Morris (Mrs. Douglas)**

# Shrimp Elégante

½ cup butter
½ cup margarine
8 Tablespoons all-purpose
   flour
2 pints half and half
3 (3-ounce) cans chopped
   mushrooms with liquid
6 green onions, finely chopped
½ teaspoon tarragon
½ teaspoon rosemary
¼ teaspoon cayenne pepper
1 Tablespoon celery seed
4 bay leaves
5 cloves garlic, crushed
Salt to taste
4 pounds shrimp, cooked
   and peeled
½ cup sherry
Toast cups:
3-4 loaves white sandwich
   bread
1 cup butter

Melt butter and margarine in a saucepan; add flour. Add cream and cook over medium heat until well blended, stirring constantly. Add mushrooms and liquid. Add green onions, tarragon, rosemary, cayenne pepper, celery seed, bay leaves, garlic and salt. Cook slowly for 15 minutes, do not boil. Add shrimp and sherry, and simmer 10 minutes. For luncheon or dinner, serve over rice. For a cocktail party, serve in toast cups.

Toast cups: Using a ½ inch cookie cutter, cut out bread (3 rounds per slice of bread). Brush melted butter on both sides of bread and press into small muffin tins. Bake at 300° for about 20 minutes, or until light brown and crusty. These can be placed in plastic bags and frozen until party time. 12 servings or 50 cocktail servings

**Nancy Kirby (Mrs. Jeff D., III)**

## Shrimp with Tarragon

1 clove garlic, finely minced
½ teaspoon salt
½ cup butter, room
    temperature
2 teaspoons finely chopped
    parsley
1 teaspoon minced fresh or
    dried tarragon
¾ cup soft bread crumbs
3 Tablespoons sherry
1 pound cooked, shelled
    shrimp (2 pounds fresh
    shrimp before shelling)

Crush garlic and salt together with back of a spoon until it is almost a purée. Cream the purée with butter, parsley, tarragon, bread crumbs and sherry. Spread half of mixture in bottom of individual ramekins. Arrange an equal portion of shrimp in each ramekin. Spread remaining butter mixture over shrimp. Bake at 400° until shrimp are done and until bread crumbs are brown, about 10 minutes depending on size of shrimp. 4 servings or 8 appetizer servings

**Jane Acker (Mrs. Reynolds B.)**
*Westport, Connecticut*

## Shrimp Asopao
A Puerto Rican peasant stew usually served as a main course

¼ cup olive oil
1½ cups finely chopped onion
1½ cups finely chopped green
    pepper
¼ pound bacon, chopped
¼ pound piece salt pork
6 cans condensed chicken
    broth
2 cups uncooked converted
    white rice
3 pounds large raw shrimp,
    shelled and deveined
1 (10 ounce) package frozen
    green peas
½ cup capers, drained
½ cup sliced stuffed green
    olives
2 pimientos, sliced
4 tomatoes, peeled, seeded
    and chopped

Heat oil in 6-8 quart kettle. Add onion, pepper, bacon and pork; cook covered over low heat 10 minutes. Add broth and 6 soup cans water. Bring to boil; add rice; return to boil; reduce heat; cook covered, stirring occasionally, 30 minutes. Add shrimp; bring to boil; reduce heat and simmer 15 minutes. Add frozen peas, capers, olives and pimientos. Return to boiling; reduce heat and cook 5 minutes or until peas are tender. Discard salt pork. Serve in deep soup plates with crusty bread and a fruit salad. 5 quarts 10-12 servings

**Pamela T. Marcus**

## Shrimp Jekyll
A good way to make shrimp go a long way!

1½ sticks butter
8 ounces fresh mushrooms, sliced
1 cup chopped onions
2 pounds small shrimp, cleaned and deveined
1 teaspoon seasoned salt
½ teaspoon lemon pepper
2 Tablespoons chopped parsley
1 Tablespoon Worcestershire sauce
½ cup grated Romano cheese
4 ounces chopped ripe olives (optional)
12 ounces thin spaghetti (Vermicelli) broken into thirds

Melt ¾ stick butter over moderate heat. Sauté mushrooms and onions in butter about 5-8 minutes. Transfer to mixing bowl. Melt ¾ stick butter in same pan and quickly cook shrimp until just pink. Transfer shrimp and liquid to same mixing bowl. Add salt, lemon pepper, parsley, Worcestershire, ¼ cup cheese and olives to shrimp-mushroom mixture. While preparing above, cook vermicelli al dente (about 9 minutes). Drain. Add to other ingredients while warm. Place in baking dish and top with remaining ¼ cup cheese. Bake at 350° for 20-30 minutes or until warmed through. This dish is best if made a few hours in advance to allow the flavors to blend. 6-8 servings

**Emy Blair (Mrs. Duane)**

## Shrimp With Fresh Mushrooms

¼ cup butter
1 pound fresh shrimp, peeled and deveined
2 Tablespoons shallots or green onions, minced
½ pound fresh mushrooms, sliced
1 Tablespoon flour
½ teaspoon salt
Freshly ground black pepper
3 Tablespoons sherry
1½ cups sour cream

Melt butter in a large skillet; add shrimp and shallots, and sauté until shrimp turn pink. Add mushroom slices and cook 5 minutes. Mix flour, salt and pepper. Sprinkle over ingredients in pan. Add sherry and sour cream, blending well; and continue heating gently. Adjust seasonings. Serve with steamed rice in a separate bowl, or spoon mixture into patty shells. 4 servings

**Joan McMahan (Mrs. James P.)**

# Shrimp Curry
An outstanding curry!

**Shrimp:**
**2 pounds raw shrimp, (18-20 count per pound)**
**1 Tablespoon salt**
**1 small onion, sliced**
**½ lemon, sliced**
**5 whole black peppercorns**
**CURRY SAUCE:**
**3 Tablespoons butter**
**1 cup finely chopped onion**
**1 cup finely chopped, pared apple**
**1 clove garlic, crushed**
**2-3 teaspoons Madras curry powder**
**¼ cup unsifted flour**
**1 teaspoon salt**
**1 teaspoon grated fresh ginger, (or ¼ teaspoon ground ginger)**
**¼ teaspoon ground cardamon**
**¼ teaspoon pepper**
**22 ounces chicken broth (undiluted)**
**2 Tablespoons fresh lime juice**
**2 teaspoons grated lime peel**
**¼ cup chopped chutney**

Rinse shrimp under cold water. Combine 1 quart water, salt, onions, lemon and pepper. Bring to a boil and add shrimp. Reduce heat and simmer 5 minutes, or until shrimp turn pink. Remove from liquid, peel and devein. Refrigerate until needed.

In a large saucepan, melt butter, and stir in curry powder. Add onions, apple, and garlic, and sauté until soft, about 5 minutes. Remove pan from heat; stir in flour and other spices. Gradually add broth, lime juice and peel. Return to heat and bring mixture to a boil, stirring constantly. Reduce heat and simmer sauce for 20 minutes. Stir occasionally. Mixture may be prepared several hours in advance, and refrigerated until serving time. Before serving, heat sauce, add shrimp and chutney. Serve hot with rice, and your choice of condiments. 6 servings Condiment suggestions: chopped peanuts, tomatoes, raisins, coconut, chopped hard-cooked eggs, green pepper.

**Susan M. Morley**

# Steamed Shrimp

**1 pound raw shrimp, unpeeled**
**½ cup sweet pickle juice**
**¾ cup cider vinegar**
**3 Tablespoons pickling spice**
**Dash garlic salt**
**2 teaspoons salt**

Place shrimp in bottom of a heavy pot. Pour sweet pickle juice and cider vinegar over shrimp. Cook over high heat until shrimp begin to turn pink. Add pickling spice, garlic salt and salt. Stir until very pink, about 3-4 minutes. Pour into bowl with juices. Cool, peel and serve. Shrimp may be prepared ahead and used as an appetizer or in a salad.
2-4 servings

**Mary Lib Dillard (Mrs. George P.)**

# Shrimp in Puff Pastry

20-24 large shrimp
Lemon juice
Salt and pepper
Worcestershire sauce
Butter
1 large onion, finely chopped
2 cloves garlic, crushed
4-5 green onions, finely
  chopped
6-8 mushrooms, thinly sliced
1 large tomato, peeled and
  diced
1 Tablespoon chives
1 bunch parsley, finely
  chopped
Salt and pepper to taste
1 sheet of puff pastry cut in
  5 x 5-inch squares
Slightly beaten egg
Sauce Bernaise

Peel and devein shrimp, and marinate in lemon juice, salt, pepper, and Worcestershire sauce in refrigerator. Melt butter in skillet large enough to hold all herbs and vegetables. Sauté onions, crushed garlic, green onions, mushrooms, tomatoes, chives and parsley, and season with salt and pepper. This should not take longer than 5 minutes. Take off stove and cool. Take about 5-6 shrimp and place on pastry squares and top with mixture divided equally among the 4 servings. Fold opposite edges of pastry and brush with egg. Bake at 400° until pastry is done. Serve topped with Sauce Bérnaise, with assorted vegetables on the side. 4 servings

**Yvette Greune**
*Old Vinings Inn*
*Atlanta, Georgia*

# Barbequed Shrimp
Give everyone a damp hot towel afterwards
Spicy and messy, but fun!

2 pounds (16-20 per pound)
  shrimp, unpeeled
6 cloves garlic, crushed
2 bay leaves
1 teaspoon rosemary
1 teaspoon oregano
1 teaspoon whole peppercorns,
  crushed
1 Tablespoon salt
2 Tablespoons Sauterne wine
4 Tablespoons olive oil

Heat oil in frying pan. Add shrimp and spices. Sauté 20 minutes. Add sauterne and simmer 5 minutes. Peel shrimp at table and dunk in sauce. Serve with hot crisp bread, also good for dunking into sauce.
4-6 servings

**Elise M. Griffin**

HINT ■■■■■■■■■■■■■■■■■■■■■■

When handling freshly caught fish, coat hands with salt for easier gripping.

## Sweet and Sour Shrimp

1 onion, sliced thin
1 green pepper, sliced or
   chopped
¼ cup butter, melted
½ cup sugar
1 (8½ ounce) can pineapple
   chunks, undrained
2 Tablespoons cornstarch
½ teaspoon dry mustard
¼ teaspoon salt
½ cup white vinegar
1 Tablespoon soy sauce
1 cup cherry tomatoes
1 pound shrimp, boiled,
   shelled and deveined
1 cup fresh Chinese snow
   peas or 1 package frozen
   peas
1 cup toasted slivered almonds
   (optional)

Sauté onion and green pepper in butter. Mix sugar, pineapple syrup, cornstarch, dry mustard, salt, vinegar and soy sauce, and add to the sautéed vegetables. Simmer for 10 minutes. Before serving, add tomatoes, shrimp, snow peas and pineapple. Cook for an additional 5-10 minutes. Serve on rice. Garnish with toasted almonds if desired.
6-8 servings

**Cile M. Davidson (Mrs. Charles, Jr.)**

## Shrimp and Wild Rice

2 (6 ounce) packages long
   grain and wild rice, cooked
2 Tablespoons butter
1 cup bias-cut celery
½ cup chopped green onions
2 (2½ ounce) jars sliced
   mushrooms, drained
2 Tablespoons chopped
   pimiento
2 cups cooked and peeled
   shrimp (more if desired)
Salt and pepper to taste
TOPPING:
1 can cream of mushroom soup
1⅓ cups sour cream
⅔ cup dry bread crumbs
2 Tablespoons chopped parsley

Melt butter and sauté celery, green onions, pimiento and mushrooms until tender. Add shrimp, salt and pepper. Add rice. Spoon mixture into a greased 2-quart casserole. Mix soup and sour cream. Spread over rice mixture. Top with bread crumbs and parsley. Bake 30 minutes at 325°. May be prepared in advance.
8 servings

**Mrs. Kirk Scruggs**

# Crabmeat Soufflé

1½ cups fresh or frozen
  crabmeat, drained and
  flaked
¼ cup butter or margarine
¼ cup flour
1 cup milk
½ teaspoon salt
1 cup shredded sharp Cheddar
  cheese
4 eggs, separated

Preheat oven to 300°. Place crabmeat in bottom of a 5-cup soufflé dish. Make a white sauce with butter, flour, milk and salt. Add cheese and stir until melted. Remove from heat. Add slightly beaten egg yolks, and cool. Beat egg whites until stiff, and fold lightly into sauce. Pour sauce over crabmeat in dish. With tip of spoon, make a slight indentation or "track" around top of soufflé, 1 inch from edge to form a top hat. Bake at 300° for 60-65 minutes, or until browned and set. Serve immediately. 4 servings

**Jeanine C. Andrews (Mrs. Edward B.)**

# Crab Imperial
This receives rave reviews in Tidewater, Virginia
where folks enjoy their seafood

2 cups backfin crabmeat
4 Tablespoons butter, melted
1 teaspoon grated onion
2 Tablespoons chopped
  pimiento
4 Tablespoons mayonnaise
2 Tablespoons cream
1 teaspoon Worcestershire
  sauce
½ cup finely chopped green
  pepper
Salt and pepper to taste
Ritz cracker crumbs

Combine all ingredients except cracker crumbs. Fill individual baking shells or 1-quart casserole. Spread top with additional mayonnaise and sprinkle with rolled Ritz cracker crumbs. Bake 30 minutes in a 350° oven. 4 servings

**Mrs. Alfred J. Westcott**
*Norfolk, Virginia*

## Crab Continental

4 Tablespoons butter
4 Tablespoons flour
Dash pepper
1 teaspoon salt
⅛ teaspoon paprika
2 cups milk
½ pound sharp yellow cheese, grated
6 hard-boiled eggs, chopped
2 Tablespoons Worcestershire sauce
1 cup stuffed olives, sliced
1 (12 ounce) can mushrooms, or fresh if desired
1 cup slivered almonds
3 cans (6 to 8 ounces) crabmeat
4 Tablespoons sherry (optional)
Parmesan cheese

Melt butter. Add flour and salt and cook until bubbly. Add heated milk gradually stirring until sauce is slightly thickened. Add paprika and pepper. Add cheese and let melt. Pour in large baking pan and add remaining ingredients. Top with Parmesan cheese. Bake 30 to 40 minutes at 350°. May also be baked and then used as a filing for patty shells. 6 servings

Beth Johnston (Mrs. J. Gibson)

## Eggplant Stuffed with Crab and Shrimp

6 medium eggplant
3 Tablespoons butter
4 green peppers, finely chopped
4 medium carrots, finely chopped
½ cup chopped parsley
½ cup finely chopped celery
3 cloves garlic, minced
1 pound white lump crabmeat
1 pound small shrimp, shelled
Salt and pepper to taste
Cup bread crumbs
Paprika
1 cup butter, melted

Boil eggplants until soft, cut in halves (or cook in microwave—place halves on tray 1 inch apart, cook 2 minutes, rotate and cook 2-3 minutes more until tender). Scoop out meat, reserve shells. Sauté vegetables in 3 Tablespoons butter until tender. Add eggplant and cook over medium heat until most of liquid has evaporated. Add shrimp and cook 15 minutes. Add crabmeat and bread crumbs, cook 3-5 minutes, and season with salt and pepper. Stuff shells with mixture, and sprinkle with paprika. Pour melted butter over, and heat in a 350° oven until thoroughly warmed. 12 Servings

Lucy Dyer

# Baked Crab

This Gulf coast specialty is the favorite of our cover artist.
It's his mother's recipe.

1 cup finely chopped celery
½ cup finely chopped parsley
1 cup finely chopped green
  pepper
1 cup finely chopped onion
3 Tablespoons bacon grease
1 pound fresh lump crabmeat
1 pound fresh claw crabmeat
2 cups milk
2 eggs, beaten
2 cups fresh bread crumbs
½ cup butter, melted
½ cup buttered bread crumbs
  for topping

In a large skillet, sauté vegetables in bacon grease until soft. Combine remaining ingredients and mix well; add sautéed vegetables. Place in a 2-quart baking dish, sprinkle with buttered crumbs and bake in 350° oven for 30-45 minutes until bubbling and nicely browned. Serve with a colorful fruit salad, a green vegetable, and a dry white wine. 8-10 servings

**Mrs. T.S. Morton, Jr.**
*Gulfport, Miss.*

# Broiled Soft Shell Crabs

8 soft shelled crabs
½ pound butter, melted
4 garlic cloves, minced
6-8 green onions, chopped
1 teaspoon salt
Pepper
Paprika

Wash crabs and drain well. Place in single layer in baking pan; use earthen-ware if possible. Mix remaining ingredients and use to brush crabs. Broil under high heat until claws are crisp. Serve with slaw and hot French bread. 4 servings

**Terry C. Morris (Mrs. Douglas)**

# Baked Scallops

1 pound scallops (if large, cut
  in 4 pieces)
Fresh bread crumbs (about 6
  slices), buttered
2 eggs, lightly beaten with
  pinch of salt
⅓ cup melted butter or
  margarine (approximate,
  add more if necessary)

Dip scallops in egg and then in crumbs. Put in shallow baking dish in single layer. Drizzle with melted butter. Can be done earlier in the day to this point and refrigerated until time to cook. Bake in 450° oven for 15-20 minutes, until brown and crisp. Serve with tartare sauce. 3-4 servings

**Virginia P. Rick (Mrs. James, III.)**

# Seafood Casserole
### Excellent for a buffet supper

2 (6-ounce) packages wild and long grain rice mix
1 pound lump crab meat, cooked and cleaned or 3 (6 ounce) cans white crab meat
1 pound fresh shrimp, cooked or 4 (4½ ounce) cans shrimp, drained
3 cans cream of mushroom soup
½ onion, grated
1 cup chopped green pepper
1 cup chopped celery
1 (14-ounce) jar pimiento, chopped
2 Tablespoons lemon juice
1 (8-ounce) can button mushrooms
1 (14-ounce) can artichoke hearts, drained well

Cook rice as label directs. Remove any cartilage from crab. Rinse shrimp in cold water and drain well. Preheat oven to 325°. Mix all ingredients and place in a greased 4-quart casserole. Bake for 1½ hours or, use two 2-quart dishes and bake for 45 minutes.
14 servings

**Constance D. Wilson (Mrs. A.E., Jr.)**

# Scallop Kabobs
### A low calorie meal

1½ pounds sea scallops
2 cups canned pineapple chunks
2 cups small, whole mushroom caps
1 medium green pepper, cut into 1-inch squares
¼ cup soy sauce
¼ cup lemon juice
¼ cup chopped fresh parsley
½ teaspoon salt
Dash pepper
½ teaspoon grated fresh ginger (optional)

Combine all ingredients in a large bowl; toss lightly but thoroughly. Let stand 30 minutes, stirring occasionally. Drain ingredients; reserve marinade and keep warm. Thread scallops, pineapple, mushrooms and green pepper, evenly divided, on each of eight 12-inch skewers. Broil on grill about 4 inches from heat source for about 5 minutes. Turn and cook 5 minutes longer. May be prepared earlier in day and refrigerated until ready to cook.
4 servings

**Dot W. Smith (Mrs. William P., III)**

# Scallop Sauté

¼ cup butter
½ teaspoon salt
⅛ teaspoon pepper
1 clove garlic, minced
½ teaspoon paprika
1 pound bay scallops
3 Tablespoons lemon juice
1 Tablespoon parsley

In a large skillet, heat ½ of the butter with the garlic and seasonings. Add scallops to cover bottom of skillet without crowding. Cook quickly on high heat, stirring occasionally until golden, about 5-7 minutes. Repeat until all scallops are cooked, keeping the cooked ones warm. In same skillet, place parsley, lemon juice and remaining butter. Pour sauce over scallops. 4 servings

**Cookbook Committee**

# Oysters Pan Roast

½ cup butter
2 slices bacon, cut in ½ inch pieces
1 bunch shallots or green onions, finely chopped
1 bunch parsley, finely chopped
1-2 cloves garlic, finely chopped
½ cup flour (or more if a thick sauce is desired)
1 quart oysters (select), undrained
¼ teaspoon seasoned pepper
½ teaspoon salt
4 Tablespoons Worcestershire sauce
¼ cup vermouth
1-2 dashes Tabasco sauce
1 cup Italian bread crumbs

Melt butter in saucepan. Sauté bacon, shallots, parsley and garlic 5 minutes over medium heat. Remove pan from heat, and stir in flour. Meanwhile, heat oysters in their liquid until the edges curl. Drain, and pour the oyster liquid gradually into the flour mixture, stirring rapidly until blended. Return to heat and cook, stirring constantly, until sauce becomes thick. Add seasoned pepper, salt, Worcestershire, vermouth and Tabasco. Taste and adjust seasoning as desired. Gently stir in oysters. Pour into buttered casserole dish and sprinkle bread crumbs on top, or use 4 individual ramekins. Bake 20 minutes at 475°. Entire dish may be made in advance and baked at the last minute. A green salad, French bread and a special dessert make this a wonderful company dish for oyster lovers. 4 servings

**Elise M. Griffin**

# Deviled Oysters

1 pint oysters with liquid
¼ cup butter, melted
1 cup oyster cracker crumbs
1 medium green pepper,
    seeded and finely chopped
¼ cup finely chopped parsley
1 medium onion, grated
2 teaspoons Worcestershire
    sauce
2 hard-cooked eggs, chopped
3 eggs, slightly beaten
½ cup light cream
1 teaspoon Dijon mustard
⅛ teaspoon cayenne pepper
½ teaspoon salt

Combine all ingredients and toss to mix well. Turn into a buttered 5-6 cup soufflé dish or casserole. Bake 30 minutes at 375° until set and lightly browned. For individual servings, spoon mixture into buttered ramekins or scallop shells and bake for 15 minutes. To serve as hors d'oeuvres, bake in buttered oyster or clam shells for 10 minutes or until set. 6 servings

**Peggy Weitnauer (Mrs. John)**

# Lobster Supreme
For a special party

8 lobster tails, split
¼ pound butter
4 Tablespoons flour
1 teaspoon salt
1 teaspoon paprika
Dash cayenne
2 cups half and half
2 teaspoons lemon juice
TOPPING:
¼ cup cracker crumbs
¼ cup grated Parmesan
    cheese
1 Tablespoon butter, melted

Boil lobster tails in salted water. Cut meat out and dice. Sauté meat in butter, remove, blend in flour, salt, paprika, and cayenne. Slowly stir in cream, cook until thick—boil one minute. Stir in lemon juice. Spoon into shells and add topping. Bake at 450°, approximately 10-12 minutes. May be refrigerated before the last cooking. Goes well with fresh asparagus topped with lemon juice, butter and toasted sesame seeds. 4 servings

**Lynn Herring (Mrs. Roy P.)**

# Lobster Thermidor

4 boxes rock lobster tails
½ pound fresh mushrooms, sliced
4 Tablespoons butter
4 Tablespoons flour
Salt and pepper to taste
⅛ teaspoon Tabasco sauce
1 teaspoon Worcestershire sauce
1 pint half and half
½ cup grated Parmesan cheese
1 cup soft bread crumbs
1 cup grated Cheddar cheese
4 Tablespoons butter

Follow package directions for boiling lobster tails. Remove from water and allow to cool. Remove lobster from shells; cut into bite-size pieces. Reserve shells for serving if desired. Melt butter in large skillet; add mushrooms and sauté over low heat. Add flour, salt and pepper, Tabasco and Worcestershire sauce. Remove from heat and add cream slowly, stirring constantly. Simmer sauce over low heat until sauce thickens. Add lobster and Parmesan cheese. Flatten lobster shells. Fill shells with mixture. Sprinkle tops with bread crumbs and grated Cheddar cheese. Dot with butter. Broil 3 minutes or until lightly browned.
4 servings

# White Clam Sauce for Spaghetti
A superb quickie—elegant and easy

1 onion chopped
1 bunch green onions and some tops, chopped
¼ cup olive oil (Berio brand)
2 cans Buitoni white clam spaghetti sauce
1 pound shrimp or lobster
¼ cup dry vermouth
1 Tablespoon Worcestershire sauce
Salt and pepper to taste
½ teaspoon sugar
Juice of ½ lemon
1 (8 ounce) package spinach noodles or vermicelli, cooked according to directions

Sauté onions gently in olive oil. Add clams, seafood and seasonings. Simmer slowly for a few minutes. Spoon over cooked spinach noodles or vermicelli.
4 servings

**George Pendley**

# Meats

# How to Stir-Fry Successfully

Three rules—cut bite-size, cook quickly, and serve immediately.

## Preparation

Meats and vegetables which are cooked together should be of equal size and thickness so cooking times will be the same.

Cut meats across the grain into thin strips. Meat will slice easier if partially frozen.

Cut celery, asparagus, and less tender vegetables diagonally to expose more surface and allow quicker cooking.

## Types of Oil

Any vegetable oil which does not have a strong flavor is acceptable for stir-frying. Peanut oil is best; it has a good flavor and does not burn easily. The Chinese prefer to use lard which gives a rich flavor and clear color, but we do not recommend its high cholesterol content. Butter, margarine, olive oil and solid shortenings are not suitable. Chicken fat gives a good flavor to certain vegetable dishes, especially Chinese cabbage.

The oil may be flavored by adding a clove of garlic and 1-2 slices of fresh ginger. Brown them in the oil, then remove before adding other ingredients.

## Method

Always stir-fry the minimum amount of time necessary. Meats will become tough if over-cooked; vegetables should remain crisp to retain color and nutrients.

Have all ingredients prepared and within reach before beginning to cook. Heat wok or large skillet over high heat, add 1-2 Tablespoons oil. Cook ingredients in small batches, over medium-high to high heat, stirring constantly adding more oil as needed for each batch. Meats and vegetables are usually cooked separately. Drain on a rack or on paper towels. If a sauce is desired, return all ingredients to the pan and add cornstarch dissolved in water, broth, or soy sauce. Use 1 Tablespoon cornstarch to 2-3 Tablespoons liquid. Additional soy sauce, sesame oil, salt and pepper, MSG and wine may be added as desired for flavor. If a marinade is used for the meat, dissolve cornstarch in marinade and add to the pan. Cook just until thickened.

A good basic marinade for beef: To 1 pound sirloin or round steak, thinly sliced, add 3 Tablespoons soy sauce, 1 Tablespoon dry sherry or Mirin, 1 teaspoon sugar and ¼ teaspoon MSG. Marinate at least 30 minutes.

## Soy Sauce

Imported Japanese soy sauce is a good all-purpose sauce to use. For variety, try experimenting with good Chinese imports; the dark variety is thick and black, the light variety is thin and more salty.

## Tournedos Sautés Aux Champignons

2 Tablespoons butter
3 Tablespoons minced shallots
½ pound mushrooms, sliced
2 Tablespoons chopped chives
1 teaspoon marjoram
Salt and pepper to taste
½ cup dry white wine
6 fillet steaks, 1 inch thick
    or 1 (3½-4 pound) tender-
    loin roast
¼ cup brandy

In skillet melt butter, stir in shallots and cook slowly 1 minute. Add mushrooms and cook 1 minute. Stir in herbs, seasonings and white wine. Cook over moderately high heat for 3 minutes. In a separate pan, sauté steaks in butter until cooked to your preference. (May be grilled if desired.) Cook the roast, uncovered, at 325° for approximately 1 hour, and cut in ¾ inch slices. Pour sauce over meat. Heat brandy, ignite and pour over meat; serve immediately. Sauce may be prepared in advance. 6 servings

**Sandy L. Carley (Mrs. George H.)**

## Tournedos in Puff Pastry
This elegant entrée may be prepared early in the day
and refrigerated until cooking time

6 tournedos (filet mignon)
5 Tablespoons butter
Salt and pepper to taste
½ pound fresh mushrooms,
    chopped
½ cup liver pâté (homemade
    or liverwurst)
3 Tablespoons sherry
6 frozen Pepperidge Farm
    Patty Shells, thawed
1 egg, separated

Sauté tournedos in 3 Tablespoons butter for 3 minutes on each side. Season and cool. Sauté mushrooms in remaining 2 Tablespoons butter; add pâté and sauté until brown. Add enough sherry to bind mixture. Spread a thin layer of pâté mixture on top of each tournedo. Cool again. Remove center portion of patty shells, and roll each into a thin round; roll out shells in the same manner. Place each of the 6 tournedos on the smaller rounds and cover with the large rounds. Paint edges with slightly beaten egg yolk and seal. Bake 10 minutes in a 400° oven until pastry is golden. Serve with Madeira Sauce (see Index). 6 servings

**Ann T. McCrory (Mrs. Charles O.)**

# Helen Corbitt's Tenderloin of Beef with Lobster

3 lobster tails
½ cup imported soy sauce
1 3-4 pound tenderloin, oven-
   ready*
2 Tablespoons grated fresh
   ginger
1 medium onion, sliced
¾ cup dry sherry
4 Tablespoons butter, melted
Chopped parsley
*An oven ready tenderloin has
   had all excess fat and
   membrane trimmed away.

Preheat oven to 350°. Split lobster tails, loosen meat. Rub with soy sauce. Bake for 10 minutes. Remove meat from shells. Preheat oven to 450°. Rub the tenderloin with soy sauce and grated ginger. Place on top of sliced onions in a broiler pan and bake for 25 minutes at 450°. Baste with half of the sherry. Split tenderloin ¾-inch deep, stuff lobster into cavity. Place under broiler just long enough to heat, basting with a mixture of the remaining soy sauce and sherry, or heat briefly in a 350° oven. Sprinkle with melted butter and chopped parsley before serving.
6 servings

# Mongolian Beef

1½ pounds beef (preferably
   sirloin), cut in thin strips
½ teaspoon MSG
¼ cup peanut oil
1 cup beef bouillon
½ teaspoon sugar
¼ teaspoon grated ginger root
1 teaspoon Japanese soy sauce
2 large ribs celery, cut bite size
2 green peppers, cut bite size
1 large onion, cut bite size
2 large tomatoes, cut in 8
   sections
2 teaspoons cornstarch
2 Tablespoons water

Sprinkle beef with MSG. Brown quickly in hot oil in a skillet or wok. Add bouillon, sugar, ginger, and soy sauce. Bring to a boil and simmer 15 minutes. Add vegetables and cook 5 minutes longer. Combine cornstarch and water, add to beef and stir until it thickens. Serve over rice.
4 servings

**Pamela T. Marcus**

# Beef and Oyster Sauce
A Chinese "stir-fry" dish

4 Tablespoons bottled oyster
    sauce (found in gourmet or
    oriental food stores)
1 teaspoon sugar
Dash pepper
1 cup beef broth
4 Tablespoons cornstarch
¼ cup Japanese soy sauce
4 Tablespoons water
2 Tablespoons peanut oil
1 onion, chopped
1 clove garlic, minced
1 teaspoon fresh ginger
1 pound sirloin or round steak,
    thinly sliced

Combine oyster sauce, sugar, pepper and broth. In another bowl, blend cornstarch, water and soy sauce to a paste. Put oil in wok or large fry pan and bring to high heat. Stir-fry onion, garlic and ginger for 30 seconds. Add beef and stir-fry until it loses its redness. Add oyster sauce mixture, heat thoroughly, and cook covered for one minute. Add cornstarch mixture to thicken. Stir well; turn on low to keep warm. Serve with steamed rice. 4 servings

**Decie Nygaard (Mrs. W.F.)**

# Blackbirds

3 pounds top round steak,
    1" thick
1 pound bacon
Salt & pepper
Celery salt
8 medium onions

Cut steak in strips ¼" wide. Lay flat and place slice of bacon on top. Roll bacon inside and insert toothpicks to hold. Place in frying pan and sear top, bottom and sides. Remove. Chop 8 onions and brown in same pan. Remove onions. Replace blackbirds and pour onions on top. Add salts, pepper and enough water to cover ⅔ of meat (about 1 cup). Cover tightly and simmer for 2 hours 15 minutes. Remove grease from top and serve. 8 servings

**Mrs. William J. Patterson**

# Pic-L-Nic Beef Roll
Great for a tailgate picnic

1 (2½ pound) flank steak
Prepared mustard
Seasoned salt, and pepper
6 dill pickles, quartered
   lengthwise
6 carrots, quartered lengthwise
6 scallions
Shortening
1 beef bouillon cube
¼ cup vinegar
2 cups water
1 cup dry red wine
1 Tablespoon whole black
   peppercorns
2 bay leaves
2 stalks celery
Parsley

Spread mustard thinly on steak and sprinkle with salt and pepper. Starting at narrow side, alternate rows of pickles, carrots and scallions on top of steak. Roll up in jelly roll fashion and tie securely with string at 1-inch intervals. Brown steak on all sides in hot oil. Pour off drippings. Add water, bouillon cube, vinegar, wine, peppercorns, bay leaf and celery. Cover and cook for 3 hours. Allow to cool in liquid and chill overnight. To serve, remove from liquid and slice diagonally ¼ inch thick. Serve cold; garnished with parsley. 6 servings

**Susan M. Morley**

# Charcoaled Flank Steak

2 flank steaks (about 2½
   pounds)
½ cup soy sauce
½ cup salad oil
3 Tablespoons wine vinegar
2 Tablespoons instant minced
   onion
¼ teaspoon garlic powder
½ teaspoon MSG
1 Tablespoon liquid smoke
2-3 Tablespoons barbecue
   sauce
2-3 Tablespoons A-1 steak
   sauce
½ cup red wine (optional)

Select top quality flank steaks. Combine all other ingredients and pour over steaks in a shallow pan. Marinate in the refrigerator for 8 to 10 hours, turning meat occasionally. Cook on a charcoal grill over a medium to high fire. Steaks should be cooked rare or medium. If cooked well done, it could be tough. To serve, carve in very thin slices (electric knife helpful) across the grain. 5-6 servings

**Mary M. Joines (Mrs. I.W.)**

## Marinated London Broil

1 (2½-3 pound) London broil
MARINADE:
1 can beer
½ cup peanut oil
1 teaspoon dry mustard
1 teaspoon ginger
1 teaspoon Worcestershire
    sauce
1 Tablespoon sugar
2 Tablespoons orange
    marmalade
1 teaspoon garlic powder
Salt and freshly ground pepper

Mix all marinade ingredients together and pour into oblong glass casserole. Place meat in mixture and spoon marinade over top and sides of meat. Cover and place in refrigerator for 24 hours. Turn meat at least twice. Barbecue to personal taste, brushing with marinade. 4-6 servings

Helen W. Ward (Mrs. William T., Jr.)

## Braised Sirloin Tips

1 pound fresh mushrooms,
    sliced
¼ cup butter, melted
1 Tablespoon salad oil
1 (3 pound) sirloin tip steak,
    cut in 1 inch cubes
¾ cup beef bouillon
¾ cup red wine
2 Tablespoons soy sauce
2 cloves garlic, minced
½ onion, grated
2 Tablespoons cornstarch
⅓ cup beef bouillon
½ (10¾ ounce) can cream of
    mushroom soup, undiluted
Salt to taste

Sauté mushrooms in 2 Tablespoons butter and spoon into 3-quart casserole. Add remaining butter and salad oil to skillet; add meat and brown. Spoon over mushrooms. Combine bouillon, wine, soy sauce, garlic and onion; add to skillet, scraping bottom to salvage all particles. Blend cornstarch with remaining ⅓ cup bouillon and stir into wine mixture. Cook, stirring constantly, until smooth and thickened. Spoon over meat, stirring gently to mix. Cover and bake at 275° for 1 hour. Add soup and season with salt. Return to oven; bake approximately 1 hour, or until tender. Serve over rice. May be frozen or prepared in advance. 6-8 servings

Mrs. John Stroop

## Beef with Artichokes

2 pounds top sirloin, cubed
⅓ cup flour
Salt and pepper
2 Tablespoons salad oil
2 (8 ounce) cans tomato sauce
1 clove garlic, crushed
1 cup dry red wine
2 beef bouillon cubes
½ teaspoon dill weed
1 can artichoke hearts, drained
1 (1 pound) can small white
    onions, drained
1 (4 ounce) can mushrooms,
    drained

Dredge meat with flour, seasoned with salt and pepper, and brown in oil; set meat aside. Add tomato sauce, garlic, wine, bouillon cubes and dill weed to skillet and mix well. Return meat to pan and simmer for 90 minutes. Add vegetables and heat 30 minutes longer. Serve with rice. 4 servings

**Helen W. Ward (Mrs. William T., Jr.)**

## Carbonnade of Beef
This is a national dish of Belgium

1 (2½ pound) round steak,
    ¼ inch thick
½ cup all purpose flour
½ cup butter or margarine
8 large onions, sliced
2 garlic cloves, minced
1 beef bouillon cube
1 teaspoon thyme leaves
2 teaspoons salt
¼ teaspoon pepper
1 (12 ounce) can beer

Cut round steak into 8 pieces. Using a meat mallet or the side of a saucer, pound ¼ cup flour into one side of steak. Repeat on the other side using remaining flour. Melt ¼ cup butter or margarine in a large skillet. Cook onions over medium heat in melted fat until golden. Drain. In the same skillet, melt remaining fat, and brown meat well on both sides, a few pieces at a time. Return meat and onions to the skillet. Add remaining ingredients. Cover and cook over low heat for 1 to 2 hours until meat is fork tender. 8 servings

**Sandra R. Pritchett (Mrs. Edwin P.)**

## Swiss Steak Supreme

½ Tablespoon butter
2 pounds round steak, sliced
    thin
1 package onion soup mix
½ pound fresh mushrooms,
    sliced
½ green pepper, sliced
Fresh ground black pepper
1 (16 ounce) can tomatoes,
    drained and chopped,
    reserve juice
¼ teaspoon salt
1 Tablespoon A-1 sauce
1 Tablespoon cornstarch
1 Tablespoon chopped parsley

Butter large 10-inch casserole.
Arrange strips of meat in
casserole, overlapping each
piece. Sprinkle with soup mix,
mushrooms, green pepper, black
pepper, tomatoes and salt. Mix
A-1 sauce and cornstarch in ½
cup tomato juice. Pour over meat.
Cover casserole with foil and seal
tightly. Bake at 375° for 2 hours.
Sprinkle with parsley and serve
with buttered noodles. 4 servings

**Dunja S. Awbrey (Mrs. James J.)**

## Beef Rouladen I

2 round steaks, cut ¼ inch
    thick
Prepared mustard
Salt and pepper
1 large onion, chopped
4 strips bacon, cut into
    small pieces
1 dill pickle, finely chopped
3 Tablespoons oil
Red wine
½ cup sour cream
2 Tablespoons flour

Cut each steak in half, and
pound to tenderize. Spread each
piece with mustard, and sprinkle
with salt and pepper. Place bacon,
onion, and dill pickle on top. Roll
each piece and secure with toothpicks. Heat oil in a Dutch oven,
and brown meat on all sides.
Cover rolls with wine, cover pot
and simmer about 1½ hours, until
rolls are tender. Combine 2
Tablespoons flour with ¼ cup
water; add to stock and simmer
until thickened. Add sour cream,
and heat through. 4 servings

**Barbara Johnson (Mrs. Larry)**

# Beef Rouladen II
A traditional German dish

3 pounds sirloin tip roast,
  sliced ¼ inch thick
2 large onions, finely chopped
1¼ cups butter
1½ pounds fresh mushrooms,
  finely chopped (save a few
  small ones for the sauce)
¾ pound cooked ham,
  julienned in strips ½ inch
  long and ⅛ inch wide
¾ cup grated Parmesan
  cheese
1 cup dry white wine
1 cup beef broth, full strength
1 teaspoon salt
Freshly ground black pepper
2 Tablespoons cornstarch
2 Tablespoons water
2 Tablespoons finely chopped
  parsley

Pound meat slices to about ¹⁄₁₆ inch thickness. Melt 2 Tablespoons butter in a skillet and saute onions about 5 minutes until soft. Transfer onions to a bowl, and sauté mushrooms 5 minutes in 2 more Tablespoons butter. Add mushrooms, ham and grated cheese to onions; mix well. Place 1 heaping Tablespoon or more of this filling on each meat slice and roll up, securing with toothpicks. In a skillet, melt 2-4 Tablespoons butter. Brown meat rolls on all sides (You may need two pans). Pour in wine and broth. Season to taste with salt and pepper. Cover and simmer for 10-15 minutes. Remove toothpicks and transfer meat to an ovenproof serving dish. Into the remaining juices and wine, stir cornstarch blended with water, and cook over medium heat until thickened. Toss reserved whole mushrooms in melted butter, and add to the sauce. Pour sauce over meat rolls on a serving plate and cover until serving time. Rolls may be prepared in advance and refrigerated at this point. Before serving, heat thoroughly, covered, in a 375° oven for 20 minutes; or for 45 minutes, if refrigerated. Garnish with parsley. This is traditionally served with potato pancakes and a Moselle wine. 8-10 servings

**Susan Morley**

## Marinated Sirloin Tip Roast

1 5-6 pound sirloin tip roast
1 Tablespoon salt
½ teaspoon pepper
Enough beef suet to cover top
   of roast
MARINADE:
1 cup thinly sliced onions
1 cup thinly sliced carrots
1 cup sliced celery stalks
   and leaves
2 cloves garlic, halved
2 bay leaves
1 Tablespoon thyme leaves
¼ cup minced parsley
5 cups burgundy
¼ cup brandy
½ cup olive or vegetable oil
Flour for thickening gravy, if
   desired

Place half the vegetables and herbs in the bottom of a large bowl. Rub the roast with salt and pepper, and place over the vegetables. Top with the rest of the vegetables and herbs. Add wine, brandy and oil; cover and marinate for 6-24 hours. Turn and baste several times. Remove meat. Put marinade in a saucepan and boil to reduce in volume by ½. Arrange suet on top of meat. Roast in a 350° oven or on a covered grill over slow coals. If gravy is desired, place roast in an ovenproof skillet or baking dish. Cook for about 20 minutes per pound for medium rare. A meat thermometer may be used. To make gravy, add water and some of the marinade to pan juices, and thicken with flour.
10-12 servings

**Cookbook Committee**

## Carl's Roast

1 (2½-3 pound) shoulder roast
1-2 cloves garlic
1-2 red peppers
2 bunches green onions
Salt and pepper
1 brown-in-bag
1 cup sauterne
1 Tablespoon Worcestershire
   sauce
Vegetables: mushrooms,
   potatoes, carrots, onions,
   celery, as desired

With a sharp knife, make slits over surface of roast at 1-inch intervals. Insert a small sliver of garlic and red pepper, and 1 green onion top into each slit. Salt and pepper roast. Prepare bag according to manufacturer's directions and insert roast and vegetables. Mix wine and Worcestershire and pour over roast. Bake at 350° for 2½-3 hours. Thicken gravy if desired.
4-6 servings

**Carl Veal**

# Chinese Pot Roast

4 pounds chuck roast
2 Tablespoons fat
1 teaspoon garlic salt
½ teaspoon dry mustard
¼ teaspoon pepper
¼ cup soy sauce
1 Tablespoon honey
1 Tablespoon vinegar
1 teaspoon celery seed
½ teaspoon ground ginger
2 Tablespoons cornstarch
¾ cup water

Brown meat in fat until browned on all sides. Mix remaining ingredients, and pour over meat. Simmer approximately 2 hours or until meat is tender. 4-6 servings

Linda D. Bobo (Mrs. Earl)

# Pennsylvania Pot Roast

1 (3-5 pound) chuck roast,
    2 inches thick
Salt
Pepper
Paprika
Flour
½ pound bacon, diced
1 cup sweet pickles, sliced
1 large onion, sliced
1 (8 ounce) can tomato sauce
1 cup water
½ cup sour cream

Rub roast with seasonings and flour. Fry bacon until crisp, drain and reserve fat. Brown roast in fat. Add all other ingredients except sour cream and bacon bits. Cover and cook at 350° for 2-3 hours. Add more water if necessary. Remove meat and thicken gravy. Add bacon bits and sour cream. Blend well. Serve with noodles. 6-8 servings

# Spicy Corned Beef
Leftovers make sandwiches that rival "Deli" corned beef

3-4 pounds corned beef brisket
    (with spices in bag if
    possible)
1 orange, sliced
1 large onion, quartered
2 stalks celery, cut in half
2 cloves garlic
1 teaspoon dill weed
1 teaspoon rosemary
6 whole cloves
3 inch stick cinnamon
1 bay leaf
Light corn syrup for glaze

Remove meat from package and place in a large, heavy pot or Dutch oven. Add enough water to barely cover meat. Add remaining ingredients, except syrup. Cover and simmer for 1 hour per pound, or until tender. Remove meat from pot and glaze with corn syrup while still hot. To serve, cool slightly, and cut into thin slices. 10-12 servings

Elise M. Griffin

## Stifado
### (Greek Stew)

3 pounds lean beef stew meat, cut into 1½-inch cubes
5 Tablespoons butter
Salt and pepper
1 medium onion, chopped
½ (6-ounce) can tomato paste
1½ cups water
2 Tablespoons red wine vinegar
1 clove garlic, minced or mashed
1 bay leaf
2 pounds small onions, peeled
¾ cup walnut halves
½ pound feta, Monterey Jack, or Gouda cheese

In a Dutch oven or heavy kettle with cover, brown meat over medium heat in butter; season lightly with salt and pepper. Add chopped onion and sauté until limp. Mix tomato paste, ½ cup water, vinegar and garlic; pour over meat. Add bay leaf. Cover kettle and simmer 1 hour; add remaining water, a little at a time, as necessary during cooking. Add onions, cover and simmer 1 hour or longer, or until onions and meat are tender. Add walnuts and feta cheese, cover and simmer 5 minutes. 6 servings

**Elise M. Griffin**

## Buffet Beef Cacciatore
### Red pepper gives this dish a spicy flavor

Olive or salad oil
2 medium onions, chopped
3 pounds lean beef, cubed
Flour
2 medium cloves garlic, minced
2 teaspoons salt
½ teaspoon oregano
½ teaspoon red pepper
1 can beef consommé
½ cup red wine
1 (16 ounce) can tomatoes
2 green peppers, cut in strips
12 ounces noodles, cooked

Lightly brown onions in oil, and remove to a bowl. Dredge beef in flour, and brown in same oil. Add onions, garlic, salt, oregano, red pepper and 1 cup of consommé. Cover and simmer on top of stove, or bake in an oven-proof dish at 350° for 2 hours, or until beef is almost tender. Add the rest of the consommé, wine and tomatoes, and simmer 10 minutes more. Stir in green pepper, and cook uncovered an additional 15 minutes. Stir in cooked noodles. Can be made ahead and reheated over low-medium heat. Add a little water if needed. 8 servings

**Edna K. Jennings (Mrs. E. Paul, Jr.)**

# Oriental Beef Stew

2 pounds lean beef stew meat
⅛ teaspoon pepper
1 Tablespoon oil
1 can golden mushroom soup
1¼ cups water
1 medium onion, thinly sliced
2 Tablespoons soy sauce
1 small head cabbage, cut in
    1-inch strips
1 (5 ounce) can bamboo shoots,
    drained
1 (7 ounce) can water
    chestnuts, drained and
    sliced

Brown meat in hot oil in skillet. Add seasonings, water, onions and soy sauce. Cover and simmer 1½-2 hours until meat is tender. Add remaining ingredients. Simmer 10-30 minutes. Serve in soup bowls. 4-6 servings

Diane Douglas (Mrs. Robert)

# Lasagne di Carnevale

TOMATO SAUCE:
¼ cup butter
½ pound ground beef
½ pound ground pork (or
    pork sausage)
1 cup chopped onion
1 clove garlic, minced
3¼ cups (1 pound-12 ounce
    can) tomatoes
2 cups tomato paste (3-6
    ounce cans)
2 cups water
2½ teaspoons salt
1 teaspoon pepper
1 teaspoon oregano
LASAGNA:
1 pound broad lasagna noodles
2 pounds Ricotta or cottage
    cheese
6 cups (1½ pounds) shredded
    Mozzarella cheese
1½ cups (6 ounces) grated
    Parmesan cheese
Paprika

Melt butter in a large skillet. Add meat and brown slowly. Add onion and garlic and saute until tender. Stir in remaining sauce ingredients. Simmer over low heat for 45-60 minutes. Preheat oven to 375°. Cook noodles according to package directions and drain well. Handle noodles carefully to prevent them from tearing. Place a layer of noodles in bottom of one 9 x 13-inch or two 8 inch buttered baking dishes. Top with a layer of tomato sauce. Sprinkle over the sauce, one-half each of the Ricotta, Mozzarella and Parmesan cheeses; repeat layers one more time, reserving a small amount of sauce to spread in center of top layer of cheese. Sprinkle with paprika. Bake approximately 30 minutes. Allow to set 10-15 minutes before cutting into squares for serving. Lasagna freezes beautifully before and after cooking. 12 servings

Lucia Sizemore (Mrs. Thomas A., III)

# Moussaka
Light, with a quiche-like texture

3 large eggplants, peeled
and sliced
½ pound potatoes, peeled
and sliced
Flour
½ pound ground beef
1 large onion, chopped
Salt
Pepper
1 teaspoon oregano
1 Tablespoon tomato sauce
Parmesan cheese (about ½
cup)
1 quart milk
1 cup flour
½ pound butter
4 eggs

Flour sliced eggplant and potatoes lightly, and fry in deep fat until golden brown. Drain on paper towels. Place ground beef in skillet with 1-2 Tablespoons water, salt and pepper to taste, and sprinkle chopped onion over top. Saute until meat is browned. Add oregano and tomato sauce and simmer until well blended. Sprinkle parmesan liberally over the bottom of a 9 x 13-inch baking dish. Layer potatoes, eggplant and meat mixture in dish.

Sauce: Heat milk. Heat butter and flour together and add milk, stirring over low heat. Beat eggs well; remove milk mixture from heat and add to eggs. Beat well, until mixture is thick and creamy (a thin pudding consistency). Pour sauce over vegetables and meat in baking dish and shake down. Bake at 350° for approximately 45 minutes or until dish is light brown on top. 8-10 servings

**Athens Pizza**
*Decatur, Georgia*

# Lemon Barbeque Meat Loaves

1½ pounds ground beef
4 slices day old bread, cubed
¼ cup lemon juice
¼ cup minced onion
1 egg, slightly beaten
2 teaspoons seasoned salt
SAUCE:
½ cup catsup
⅓ cup brown sugar
1 teaspoon dry mustard
¼ teaspoon allspice
¼ teaspoon ground cloves
GARNISH:
6 thin lemon slices

Preheat oven at 350°. In a large bowl, combine ground beef, bread, lemon juice, onion, egg and salt. Mix well. Shape into 6 small individual loaves and place in a baking pan. Bake 15 minutes. In a small bowl, combine sauce ingredients. Cover loaves with sauce and top each with lemon slices. Bake 30 minutes longer, basting occasionally with sauce from pan. Serve sauce over loaves. 6 servings

**Pat Adams (Mrs. P.H.)**

# Indian Beef Curry

3 pounds chuck or stew beef,
    cut in ½-inch cubes
3-4 Tablespoons olive oil
1 cup seedless raisins
2 sticks cinnamon
3-4 bay leaves
SAUCE:
3 onions chopped
3-4 Tablespoons olive oil
3-4 Tablespoons curry powder
1 teaspoon powdered
    cardamon
2 teaspoons salt
1 Tablespoon brown sugar
1 quart buttermilk

In a large Dutch oven, brown meat in olive oil. Add raisins, cinnamon and bay leaves. Cover and simmer over very low heat while preparing sauce. Cook onions in olive oil until tender. Add spices and simmer gently 5-6 minutes; then add half of the buttermilk. Cover and simmer over very low heat until sauce is well blended. Watch carefully to avoid scorching! Add sauce to meat and simmer for about 3 hours. Add last half of buttermilk as needed to make a moderately liquid sauce. Serve the curry over steamed rice and let each guest serve himself from a tray of the following condiments:
chopped peanuts
4-5 chopped hard-boiled eggs
1-2 chopped green peppers
2 chopped cucumbers
2 bunches chopped green onions
1 can shredded coconut, toasted
2 (14 ounce) cans crushed
    pineapple, drained
1 large bottle good quality chutney
Hint: Curry may be prepared in advance and reheated, or may be frozen. 6 servings

**Mrs. Joann Forney**

---

HINT ■■■■■■■■■■■■■■■■■■■■■■■■

Keep fresh ginger root in a plastic bag in the freezer. Peel and slice or grate as needed, no need to thaw. Another method is to keep small pieces covered with dry sherry or rice wine in a jar in the refrigerator. The ginger adds a delicious flavor to the wine.

# Zucchini Lasagna
A delicious variation!

1 pound lean ground beef
1 onion, chopped
1 Tablespoon chopped green
  pepper (optional)
1 teaspoon salt
¼ teaspoon pepper
1 small can tomato paste
2 small cans water
1 can tomato soup
½ teaspoon oregano
3 medium zucchini squash
12 ounce container small curd
  cottage cheese (can be low
  calorie)
½ cup Parmesan cheese
1 Tablespoon parsley flakes
2 eggs, beaten
1½ teaspoons salt
½ teaspoon pepper
12 ounces mozzarella cheese,
  thinly sliced

Brown meat; spoon off any excess grease. Add onions and green peppers, salt and pepper. Cook until onions are tender. Add tomato paste, water and soup. Cook slowly about 30-45 minutes. Add oregano last. Slice zucchini lengthwise after trimming ends. Lightly skim peeling off opposite sides of zucchini so that zucchini lies flat. Layer sliced zucchini as you would lasagna noodles in 13 x 9 x 2-inch baking dish. Mix cottage cheese, Parmesan cheese, parsley flakes, eggs, salt and pepper together. Spread half of this mixture over zucchini slices. Add half of mozarella cheese and top with half of meat sauce. Repeat layers. Bake at 350° about 40-45 minutes. Let stand 10 minutes before cutting into squares. For microwaves, bake 15 minutes on medium-high setting. Cover with plastic wrap and let stand 5 minutes. May be prepared in advance and refrigerated for a couple of days. Freezes well.
8 servings

**Beth C. Benefield (Mrs. Phillip D.)**

To peel garlic easily, strike clove with the flat side of a knife.

# Chili

2 pounds ground round or
   chuck
1 pound ground pork
3 medium onions, chopped
4 cloves garlic, chopped
4-6 Tablespoons chili powder
1 Tablespoon flour
2 small cans chopped green
   chilis
3 (16 ounce) cans tomatoes,
   crushed
3 bay leaves
1 Tablespoon salt
1 Tablespoon oregano
1 Tablespoon red wine vinegar
1 Tablespoon brown sugar
3 (16 ounce) cans pinto beans

Brown meat, onions and garlic in a large heavy pot. Drain off fat. Add flour and chili powder, stirring to coat well. Add chilis, tomatoes, bay leaves, salt, oregano, vinegar and brown sugar. Cover and cook slowly for 2 hours. Add beans and cook uncovered 30 minutes more. Serving Suggestion: pass bowls of crushed corn chips, shredded sharp cheese and shredded lettuce. Let each guest add these to his bowl of chili. 12 servings

**Barrie C. Aycock (Mrs. Robert R.)**

# Taco Casserole

1 medium onion, chopped
1 large clove garlic, crushed
1½ pounds lean ground beef
1 (8 ounce) can tomato sauce
⅓ cup water
1 Tablespoon or more chili
   powder
1 teaspoon oregano
⅛ teaspoon ground cloves
1 (8 ounce) package corn chips
1 (16 ounce) can kidney beans
   (optional)
TOPPING:
2 cups finely shredded lettuce
1 cup grated Cheddar or
   Monterey Jack cheese
1 red onion, sliced and
   separated into rings
Diced tomatoes (optional)

Sauté onion and garlic in a small amount of oil until golden. Add beef and brown quickly. Drain off fat. Reduce heat and add tomato sauce and water. Stir in seasoning and kidney beans. Place half the corn chips in a buttered 2-quart baking dish. Spoon half the meat mixture over chips. Repeat, ending with meat. Bake in a 325° oven for 20 minutes until heated thoroughly. Remove from oven and garnish with shredded lettuce, grated cheese and onion rings. Diced tomatoes may be added if desired. 6 servings

**Patricia H. Adams (Mrs. P.H.)**

## Meat Sauce for Pasta

2 Tablespoons olive oil
1 cup diced onion
2 garlic cloves, minced
1½ cups grated carrots
1 pound lean ground beef
1 (28 ounce) can tomato purée
    or Italian plum tomatoes
1 (8 ounce) jar marinara sauce
    (seasoned herb tomato
    sauce may be used)
1 (6 ounce) can tomato paste
½ pound mushrooms, thinly
    sliced
½ cup diced green pepper
1 Tablespoon chopped parsley
1 teaspoon salt
1 teaspoon dried oregano
1 teaspoon dried basil
1 bay leaf
½ teaspoon white pepper
½ teaspoon allspice
⅛ teaspoon crushed red pepper
½ cup dry red wine

Heat oil in 4-5 quart saucepan over medium-high heat. Add onion and garlic. Sauté, stirring constantly, until lightly browned. Reduce heat to medium, add carrots and cook, stirring, until softened. Add meat and cook, stirring, until crumbly and all liquid has evaporated. Reduce heat to low. Add all remaining ingredients except wine and simmer uncovered 1½ hours, stirring occasionally. Blend in wine and simmer ½ hour more. Adjust seasonings, if necessary. Serve over green spinach noodles or pasta of your choice. Sauce may be refrigerated up to 5 days or frozen up to 4 months.

**Jane H. Nardone (Mrs. Joseph A.)**

## Pita Sandwiches

1 pound ground lean beef
1 large onion, chopped
2 cloves garlic, minced
1 Tablespoon vegetable oil
1 (16 ounce) can tomatoes
½ cup sliced stuffed olives
2 Tablespoons chopped
    almonds
1 teaspoon capers
½ teaspoon chili powder
¼ teaspoon salt
⅛ teaspoon pepper
4 pita bread (Middle Eastern
    pocket bread found in most
    supermarkets, or see index)

In large skillet, cook and stir beef, onion and garlic in oil until meat loses its color. Add remaining ingredients except pita bread. Reduce heat and simmer 30 minutes, stirring occasionally. Cut a large slit in side of pita breads; fill with meat mixture. 4 servings

**Trina Graham**
*Atlanta Gas Light Company*

## Pizza Casserole

1 (4 ounce) package sliced
   pepperoni
1 medium onion, chopped
2 (8 ounce) cans tomato sauce
⅓ cup melted butter
6 ounces thin spaghetti,
   cooked
1 cup (4 ounces) grated
   Swiss cheese
1 pound mozzarella cheese,
   sliced
1 (4 ounce) can mushroom
   stems and pieces, drained
½ teaspoon oregano
½ teaspoon basil

Boil pepperoni for 5 minutes in water to cover; drain well. Sauté onion in 1⅓ Tablespoons butter until golden brown. Pour remaining ¼ cup butter into 11 x 7 x 2-inch baking dish. Toss spaghetti in buttered dish. Cover with 1 can tomato sauce. Add half of the Swiss cheese, pepperoni and mozzarella cheese, and all of the mushrooms and onions. Sprinkle with oregano and basil. Top with remaining Swiss cheese, pepperoni, tomato sauce and mozzarella cheese. Bake at 350° for 20-25 minutes or until casserole bubbles. 8 servings

**Margaret Newsome (Mrs. James L.)**

## Pizza By The Yard
Wonderful for a crowd of hungry teenagers

1 (18-inch loaf) French bread
1 pound lean ground beef
⅓ cup grated Parmesan
   cheese
¼ cup finely chopped onion
¼ cup finely chopped olives
1 teaspoon oregano
Salt and pepper to taste
1 (6 ounce) can tomato paste
3 tomatoes, sliced
Sliced mozzarella cheese

Split French bread in half lengthwise. Mix next 7 ingredients and spread on both halves of bread, covering edges well (so they will not burn). Broil 12 minutes. Arrange alternate and overlappng slices of cheese and tomato on top of meat, and broil 2 minutes more. Slice in serving size portions and feed to a hungry crowd. The entire loaf may be frozen without the cheese and tomato. Thaw completely before broiling. 8 servings

**Cookbook Committee**

# Pizza Popover
Serve with beer for a post-football supper

1 pound ground beef or pork
1 medium onion, chopped
16 ounces good marinara
    sauce or spaghetti sauce
6 ounces Mozzarella cheese,
    sliced
POPOVER BATTER:
2 eggs, beaten
1 cup milk
1 Tablespoon oil
1 cup flour
½ teaspoon salt
TOPPING:
½ cup grated Parmesan
    cheese

Brown meat and onion. Combine with sauce and simmer 12 minutes. Spoon meat sauce into a greased 13 x 9½ x 2-inch baking pan and top with Mozzarella cheese. Bake at 400° for 10 minutes. Combine eggs, milk and oil in small bowl; add flour and salt, mixing well. Yield is about 2 cups. Remove meat mixture from oven; pour popover batter over top, and sprinkle with Parmesan cheese. Bake at 400° for an additional 30 minutes. May prepare batter and meat sauce separately; then combine right before baking. 6-8 servings

**Susan M. Morley**

# Marinated Roast Leg O' Lamb

5 cups red wine
½ cup gin
¼ cup olive oil
2 Tablespoons dried thyme
3 whole cloves
2-3 small cloves garlic, crushed
1 (5 pound) leg of lamb
10 peppercorns, crushed
1 Brown-In-Bag

Prepare marinade by combining wine, gin, oil and spices in a saucepan. Bring to a boil. Lower temperature and simmer 5 minutes. Cool. Place lamb in an oven bag. Pour cooled marinade over meat. Seal and refrigerate 5 days, turning over meat each day. Place bag in a shallow roasting pan, make slits in top according to manufacturer's directions. Roast at 325° for 35 minutes per pound if desired well-done, reduce cooking time for a more rare roast. Meat thermometer may be used. 6-8 servings

**Susan M. Morley**

# Portuguese Roast Lamb

6-8 pound leg of lamb
½ cup chopped parsley
3 Tablespoons chopped
  rosemary
4 cloves garlic, minced
½ teaspoon ground cardamon
1 Tablespoon olive oil
Salt and pepper to taste
BASTING SAUCE:
1 cup white wine
3 Tablespoons olive oil

Slash lamb in several places with a knife and stuff slashes with herbs mixed with oil. Sprinkle lamb with salt and pepper to taste. Roast at 450° for 15 minutes. Reduce heat to 300° and roast 4 hours, basting with sauce occasionally. 8 servings

**Mrs. Elsie B. Manry**
*Tampa, Florida*

# Lamb Shoulder Chops, Family Style
Using shoulder chops is an economical way to serve lamb

Lamb shoulder chops
1 clove garlic, crushed
Olive oil
Lemon pepper seasoning
Butter

Rub chops well with crushed garlic, coat generously with olive oil and sprinkle with lemon pepper seasoning. Cover and marinate at room temperature for 1 hour. Broil 4 inches from heat 5 minutes per side, place a pat of butter on each chop and serve immediately. Simple and delicious.

**Decie Nygaard (Mrs. William)**

# Pork Chops in Cream Sauce

4 medium pork chops
Salt and pepper
2 Tablespoons salad oil
1 can beef broth
1 cup heavy cream
2 Tablespoons spicy brown
  mustard

Season chops with salt and pepper. Brown in oil; add broth and cook until tender. Just before serving, combine mustard and cream and pour over chops in pan. Heat. Serve with rice. 4 servings

**Patricia King**
*Cairo, Georgia*

## Pork Tenderloin Lorraine

1 (1½-2 pound) pork tenderloin
2 Tablespoons butter
Fine bread crumbs to cover
   tenderloin
1 medium onion
1 shallot
1 clove garlic
2-3 sprigs parsley
1 cup stock (beef or chicken)
1 Tablespoon wine vinegar

In a small roasting pan on top of stove, brown meat on all sides in butter. Cover with a generous layer of fine bread crumbs that have been mixed with salt and pepper. Mince onion, shallot, garlic and parsley and sprinkle on meat. Hint: Make fresh bread crumbs in your food processor. Add the onion, shallot, garlic and parsley. Process for 60 seconds and check to see if all is chopped well. Sprinkle this on the meat and brown. Add salt and pepper. Put roast in a 500° oven to brown the layer of bread crumbs, basting several times with the melted butter. Once the crumbs are brown, lower the oven temperature to 350°. Add 1 cup of stock to pan. Cover roast and cook until done, about 50 minutes. Uncover and raise temperature; brown crumbs for 10 minutes. Put on a hot platter and stir 1 Tablespoon of wine vinegar into sauce before serving.
4-6 servings

**Kathy Messer (Mrs. Thomas)**

## Stuffed Pork Loin with Savory Gravy

¾ cup sauerkraut, drained
½ medium onion, chopped
¼ cup or more brown sugar
   to taste
1 (4 pound) pork loin
GRAVY:
Pork drippings
½ onion, sliced
1 teaspoon caraway seed
½ cup water
1 can cream of celery soup
1-2 Tablespoons horseradish
½-1 teaspoon Dijon mustard

In a mixing bowl, combine sauerkraut, onion and sugar. Make 8 slits in roast almost to the bone. Spoon 2 Tablespoons of mixture into each slit. Tie together with string at 2-inch intervals. Roast fat side up at 325-350° for 2½ hours (35-40 minutes per pound). After roasting, transfer meat to a warm platter and combine ingredients for gravy. Serve with a chilled Rhine wine. 6-8 servings

**Susan M. Morley**

# Chinese Pork Rolls
### Serve with other Chinese entrées or alone with rice

1 pound pork loin, cut into
  ¾ inch slices
2 Tablespoons soy sauce
1 Tablespoon dry white wine
2 Tablespoons safflower oil
1 cup fresh green beans,
  French cut
½-¾ cup fresh carrots, cut
  same size and shape as
  beans
1½-2 cups shredded cabbage
1 teaspoon salt
1 teaspoon MSG
1 teaspoon lemon juice
SAUCE:
5 Tablespoons sugar
5 Tablespoons vinegar
1 teaspoon soy sauce
1 cup hot water
3 Tablespoons cornstarch

Pound pork slices on both sides, both ways with back of cleaver until very thin (⅛ inch thick). Marinate slices in soy sauce and wine on plate; turn and move pieces around so they are covered at least 10 minutes or up to several hours. Heat oil in pan; sauté beans, carrots and cabbage until limp; add salt, MSG and lemon juice while cooking. Reserve juices in pan. Arrange cooked vegetables on pork and roll up, securing with a toothpick. Prepare sauce in pan in which vegetables were cooked: combine sugar, vinegar, soy sauce, hot water and cornstarch (mix cornstarch with cold liquids until dissolved). Pour over pork rolls. Bake 20 minutes at 450° uncovered. Remove toothpicks and cut in bite size pieces.
4 servings

**Barbara R. Schuyler (Mrs. Lambert, Jr.)**

# Pork Chop Scallop

12 rib pork chops, thin cut
Salt and pepper
4 Tablespoons butter
3 onions, thinly sliced
4 medium potatoes, thinly
  sliced
3 cups beef bouillon
½ cup white wine
2 cloves garlic, crushed
¼ teaspoon thyme leaves
1 bay leaf
1 sprig parsley

Sauté onions in 2 Tablespoons butter until soft. Add garlic and potatoes; season with salt and thyme, toss well and set aside. Season chops with salt and pepper and brown lightly in 2 Tablespoons butter. Remove chops from pan. Add bouillon and wine to pan drippings and scrape browned bits from bottom of pan. Add bay leaf and parsley and cook for a few minutes, until liquid is reduced slightly. Remove herbs. In a 2-quart casserole, alternately layer chops and potatoes. Pour broth over, and bake at 375° for 45 minutes. 6 servings

**Helen Ward (Mrs. William T.)**

## Noisettes de Porc Aux Pruneaux

8 (3 ounce) noisettes of pork
    tenderloin (boned pork-
    chops or slices of
    tenderloin)
1 pound large California prunes
½ bottle dry white wine
2 Tablespoons flour
4 Tablespoons butter
Salt and fresh ground pepper
1 Tablespoon red currant jelly
1 Tablespoon lemon juice
1 cup heavy cream

Soak prunes in wine overnight. Remove 3 Tablespoons liquid from prunes and reserve. Cover pan of prunes and place in a 250° oven for 1 hour or more. Season and flour pork. Saute in butter, being careful not to allow butter to brown. Add 3 Tablespoons reserved prune liquid, cover pan and simmer meat for 20-40 minutes or until fork tender. Pour juice from prunes over meat and bring to a boil for 3-4 minutes. Put pork and prunes on a warm platter to keep hot. Add currant jelly to wine sauce; stir well. Add lemon juice, blend, and add cream very slowly to thicken. Pour over meat and serve. 4 servings

**Cookbook Committee**

## Rio Grande Pork Roast

1 (4-5 pound) boneless rolled
    pork loin roast
½ teaspoon salt
½ teaspoon garlic salt
½ teaspoon chili powder
½ cup apple jelly
½ cup catsup
1 Tablespoon vinegar
½ teaspoon chili powder
1 cup corn chips, crushed

Place pork, fat side up, on rack in shallow roasting pan. Combine the salts and ½ teaspoon chili powder; rub into roast. Roast in a 320° oven for 2-2½ hours or until meat thermometer registers 165°. In a small saucepan, combine jelly, catsup, vinegar and the remaining chili powder. Bring to a boil; reduce heat and simmer, uncovered, for 2 minutes. Brush roast with glaze; sprinkle top with corn chips. Continue roasting 10-15 minutes more or until thermometer registers 170° Remove roast from oven. Let stand 10 minutes. Measure pan drippings, including any corn chips. Add water to make 1 cup. Heat to boiling and pass with meat. Serve with Bean and Avocado Boat Salad. (see Index) 6-8 servings

**June L. Wagner (Mrs. James)**

# Baked Barbecue Spareribs
Sauce may also be used for chicken and pork chops

3-4 pounds spareribs
Salt
1 large onion, thinly sliced
1 lemon, thinly sliced
1 cup catsup
⅓ cup Worcestershire sauce
1 teaspoon chili powder
1 teaspoon salt
⅛ teaspoon Tabasco sauce
1½ cups water

Salt ribs. Place in shallow roasting pan, meat side up. Roast at 450° for 30 minutes. Drain fat. Top each piece with a slice of onion and a slice of lemon. Combine remaining ingredients in a saucepan and bring to a boil. Pour over ribs. Lower oven to 350° and bake 1½ hours. Baste every 15 minutes. 4 servings

**Jerry P. Connor (Mrs. Paul)**

# Oriental Ribs

½ Tablespoon salt
2 Tablespoons vinegar
3 pounds lean pork ribs or backbone
⅓ cup catsup
⅓ cup vinegar
2 or more Tablespoons soy sauce
Dash of pepper sauce
½ cup brown sugar
¼ cup peach preserves
1 teaspoon grated fresh ginger
1 teaspoon salt
Dash coarsely ground black pepper

Place ribs in a large pot and cover them with water. Add ½ Tablespoon salt, 2 Tablespoons vinegar and parboil for 30 minutes. Combine remaining ingredients in a saucepan and simmer for 10 minutes. Dip ribs in sauce, coating well. Grill over slow coals 20-30 minutes, or bake at 350° for 30 minutes. Baste frequently with sauce; turn once. Hint: Ribs may be parboiled or microwaved in advance. Refrigerate until cooking time; reheat sauce and complete cooking on grill or in oven. 4 servings

**Barrie C. Aycock (Mrs. Robert R.)**

# Grilled Ham Slice

1 ham slice, 2 inches thick
2 Tablespoons brown sugar
Gingerale

Cook ham on grill basting with sauce made of brown sugar and gingerale. 4 servings

**Ned Stuart**

# Glazed Ham Loaves
The cold sauce makes this different

2 pounds lean ham, ground
2 pounds lean pork, ground
1½ cups cracker crumbs
1⅓ cups chopped onion
3 eggs, well beaten
1½ teaspoons salt
2 cups milk
2 teaspoons parsley
¼ teaspoon pepper
GLAZE:
1 cup brown sugar
⅓ cup cider vinegar
1 Tablespoon dry mustard
Boil 1 minute.
COLD SAUCE:
½ cup mayonnaise
½ cup sour cream
¼ cup prepared mustard
1 Tablespoon chives
1½ Tablespoons horseradish
Add salt and lemon juice to
    taste

Mix together by hand or in a food processor. Bake in 2 loaf pans at 350° for 30 minutes. Freeze 1 loaf if desired. Pour glaze mixture over loaf and bake 1 hour longer. Serve with Cold Sauce. 12-14 servings

Sallie Smith (Mrs. Tommy W.)
Dede Slappey (Mrs. George N.)

# Stuffed Ham Slices
Great for picnics!

1 loaf unsliced French/Italian
    bread
¼ cup mayonnaise
⅓ cup chopped parsley
1 (8 ounce) package cream
    cheese
¾ cup finely chopped celery
½ cup shredded Cheddar
    cheese
2 Tablespoons finely chopped
    onion
¼ teaspoon salt
1 teaspoon lemon juice
1 Tablespoon Worcestershire
8 slices boiled ham
Dill pickle, sliced lengthwise

Slice bread in half, Hollow out each half with fork leaving ½ inch thick shell (save inside for crumbs). Spread hollow with mayonnaise. Sprinkle with parsley. Blend cream cheese, celery, Cheddar cheese, onion, salt, lemon, and Worcestershire; spoon into halves and pack down, leaving ridge in center. Roll pickles in ham slices. Place rolls end to end down center of loaf. Put bread halves together. Wrap and chill. Before serving, slice in sandwich-size portions. 6 servings

Diane Mahaffey (Mrs. Randy)

# Baked Ham

1 (5-6 pound) butt end ham
Cavender's Greek seasoning or
   your favorite (lemon pepper
   or other dry seasonings)

Rub ham all over with seasoning. Place in brown grocery bag. Turn edges over several times and staple shut. Place in a roasting pan. Bake 3 hours at 350°. Ham may be glazed in a warm oven after removing from bag. 10-12 servings

**Mildred Hodsdon (Mrs. Nicholas)**

# Hot Dogs Creole

2 Tablespoons margarine
¼ cup chopped onion
¼ cup chopped celery
⅓ cup Madeira
2 teaspoons Dijon mustard
1 Tablespoon Worcestershire
   sauce
½ cup chili sauce
1 Tablespoon brown sugar
⅛ teaspoon cayenne pepper
Dash Tabasco Sauce
8 frankfurters
8 buns

In a skillet, sauté onion and celery in margarine until lightly browned. Add remaining sauce ingredients and simmer 5 minutes. Prick the skins of frankfurters, place them in the sauce, cover and simmer slowly about 15 minutes until thoroughly heated. Lightly butter buns and warm in moderate oven. Place frankfurters in buns and spoon on sauce. 8 servings

**Barrie C. Aycock (Mrs. Robert R.)**

# Sherried Veal

1 pound veal cutlets
Salt and pepper to taste
1 egg, beaten
½ cup dry bread crumbs
3 Tablespoons olive oil
Juice of ½ lemon
1½ cups chicken broth
1 small can sliced mushrooms
   plus liquid
¼ cup dry sherry

Pound veal thin between two sheets of wax paper, and cut into serving-sized pieces. Dip in egg and coat with bread crumbs. Brown quickly in hot olive oil. Add lemon juice, half of broth and mushroom liquid. Reduce heat, cover and simmer until sauce thickens. Add rest of broth and simmer 5 to 10 minutes. Add mushrooms and wine and serve hot. Sprinkle with Parmesan cheese, if desired. 6 servings

**Mrs. Elsie B. Manry**
*Tampa, Florida*

# Escalopes of Veal Italienne
A favorite of students at Rich's Cooking School

4-8 veal escalopes (about
   1½ pounds)*
¼ cup oil and butter, mixed
1 onion, finely chopped
¼ cup Marsala or sherry
1 Tablespoon flour
1½ cups beef stock or bouillon
1½ teaspoons tomato paste
1 bay leaf
Salt and pepper
FOR GARNISH:
1½ pounds fresh or 2
   packages frozen spinach
1 Tablespoon butter
2 tomatoes, peeled, seeded,
   and sliced
1 clove of garlic, crushed
5-6 Tablespoons heavy cream
4 large slices of Gruyere or
   Muenster cheese
*Boned chicken breasts may
  be used instead of veal;
  flatten slightly with handle
  of a knife.

In a skillet heat the oil and butter, sauté escalopes quickly, about 1-2 minutes on each side until golden brown and remove. Add the onion and cook until soft. Replace escalopes, pour over Marsala or sherry and flame. Take out the escalopes again, boil liquid to reduce slightly, then stir in flour and add stock, tomato paste, bay leaf and seasoning. Bring to a boil stirring, put back escalopes, cover and simmer gently for 7-10 minutes, or until tender. To prepare the garnish: cook fresh spinach in plenty of boiling salted water for 5 minutes or until just tender; defrost the frozen spinach. Drain well, pressing between 2 stacked plates to remove excess water. Melt butter in a frying pan, add tomatoes with garlic and seasoning, sauté briskly for 1-2 minutes or until just cooked. Put the spinach in a pan with cream, reheat well, stirring, and arrange down center of a long ovenproof platter. Drain the escalopes, arrange them, overlapping, on top of the spinach, with a slice of cheese (halving slices if escalopes are small) and 1-2 tomato slices on top of each escalope and brown under the broiler. Reheat sauce, strain, pour a little around the dish and serve the rest separately. 4-6 servings

**Nathalie Dupree**
*Rich's Cooking School*

## Veal Scaloppine Al Limone

1½ pounds veal scallops
Salt and freshly ground pepper
¼ cup flour
4 Tablespoons butter, divided
3 Tablespoons olive oil
¾ cup beef bouillon
6 lemon slices, cut paper thin
1 Tablespoon lemon juice

Pound veal slightly, season and coat with flour. Sauté veal in mixture of 2 Tablespoons butter and olive oil until golden. Remove veal. Drain most of fat. Add ½ cup bouillon and boil, scraping browned bits from bottom of pan. Return veal to skillet with lemon slices on top. Cover and simmer 10 minutes or until veal is tender. To serve, arrange veal and lemon slices on a heated platter. Add ¼ cup bouillon to juices in skillet and boil until reduced to a syrupy glaze. Add lemon juice and cook, stirring for 1 minute. Remove from heat, stir in remaining butter and pour sauce over veal. 4 servings

**Barbara H. Stuart (Mrs. Edward)**

## Venison Roast

1 Venison roast (about 3
    pounds)
½ cup vinegar
1 Tablespoon black pepper
1 clove-garlic, mashed
    (optional)
1 cup red wine (optional)
12-15 small whole onions,
    peeled
1 pod red pepper (optional)
Aluminum foil

Place roast in a container with cover. Add vinegar and pepper, garlic and wine (optional), and enough water to cover meat. Marinate covered for 6 hours or overnight. Remove roast from marinade. If desired, brown roast in a skillet with a little fat added. Place meat on a large sheet of aluminum foil, add onion and red pepper, wrap tightly and place in a 300° oven. Cook for 4-5 hours, or until fork tender. 6 servings

**Grace Acree (Mrs. Charles)**
*Dalton, Georgia*

# Venison Steaks
For all deer hunters

4 venison steaks
MSG
½ cup salad oil
¼ cup cider vinegar
¼ cup chopped onion
2 teaspoons Worcestershire
    sauce

The night before serving, remove all fat from steaks. Sprinkle steaks with MSG and pound well on both sides. Combine salad oil, cider vinegar, chopped onion and Worcestershire sauce. Pour sauce over steaks and marinate overnight. Grill over coals, basting often with marinade until meat is cooked to your preference. 4 servings

**Barbara R. Johnson (Mrs. Larry)**

# Old #7
Popular at a downtown tea room

Sliced French bread
Thinly sliced ham
Thinly sliced turkey
Sliced swiss cheese
Shredded lettuce
Butter
Anchovie paste (optional)
Tomato wedges
Sliced hard cooked eggs
Olives
RUSSIAN DRESSING:
2½ cups real mayonnaise
2 cups finely diced celery
¼ cup finely chopped green
    pepper
¼ cup chili sauce
2 Tablespoons catsup
Dash Worcestershire sauce
½ teaspoon cider vinegar

Mix all dressing ingredients together and chill until ready to serve.

Spread slices of bread with mixture of butter and anchovie paste (be sparing with the paste as it is strong in flavor). Place sliced ham, turkey, and cheese on each bread slice (about 2 slices per person). Cover completely with shredded lettuce. Pour liberal amount of dressing over sandwich. Garnish plate with tomatoes, sliced eggs and olives.

This is a complete meal. Only a beverage and dessert is needed to finish the meal.

**Mrs. Edward L. Traylor**

# Tourtière

Traditionally served in French-Canadian homes
after the Christmas Eve midnight Mass
Pass around a good mushroom gravy with this dish

1 pound lean ground beef
½ pound lean ground pork
　and/or veal
1 cup diced onion
½ cup grated carrot
½ teaspoon dry mustard
½ teaspoon thyme
¼ teaspoon sage
1 teaspoon salt
⅛ teaspoon ground cloves
½ cup water
1 recipe, double crust pie
　pastry

Place all ingredients in a frying pan and cook together slowly until pink of meat disappears. Continue to simmer for 20 minutes. Remove all grease. Allow mixture to cool. Place in an uncooked pie crust shell; cover with top crust, and cut vents in top in the shape of a star. Bake at 400° for 25-30 minutes. Cut pie in wedges to serve. May be frozen after cooking completely. Should be frozen if prepared more than a day in advance. 6-8 servings

**Judith O'Shea (Mrs. Timothy)**

# Brunswick Stew

6 pounds chicken
3 pounds lean pork roast (loin)
3 pounds lean beef roast
3 (16 ounce) cans creamed
　corn
2 (28 ounce) cans whole
　tomatoes
1 (14 ounce) bottle catsup
1 (5 ounce) bottle
　Worcestershire sauce
2 lemons, thinly sliced,
　seeds removed
1 cup chopped onions
1 stick butter
1 teaspoon tabasco sauce
　(or to taste)
1 Tablespoon salt (or to taste)
1 Tablespoon sugar
½ teaspoon black pepper

Simmer meat in water or stock until meat falls off bones. Several large pots will be needed to do this. Shred the meat, discarding all waste (this amount requires approximately one hour to shred— can be done ahead of time). Add remaining ingredients to meat. Cook slowly 2 to 3 hours, stirring frequently to keep from sticking. Makes approximately 6 quarts of stew. Serve alone or with barbecue, ribs, cole slaw, bread and pickles. Freezes well. 18-20 servings

**Emy Blair (Mrs. H. Duane)**

# Poultry

# Crab Stuffed Chicken

4 large chicken breasts (12
  ounces each), halved,
  skinned and boned
3 Tablespoons butter or
  margarine
¼ cup all-purpose flour
¾ cup milk
¾ cup chicken broth
⅓ cup dry white wine
¼ cup chopped onion
1 Tablespoon butter or
  margarine
1 (7½ ounce) can crab meat,
  drained, flaked and
  cartilage removed
1 (3 ounce) can chopped
  mushrooms, drained
½ cup coarsely crumbled
  saltine crackers
2 Tablespoons snipped parsley
½ teaspoon salt
Dash pepper
1 cup shredded Swiss cheese
½ teaspoon paprika

Place 1 chicken piece, boned side up, between 2 pieces of waxed paper. Working from center out, pound chicken lightly with meat mallet to make a cutlet about ⅛-inch thick (8 x 5 inches). Repeat with remaining chicken. Set aside. In saucepan, melt 3 Tablespoons butter or margarine; blend in flour. Add milk, chicken broth and wine all at once; cook and stir until mixture thickens and bubbles; set aside. In skillet, cook onion in 1 Tablespoon butter until tender, not browned. Stir in crab, mushrooms, cracker crumbs, parsley, salt and pepper. Stir in 2 Tablespoons of the sauce. Top each chicken piece with about ¼ cup crab mixture. Fold sides in; roll up. Place seam side down in 12 x 7½ x 2-inch baking dish. Thin sauce slightly with extra broth, if necessary. Pour remaining sauce over all. Bake, covered, in a 350° oven for 1 hour or until chicken is tender. Uncover; sprinkle with cheese and paprika. Bake 2 minutes longer or until cheese melts. Serve with rice and spoon sauce over. 8 servings

**Malinda Steed (Mrs. Richard)**

HINT

Use dental floss to truss the turkey for roasting.

# Phoenix Emperor Chicken

6 boneless chicken breasts,
    skinned
4 Tablespoons soy sauce
3 slices ham (boiled
    Danish style)
1½ cups flour
1 cup water
1 egg
1 teaspoon baking powder
½ teaspoon salt
2 packages frozen leaf spinach,
    thawed and drained
    thoroughly
1 small can pineapple chunks
1 package almond slices
¾ cup oyster sauce
½ pound fresh or frozen pea
    pods
1 quart peanut oil

Spread inside of chicken breasts with soy sauce. Place ½ slice of ham inside chicken and roll chicken around ham. Refrigerate for 2 hours. Make a batter with flour, water, eggs, baking powder and salt. Refrigerate at least 1 hour. Heat oil in a pot which is large enough to hold 3 chickens. Bring oil to 375°. (Do not let the oil get hotter than this or it will burn. Try to keep it above 350° so that the coating will not get soggy or greasy.) With a pair of tongs carefully dip rolled chicken in batter until completely coated. Then place in hot oil. You may cook as many at a time as the pan will hold provided the oil stays above 350°. When the coating has turned golden brown place in oven (350°) to finish cooking and to keep warm until ready to serve. While chickens are cooking, fill a saucepan ½ full of water and bring to a boil. Place spinach in a wire strainer and dip into boiling water. Cook spinach just a few minutes until it is hot. Drain water out by pressing with a large spoon. Have serving plates ready. Have pineapple can opened and drained, almonds and oyster sauce at hand. Put fresh pea pods in boiling water for about 1 minute, until they turn bright green. 6 servings

To assemble plates: Work fast to keep food warm. Make a bed of hot spinach on each plate. Then put chicken down and slice 3 times ¾ way through on 45° angle. Place pea pods in these slits so they stand up out of top of chicken rolls. Pour a line of oyster sauce on top of chicken and pea pods. Garnish chicken with almonds and pineapple chunks and serve immediately.

**Sidney's Just South Restaurant**
*Atlanta, Georgia*

# Chilled Chicken Breasts with Green Peppercorn Sauce
Delicious for a summer luncheon; serve with
Chilled Lemon Broccoli (see Index)

**CHICKEN:**
**3 whole chicken breasts,**
**skinned, boned and halved**
**¾ cup white wine**
**1 bay leaf**
**3 Tablespoons butter**
**6 whole peppercorns**
**6 Tablespoons chopped fresh**
**parsley**
**Water to cover**
**GREEN PEPPERCORN SAUCE:**
**2 Tablespoons Dijon mustard**
**2 Tablespoons white wine**
**2 teaspoons sugar**
**½ teaspoon salt**
**¼ teaspoon white pepper**
**2 egg yolks**
**2 Tablespoons green**
**peppercorns, rinsed and**
**drained (available in**
**gourmet food stores)**
**1 Tablespoon butter**
**½ cup heavy cream**

Place wine, bay leaf, butter, peppercorns and parsley in a large skillet; add chicken, and water to barely cover chicken. Simmer 7 to 10 minutes, just until breasts are no longer pink (further cooking toughens the meat and spoils the texture). Test for doneness by inserting a knife in the center of the breast, meat should be white, not pink. Remove chicken from liquid, cover, and chill thoroughly. Serve with Green Peppercorn Sauce spooned over each breast. 3-6 servings

Sauce: Place mustard, wine, sugar, salt, pepper and egg yolks in top of double boiler. Cook over hot, not boiling water, stirring constantly with a whisk, until mixture has thickened, about 5 minutes. Remove from heat and stir in green peppercorns and butter. Whip cream until stiff and fold into mustard mixture. Cover and chill at least 8 hours. Sauce will keep about a week in refrigerator. 1½ cups

**Elise M. Griffin**

# Chicken With Apples

**2-3 apples, sliced**
**¼ cup raisins**
**2 Tablespoons sugar**
**¼ teaspoon cinnamon**
**1½ pounds chicken breasts**
**Seasoned salt to taste**
**GLAZE:**
**¼ cup white wine**
**2 Tablespoons sugar**
**Juice and grated rind of ½**
**orange**

In buttered casserole place apples, raisins, sugar and cinnamon. Season chicken breasts with seasoned salt and let dry 30 minutes. Place chicken on top of apples. Bake uncovered for 1 hour at 325°. 6 servings

Glaze: Simmer glaze ingredients together for 15 minutes. Glaze chicken. Bake 30 minutes longer.

**Martha H. Whitehead (Mrs. Richard K.)**

# Chicken and Snow Peas

1½ pounds chicken breasts
1 teaspoon ginger
2 teaspoons sugar
1 Tablespoon cornstarch
6 Tablespoons soy sauce
  (imported)
⅓ cup sherry
2 6 ounce packages frozen
  snow peas
¼ cup oil
¾ cup whole blanched
  almonds
Sliced fresh mushrooms
  (optional)

Skin, bone and cut chicken into ½ inch cubes. In bowl, mix ginger, sugar, cornstarch, soy sauce and sherry. Thaw snow peas. In a wok or large skillet heat oil over medium heat. Add almonds. Stir and cook about 3 minutes. Add chicken and cook just until meat turns white. Drain. Pour in sherry mixture. Cook until sauce thickens. Add pea pods and mushrooms; stir fry until hot and glazed. Serve at once.
4 servings

**Joe Nardone**

# Abu Faruque's Homestyle Chicken Curry
This is a mild curry which may be
spiced up according to taste

9-12 pieces chicken, skinned
1 jumbo yellow onion, slivered
1½ ginger root, freshly
  grated
2-3 garlic cloves, crushed
1 Tablespoon ground turmeric
½ Tablespoon chili powder
1½ Tablespoons cumin powder
½ Tablespoon coriander
1 cinnamon stick
5-6 whole cardamon pods
½ cup vegetable oil (pure
  mustard oil or ghee—
  clarified butter—is best)
2½ cups water
1 teaspoon salt

Heat oil in Dutch oven until very hot, but not smoking. Add onions and cook until translucent, stirring constantly. Add all the spices and ½ cup water. Cook 12-15 minutes over medium-high heat, stirring constantly, until mixture becomes thick, almost dry. Stir chicken, salt, and 2 cups water into onion mixture. Bring to a boil and cover. Cook over high heat, stirring occasionally, until thickest pieces are tender— about 15-20 minutes. Spoon chicken and sauce into a warm serving dish. 6 servings
  Variation: ¼ head of cabbage, sliced, may be added to chicken for last 5-7 minutes to make the sauce milder.
  This dish may be made with lamb, beef or pork—only the cooking time of the meats would differ.

**ANARKALI Indian Restaurant**
*Decatur, Georgia*

## Chicken Rococo

1 (10 ounce) stick medium
   Cheddar cheese
4 chicken breasts, boned
   and skinned
2 eggs, beaten
¾ cup dry bread crumbs
4 Tablespoons margarine
1 chicken bouillon cube
1 cup boiling water
½ cup chopped onion
½ cup sliced fresh mushrooms
½ cup chopped green pepper
⅓ cup margarine
2 Tablespoons flour
1 teaspoon salt
¼ teaspoon pepper
2 cups white rice, cooked
1 cup wild rice, cooked

Heat oven to 400°. Cut cheese into 8 equal lengthwise sticks. Cut chicken breasts in half; flatten each to ¼ inch thickness. Roll each piece around stick of cheese. Secure with toothpicks. Dip in eggs, then in bread crumbs. Cook in margarine until brown and test for doneness. Dissolve bouillon cube in water. Cook onions, mushrooms and green pepper in ⅓ cup margarine until tender. Add flour, seasonings and bouillon. Cook until thickened. Add rices and pour into a 10 x 8-inch baking dish. Top with chicken. Bake at 400° for 20 minutes. Can be prepared in advance and baked at the last minute. Serve with a green vegetable and fresh avocado or fruit salad. 8 servings

**Jeanine C. Andrews (Mrs. Edward B.)**

## Curried Orange Chicken

6 chicken breasts, boned
1-2 Tablespoons curry powder
½ cup orange juice
¼ cup honey
2 Tablespoons mustard
2 teaspoons cornstarch
2 Tablespoons water
Salt to taste

Sprinkle curry powder onto chicken breasts and rub in well. Arrange chicken breasts in a flat baking dish. Combine orange juice, mustard, and honey. Pour over chicken. Bake uncovered at 375° for 1 hour, basting several times while cooking. Combine cornstarch and water, blending well. Drain pan juices, add to sauce, and cook over low heat until thickened. Add salt, if necessary. Pour over chicken when ready to serve. 4-6 servings

**Cheryl I. Fletcher (Mrs. John S., Jr.)**

# Party Casserole
A wonderful answer for a large dinner party

8 whole chicken breasts, cooked and cut into large cubes
4 pounds shrimp in shell, boiled and peeled or 2 pounds cooked shrimp
3 (14 ounce) cans plain artichoke hearts, quartered
3 pounds fresh mushrooms, sauteed in butter
6 cups medium white sauce (see Index)
2 Tablespoons Worcestershire sauce
1 cup sherry or white wine
½ cup freshly grated Parmesan cheese

Divide chicken, shrimp, artichokes, and mushrooms equally in two greased 3-quart (9 x 13-inch) casseroles. Prepare white sauce adding Worcestershire sauce and wine. Pour over casseroles. Top with cheese. Bake uncovered at 375° for 40 minutes until bubbly. The chicken and shrimp can be prepared in advance. Assemble day of party. Refrigerate and allow extra cooking time. 18-20 servings

Carolyn B. Hoose (Mrs. Kenneth A.)

# Honolulu Kabobs

MARINADE:
Liquid from 1 (1 pound) can pineapple chunks
½ cup soy sauce (Kikkoman)
¼ cup cooking oil
1 teaspoon dry mustard
1 Tablespoon brown sugar
2 teaspoons ground ginger
1 teaspoon garlic salt
¼ teaspoon pepper
6 chicken breasts, boned and cut in 1 inch cubes
Sliced green pepper
1 can water chestnuts
Cherry tomatoes
Fresh mushrooms
Pineapple chunks

For 1¼ cups marinade: Combine in saucepan, ½ cup pineapple juice (drained from can of chunks), soy sauce, oil, dry mustard, brown sugar, ginger, garlic salt and pepper. Simmer for 5 minutes. Cool. Marinate chunks of chicken for 1 hour.
   Thread chicken, pineapple chunks, green pepper slices, water chestnuts, cherry tomatoes and mushrooms on skewers. Grill for 20 minutes, turning often on low gas setting or on upper rack, basting with remaining sauce. Serve with stir-fried rice.
4-6 servings

Jane H. Nardone (Mrs. A. Joseph, Jr.)

## Chinese Chicken & Cashews
A Chinese "Amah" (friend) offers this to be eaten with chop sticks

3 whole chicken breasts
5 Tablespoons soy sauce
1 Tablespoon dry white wine
   or sherry
1½ Tablespoons cornstarch
¾ Tablespoon sugar
⅛ teaspoon MSG
1 clove garlic, crushed
¾ cup raw cashews (can use
   regular cashews; not dry
   roasted)
3 green peppers, cut bite-size
1 medium onion, cut bite-size
6 Tablespoons safflower oil
½ teaspoon salt

Skin, bone and cut the chicken into ¾ inch cubes. Marinate for one to two hours in the refrigerator in soy sauce, wine, cornstarch, sugar, MSG and garlic. Boil raw nuts in water 10-15 minutes. Drain. Heat 2 Tablespoons oil in wok or frying pan. Cook cashews until golden, about 10 minutes. If using regular cashews cook 1 to 2 minutes only. Wipe pan and add 3 Tablespoons oil; add chicken and marinade, and stir-fry over high heat until meat is no longer pink, about 5 minutes. Remove chicken onto plate. Wipe pan and heat 1 Tablespoon oil—cook green pepper and onion about 3 minutes. Add chicken and cashews and stir quickly until all is very hot. Arrange on a platter and serve immediately. Ingredients should be prepared in advance and cooked at the last minute.
4 servings

**Barbara R. Schuyler (Mrs. Lambert, Jr.)**

## Lemon Barbecued Chicken
Outstanding for summertime entertaining

Meaty pieces of 2 chickens,
   skinned (or breasts only)
1 cup salad oil
½ cup fresh lemon juice
1 Tablespoon salt
1 teaspoon paprika
2 teaspoons onion powder
2 teaspoons basil
½ teaspoon thyme
½ teaspoon garlic powder

Place chicken in shallow pan. Pour marinade over. Cover and refrigerate overnight. Remove to room temperature 1 hour before grilling. Grill 10-12 minutes per side, basting often. 6 servings

**Cookbook Committee**

# Chicken Sari
The use of Hungarian paprika is the secret

6 large chicken breasts,
  skinned, boned and halved
¾ cup flour
1½ teaspoons salt
1½ teaspoons Hungarian
  paprika (found in gourmet
  shops or gourmet sections
  of super market)
¼ cup finely chopped onions
2 Tablespoons butter
SAUCE:
2 Tablespoons butter
2 Tablespoons flour
1 cup good quality chicken
  stock (preferably
  homemade)
⅔ cup milk
1½ Tablespoons Hungarian
  paprika
1½ cups sour cream

Coat chicken breasts with mixture of flour, salt and paprika. Sauté onion in 2 Tablespoons butter until transparent. Remove onions. Brown chicken breasts lightly. Meanwhile make sauce in saucepan: melt butter and stir in flour; cook until mixture bubbles, stirring constantly. Remove from heat and gradually add chicken stock. Return to heat, bring to boil and cook 1-2 minutes; add the milk and paprika, stirring constantly; when warmed remove from heat; beat with wire whisk and blend in sour cream. Stir in onion and pour sauce over chicken in pan. Cook over low heat, stirring, 3-5 minutes. Do not boil. Cover skillet tightly, turn off heat and let stand 1 hour. Reheat before serving. 12 servings

**Ron Cohn**
*Hal's Restaurant*
*Atlanta, Georgia*

# Sautéed Chicken with Wine and Brandy Sauce

1 fryer, cut up
Salt and pepper to taste
1½ Tablespoons butter
1½ Tablespoons oil
¼ pound mushrooms, sliced
¼ teaspoon marjoram
¼ teaspoon thyme
2 fresh tomatoes, peeled and
  cut in quarters
½ cup dry white wine
½ cup chicken broth
1 Tablespoon finely chopped
  parsley
2 Tablespoons minced onion
1 ounce brandy

Rub chicken pieces with salt and pepper; brown chicken in butter and oil over medium high heat, turning frequently. Add mushrooms, marjoram, thyme and tomatoes. Simmer for 5 minutes. Add wine and broth. Season with salt and pepper; cook slowly until tender, about 30 minutes. Remove chicken to a warm platter while preparing sauce. Add finely chopped parsley and minced onion to the liquid in the pan. Cook slowly for 10 minutes. Remove from heat and add brandy. Stir well and pour sauce over chicken. Serve with rice. 4 servings

**Barrie C. Aycock (Mrs. Robert R.)**

# Pollo Alla Cacciatora

1 (3 pound) frying chicken, cut up
3 Tablespoons olive oil or vegetable oil
2 bay leaves
1 cup dry white wine
1 chicken bouillon cube
1-1½ teaspoons salt
Freshly ground pepper
BATTUTO:
1 Tablespoon fresh parsley
1½ celery stalks with leaves
1 clove garlic

Finely mince battuto ingredients almost to a paste. Brown chicken pieces in olive oil over high heat. Add the battuto and cook over medium-high heat until well browned, turning frequently to keep ingredients from sticking and burning. Add bay leaves, wine and chicken bouillon cube and cook over high heat until wine is almost evaporated. With a wooden spoon, scrape all the browned bits from the bottom and sides of the pan. Add salt and pepper. Simmer for 20 minutes until chicken is tender. Serve with Italian Bread which is delicious dipped into the sauce. 4 servings

**Barrie C. Aycock (Mrs. Robert R)**

# Chicken Paulette

6 pieces of chicken (one per person)
Oil
1 small onion or 8 spring onions (white part only)
1 carrot
3 mushrooms
Pinch of ginger
Pinch of mace
Salt & pepper to taste
3 ounces of sherry
5 ounces chicken stock
2 Tablespoons Dijon mustard
5 ounces heavy cream
Cornstarch

Brown chicken pieces in hot oil in large casserole. Take out and set aside. Finely chop the onion, carrot and mushrooms; add to casserole, cover and cook gently for a few minutes. Replace chicken, add spices, sherry and stock. Cover and cook gently for 40 minutes. Remove chicken. Reduce sauce a little by boiling. Add mustard and cream. Bring to boil and thicken with cornstarch mixed with water. The sauce should be thick enough to cling nicely to chicken. Spoon sauce over chicken. Serve with saffron rice. 6 servings

**Matte Campbell (Mrs. Gilbert R., Jr.)**

# Chicken Paprikas with Spatzle

**CHICKEN:**
1 large onion, sliced in rings
5 Tablespoons butter
1½ Tablespoons Hungarian
   paprika
1 small chicken (about 2½
   pounds), cut into serving
   pieces
1 green pepper, sliced
1 tomato, sliced
¼ pound mushrooms (optional)
½ cup sour cream (optional)
**SPATZLE:**
2¼ cups flour
1 teaspoon salt
1 Tablespoon cream of wheat
2 eggs
1 cup water
1 Tablespoon butter, melted

Sauté onion rings in butter in Dutch oven until transparent. Remove from heat; add paprika, chicken, half of green pepper and half of tomato. Stir to coat chicken. Cover and simmer slowly for 1½ hours turning pieces occasionally to cook evenly. Add small amounts of water if necessary. If mushrooms are used, add during last 15 minutes. When meat is tender, transfer to baking dish; add a little water to pan, scraping onion from pan. Pour over chicken. Garnish with remaining tomato and pepper. Cover with foil and keep warm in oven at low heat. Sour cream may be added to gravy if you prefer. Serve with Spatzle.

Spatzle: Put flour, salt and cream of wheat in a bowl. Make a well in middle and add eggs, water and butter. Stir until batter is smooth. Drop by teaspoons into 8 cups boiling water with 2 teaspoons salt. Avoid crowding. Stir bottom so dumplings will rise to top. After they rise to top, cook gently 1-2 minutes. Remove with slotted spoon. Lightly toss with 4 Tablespoons melted butter. Sauce from chicken may be poured over spatzle.

# Spicy Chicken

1 cup orange juice
1 Tablespoon vinegar
2 Tablespoons brown sugar
½ teaspoon nutmeg
½ teaspoon basil
1 clove garlic, whole
¼ cup flour
1 teaspoon salt
⅛ teaspoon pepper
1 frying chicken, cut up
¼ cup shortening
1 orange, sectioned

In a saucepan mix orange juice, vinegar, brown sugar, nutmeg and basil. Add garlic. Bring to a boil and simmer 10 minutes. Remove garlic. Mix flour, salt and pepper in paper bag. Add chicken pieces and shake well. In a skillet brown chicken on both sides in shortening. Pour off drippings. Pour sauce over chicken. Cover and simmer 20-30 minutes or until chicken is tender. Add orange sections and cover. Simmer another 5 minutes. May be prepared in advance. Serve with rice. 4 servings

**Alice D. Remigailo (Mrs. Richard)**

# Chicken Enchiladas with Sour Cream Sauce

2 whole chicken breasts or
   1 whole chicken, cut up
1 medium onion, chopped
1 green pepper, chopped
½ teaspoon chili powder
¼ teaspoon garlic powder
1 (12 ounce) bottle chili sauce
1 dozen tortillas
SOUR CREAM SAUCE:
2 Tablespoons butter
3 Tablespoons flour
Hot water
1 cup milk
2 cups sour cream
3 Tablespoons chives
Salt to taste
¼ pound Monterey Jack
   cheese, grated

Boil chicken in a very small amount of water. When tender, take chicken off bone. Add onion and pepper to stock; cut up chicken and return to stock. Cook until juice is evaporated. Add chili powder and garlic powder. Add chili sauce (¾ of bottle may be enough). Simmer; sauce should be thick.

Sour Cream Sauce: Melt butter; add flour. Mix. Add enough hot water to make thin. Add milk. Cook until sauce begins to thicken. Add sour cream, chives and salt. Roll chicken mixture in uncooked tortillas. Place in oven proof 9 x 13-inch pan, seam side down. Pour sour cream sauce over and top with grated Monterey Jack cheese. Warm in oven or if chicken mixture is already warm, just melt cheese under broiler. Note: Soften tortillas in damp cloth to prevent cracking. 4 servings

**Judy George (Mrs. Graham W., Jr.)**

## Chicken-Shrimp Tetrazzini

2 whole chicken breasts
6 ounces vermicelli
½ cup chopped onion
1 clove garlic, chopped
⅓ cup chopped green pepper
1 cup chopped celery
¼ cup butter or margarine
1 teaspoon snipped parsley
1 Tablespoon Worcestershire
    sauce
1 (4½ ounce) can shrimp,
    drained
1 can cream of mushroom soup
1 (8 ounce) can tomato sauce
Shredded sharp Cheddar
    cheese

Simmer chicken in water until tender, seasoning with salt to taste; cool. Remove meat from bones and cut into bite size pieces. Cook vermicelli according to package directions. Over low heat sauté onion, garlic, green pepper and celery in butter. Add parsley and Worcestershire sauce; stir in chicken, vermicelli, shrimp, soup and tomato sauce. Turn into greased shallow 2½-quart casserole; top with cheese. Bake in 350° oven 45-50 minutes. 4-6 servings

**Trina Graham**
*Atlanta Gas Light Company*

## Chicken in a Ring with Mushroom Sauce
A nice company dish for a small group

½ cup chopped onion
¼ cup chopped celery
¼ cup butter, melted
¾ cup sliced mushrooms
1 Tablespoon lemon juice
2 cups cooked, diced chicken
¼ cup mushroom soup
½ teaspoon garlic salt
¼ teaspoon black pepper
DOUGH:
2 cups biscuit mix
½ cup milk
1 egg
1 Tablespoon water
SAUCE:
1½ cups sliced mushrooms
2 Tablespoons butter
½ cup mushroom soup
2 Tablespoons chopped
    parsley
2 Tablespoons lemon juice

Sauté onion and celery in butter. Add mushrooms and lemon juice and sauté 2-3 minutes. Combine with chicken, mushroom soup, garlic salt and pepper. Cover and chill 1 hour.

Dough: Make dough by combining mix with milk. Knead 8-10 times on a floured board. Roll into an 18 x 7-inch rectangle. Spread chicken mix evenly over dough. Roll up jelly-roll fashion. Press seam to seal. Moisten ends and shape into a ring, pinching ends to seal. Cut 12 slits around ring. Brush with the egg beaten with water. Slide onto a greased baking sheet. Bake 20-25 minutes at 400°.

Sauce: Make sauce by sauteing mushrooms in butter for 2-3 minutes. Add mushroom soup, parsley and lemon juice. Stir constantly but do not boil. Serve sauce separately. 6 servings

**Lucia Sizemore (Mrs. Thomas A., III)**

# Chicken with Wild Rice

2 (3 pound) whole fryer
  chickens
1 cup water
1 cup dry sherry
1½ teaspoons salt
½ teaspoon curry powder
1 medium onion, sliced
½ cup sliced celery
1 pound fresh mushrooms
¼ cup butter or margarine
2 (6 ounce) packages long
  grain and wild rice with
  seasonings
1 cup sour cream
1 can cream of mushroom
  soup

Place chickens in a deep kettle; add water, sherry, salt, curry powder, onion and celery. Cover and bring to a boil; reduce heat and simmer for 1 hour. Remove from heat; strain broth. Refrigerate chicken and broth at once, without cooling first. When chicken is cool, remove meat from bones and cut meat into bite-size pieces. Rinse mushrooms and pat dry; slice and saute in butter until golden, about 5 minutes, stirring constantly. (Reserve enough whole caps to garnish top of casserole; they may be sauteed along with sliced mushrooms.) Measure chicken broth; use as part of the liquid for cooking rice, following directions for firm rice on the package. Combine chicken, mushrooms and rice in a 3½ or 4 quart casserole dish. Blend in sour cream and mushroom soup and toss with the chicken and rice mixture. Arrange reserved mushroom caps in a circle over the top of the casserole. Cover; refrigerate overnight if desired. To heat, bake, covered, at 350° for 1 hour. The casserole may be completely prepared and frozen ahead of time. 8-10 servings

**Mrs. William F. Bell, II**

## HINT

When barbecuing poultry and pork, longer cooking over a low fire means less shrinkage and more tender meat. Let your fire burn down to glowing coals before you begin cooking.

# Chick'N Puffs
Good luncheon main dish or use as
an interesting appetizer

⅓ cup crushed seasoned
    croûtons
¼ cup finely chopped pecans
1 (3 ounce) package cream
    cheese
2 Tablespoons butter, softened
½ teaspoon lemon-pepper
    seasoning
1 cup cooked chicken, finely
    chopped
⅓ cup (2 ounce can)
    mushrooms, drained and
    finely chopped
1 can Pillsbury Refrigerated
    Crescent Dinner rolls*
3 Tablespoons melted butter
*Substitute 1 (10 ounce)
    package Pepperidge Farm
    Patty Shells for Crescent
    Rolls, if desired.
    (see variation)

Place croûtons and pecans in small bowl; set aside. In medium bowl, combine cream cheese, 2 Tablespoons butter and seasonings; stir in chicken and mushrooms. Separate crescent dough into 8 triangles; place 2 heaping Tablespoons mixture on triangles. Roll up starting at shortest side of triangle and roll to opposite point. Tuck sides and point under to seal completely. Dip rolls in melted butter; coat with crumb-nut mixture. For use as an appetizer, cut rolls in half crosswise. Bake on ungreased cookie sheet at 375° for 15-20 minutes until golden brown. May be prepared up to 2 hours before serving; prepare, cover and refrigerate, bake 20-25 minutes. 8 servings.

Variation using Pepperidge Farm Patty Shells: Can be frozen. Double quantity of filling in recipe. Thaw patty shells slightly. Dust with a small amount of flour and roll into approximate 6 inch circles. Place ⅓-½ cup filling on each circle, fold over and seal edges. Dip in melted butter, and coat with crumb-nut mixture. Follow preceding directions for baking, or freeze on cookie sheet and transfer to plastic bag. Thaw before cooking.

**Jeanette James (Mrs. T. Allen)**

# Chicken Crêpes

1 recipe Crêpes (see Index)
¼ cup butter or margarine
¼ cup flour
½ teaspoon salt
½ teaspoon pepper
1¾ cup milk
1 (5 ounce) can boned chicken, cut up
1 (2½ ounce) jar mushrooms, drained and chopped
3 Tablespoons sherry
1 cup grated sharp Cheddar cheese
1 (15 ounce) can extra long green asparagus spears, drained

In medium saucepan melt butter; stir in flour, salt and pepper until smooth. Stirring constantly, slowly add milk and cook over medium heat until thickened. Add chicken, mushrooms, sherry and ¾ cup cheese; cook until cheese is melted. Place 2 asparagus spears atop each crêpe; top with 2-3 Tablespoons sauce. Roll up and place seam side down, in shallow 3-quart baking dish. Top with remaining sauce and cheese. Bake in 350° degree oven 10-15 minutes, or until heated through. 4-6 servings

**Trina Graham**
*Atlanta Gas Light Co.*

# Stuffed Roast Chicken
The stuffing goes between the skin and the meat

½ cup butter
2 small cloves garlic, minced
3 green onions, minced
1 Tablespoon parsley
¼ teaspoon dried chives
¼ teaspoon dried chervil
¼ teaspoon thyme
1¼ cups bread crumbs
3-4 pound chicken, whole
3 Tablespoons butter, melted
½ cup white wine
2 Tablespoons butter

In food processor, cream butter with garlic, green onions and herbs. Add bread crumbs. Loosen skin around breast of chicken and fill with stuffing. You must use your fingers to place stuffing between skin and meat. Fill cavity with remaining stuffing. Truss chicken. Brown on all sides in 3 Tablespoons butter. Roast in covered pan small enough to crowd chicken at 350° for 1 hour. Remove chicken from pan. To deglaze pan juices, place pan over direct heat, add wine, scrape browned bits and let juices boil 1 minute. Swirl in 2 Tablespoons butter. 2-4 servings

**Sylvia Dorough (Mrs. Don)**

# Chicken Kiev

8 whole chicken breasts,
   boned, skinned and halved
1 cup unsifted flour
2 cups dry bread crumbs
4 eggs, well beaten
Oil for deep frying
HERB BUTTER:
1⅓ cups soft butter
2⅔ Tablespoons chopped
   fresh parsley
2 teaspoons dried tarragon
⅛ teaspoon garlic powder
1 teaspoon salt
¼ teaspoon pepper
1 Tablespoon chives
1 teaspoon rosemary

Herb Butter: Combine all ingredients and whip. Spread out in bottom of square pan. Chill until firm and cut into 16 pieces.

Chicken: Pound breasts to ¼ inch thickness. Place pat of butter in center of each piece of chicken. Fold and fasten with a toothpick so that butter is completely enclosed. Roll each breast in the flour, dip in beaten egg and roll in crumbs. Refrigerate at least 1 hour or overnight. Heat oil (1-2 inches deep) to 360°. Add chicken. Fry, turning with tongs, until brown. Keep warm in 200° oven for no more than 15 minutes.

To Freeze and Serve Later: Fry, as above, and cool. Wrap in freezer wrap and freeze. To serve, unwrap, but do not defrost. Bake, uncovered, 35 minutes at 350° Fry a little less time if you plan to freeze. 16 servings

**Betty Jo Ridley (Mrs. William E.)**

# Chicken Parmigiana

3 whole chicken breasts (about
   12 ounces each), split,
   skinned and boned
2 eggs, slightly beaten
1 teaspoon salt
⅛ teaspoon pepper
¾ cup fine dry bread crumbs
½ cup salad oil
2 cups tomato sauce
¼ teaspoon basil
⅛ teaspoon garlic powder
1 Tablespoon margarine
½ cup grated Parmesan cheese
8 ounces Mozzarella cheese,
   sliced and cut in triangles

Place chicken breasts on cutting board; pound lightly with side of heavy knife until about ¼ inch thick. Combine eggs, salt and pepper. Dip chicken into egg mixture, then crumbs. Heat oil in frying pan to 350°. Brown chicken on both sides, remove to shallow baking dish. Pour excess oil from frying pan, then add tomato sauce, basil, and garlic powder. Heat to boiling; simmer for 10 minutes or until thickened. Stir in margarine. Pour over chicken; sprinkle with Parmesan cheese. cover. Bake at 350° for 30 minutes; uncover. Place mozzarella cheese over chicken. Bake 10 minutes longer or until cheese melts. 6 servings

**Trina Graham**
*Atlanta Gas Light Company*

# Boneless Chicken Breasts, Italian Style
Good to prepare ahead for a crowd

6 whole chicken breasts,
   boned, skinned and halved
Salt and pepper
4 cloves garlic, crushed
½ cup flour
3 Tablespoons butter
3 Tablespoons oil
½ teaspoon dry tarragon
1½ cups chicken broth
½ cup dry white wine
12 slices boiled ham
12 thin slices mozzarella
   cheese

Season chicken with salt and pepper and spread with crushed garlic. Flour and sauté in oil and butter until light brown. Place in shallow casserole and sprinkle with tarragon. Add broth to skillet and heat while scraping brown particles from bottom of pan. Add wine and pour over chicken. Cover and bake at 350° for 30 minutes. Uncover and top each breast with ham slice. Bake 20 minutes, add cheese 5 minutes before serving and bake uncovered until cheese melts. To freeze: after adding the wine mixture to chicken, cover and freeze. Allow casserole to thaw 1-2 hours, then bake, covered 1 hour. Finish as directed. 12 servings

**Elise M. Griffin**

# Chicken and Lobster in Madeira Sauce

SAUCE:
1 cup butter
2 Tablespoons chopped onion
2 Tablespoons chopped celery
1 cup flour
¼ teaspoon thyme
¼ teaspoon rosemary
2 small bay leaves
2 cloves garlic, minced
2 Tablespoons tomato puree
6 cups beef bouillon
2 Tablespoons orange juice
2 Tablespoons sugar
½ cup Madeira wine
4 cups cooked lobster meat
4 cups cooked chicken, boned
   and cut in large pieces

Melt butter in a skillet until it foams. Add onion and celery and sauté 5 minutes. Stir in flour, spices and tomato purée; cook slowly 5 minutes stirring. Add bouillon, cover and bring to a boil, simmer slowly 1 hour. Strain sauce. Cook orange juice and sugar until caramel colored. Add wine and cook until sugar dissolves. Add lobster and chicken and strained sauce, and heat all together. 8 servings

**Helen Ward (Mrs. William T.)**

## Chicken with Green Noodles

¼ pound butter
¼ pound fresh mushrooms
1 pint heavy cream
1 Tablespoon sherry
1 Tablespoon dry white wine
2 chickens, cooked and diced
2 Tablespoons flour
2 Tablespoons butter
½ package green noodles,
    cooked and drained
Parmesan cheese

Melt butter. Sauté mushrooms. Add cream, sherry, wine and chicken. Make a paste of the butter and flour and stir into chicken mixture. Put noodles into bottom of a greased 2½-quart casserole. Put chicken mixture on top. Sprinkle with Parmesan cheese. Bake at 350° for 30 minutes. 4-6 servings

**Kenney K. Linton (Mrs. Sidney E.)**

## Chicken Spaghetti
This gets better every time it is reheated

2 fryer hens
2 large onions, chopped fine
4 ribs celery, chopped
1 green pepper, chopped
½ stick butter, melted
1 (6 ounce) package vermicelli
2 Tablespoons chili powder
2 Tablespoons chopped parsley
1 small jar pimiento, chopped
    fine
2 cans cream of mushroom
    soup
1 small can mushrooms,
    drained
½ pound Cheddar cheese,
    grated

Boil chicken, debone and save chicken stock. In a skillet, sauté onions, pepper and celery until tender in butter. In another saucepan, boil vermicelli in chicken stock following cooking directions on vermicelli package. Drain. In a large pan, combine chicken, sautéed onions, pepper and celery with vermicelli. Combine chili powder, parsley, pimiento, soup and mushrooms. Mix thoroughly. Cover and refrigerate 24 hours. Place in a large buttered casserole. Sprinkle cheese on top. Bake at 350° for 1 hour. May be frozen. 6 servings

**Karen V. Shinall (Mrs. Myrick C.)**

## Tina's Chicken Divan

3 cups cooked chicken
2 (10 ounce) packages broccoli
  cooked and drained
2 Tablespoons butter
Salt and pepper
1 can mushroom soup
½ cup cream
½ cup white wine
2 cups grated sharp cheese
1 teaspoon lemon juice
½ cup mayonnaise
Parmesan cheese

Butter casserole; layer chicken and broccoli; dot with butter; sprinkle with salt and pepper. Heat soup and cream; when hot, add wine, cheese, and lemon juice; add mayonnaise after cheese melts; pour over chicken and broccoli; sprinkle with Parmesan cheese. Bake at 350° until sauce bubbles, approximately 25 minutes. Casserole may be assembled ahead of time.
6 servings

**Joan M. Adams (Mrs. John P., Jr.)**

## Chicken Livers with Poppy Seeds
A divine dish

4 medium onions, sliced
6 Tablespoons butter
1½ teaspoons marjoram
¼ teaspoon salt
1 pound chicken livers
1 Tablespoon poppy seeds
2 cloves garlic, minced
3 Tablespoons flour
½ teaspoon freshly ground
  pepper
1 teaspoon paprika
⅔ cup dry sherry

In a skillet with cover, sauté onions in 3 Tablespoons butter for 10 minutes. Add 1 teaspoon marjoram and ¼ teaspoon salt. Stir, cover and keep warm. Wipe livers with damp cloth and leave whole. Bruise poppy seeds. Heat remaining 3 Tablespoons butter in a second skillet. Add livers, poppy seeds, garlic, and remaining ½ teaspoon marjoram. Stir well and cook for 5 minutes at high heat. Stir often. Sift in flour, pepper and paprika. Stir and cook for 5 minutes longer. Add salt if needed. Lift out livers. Place atop onions. To the liver skillet, add the sherry and heat to boiling, stirring to loosen and blend the residue from the frying pan. When boiling, pour over the livers and onions, cover the skillet and cook at low heat for 30 minutes, leaving the cover off part of the time so the wine reduces slightly. Do not stir. 4 servings

**Cookbook Committee**

## Cornish Hen with Rice and Curry

2 Rock Cornish hens
¼ cup butter, melted
1 (6 ounce) package curry rice
SAUCE:
1 (1 pound, 1 ounce) can
   apricots
¼ cup butter
½ cup sliced onion
½ cup sliced celery
2 Tablespoons flour
1 teaspoon curry powder
1 cup water
½ cup apricot syrup from fruit
2 chicken bouillon cubes
¼ cup medium size pitted
   ripe olives
Parsley for garnish

If hens are frozen, thaw and remove giblets. Split hens. Place in 13 x 9-inch baking pan, skin side up. Brush with butter. Bake at 350° for 1-1¼ hours, basting occasionally with remaining butter, until fork tender. While hens are baking, bake rice in a 1½-quart covered casserole according to directions on package.

Sauce: Drain apricots, reserving syrup. In saucepan, melt butter. Sauté onion and celery until almost tender. Stir in flour and curry powder. Remove from heat. Gradually stir in water and ½ cup reserved syrup; add bouillon cubes. Cook, stirring constantly, until mixture thickens and cubes melt. Cook 2 additional minutes. Add drained apricots and olives. Heat to serving temperature. To serve: On heated platter, arrange rice, Cornish hens, apricots and olives. Garnish with parsley. Accompany with remaining sauce. Delicious! 4 servings

**Joartis Sims**
*Fort Worth, Texas*

## Cornish Hens Andalusia

2 Rock Cornish hens, split
  in two
2 Tablespoons minced parsley
¼ cup minced onion
½ teaspoon minced garlic
2 cups orange juice
Melted butter
¼ cup butter
1 Tablespoon cornstarch
¼ cup raisins
¼ cup slivered almonds
Warmed orange sections
Ripe olives

Marinate Cornish hens for 1 hour in mixture of parsley, onion, garlic and orange juice. Wipe hens dry, baste with butter and roast in uncovered baking pan in 300° oven for 30 minutes. In a small skillet melt ¼ cup butter, add cornstarch and cook 2-3 minutes stirring. Add marinade to this. Pour sauce over hens; sprinkle with raisins and slivered almonds. Bake covered in a 350° oven for 30 minutes. Remove cover and brown under broiler. Garnish with warmed orange sections and ripe olives. Serve over rice. 2-4 servings

**Rachel Greenland**

## Smoked Turkey on a Weber Grill

1 (16-18 pound) butterball
  turkey
Salt
Black pepper
1 (10 pound) bag charcoal
1 bag hickory chips soaked in
  water

Thaw turkey. Remove giblets. Dry bird thoroughly with paper towels. Rub well with salt and pepper, inside and out. Insert meat thermometer. Start charcoal fire using about 40 briquets. When coals are very hot and white, about 30 minutes, rake ½ of coals to each side of grill. Add a generous handful of hickory chips to coals. Place turkey in a large iron skillet or similar pan. Put pan in center of grill. Cover grill. Every 30 minutes, baste turkey with pan juices; add more hickory (for first 2 hours) and add more charcoal as needed. Don't be stingy with the hickory if a good smoked flavor is desired. Cook approximately 20 minutes per pound or until meat thermometer registers proper temperature.

**Joe Scroggs**

# Fillet of Turkey with Olive Sauce
An old family recipe that makes an unusual Thanksgiving dinner

**TURKEY:**
6 slices uncooked turkey
   breast
1 egg, beaten
½ cup flour
Salt and pepper
2 Tablespoons cooking oil
**OLIVE SAUCE:**
5 Tablespoons butter
4 Tablespoons flour
2 cups milk
½ teaspoon salt
Dash of pepper
½ teaspoon dry mustard
1 egg yolk, beaten
½ cup sliced olives

Turkey: Cut turkey breast in slices ⅓ inch thick. Dip in egg; then coat with flour that has been mixed with salt and pepper. Sauté in hot oil until golden brown. Place slices on toast or rice and pour Olive Sauce over all.

Olive Sauce: Melt butter in top of double boiler. Blend in flour. Add milk slowly and stir until blended. Add salt, pepper and mustard and cook over hot water until thickened. Pour egg yolk slowly into hot mixture, stirring constantly. Cook for 1 minute longer. Stir in olives. 6 servings

**Martha Herod (Mrs. James V.)**

# Baked Turkey Croquettes

2 Tablespoons butter
1 Tablespoon finely chopped
   onion
¼ cup all-purpose flour
½ Tablespoon salt
⅛ teaspoon pepper
1 cup milk
2 cups finely chopped
   cooked turkey
2 Tablespoons minced parsley
1 package seasoned coating
   mix for chicken
1 cup medium white sauce
   (see Index)
1 Tablespoon chopped green
   pepper
1 Tablespoon minced onion
1 Tablespoon chopped
   pimiento

Melt butter in a skillet; sauté onions until clear. Remove from heat. Add flour, salt, pepper and milk all at once. Return to medium heat and cook until thick, stirring continuously, approximately 1 minute. Add turkey and parsley. Pour mixture into greased 8 x 8 x 2-inch pan. Chill several hours. Shape mixture into balls and brush lightly with milk. Roll the balls in coating mix and place them on a wire rack to dry. Chill for 1 hour. Bake in greased shallow pan at 400° for 20 minutes. Turn and bake 10 minutes longer. Serve with 1 cup medium white sauce (see Index) to which the green pepper, onion and pimiento have been added. 4-6 servings

**Susan M. Morley**

# Turkey Casserole
A noble way to fix leftovers

1 (8 ounce) package egg
   noodles
3 cups cooked turkey or
   chicken, cut up
2 cans cream of chicken soup
2 cups sour cream
1 teaspoon thyme
1 cup buttered dry bread
   crumbs
2 Tablespoons poppy seeds

Cook noodles as directed. Add meat to soup, sour cream and thyme. Stir in noodles. Turn into a large shallow pan that has been buttered. Sprinkle with buttered bread crumbs and then poppy seeds. Bake uncovered for 30 minutes at 350°. This is lovely served with Peach Aspic (see Index). 8 servings

**Mickey Hutchinson (Mrs. James)**

# Roast Duckling with Honey Sauce

1 (5 pound) duckling, quartered
Honey for glazing
SAUCE:
4 Tablespoons lemon juice
3 Tablespoons honey
2 Tablespoons Japanese soy
   sauce
2 Tablespoons butter, melted
2 Tablespoons dry sherry
1 clove garlic, crushed

Blend sauce ingredients and let stand 1 hour. Roast quartered duckling in shallow pan at 325° for 1 hour piercing the skin frequently and basting with sauce. Turn on broiler and brown, basting with sauce, for 5 minutes on each side. Brush with honey, skin side up, and brown 1 minute more. Spoon remaining sauce over duck and serve. 4 servings

**Elise M. Griffin**

**MICROWAVE HINT**

Approximate conversion table for microwave cooking
Conventional cooking time ÷ 4 less 2
Example: 60 minutes ÷ 4 = 15 minutes, less 2 minutes = 13 minutes

# Peking Duck with Mandarin Pancakes

One of the most famous of all Chinese banquet dishes;
Our version is a little different, but we think it's a dish that's
well worth trying.

1 (4-5 pound) duck (the larger
  the better)
1 Tablespoon water
5 Tablespoons dark brown
  sugar
2 Tablespoons salt
2½ Tablespoons black pepper

MANDARIN PANCAKES:
1¾-2 cups all-purpose flour
¾ cup boiling water
2 teaspoons sesame oil
Non-stick 8-10 inch skillet
Hoisin sauce (available at
  Oriental food stores)
12 green onions

DIRECTIONS FOR GREEN
ONION BRUSHES:
  With a paring knife, cut the
  white bulb of the onion into
  fine bristles. Trim off green
  so total brush length is
  2 inches.

To serve: When duck is ready,
allow to cool enough to handle.
Pull meat off bones. Tear skin
into small pieces. Using a green
onion brush, spread 1 Tablespoon
Hoisin onto a pancake, top with
some of the meat and skin. Place
brush on top and roll up like a
crêpe. Serve immediately.
Makes 12 pancakes

Preheat oven to 350°. Prepare
the duck: Pull off excess fat and
neck skin. Remove giblets. Snip
off top half of wings. Dry duck
well. Make a thick paste of water,
sugar, salt and pepper. Put 1
Tablespoon paste in duck cavity.
Place duck breast side up on tray
of roasting pan. Using a pastry
brush, paint top side well with
paste. Turn duck over and paint
backside. Place, backside up, in
350° oven. After 45 minutes, baste
again. Cook 45 minutes more,
baste and turn duck over. Repeat
process. Total cooking time:
3 hours.

Mix 1¾ cups flour and water
in bowl. As soon as hands can
stand the heat, knead dough
together. Add other ¼ cup flour
if needed to make a smooth
dough. Continue kneading for
about 5 minutes until smooth and
elastic. Cover with damp towel
and let rest for at least ½ hour.
On floured surface, roll dough ¼
inch thick. Cut into 2 inch circles.
Brush 1 side with sesame oil and
sandwich 2 circles together (oiled
sides together). Carefully roll out
sandwiches to 6 inch circles; turn
over often; try to keep top and
bottom circles even. Heat skillet
on high for 30 seconds. Reduce
heat to moderate. Cook each
pancake until light brown spots
appear: about 1 minute per side.
Remove from pan and gently
separate halves. Cool slightly;
serve warm. May be refrigerated
or frozen. Heat in foil in oven for
10 minutes at 350°.

**Cookbook Committee**

HINT

Tie turkey legs with rolled gauze bandage.

# Smoked Wild Duck

Wild ducks
Hickory
SAUCE:
½ stick butter
¾ cup vinegar
¼ cup water
1½ Tablespoons salt
2 Tablespoons sugar
1¼ teaspoons Tabasco

Cut ducks in half down backbone. Simmer in water for 2 hours or until tender. Soak hickory chips in water for an hour. Place wet chips on low charcoal fire. Barbecue ducks over low fire (covered) and baste with sauce frequently. Be sure to keep fire low and chips wet so the ducks have smoked taste. Grill for 1 hour or until dark.

**DeDe T. Slappey (Mrs. George N.)**

# Quail with Green Grapes

4 quail
Salt, pepper and flour
¼ cup butter
½ cup water
½ cup seedless green grapes
2 Tablespoons toasted
    almonds, sliced or slivered
1 Tablespoon lemon juice
4 toast slices, buttered

Sprinkle quail inside and out with salt, pepper and flour. Melt butter in skillet; add quail and brown on all sides. Add water. Cover and cook over low heat 15 minutes or until tender. Add grapes and cook 3 minutes longer. Stir in nuts and lemon juice. Serve quail on buttered toast with pan sauce. 4 servings

**Judy Carlsen (Mrs. Alfred M., III)**

# Quail and Oysters

Quail
3 oysters per quail
Melted butter
Corn meal
Flour
Butter
Salt and pepper
Bacon

Wipe birds inside and out with damp cloth. Dip oysters in melted butter, then in cornmeal and place inside bird. Make flour and butter into a paste and rub breasts well with the paste. Put birds in baking dish with a strip of bacon across each bird. Bake for 30 minutes, basting well with butter. Serve on toast or wild rice with a green vegetable.

**Judy Carlsen (Mrs. Alfred M.)**

## Quail Normande

6-8 quail
Flour, seasoned with salt
  and pepper
2 or more Tablespoons butter
4 shallots, chopped
1 wine glass Calvados (apple
  Brandy), warmed
3 apples, peeled, cored, and
sliced
Salt and pepper to taste
½ pint chicken stock
Bouquet garni
2 Tablespoons whipping
  cream, warmed

Coat quail well with seasoned flour and brown in melted butter in a skillet, adding more butter if needed. Reduce heat, add shallots and cook until golden. Pour warm Calvados over quail and ignite. Add the apples and bouquet garni, and season with salt and pepper. Bring to a boil, then cover and cook over low heat for 30-40 minutes until tender. Remove quail to a heated platter. Strain pan juices, add cream and pour over quail. Serve with wild rice.
3-4 servings

**Southern Plantation Cookbook**
*Corinne Carlton Geer*

## Wild Duck and Oyster Gumbo

1 wild duck (domestic may be
  used)
2 Tablespoons shortening
2 Tablespoons flour
1 cup chopped onion
2 dozen oysters with liquid
2 quarts hot water
1 teaspoon garlic salt
¼ cup fresh parsley, minced
¼ cup green onion tops,
  minced

Cut duck into 4-6 pieces and season with salt and pepper. Brown in shortening. Remove duck from pan and pour off all but 2 Tablespoons fat. Add flour to fat and mix well. Add onions and cook until tender. Add duck, hot water and garlic salt. Simmer slowly until duck is tender, about 2 hours. Add oysters and liquid, making sure both are free of grit and shell. Add parsley and green onion tops. Season to taste. If oysters are preferred nearly raw, and parsley and onion tops, crisp, then serve immediately; or keep warm until needed. Serve over rice. 4-6 servings

**Mrs. Alma DuPont**

# Doves in Wine Sauce
Outstanding with hot curried fruit, wild rice,
a green vegetable and red wine

4 Tablespoons butter
1 medium onion, chopped
16 dove breasts
1 teaspoon salt
1 teaspoon pepper
2 teaspoons parsley, fresh or
    dried
2 teaspoons Worcestershire
    sauce
¼ teaspoon thyme
½ cup dry red wine
1 beef bouillon cube, dissolved
    in 1 cup boiling water
2 Tablespoons butter, softened
2 Tablespoons flour

In large skillet, melt butter and sauté onions until tender, about 5 minutes. Remove onions and lightly brown doves in same skillet. Reduce heat to simmer. Arrange doves, meat side up. Return onions to skillet. Add salt, pepper, parsley, Worcestershire sauce, thyme, and wine. Simmer uncovered for 15 minutes. Add bouillon; cover and simmer 1-1½ hours until meat is tender.

Remove doves to a warm platter. Mix flour and soft butter to form a roux. Add to the liquid in pan and cook until smooth. Pour thickened sauce over doves.
Serves 4-6

**Molly Ahlquist (Mrs. Ernest, Jr.)**

# Smothered Georgia Doves

Doves
Flour
Salt
Pepper
Crisco
Water
Sugar
Kitchen Bouquet

Roll doves in flour, sprinkle with salt and pepper and fry in Crisco until light brown. Remove doves to Dutch oven or electric skillet. Add water to almost cover birds. Add 1 teaspoon Kitchen Bouquet, salt, pepper and sugar to taste. If necessary thicken gravy with cornstarch and water. Cover and simmer in gravy for several hours. Serve over wild rice.

**DeDe T. Slappey (Mrs. George N.)**

# Vegetables

## Asparagus Supreme Casserole

3 hard boiled eggs, sliced
2 (14½ ounce) cans green
  asparagus spears
1 (8 ounce) can water
  chestnuts, thinly sliced
6 Tablespoons flour
½ cup whole milk
¼ cup butter
½ teaspoon salt
¼ teaspoon black pepper
1 cup grated sharp Cheddar
  cheese
2 Tablespoons diced pimiento
1 cup seasoned bread crumbs

Drain asparagus and water chestnuts, saving 1½ cups of combined liquids. Mix flour and milk until smooth. Combine with vegetable liquids, butter, seasonings and cheese. Cook over medium heat, stirring constantly, until thickened. Add pimiento. Arrange asparagus in oblong shallow casserole. Top with water chestnuts; then cover with egg slices. Pour sauce over all. Sprinkle with crumbs. Bake in a 375° oven for ½ hour or until top is lightly browned and sauce is bubbly. May be prepared in advance. 8 servings

Constance D. Wilson (Mrs. A.E., Jr.)

## Crunchy Asparagus

Fresh asparagus spears
4 Tablespoons oil
SEASONINGS:
1-2 teaspoons accent or salt,
  freshly ground black
  pepper, and oregano to
  taste

Slice asparagus diagonally into ½-1 inch lengths. Place oil in fry pan and heat slightly. Add asparagus, and your choice of seasonings to pan. Cover and shake over medium high heat until asparagus are crispy, about 7 minutes.

Dr. Ruth Kalish

**MICROWAVE HINT** ■■■■■■

*Standing time* is essential in microwave cooking. Allow all foods to stand from 2 to 10 minutes after cooking. Wrap in a towel to keep warm. Length of standing time depends on the volume of food cooked. For example: a baked potato—2 minutes, a large casserole—10 minutes.

# Winter Artichokes
This rich Cuban dish goes well with a light meal

4 large artichokes
¼ cup dried bread crumbs
¼ cup grated Parmesan
   cheese
½ cup chopped parsley
¼ cup chopped chives
1 Tablespoon grated onion
½ clove garlic, grated
4 Tablespoons melted butter
Olive oil (about ⅓ cup)

Wash and trim artichokes. Mix bread crumbs, Parmesan cheese, parsley, chives, onion, garlic and butter to make a stuffing. Press stuffing mixture well down into leaves of artichokes and into and across tops. Stand in earthenware casserole with about ½ inch water in bottom. Dribble oil over artichokes. Cover and bake at 325° for 1½ hours or until thoroughly tender and leaves pull away easily. Serve warm with melted butter as a first course. May be cooked ahead and reheated. 4 servings

**Cookbook Committee**

# Bill's Banana Pepper Bake

10 banana peppers
½ cup or more corn oil
6 American cheese slices
½ small package Pepperidge
   Farm herb dressing mix
   (approximately)

Cut tops from peppers. Cut down one side and remove seeds. Pour oil in glass 8 x 8-inch baking dish. Add peppers turning to coat. (You may need more oil.) Cover peppers with cheese slices. Sprinkle with dressing mix until well covered. Bake at 350° for 30-40 minutes until peppers are soft.

**Caroline McPheeters (Mrs. Hal)**

## MICROWAVE HINT

Always prick foods which are covered by a skin or membrane, such as sausages, baking potatoes, squash, egg yolks and chicken livers, to keep them from bursting.

## MICROWAVE HINT

To clarify butter, heat until bubbling and pour off clear liquid, discard residue.

## Green Beans Horseradish

2 cans whole green beans
1 large onion, sliced
Several bits of bacon
1 cup mayonnaise
2 hard boiled eggs, chopped
1 heaping Tablespoon
   horseradish
1 teaspoon Worcestershire
   sauce
Salt and pepper to taste
Garlic salt to taste
Celery salt to taste
1½ teaspoon chopped parsley
Juice of 1 lemon

Cook beans with bacon and onion for ½ hour. Blend rest of ingredients and allow to come to room temperature. When ready to serve, drain beans and add horseradish sauce to beans. May be prepared ahead. Do not freeze. 6-8 servings

Jane G. Skelton (Mrs. W. Douglas)

## Green Beans with Salted Peanuts

2 slices bacon, diced
⅔ cup sliced onions
4 cups cooked green beans
2 Tablespoons wine vinegar
¼ teaspoon pepper
1½ teaspoons salt
½ cup salted peanuts

Fry bacon and remove from pan. Saute onions in bacon grease until golden. Add cooked green beans, vinegar, salt and pepper. Simmer 12 minutes. Add peanuts and cook 5 minutes longer. Serve with crisp bacon bits on top. 8 servings

Julia W. Ray (Mrs. Frederick C., Jr.)

HINT ▬▬▬▬▬▬

Tomatoes have a better flavor if not refrigerated. Even the super-market variety will improve in color and texture if allowed to sit in a sunny window for a day or two.

## "Skinny" Green Beans
A "non fattening" favorite—no grease

4 cups water
2 beef bouillon cubes
1 teaspoon sugar
2 pounds fresh green beans, washed, strings removed.
Dash Tabasco sauce
Dash freshly ground black pepper

Place bouillon cubes in water and bring to boil. Add sugar and beans to bouillon. Cover and cook until tender over medium heat, about 1 hour. Check bouillon and add more water if necessary. During last 15 minutes add Tabasco sauce and pepper. Hint: Use leftovers in vegetable salads. 6-8 servings

**Jeanine C. Andrews (Mrs. Edward B.)**

## Green Beans Tivoli
Wonderful to take on a Stone Mountain picnic

1 pound crisp young green beans
¼ cup minced green onions
1 Tablespoon cider vinegar
2 Tablespoons lemon juice
2 teaspoons sugar
2 Tablespoons Dijon mustard
⅓ cup olive oil
1 Tablespoon chopped parsley
3 Tablespoons fresh or dried dillweed
Salt
¼ teaspoon fresh ground pepper
GARNISH:
⅓ cup sliced radishes
⅓ cup coarsely chopped walnuts

Snap ends of beans and cook 5-7 minutes or until just tender. Drain and cool under cold water. Mix all ingredients except radishes and walnuts and pour over vegetables. Refrigerate at least 2 hours. Before serving, stir in radishes and walnuts. Note: Red on radishes will bleed if stirred into beans more than 1-2 hours in advance. Wonderful leftovers if you don't mind red radish slices.

4-6 servings

**Cookbook Committee**

## Jim's Favorite Beans

¾ cup sliced apples
½ cup chopped onion
1 (31 ounce) can or 2 (16
   ounce) cans pork and beans
6 ounces smoked sausage
   links, thinly sliced
¼ cup raisins
2 Tablespoons catsup
2 teaspoons prepared mustard
¼ teaspoon ground cinnamon
Dash cayenne

Cook apples and onion in small amount of water until crisp and tender, about 5 minutes, and drain. Mix with all other ingredients and turn into bean pot or casserole. Bake, uncovered, in a 375° oven (or less) for 1-1¼ hours STIRRING ONCE. Serve with corn muffins. 8-10 servings

Joan McMahan (Mrs. James P.)

## Black Beans and Rice

1 pound dried black beans
10 cups water
1 green pepper, diced
⅔ cup olive oil
1 large onion, chopped
Garlic salt to taste
¼ pound bacon, diced
1 green pepper, diced
4 teaspoons salt
½ teaspoon pepper
2 Tablespoons olive oil
WHITE RICE:
3 Tablespoons oil
3 cups water
1 Tablespoon salt
1 pound rice
1 pint sour cream (optional)

Wash beans and soak with 1 diced green pepper in water 6-8 hours or overnight. Boil beans in this water for 45 minutes or until tender. Heat olive oil in skillet; add onion, green pepper, garlic salt and bacon; cook until light brown. Pour mixture into beans; add salt and pepper. Cook 1 hour longer. Add 2 Tablespoons olive oil when ready to serve.

To cook rice, combine water, oil and salt; bring to a full boil. Add rice. When it comes to a boil, reduce heat to simmer and cook 30 minutes or until done. Serve black beans over rice with chopped raw onions and a dollop of sour cream (optional) on top. Can be a main dish or an accompaniment to pork roast. Add more liquid to make black bean soup. 8 servings

Patricia Barton (Mrs. William L.)

# Red Beans and Rice

6 cups water
1 pound dried small red beans
    or 1 pound dried red kidney
    beans
4 Tablespoons butter
1 cup finely chopped green
onions, divided
½ cup finely chopped onions
1 teaspoon finely chopped
garlic
2 (1 pound) smoked ham hocks
or ham bones with meat
1 teaspoon salt
½ teaspoon black pepper
6-8 cups cooked long grain
    rice

Rinse beans in cold water. In 3-4 quart saucepan, bring 6 cups water to boil. Drop beans in and boil briskly for 2 minutes. Turn off heat and let beans soak for 1 hour. Drain beans; save liquid; add more water to make 4 cups. Melt butter in heavy 4-5 quart kettle. Sauté ½ cup of the green onions, onions and garlic for about 5 minutes until they are soft and translucent. Stir in beans, their liquid, ham hocks, salt and pepper. Bring mixture to a boil, reduce heat to low and simmer about 3 hours, covered, or until beans are very soft. Check pot from time to time, adding more water (up to 1 cup) if beans seem too dry. During last 30 minutes, stir frequently and crush beans against the sides of pan to form a thick sauce. Remove ham bones to cutting board; cut meat from bone into bite size chunks. Return ham to beans. Discard bones. Serve mixture over rice with ½ cup green onions sprinkled on top. May be prepared in advance.
6 servings

**Jane H. Nardone (Mrs. A. Joseph, Jr.)**

---

**HINT**

Add ½ teaspoon sugar to vegetables such as corn, peas or carrots, when cooking, to help bring out the flavor.

# Kidney Bean Casserole
A must for an outdoor cookout

2 (15 ounce) cans kidney
    beans, partially drained
1 green pepper, coarsely
    chopped
2 small onions, coarsely
    chopped
2 tomatoes, cut into small
    chunks
1 strip raw bacon, finely
    chopped
½ cup brown sugar
½ (14 ounce) bottle catsup or
    chili sauce

Combine all ingredients in casserole dish and bake, covered, for 2 hours at 325°. May be prepared in advance, and is good reheated. 6 servings

**Judy L. O'Shea (Mrs. Timothy)**

# Southern Baked Beans

1 pound dried navy beans
6 cups water
2 minced garlic cloves
2 large onions, sliced
1 dried hot red pepper, small
1 bay leaf
¾ pound sliced salt pork or
    4 strips bacon
3 Tablespoons molasses
¼ cup catsup
1 teaspoon dry mustard
½ teaspoon ground ginger
1½ teaspoons Worcestershire
½ teaspoon salt
¼ cup brown sugar, firmly
    packed

Cover beans with water and bring to a boil, boiling for 2 minutes. Cover and let stand one hour. Add next 5 ingredients and cook until beans are tender. Drain, save liquid. Add remaining ingredients, except sugar, to two cups of liquid. Place beans in a shallow 2-quart baking dish. Arrange slices of pork on top and add liquid. Sprinkle with brown sugar. Bake at 400° for 1 hour.

**June Parker (Mrs. Charles)**

## Stir Fried Broccoli

2 pounds fresh broccoli
2 Tablespoons oil
2 Tablespoons chicken stock
1 teaspoon salt
½ teaspoon sugar
1 teaspoon cornstarch
    dissolved in 1 Tablespoon
    stock

Divide broccoli into florets;
Peel stems. Heat oil and stir fry
broccoli about 1 minute. Add
chicken stock, salt and sugar.
Cover and cook 3-4 minutes.
Lower heat and add cornstarch
dissolved in stock; stir briefly to
thicken. Serve immediately. Will
hold warm for a few minutes.
6 servings

**Pamela T. Marcus**

## Sesame Broccoli

2 pounds fresh broccoli, cut
    into 2-inch pieces
2½ Tablespoons sugar
2 Tablespoons sesame seeds,
    toasted
2 Tablespoons oil
2 Tablespoons vinegar
2-3 Tablespoons Japanese soy
    sauce

Cook broccoli in small amount
of boiling, salted water until
tender—about 7 minutes. Drain
and keep warm. Combine
remaining ingredients in small pan
and bring to boil over medium
heat. Pour over broccoli, coating
well. Serve immediately. Serves 6

**Cookbook Committee**

## Chilled Lemon Broccoli
### An excellent summertime vegetable

1 bunch fresh broccoli
Juice of 1 lemon
3 Tablespoons olive oil
Salt to taste
¼ cup pine nuts or sliced
    almonds

Divide broccoli into florets.
Steam over boiling water 5 minutes
only. Drain. Pour several changes
of ice water and ice cubes on
broccoli to retain color. Chill. Mix
lemon juice, oil and salt. Pour
over broccoli. When ready to
serve, sprinkle with pine nuts (or
almonds). Recipe can be doubled
easily. 4 servings

**Elise M. Griffin**

# Broccoli Rice Casserole

1 medium onion, chopped
¼ cup chopped celery
½ stick butter
1 (10 ounce) package frozen chopped broccoli, or 1 bunch fresh broccoli (chopped), cooked and drained well
2½ cups cooked rice
1 can condensed cream of chicken soup
4 ounces Cheese Whiz
Dash Tabasco
Pepper to taste

Sauté onion and celery in butter until tender. Combine with other ingredients. Pour into greased 1½-quart baking dish. Bake at 350° until bubbly; about about 30-35 minutes. May be frozen. Best when prepared a day ahead. 6 servings

**Lachlan M. Fiveash (Mrs. Charles)**

# Brandied Carrots

Enough slender carrots to serve 4-6 people
½ stick butter (approximately)
Brown sugar
⅓ cup brandy

Scrape carrots and cut in thirds. Layer carrots in a buttered baking dish. Dot each layer with butter and sprinkle with brown sugar. Pour brandy over top. Cover dish and bake at 350° about 1 hour. 4-6 servings

# Gingered Carrots

1 pound carrots
½ cup water
Salt
1 teaspoon ground ginger
1 Tablespoon brown sugar
2 Tablespoons butter

Cut carrots in lengthwise strips or crosswise circles. Cook in water seasoned with salt for 10 minutes or until tender; drain. In skillet melt butter; add ginger and sugar and cook 2-3 minutes turning carrots several times until well glazed. 4 servings

**Cookbook Committee**

# Carrot Mold with French Peas

A rich and delicious way to serve carrots
The cake-like texture of the mold eliminates the need to serve bread

**CARROT MOLD:**
1½ sticks butter, softened
½ cup brown sugar, firmly
    packed
2 eggs, separated
1½ cups finely grated raw
    carrots (approximately
    ½ pound)
1 Tablespoon cold water
1 Tablespoon lemon juice
1 cup plain flour
½ teaspoon baking soda
1 teaspoon baking powder
½ teaspoon salt
Breadcrumbs
**FRENCH PEAS:**
3 Tablespoons butter
¼ cup lettuce, finely chopped
1 box frozen green peas (top
    quality)
¼ cup minced shallots or
    green onions
1 large sprig parsley
2 teaspoons sugar
½ teaspoon salt
Dash of white pepper

Preheat oven to 350°. In mixer, cream butter and brown sugar. Add egg yolks and beat until thick. Add carrots, water, lemon juice, flour, soda, baking powder and salt. Mix thoroughly.* Beat egg whites until stiff peaks form and fold into carrot mixture. Generously oil 1½ quart ring mold and dust with breadcrumbs. Turn mixture into mold. Bake for 45 minutes or until firm. Turn onto serving dish. Fill with French peas.
*May be prepared ahead to this point.

Melt butter in saucepan. Place lettuce on top of butter. Add remaining ingredients. Simmer covered 5-7 minutes, stirring occasionally until peas are tender. Remove parsley. Serves 4

**Cookbook Committee**

# Dressed-Up Cabbage

1 head cabbage, cut in bite
    size pieces
1 cup thick white sauce (see
    Index)
2 Tablespoons catsup or chili
    sauce
½ cup grated Cheddar cheese
½ cup mayonnaise or salad
    dressing
½ small green pepper, minced
½ small onion, minced

Cook cabbage in boiling salted water until barely tender, about 8 minutes. Drain and put in buttered casserole. Make a thick white sauce and pour over cabbage. Bake covered for 30 minutes. Cover with a mixture of chili sauce, cheese, mayonnaise, pepper and onion. Serve immediately. Serves 6-8

**Doris Dixon**
*Tampa, Florida*

# Cauliflower-Cheese Fritters
A deliciously different fritter; great with ham

1 large head cauliflower
   or 1 (20 ounce) bag frozen
   cauliflower
¾ teaspoon salt
3 cups grated sharp Cheddar
   cheese
2 eggs, slightly beaten
½ teaspoon baking powder
BATTER:
4 eggs, separated
12 ounces beer
2 cups sifted flour
1½ teaspoons salt
¼ teaspoon pepper
2 ounces butter, melted
4 cups cooking oil

Several hours before serving, remove core from fresh cauliflower and separate into florets. Cook cauliflower in boiling salted water until tender; crush into small pieces. Add cheese, eggs and baking powder. Spread mixture onto a pie plate and refrigerate several hours.

Prepare Batter: Beat egg yolks until light. Add beer and flour. Add salt, pepper and butter. Let stand at least 1½ hours. Twenty minutes before serving time, beat egg whites until stiff. Gently fold into batter.

Heat oil in a large pan to 375° Shape cauliflower mixture into 1-inch balls, dip in batter and fry in hot fat until brown. Serve immediately. Variation: Substitute eggplant or minced mushrooms for cauliflower.

**Laura G. Ward (Mrs. Peter C.)**

# Sesame Cauliflower

1 medium head cauliflower
Salt and pepper to taste
1 cup sour cream at room
   temperature
1 cup (¼ pound) shredded
   Cheddar cheese
2 teaspoons toasted sesame
   seeds

Rinse cauliflower and separate into small florets. Cook in 2-quart covered saucepan in 1-inch boiling salted water 8-10 minutes or until tender; drain well. Place half of cauliflower in a 1-quart casserole; sprinkle with salt and pepper. Spread half of sour cream over cauliflower; sprinkle half of grated cheese over sour cream and top with 1 teaspoon sesame seeds. Repeat layers. Bake at 375° for 15 minutes or until heated through. May be prepared in advance. If refrigerated, heat for about 20 minutes. 6 servings

**Joan M. Adams (Mrs. John P., Jr.)**

# Microwave Corn on the Cob
This American summertime favorite is spectacular
cooked in the microwave

Carefully strip back the husks of each ear of corn and remove the silks, brush corn generously with melted butter and pull the husks back into place. Tie with string around the tip of each ear. When cooking more than 4 ears, remove silks and husks and place in a 3-quart casserole dish. Cover and cook. Allow corn to stand covered 3-5 minutes after cooking.

| No. of Ears | Cooking Time in Minutes |
|---|---|
| 1 | 3-4 |
| 2 | 5-6 |
| 3 | 8-10 |
| 4 | 12-14 |
| 5 | 15-18 |

**Cookbook Committee**

# Eggplant, Peppers, and Onions

**1 eggplant, peeled and sliced**
**½ teaspoon salt**
**3 Tablespoons olive oil**
**2 small onions, chopped**
**½ pound ripe tomatoes,**
**  seeded and chopped**
**Seasoned salt**
**Freshly ground black pepper**
**3 large green peppers, or 6**
**  large banana peppers,**
**  chopped**
**2 sprigs fresh basil, or ½**
**  teaspoon dried basil**
**½ teaspoon sugar**

Sprinkle eggplant with salt and let drain in a colander for 1 hour. Rinse, dry and chop eggplant. Heat oil in a heavy pan and sauté onions until soft. Add tomatoes and season with salt and pepper. Add peppers and eggplant, and sauté for about 5 minutes. Add basil and sugar, and check seasonings. Stir well and cook, covered, over low heat for 30 minutes. 4 servings

**Decie Nygaard (Mrs. W.F.)**

## MICROWAVE HINT

A round cooking dish is best for cooking chicken, meatballs, whole vegetables, etc. Arrange foods of uniform size in a circle, leaving the center empty.

# Fried Eggplant Strips

1 medium eggplant, peeled
  and cut into finger-sized
  strips
1½ teaspoons salt, divided
1 cup all-purpose flour
1 egg, slightly beaten
1 cup milk
1 Tablespoon salad oil
Salad oil for frying

Sprinkle eggplant strips with 1 teaspoon salt. Place in a bowl, cover with cold water and let stand for 1 hour. Drain and pat dry with paper towels. Meanwhile, combine flour and ½ teaspoon salt in a mixing bowl. Add egg, milk and 1 Tablespoon salad oil, beat until smooth. Dip eggplant strips in batter and deep fry in hot oil until golden brown. Drain well on paper towels. 6 servings

**Pamela T. Marcus**

# Fresh Mushroom Casserole

8 slices white bread, cubed
4 Tablespoons margarine
1 pound fresh mushrooms,
  sliced
½ cup chopped onion
½ cup chopped green pepper
½ cup mayonnaise
2 beaten eggs
1 cup mushroom soup
1½ cups milk
¾ teaspoon salt
Grated sharp cheese

Cut bread into cubes (may trim edges). Sauté mushrooms, onion and green pepper in margarine. Mix mayonnaise, eggs, soup, milk and salt. Grease a 2-quart casserole. Put bread cubes in bottom and up sides. Mix other ingredients together, pour over bread and mix gently but thoroughly. Let stand overnight in refrigerator. Cook uncovered at 350° for 40 minutes. Remove and cover with sharp grated cheese; return to oven and cook 10 minutes longer. 8 servings

**Eleanor R. McCormack (Mrs. T. Wayne)**

# Mushroom Pie

2 medium onions, chopped
  or sliced
⅓ cup butter
1 pound mushrooms, cleaned
  and thinly sliced
1 Tablespoon flour
½ cup half and half
1 Tablespoon sherry
Salt and pepper to taste
Double pie crust

Sauté onions in butter until golden, stirring often. Add mushrooms and cook 1-2 minutes, stirring occasionally. Add flour and toss mixture until blended. Add cream and bring to boil. Stir to thicken, adding more flour if needed. Add sherry and seasonings. Cool. Fill pastry lined pie plate with mushroom mixture. Lace top of pie with ½ inch strips. Flute edges. Bake on lower rack at 450° for 20 minutes. May be prepared in advance. 6-8 servings

**Dona B. Ansley (Mrs. Wiley S.)**

# Mushrooms Polonaise

½ cup butter
1½ pounds fresh mushrooms,
  sliced
¼ cup sherry (optional)
1 medium onion, minced
2 Tablespoons flour
1 cup sour cream
¼ cup heavy cream
Salt and pepper to taste
¼ teaspoon nutmeg
2 Tablespoons chopped fresh
  parsley
¼ cup soft bread crumbs,
  tossed in ¼ cup melted
  butter

Melt butter in heavy skillet;* add mushrooms and sauté until browned slightly and liquid is evaporated. Add onion and sauté until soft. Stir in flour; cook 5 minutes over low heat, stirring constantly. Blend in sour cream and cream. Add salt, pepper and nutmeg and cook until thickened. Stir in parsley. Pour into buttered casserole and sprinkle with bread crumbs. Bake in a 325° oven for 35 minutes or until lightly browned. 6 servings
*¼ cup sherry may be added to the butter when sautéing mushrooms, if desired.

**Betty Jo Ridley (Mrs. William E.)**

# Southern Okra and Tomatoes

1 cup okra, cut in ½ inch
   slices
½ cup chopped onion
¼ cup chopped green pepper
3 Tablespoons margarine or
   bacon fat
4 quartered tomatoes (peeled
   if desired)
1 teaspoon salt
¼ teaspoon pepper
1 cup fresh corn (optional)

Sauté okra, onion and green pepper in margarine or bacon fat over low heat. Add tomatoes and seasonings. Cook until tender, stirring as little as possible. One cup fresh corn cut from cob may be added. May be prepared in advance. 4 servings

**Jeanine C. Andrews (Mrs. Edward B.)**

# Onion Pie
Absolutely delicious!

1 cup finely crumbled Ritz
   cracker crumbs
½ stick butter, melted
2 cups yellow onions, thinly
   sliced (Vidalia's are best)
2 Tablespoons butter
2 eggs
¾ cup milk
¾ teaspoon salt
Dash pepper
¼ cup grated sharp Cheddar
   cheese
Paprika
Parsley

Mix cracker crumbs with melted butter; press into 8-inch pie plate. Sauté onions in 2 Table-spoons butter until clear, but not brown. Spoon into crust. Beat eggs together with milk, salt, pepper and pour over onions. Sprinkle with cheese and paprika. Bake at 350° for 30 minutes, or until a knife inserted in the center comes out clean. Sprinkle with parsley before serving. Serves 6-8

**Fran Scott (Mrs. Romney E.)**

---

**HINT** ■■■■■■■■■■■■■■■

To remove skins easily from tomatoes, place in a brown paper bag in the sink, make a cuff around top of bag and fill it with boiling water. The bag generally splits after 15 to 20 seconds. After draining, refrigerate tomatoes. They are ready to skin. Cherry tomatoes can be fixed this way for marinating.

# Fabulous Fried Onion Rings

1½ **cups all-purpose flour**
1½ **cups beer (active or flat;**
    **cold or room temperature)**
1 **teaspoon salt**
3 **large yellow onions**
3-4 **cups shortening or**
    **vegetable oil**

Combine flour, beer and salt in large bowl using a whisk. Cover bowl and allow batter to sit at room temperature for no less than 3 hours. Twenty minutes before batter is ready, preheat oven to 200°. Place brown paper bag or layer of paper toweling on a cookie sheet. Peel onions and cut into ¼ inch thick slices. Separate slices into rings. On top of stove, melt shortening in a 10-inch skillet to a depth of 2 inches. Heat shortening to 375°. With metal tongs, dip a few onion rings into batter. Carefully place in hot fat. Fry rings, turning once or twice, until evenly browned. Transfer to brown paper in pan and place on middle shelf in oven. Keep in oven until all rings are fried. To freeze, fry rings and drain on brown paper. Let rings reach room temperature. Arrange on cookie sheet and freeze. When frozen, place in plastic bags and return to freezer. Reheat on cookie sheet in a 400° oven for 4-6 minutes. 6 servings

**Jeanine C. Andrews (Mrs. Edward B.)**

## HINT

To keep sweet white onions such as Vidalias fresh longer, tie them in a stocking with a knot between each onion so they do not touch, and hang from a hook.

# Onion Ring Casserole
A good recipe for your outdoor gas grill

1 pound onions
Salt and pepper
⅓ cup water
2 Tablespoons butter or
   margarine
½ cup milk
1 egg, well beaten
½ cup shredded sharp
   Cheddar cheese
Paprika

Peel and slice onions ¾ inch thick; separate into rings. Place onion rings in 9-inch foil pan; season to taste with salt and pepper. Add water. Cover snugly with foil. Preheat grill. With cover down, cook on low setting 20 minutes, or until onions are tender. Uncover; dot with butter, stirring as butter melts. Combine milk and egg; pour over onions. Top with cheese, then sprinkle with paprika. Replace foil. With cover down, cook on low setting 10 minutes, or until "set". To cook in oven, cook in a covered casserole dish at 350° for 1 hour. 4 servings

**Trina Graham**
*Atlanta Gas Light Company*

# Chinese Pea Pods

1 (6 ounce) package Chinese
   pea pods, plain or with
   water chestnuts
⅓ cup diced green onion
   (with tops)
1 (3 ounce) can (or smaller)
   mushrooms and juice
2 Tablespoons butter
¾ cup chicken broth
2 teaspoons cornstarch
2 Tablespoons pale or medium
   sherry
1 teaspoon sugar
1 Tablespoon Japanese soy
   sauce
⅛ teaspoon garlic powder
2 Tablespoons toasted almonds

Thaw pea pods and drain off all water. Sauté onions and mushrooms in butter and small amount (¼ cup) chicken broth for 10 minutes. Add all other ingredients except pea pods and almonds. Cook for 5 minutes until sauce thickens slightly. Add pea pods and cook for 3 minutes (do not boil). Serve immediately with almonds sprinkled on top. Note: Sauce can be cooked ahead of time and chilled. Diced cooked pork or chicken can be added to this sauce for a main dish. 4 servings

**Jerry P. Connor (Mrs. Paul)**

# French Peas in Cream

1 cup fresh sliced mushrooms
2 Tablespoons melted butter
4 slices chopped bacon
1 Tablespoon chopped onion
1 Tablespoon all-purpose flour
1 cup half and half
1 (17 ounce) can green peas, drained
Salt and pepper to taste

Sauté mushrooms in butter about 1 minute. Cook bacon in large saucepan until bacon starts to brown. Add onions and sauté until tender. Bacon bits should be crisp. Blend in flour and cook until mixture bubbles. Gradually add half and half; cook until smooth and thick, stirring constantly. Add mushrooms, peas and salt and pepper. May be prepared earlier and reheated at serving time.
6 servings

# Pea Puff
### An unusual dish to complement ham or barbeque

2½ cups cooked, drained blackeyed peas
¼ cup bacon drippings
1 egg, beaten
1½ cups shredded sharp Cheddar cheese
1 medium onion, chopped
½ cup chopped green pepper
½ teaspoon pepper
1 teaspoon salt
1 teaspoon garlic powder
TOPPING:
½ cup shredded Cheddar cheese
Several rings of green pepper and onion

Purée peas in blender or food processor (add pea liquid if needed to purée). Combine remaining ingredients with peas and spoon into well greased 1-quart casserole. Bake at 300° for 40-60 minutes. top with onion and pepper rings and cheese. Brown briefly under broiler.
1 quart

**Susan M. Morley**

# The Potato
Variation on a theme

4 russett potatoes, cleaned
1 stick butter or margarine
2 medium Vidalia onions,
   sliced thin (or other sweet
   yellow onions)
Salt and pepper to taste
Aluminum foil

Preheat oven to 350°. Cut each potato into ½-inch thick slices, butter each slice generously on both sides, and sprinkle with salt and pepper. Place one onion slice (all rings together) between each slice of potato, forming potato back together. Wrap each potato in aluminum foil and bake for 1 hour. Great for barbeque: can be cooked on the grill.

**Terry C. Morris (Mrs. Douglas)**

# Stuffed Baked Potatoes

6 baking potatoes
½ stick butter or margarine,
   softened
3 ounces cream cheese,
   softened
¼ cup Parmesan cheese
½ cup sour cream
½ cup grated Cheddar cheese
Milk, if needed
Salt to taste

Scrub, dry, (and grease, if desired) 6 potatoes and bake at 400°-425° until done, approximately 1-1¼ hours. Immediately remove from oven and using oven mits or potholders to prevent burning hands, slice potato lengthwise about ¼ inch from top. Carefully, scoop out potato meat and put in a mixing bowl. Save shells. Add butter, cream cheese, Parmesan cheese and sour cream. Cream thoroughly. Add a small amount of milk if mixture is too stiff. Add salt to taste. Fill potato shells with mixture and top with grated Cheddar cheese. Heat 10-15 minutes at 400°. This freezes well. Prepare early in the day or well in advance and freeze. Thaw before heating. 6 servings

**Jeanette G. James (Mrs. T. Allen)**

## Easter Potato Casserole

6 medium potatoes
¼ cup butter
1 pint sour cream
1 can cream of chicken soup
⅓ cup chopped green onions
1 cup shredded sharp Cheddar
   cheese
Paprika

Note: It is important to boil the potatoes a day before preparing and leave them in the refrigerator overnight. Shred potatoes into a greased 9 x 13-inch casserole dish. Melt butter in a saucepan. Add sour cream, cream of chicken soup, onions and cheese. Stir until cheese is melted. Spread evenly over potatoes and mix well with a fork. Sprinkle top with paprika and bake at 350° for about 45 minutes. 10 servings

**Melva Jansen (Mrs. Klaus)**

## Plantation Sweet Potato Pone

2 cups finely grated raw sweet
   potatoes
1 cup (1½ small cans)
   evaporated milk
2 eggs, well beaten
¾ cup dark Karo syrup
¼ cup melted butter
1 teaspoon grated lemon rind
2 teaspoons lemon juice
½ teaspoon salt
½ teaspoon nutmeg
½ teaspoon cinnamon
½ cup brown sugar

Grate potatoes into bowl of milk so they will not darken. Mix ingredients in order given. Pour into a greased shallow baking pan. Bake in a 350° oven for 30 minutes; then stir with fork. Bake 15 minutes longer or until brown and crusty on top. 6-8 servings

**Lucy C. White (Mrs. Richard A.)**

## Senator Russell's Potatoes

3 cups cooked, mashed sweet
   potatoes
1 cup sugar
2 eggs
1 Tablespoon vanilla
½ cup butter
TOPPING:
1 cup light brown sugar,
   packed
⅓ cup flour
1 cup chopped pecans
⅓ cup butter

Combine potatoes, sugar, eggs, vanilla and butter. Beat with electric mixer for 2 minutes and pour into a buttered casserole.
Topping: Mix topping ingredients with fork and sprinkle on top of potatoes. Bake in a 350° oven for about 30 minutes. May be prepared in advance.
4 servings

**Beth M. Johnston (Mrs. J. Gibson)**

## Italian Spinach Pie

1 (9 inch) pastry shell, uncooked
1 10 ounce package chopped
   spinach, cooked and drained
4 Tablespoons butter
Salt and pepper to taste
½ pound Ricotta cheese
3 eggs, slightly beaten
½ cup finely grated Parmesan
   cheese
½ cup heavy cream (or milk)
Dash of nutmeg

Prick pastry shell and bake for 10 minutes at 450°. Cool. Mix cooked spinach with other ingredients. Pour into shell and bake at 375° for 30 minutes or until custard has set. Serves 8

**Susan Cuda**
*Tucson, Arizona*

## Creamed Spinach and Artichokes

1 small jar marinated artichoke
   hearts, drained
1 small onion, finely chopped
2 Tablespoons butter
2 packages frozen creamed
   spinach, cooked
½ cup freshly grated
   Parmesan cheese
¼ teaspoon nutmeg

Place artichoke hearts in bottom of a casserole. Sauté onion in butter until transparent. Season spinach with onion, ¼ cup cheese and nutmeg; pour over artichoke hearts. Sprinkle remaining ¼ cup cheese on top. Bake at 350° until hot, about 15 minutes. May be prepared in advance. 6-8 servings

**Lynn H. Barnes**

## Spinach Soufflé

3 eggs, beaten
3 Tablespoons flour
1 (9 ounce) package frozen
    chopped spinach, defrosted
    but not drained
1 cup creamy cottage cheese,
    small curd
⅓ pound Cheddar or Colby
    cheese, grated
⅓ cup melted butter
1 teaspoon lemon juice
Dash nutmeg
Salt and pepper to taste

Beat eggs with flour. Add defrosted spinach, cottage cheese, grated cheese, butter, nutmeg, salt and pepper. Put in 1½-quart greased casserole. Bake at 350° 55-60 minutes or until set. During last 10 minutes of baking add additional grated cheese. To freeze, cook for ½ hour, cool, freeze; later bake at 350° 50-60 minutes to serve. May also be prepared in advance, refrigerated and heated through to serve. Note: Do not squeeze moisture from spinach and do not overcook. 8 servings

**Carolyn B. Hoose (Mrs. Kenneth)**

## Spinach with Olives and Raisins
A deliciously different vegetable combination

2 pounds fresh spinach or 2
    packages chopped frozen
    spinach
1 teaspoon salt
¼ cup oil (olive oil or half
    olive, half vegetable oil)
3 Tablespoons sliced almonds
    or pine nuts
¼ cup sliced pimiento stuffed
    green olives
¼ cup sliced ripe olives
1 Tablespoon capers, drained
3 Tablespoons seedless raisins

Wash and drain spinach. Place in skillet, sprinkle with salt, cover and cook 5 minutes (only until spinach wilts). If frozen spinach is used, cook 1 minute less than package directs. Drain cooked spinach and chop if leaf spinach is used. Heat oil in skillet; stir in nuts and sauté until golden. Add the olives, capers and raisins, mixing until heated. Add the spinach, stir until heated through. Serve warm. Note: Spinach must not be overcooked. These various flavors and textures are best complemented by a roasted meat. 6 servings

**Phyllis K. Kennedy**

# Baked Yellow Squash

2 Tablespoons butter, melted
Juice of ½ lemon
¾ teaspoon thyme
¼ teaspoon salt
⅛ teaspoon pepper
4-5 medium yellow squash,
    halved lengthwise

Pour melted butter into a 9-inch pan or baking dish. Add lemon juice, thyme, and salt and pepper to the butter; stir with a fork until mixed. Place squash in pan, cut side down. Cover and bake at 350° for 30 minutes or until squash is tender. Or microwave in a pyrex dish for about 8 minutes, turn once. This is especially attractive when served around a carved roast.

**Cookbook Committee**

# Microwave Squash Casserole

2 Tablespoons butter
½ cup Ritz Cracker crumbs
    or ¼ cup chopped pecans
    and ¼ cup crumbs
¼ cup water
½ teaspoon salt
1 pound yellow squash, sliced
¼ cup mayonnaise
1 egg, beaten
½ cup grated Cheddar cheese
2 Tablespoons butter, melted
1 teaspoon sugar
¼-½ teaspoon instant minced
    onion
½-1 teaspoon horseradish

In a 1-quart casserole, melt butter on high temperature ½-1 minute until melted; add crumbs and cook on high 2 minutes. Stir after 1 minute. Place on wax paper and set aside. Place water, salt and squash in casserole, cover. Cook on high 8-10 minutes or until tender. Stir after 4 minutes; drain squash. Mix remaining ingredients in casserole, add squash and cook uncovered at medium temperature for 4 minutes. Add crumb topping. Cook 2-4 minutes more until center is set. Let stand 5 minutes before serving.
4 servings

**Cookbook Committee**

# Acorn Squash in the Microwave

1 (1½ pound) acorn squash
1 Tablespoon brown sugar
1 Tablespoon butter

Pierce squash with fork. Place on paper plate in microwave and cook 4 minutes. Give ½ turn, cook 4 minutes more. Remove from oven and let stand 2 minutes. Cut in half and remove seeds. Mix butter and brown sugar and fill each cavity with mixture. Cook 2 to 4 minutes more. Total cooking time 8 to 10 minutes. 2 servings

**Georgia Power Company**
*Home Economist*

# Crusty Tomato Scallop

2½ cups canned tomatoes
1 cup dry bread cubes
1 Tablespoon minced onion
¼ cup butter
1 Tablespoon flour
1 teaspoon salt
¼ teaspoon pepper
1 Tablespoon sugar
1 teaspoon prepared mustard
2 slices bread, buttered and
    cubed

Combine tomatoes, dry bread cubes and onion. In a saucepan, melt butter, add flour, seasonings and mustard and cook over low heat until smooth. Add tomato mixture and pour into greased 1½-quart baking dish. Sprinkle buttered, cubed bread over tomatoes. Bake in a 400° oven for 30 minutes. May be prepared in advance. 6 servings

**Jeneal L. Benton (Mrs. Gene R.)**

# Tomato Pie

2 ripe tomatoes
¾ cup chopped green pepper
1 onion, chopped
1 cup shredded Mozzarella or
    Swiss cheese
⅔ cup mayonnaise
1 large can refrigerator
    biscuits

Butter 8 or 9-inch pie pan. Pat canned biscuits out to form crust. Slice tomatoes to cover biscuits. Sauté green pepper and onion in butter. Spread over tomatoes. Mix cheese and mayonnaise together. Add more mayonnaise if mixture is too thick. Spread over top of pie. Bake at 350° for 40-45 minutes. Allow to cool and set for about 30 minutes before serving. 8 servings

**Barbara Withers (Mrs. David)**

# Mushroom Stuffed Tomatoes

6 tomatoes, red, but very firm
Salt
Pepper
Sugar
1 bunch green onions,
    chopped
3 Tablespoons butter
¾ pound mushrooms, sliced
Juice of ½ lemon
1 teaspoon paprika
¾ cup heavy cream
¼ pound freshly grated
    Parmesan cheese
¼ pound Gruyère cheese,
    grated

Cut ½ inch from top of tomatoes and scoop out shell. Chop pulp and drain. Sprinkle pulp and inside of shells with salt, pepper and sugar. Invert shells on paper towels and drain at least 30 minutes. Arrange shells in lightly buttered baking dish, top side up, and bake at 350° for 15 minutes. Drain any liquid that accumulates. In a large skillet, sauté chopped onions in butter until soft. Add mushrooms and sauté until golden. Add tomato pulp, lemon juice, paprika, salt and pepper. Sauté for 2 minutes. Increase heat to high, add cream and stir until mixture is thickened. Fill tomatoes with mushroom mixture and top with 2 teaspoons each of grated Parmesan and Gruyère cheese. Bake at 400° for 10 minutes and serve hot. Mushroom mixture and first baking of tomatoes may be done in advance. Tomatoes will get soggy if filled too far in advance. 6 servings

**Phyllis K. Kennedy**

# Scalloped Tomatoes and Artichoke Hearts
Great winter vegetable

1 (2 pound 3 ounce) can
    whole plum tomatoes
1 (14 ounce) can artichoke
    hearts
½ cup finely chopped onion
1 clove garlic or 2 Tablespoons
    finely chopped shallots
1 stick butter, melted
½ teaspoon basil
2 Tablespoons sugar
Salt and pepper to taste

Preheat oven to 325°. Grease shallow ovenproof casserole; drain tomatoes and artichokes; rinse and quarter artichokes. Sauté onions and garlic (or shallots) until tender in melted butter. Add tomatoes, artichokes and basil; heat 2-3 minutes. Season with sugar, salt and pepper. Bake in prepared casserole 10-15 minutes or until hot. 4 servings

## Vera Cruz Tomatoes
Especially pretty at Christmas around sliced roast beef or turkey

3 strips bacon
¼ cup chopped onion
8 ounces fresh spinach or
    frozen chopped spinach
1 cup sour cream
Pepper to taste
4 tomatoes
Shredded cheese

Cook bacon until crisp. Drain, reserving 2 Tablespoons of bacon grease. Crumble bacon and set aside. Cook onion in reserved drippings until tender. Stir in spinach. Cook covered until tender, about 3-5 minutes. Remove from heat and stir in sour cream, bacon and pepper. Cut tops from tomatoes; remove centers leaving shells. Drain. Salt shells and fill with spinach mixture. Place in 8 x 8 x 2-inch baking pan. Bake in a 375° oven for 20-25 minutes. Top with shredded cheese and return to oven for 2-3 minutes. May be prepared early on the day it is to be served. 4 servings

**Myrick L. King (Mrs. David L.G., Jr.)**

## Zucchini and Tomatoes Parmesan

¼ cup butter
3 small  zucchini, sliced
    (not peeled)
1 bunch green onions,
    chopped
2 medium tomatoes, sliced
Salt and pepper to taste
⅓ - ½ cup Parmesan cheese

Melt butter in a skillet and sauté zucchini and onions for 5 minutes, add tomatoes and cook 2 minutes more. Stir ½ of cheese into vegetables, and pour into an ovenproof casserole. Sprinkle remaining cheese on top. Cover and bake at 250° for 30 minutes. 4 servings

**Nancy Wactor (Mrs. William R.)**

## Ethiopian Vegetable Sauté

3 potatoes, cut in ⅓ inch-slices
¼ cup olive oil or vegetable oil
2 onions, minced
2 cups fresh green beans, broken into 1-inch pieces
1½ teaspoons tumeric
2 tomatoes, peeled and chopped
⅓ cup water
2 garlic cloves, minced
Salt and pepper to taste

Peel potatoes and cut into ⅓-inch slices; place in cold water to soak. In a skillet heat oil and sauté onions until golden. Add beans and tumeric and sauté for 10 minutes. Add tomatoes; saute 2 minutes over moderately high heat. Add drained potatoes, water and garlic cloves. Simmer, covered, for 15-20 minutes or until potatoes are tender, stirring occasionally. Season with salt and pepper. Can be prepared in advance and reheated at serving time.
4 servings

**Phyllis K. Kennedy**

## Jeanine's Vegetable Casserole
A good casserole to take to new neighbors

2 large cans green asparagus, reserve juice
2 small cans hearts of artichokes, reserve juice
2 small cans water chestnuts, reserve juice
½ pound butter
1 cup flour
2 cups grated New York sharp cheese
½ cup sherry
Salt and pepper to taste
MSG to taste
Sliced almonds

Melt butter; brown flour slowly in butter. Add juice from vegetables. If needed, add a little water, sauce should be thick. Add grated cheese and sherry. Season with salt, pepper and MSG. Layer ingredients in casserole dish, ending with sauce on top. Sprinkle with almonds. Bake at 350° for 30-35 minutes or until bubbly. May be frozen or prepared in advance. 8 servings

**Judy R. Carlsen (Mrs. Alfred M., III)**

# Six Vegetable Medley

6-8 carrots, cut in 2-inch lengths
2 cups fresh broccoli
   florets
½ green pepper, cut in 1 inch
   strips
1 medium onion, thinly sliced
2 stalks celery, sliced
10 medium mushrooms,
   quartered
Salt and pepper to taste
2 Tablespoons chopped parsley

Steam carrots and broccoli separately until crisp and tender. Sauté onion, green pepper and celery in butter until soft. Cover for a few minutes. Remove cover, add mushrooms and stir-fry until crisp and tender. Add carrots and broccoli, stir until warm, sprinkle with salt, pepper and parsley. 6 servings

**Sylvia Dorough (Mrs. Donald)**

# Two Beans and a Pea

1 box frozen green beans
   (French-cut)
1 box frozen green peas
1 box frozen lima beans
SAUCE:
2 cups mayonnaise
4 hard-boiled eggs, chopped
1 grated onion
1 Tablespoon prepared mustard
1 teaspoon Worcestershire
   sauce
2 Tablespoons salad oil

Cook vegetables separately, as directed on packages; layer in deep casserole. Dot with butter, salt and pepper to taste.
Mix all sauce ingredients together and refrigerate. When ready to serve, pour sauce on top of hot vegetables. 10 servings

**Betty Jensen (Mrs. Peter A.)**

# Luncheon Vegetables
### A breeze in the microwave

1 package frozen artichoke
   hearts
1 package frozen green beans
1 package frozen baby lima
   beans
4 Tablespoons melted butter
½ cup lemon juice

Cook frozen vegetables separately according to package directions, drain and mix. Combine butter and lemon juice and pour over vegetables. Other combinations of frozen vegetables may be used including peas, Brussels sprouts, broccoli or asparagus. 8 servings

**Doris Dixon**
*Tampa, Florida*

# Sherried Fruit Casserole
Excellent with ham as a buffet dish for brunch or dinner

**12 coconut macaroons**
**1 (1 pound 13 ounce) can**
  **peach slices**
**1 (1 pound 13 ounce) can pear**
  **halves, chunked**
**1 (1 pound 4 ounce) can**
  **pineapple chunks**
**1 (1 pound) can whole apricots,**
  **pitted and halved**
**2 (8¼ ounce) cans green grapes**
**½ stick butter**
**⅓ cup dark brown sugar**
**½ cup sherry**
**Slivered almonds**

Drain juices from fruit. Crumble half of the macaroons on bottom of a buttered 2-quart casserole. Arrange fruit on top; melt butter with brown sugar and sherry; pour over fruit. Top with crumbled macaroons. Bake 30 minutes at 350°; sprinkle with almonds and bake 5 minutes more. 12 servings

**Jeneal L. Benton (Mrs. Gene R.)**

# Peppered Oranges
An unusual accompaniment for meat

**2 navel oranges**
**2-4 teaspoons freshly ground**
  **black pepper**
**½ cup olive oil (Berio or**
  **similar brand)**
**Parsley or green grapes for**
  **garnish**

Trim off and discard a slice from the ends of each orange. Cut oranges into ⅛-inch slices, place in bowl, and sprinkle generously with pepper. Pour olive oil over, and marinate for 1 hour or more. Drain and arrange slices in an overlapping pattern in a serving dish, or around a platter of meat. Garnish with parsley or green grapes. Excellent with roast beef, pork, or chicken. 6 servings

**Jeanine Andrews (Mrs. Edward B.)**

# Grilled Pineapple Slices
Wonderful with ham—a little different, and easy

**Fresh pineappple, sliced**
**Sugar**
**Butter**

Melt butter in skillet. Dip pineapple slices in sugar and sauté in butter. Hint: Pluck a leaf from the pineapple's crown. If it pulls out easily, the fruit is ripe. 4-6 servings

**Jeanine C. Andrews (Mrs. Edward B.)**

# Holiday Ambrosia

1 cup seedless grapes
1½ cups mandarin orange
    sections (or fresh orange
    sections)
1 cup pineapple chunks
2 medium apples, unpeeled,
    cored and cubed
1 cup halved maraschino
    cherries
1 Tablespoon sugar
½ cup flaked coconut, toasted
1 cup sour cream
2 Tablespoons mayonnaise
1 Tablespoon light cream
Lettuce
½ cup sliced almonds, toasted

Combine fruits, sprinkle with sugar, add coconut and toss lightly. Mix sour cream, mayonnaise and cream; then fold into fruit. Serve on lettuce cups and garnish with almonds. Do not add dressing until serving time. Variation: Leave out sour cream mix and saturate fruit with sherry.
6 servings

**Cookbook Committee**

# Apple Cheese Salad
An excellent salad for fall and winter months
when there is a shortage of good produce for salad

2-3 tart red apples (Stayman,
    Rome)
1 cup thinly sliced celery
¾ cup pineapple chunks,
    drained (crushed may be
    used if well drained)
½ cup diced medium Cheddar
    cheese
¼ cup mayonnaise
¼ cup sour cream
1 teaspoon vinegar
Dash tarragon
1 Tablespoon prepared
    horseradish
Salad greens

Core and dice apples, or slice in food processor. Mix with celery, pineapple and cheese. Blend mayonnaise, sour cream, vinegar, tarragon and horseradish to make dressing and toss well with first mixture. Chill. Salad may be served on greens, or 1 cup of broken iceberg lettuce may be tossed with salad at serving time.
4-6 servings

**Phyllis K. Kennedy**

## Apple Cider Salad

1 (6 ounce) package orange
   flavored gelatin
3 cups hot cider or apple juice
1 cup crushed ice
1 (1 pound) can apricot halves,
   drained
2 bananas, sliced
1 small apple, unpeeled and
   diced (optional)

Add gelatin to the hot cider, and stir to dissolve gelatin. Add the ice, and stir until it melts. Add fruit. Pour into a 3-quart mold. Chill until firm. 8 servings

## Frozen Yogurt Fruit Salad

1 (8 ounce) carton peach yogurt
1 (8 ounce) carton sour cream
¾ cup sugar
Juice of large lemon
2 bananas, sliced
1 (8¼ ounce) can crushed
   pineapple, drained
¼ cup maraschino cherries,
   sliced
Dash salt
¼ cup chopped nuts (optional)

Mix yogurt, sour cream and sugar together. Add other ingredients and stir well. Pour into oiled mold (individual or other) and freeze. Take out of freezer and let stand at room temperature 30-45 minutes. Slice and serve on lettuce with mayonnaise as a topping. Will keep in freezer for 1 month. 8-10 servings

## Sacramento Fruit Bowl
In-season fruit may be substituted
The interest lies in the syrup

2 cups water
1½ cups granulated sugar
3 Tablespoons lemon juice
2 Tablespoons anise flavoring
½ teaspoon salt
1 small pineapple
1 small honeydew melon
1 small cantaloupe
2 oranges
2 nectarines or 4 apricots
2 purple plums
1 cup seedless green grapes
1 lime, sliced

In medium saucepan, combine 2 cups water with sugar, lemon juice, anise and salt. Cook over medium heat 15 minutes until mixture reaches light syrup consistency; chill 6 hours or overnight. Peel pineapple, melon, cantaloupe and oranges, and cut into bite-size chunks. Slice nectarines and plums into wedges. In large bowl combine cut up fruits with grapes and lime slices. Pour chilled syrup over fruits. Refrigerate, stirring occasionally, until chilled. 10 servings

**Penny P. Jennings (Mrs. H. Todd)**

# Cherry Almond Salad

¼ pound almonds
1 (16 ounce) can or 2 (8¾
ounce) cans white cherries,
drained
1 (1 pound 4 ounce) can
sliced pineapple, drained
1 cup mayonnaise
1 envelope unflavored gelatin
¼ cup cold water
1 cup boiling water or juice
from fruits
½ pint heavy cream, whipped

Blanch almonds and cut in pieces. Stone cherries, keeping as whole as possible; cut up pineapple. Mix fruit and mayonnaise. Soak gelatin in cold water then dissolve in 1 cup boiling water or juice. Strain into fruit mixture; cool. Add whipped cream. Pour into mold and refrigerate until firm. Make day before serving. 8-10 servings

**Mrs. Fran A. Spencer**

# Carrot Salad

1 (3 ounce) package lemon
flavored gelatin
1 (3 ounce) package orange
flavored gelatin
1 cup boiling water
1 (1 pound, 12 ounce) can
crushed pineapple and
juice (3½ cups)
1 cup diced celery
1 cup grated carrots
¾ cup chopped nuts
2 cups cottage cheese
1 cup heavy cream, whipped
½ cup mayonnaise

In a large bowl, dissolve gelatins in boiling water; add pineapple, celery, carrots, nuts and cottage cheese; fold in whipped cream and mayonnaise. Pour into a 3-quart mold. Refrigerate for 24 hours. If a firmer salad is desired, pineapple may be drained. Serve on lettuce with additional mayonnaise on top. This makes a pretty luncheon plate served with chicken salad. 16 servings

**Sarah Looper (Mrs. Joseph W.)**

# Emerald Isle Mousse

1 (3 ounce) package lime
flavored gelatin
1 cup boiling water
1 (8¼ ounce) can crushed
pineapple in syrup
2 Tablespoons green crème
de menthe
1 cup heavy cream, whipped ·

Dissolve gelatin in boiling water; add pineapple with syrup and crème de menthe. Chill until thickened, stirring often. Fold in whipped cream and spoon into a 1 quart mold or 6 individual molds. Chill. Serve on a bed of crisp lettuce. 6 servings

**Dr. Carol Marie Thigpen**

## Apricot Congealed Salad

2 (3 ounce) packages apricot
   or orange flavored gelatin
1 package unflavored gelatin
2 (1 pound) cans apricots,
   drained; reserve syrup
1 (1 pound 4 ounce) can
   crushed pineapple, drained;
   reserve syrup
1 pint sour cream
1 cup chopped nuts

To syrup from fruit, add water
to make 3 cups, and heat.
Dissolve gelatins in syrup. Mash
apricots and mix with pineapple
and sour cream. Add nuts.
Refrigerate until firm. 8 servings

**Constance Wilson (Mrs. A.E., Jr.)**

## Cranberry-Raspberry Salad

This is a good accompaniment to any holiday dinner
or use it to make an everyday dinner special.

1 (3 ounce) package raspberry
   flavored gelatin
1 (3 ounce) package lemon
   flavored gelatin
1½ cups boiling water
1 (10 ounce) package frozen
   raspberries
1 (16 ounce) can jellied
   cranberry sauce
1 (7 ounce) bottle lemon-lime
   carbonated beverage

Dissolve gelatins in boiling
water. Stir in frozen berries,
breaking up large pieces. Break
up cranberry sauce with fork. Stir
into mixture. Chill until partially
set. Carefully pour in soda, stirring
gently. Turn into 6-cup mold. Chill
5-6 hours or overnight. Unmold
onto crisp greens. Garnish with a
poached sliced apple.
8-10 servings

**Maddy S. Kligora (Mrs. H. John)**

## Tomato Lemon Aspic

1 can stewed tomatoes
1 (3 ounce) package lemon
   flavored gelatin
¾ cup mayonnaise
½ cup diced green pepper
1 cup diced celery
1 medium onion, diced

Boil tomatoes; add gelatin
straight from package. Stir and
cool. Do not boil gelatin. Add
mayonnaise, pepper, onion and
celery. Pour into a suitable
container. Refrigerate until firm.
8-10 servings

**Angela Waller (Mrs. Jerry M.)**

# Georgia Peach Aspic

1 envelope unflavored gelatin
¼ cup cold water
2 (3 ounce) packages peach
   flavored gelatin
1¼ cups boiling water
1 cup orange juice
Grated rind of 1 lemon
3 Tablespoons lemon juice
1½ cups puréed fresh Georgia
   peaches
¼ cup sugar, if necessary
CREAM CHEESE DRESSING:
1 (3 ounce) package cream
   cheese
1 Tablespoon mayonnaise
1 peach, puréed

Soften plain gelatin in ¼ cup cold water. Dissolve both unflavored and peach gelatins in 1¼ cups boiling water. Add orange juice, rind of lemon and lemon juice. Add puréed peaches; sweeten, if necessary. Pour into 1½ quart mold and chill until set. Serve with Cream Cheese Dressing.

Dressing: Cream the cream cheese until smooth. Add mayonnaise, blending well. Add puréed peach; mix. 8 servings

**Joan M. Adams (Mrs. John P., Jr.)**

# Pineapple Cream Salad
Light and fluffy

1 cup evaporated milk
1 (1 pound 4 ounce) can
   crushed pineapple,
   undrained
½ cup sugar
1 (3 ounce) package lemon
   flavored gelatin
1 (3 ounce) package cream
   cheese
DRESSING:
1 cup sugar
1 egg
⅓ cup orange juice
2 Tablespoons lemon juice

Place evaporated milk in freezer until partially frozen. Bring pineapple and sugar to a boil; add lemon gelatin and cream cheese; let melt. Stir until smooth. Cool. Whip milk until very thick; fold into gelatin mixture. Pour into a 1½ quart mold and refrigerate.

Dressing: Combine sugar, egg, orange juice and lemon juice and place in a saucepan. Let come to a hard boil, stirring well. When cool, refrigerate and serve over salad. 8-10 servings

**Agnes Seibert (Mrs. "Sam")**

## Green Bean Salad Mold

1½ packages frozen French green beans
2 cups green bean liquid and water
1 (3 ounce) package lemon flavored gelatin
1 (3 ounce) package lime flavored gelatin
½ cup chopped onion
2 Tablespoons lemon juice
1 Tablespoon vinegar
1 cup chopped celery
1 cup chopped nuts (optional)
1 small jar pimiento, drained
Salt and pepper to taste
SAUCE:
½ cup mayonnaise
2 teaspoons horseradish
2 Tablespoons lemon juice

Cook frozen French green beans. Save liquid; add water to make 2 cups. Heat this liquid and use to dissolve both packages of gelatin. Add chopped onion, lemon juice, vinegar, celery, nuts, pimientos, and salt and pepper. Chill. Serve with sauce.
8 servings

Mary Anna Hunter (Mrs. Jack D., Jr.)

## Spinach Salad Mold

1 Tablespoon unflavored gelatin
¼ cup water
1 (3 ounce) package lime flavored gelatin
1 cup boiling water
1½ cups cottage cheese
½ cup mayonnaise
1 small cucumber, chopped
1 small onion, chopped
2 stalks celery, chopped
1 teaspoon salt
1 package frozen spinach, thawed and drained well

Soften unflavored gelatin in ¼ cup water. Dissolve lime and unflavored gelatins in 1 cup boiling water. Cool. Add cottage cheese and mayonnaise. Add cucumber, onion, celery and salt. Squeeze spinach between 2 stacked plates to drain very well. Add to above and pour into a mold prepared with either oil or a non stick spray. Refrigerate until firm. 6 servings

Jane H. Thrash (Mrs. Elmore C., Jr.)

# African Salad
An interesting combination of greens and fruit

4 **medium apples, peeled
and diced**
1 **medium grapefruit, sectioned**
1 **(1 pound 4 ounce) can
pineapple chunks, drained**
1 **teaspoon ground coriander
(optional)**
½ **cup raisins**
¼ **cup sunflower seed kernels**
2 **cups (approximately) fresh
greens: spinach, romaine,
iceberg lettuce**
**DRESSING:**
1 **Tablespoon honey**
1 **Tablespoon lemon juice**
2 **Tablespoons vegetable oil**
1 **Tablespoon vinegar**
1 **Tablespoon grated lemon rind**
½ **teaspoon white pepper**
1 **teaspoon salt**

Mix apples, grapefruit,
pineapple, coriander, raisins,
sunflower seeds, and greens
together in a salad bowl. Then
mix remaining ingredients to make
salad dressing. Note: Salad
dressing ingredients may need
to be doubled depending on
amount of greens used.
8-10 servings

**Carol Stallings**

# Jackson Salad

**Iceberg lettuce**
**Romaine**
6 **hard cooked eggs, sliced**
2 **avocados, sliced**
6 **slices bacon, cooked
and crumbled**
**DRESSING FOR 6 SALADS:**
6 **Tablespoons olive oil**
3 **Tablespoons wine vinegar**
3 **teaspoons dry mustard**
**Salt and pepper to taste**

Fill large bowl with torn lettuce,
Romaine, bacon, egg and
avocado. Pour some dressing
on salad and toss. Serve other
dressings "on the side".
6 servings

**Terry C. Morris (Mrs. Douglas)**

## Esquire Salad

Your choice, mixed greens to equal 2 large heads (iceberg lettuce, fresh spinach, Boston lettuce, etc.)
3 tomatoes, cut in eighths
1 pound mushrooms, thinly sliced
1 can hearts of palm, diced
6 slices bacon, crisply cooked and crumbled
1 (15½ ounce) can garbanzo beans (Pour water off garbanzos and refill can with vinegar; let sit in refrigerator overnight. Drain before mixing.)
SALAD DRESSING:
1 cup oil
½ cup wine vinegar
Juice of ½ lemon
2 cloves garlic, minced
½ teaspoon Worcestershire sauce
2 Tablespoons chili sauce
1 teaspoon prepared mustard
4 Tablespoons Parmesan cheese
Dash oregano
Salt and pepper to taste

Mix all salad ingredients. Mix dressing together in jar, and pour over salad. Toss lightly.
12 servings

## Pennsylvania-Dutch Wilted Lettuce

5 slices uncooked bacon, diced
5 slices bacon, cooked and crumbled
1 beaten egg
¼ cup minced onion
¼ cup sugar
½ teaspoon salt
⅓ cup vinegar
¹⁄₁₆ teaspoon white pepper
1 bunch leaf lettuce
2 medium heads Boston lettuce, washed, dried and crisped

Cook diced bacon in a skillet until crisp. Combine other ingredients except lettuce; add to bacon. Heat just to boiling, stirring constantly. Tear lettuce into bowl, pour hot dressing over and toss lightly. Put on salad plates and sprinkle with extra crumbled bacon. Serve immediately.
6-8 servings

**Carolyn B. Hoose (Mrs. Kenneth A., Jr.)**

## Artichoke Mixed Salad

Serve this salad as a separate course so guests
can appreciate the flavors.

**2 packages frozen artichoke
hearts
½ cup dry white wine
½ cup water
2½ cups thinly sliced raw
mushrooms
2 avocados, diced
1 can filets of anchovy, drained
French Dressing (see below)
Salt and freshly ground black
pepper to taste
Watercress and romaine
Mayonnaise thinned with
lemon juice
FRENCH DRESSING: 2 cups
½ cup fresh lemon juice
1½ cups olive oil
2 teaspoons salt
¼ teaspoon pepper
1 teaspoon dry mustard
Dash cayenne
2 garlic cloves, crushed**

Cook artichoke hearts in white
wine and water until fork tender.
Drain and cut into ½ inch slices
and marinate with mushrooms in
French Dressing. Artichokes and
mushrooms should marinate for at
least 30 minutes. Dice avocados
and sprinkle them very well with
lemon juice to keep them from
turning dark. Drain anchovies and
cut into very small pieces. Drain
artichokes and mushrooms and
add the avocado and anchovies.
Season with salt and pepper. Line
a salad bowl with watercress and
romaine. Arrange the vegetables
in the middle to form a dome.
Serve mayonnaise separately.
8 servings
French Dressing: Mix all
ingredients in a 1 quart jar; cover
tightly and shake until thoroughly
blended.

## Artichoke Asparagus Tossed Salad

**1 head lettuce
1 large can cut-up asparagus,
drained
1 jar Cara Mia marinated
artichoke hearts, drained
Croûtons, seasoned type
Italian Dressing**

Combine lettuce, asparagus,
artichoke hearts and croûtons.
Toss with prepared Italian
dressing. 4-6 servings

**Diane D. Mahaffey (Mrs. Randy)**

## Stuffed Lettuce Salad

2 medium heads lettuce
2 Tablespoons bleu cheese
1 Tablespoon minced green
  pepper
1 Tablespoon minced green
  onion and stems
1 (3 ounce) package cream
  cheese
2 Tablespoons grated carrot
2 Tablespoons diced tomato
⅛ teaspoon pepper
½ teaspoon salt
DRESSING:
1 Tablespoon sugar
1 teaspoon paprika
¼ teaspoon pepper
¾ cup salad oil
1 teaspoon salt
1 teaspoon dry mustard
¼ cup vinegar

Core lettuce; wash and drain well. Mix all stuffing ingredients; cheeses first, tomatoes, last. Stuff lettuce ahead of time. May be done the day before and wrapped tightly in plastic wrap. Store in refrigerator. Quarter lettuce and serve with dressing on table.
8 servings
Dressing: Mix dressing ahead of time and store unrefrigerated in cool place. Keep tightly covered. Serves 8-10. Dressing may be used on tossed salads later.

**Betty Jo Ridley (Mrs. William E.)**

## Avocado Halves, California Style

2 Tablespoons chili sauce
2 Tablespoons catsup
1 Tablespoon vinegar
1 Tablespoon sugar
½ teaspoon Worcestershire
  sauce
6 dashes Tabasco
5 Tablespoons lemon juice
4 medium-sized, ripe avocados,
  chilled and sliced
3 pink grapefruit, peeled and
  sectioned

Sauce: Combine chili sauce, catsup, vinegar, sugar, Worcestershire sauce, Tabasco and 2 Tablespoons lemon juice; mix well. Refrigerate several hours.
Salad: Pit avocados and slice. Brush with remaining lemon juice. Arrange avocado slices with grapefruit. Spoon on sauce. May be served as a first course.
8 servings

**Susan M. Morley**

# Garden Party Salad
Lovely served in a clear crystal bowl so that
the layers show through

1 head lettuce, torn into bite
  size pieces
3 carrots, thinly sliced
½ head purple cabbage,
  shredded
1 (10 ounce) package frozen
  English peas (1 can may be
  used, but frozen is better)
3 yellow squash, thinly sliced
½ cup diced celery
½ cup diced onion
½ cup chopped green pepper
3 hard cooked eggs, sliced
6 slices bacon, cooked and
  crumbled
TOPPING:
3 cups mayonnaise
1½ cups grated cheese
  (Parmesan or Cheddar)

Layer in large bowl in order
of listing. Seal with 3 cups
mayonnaise spread over entire
top. Top with grated cheese.
Cover with plastic wrap.
Refrigerate overnight. May be
prepared 2 days ahead. Note:
Amount of mayonnaise and grated
cheese may vary according to
individual taste and size of
ingredients used. 8-12 servings

**Edna K. Jennings (Mrs. E. Paul, Jr.)**

# Spinach Salad and Dressing
A delightful change for spinach salad

DRESSING:
½ cup soy sauce
1 ounce fresh lemon juice
½-¾ teaspoon freshly ground
  black pepper
1½ teaspoons sugar
1 Tablespoon minced onion
1½ teaspoons sesame seeds
1 cup peanut oil
SALAD:
3 cups mixed Romaine and
  Bibb lettuce
3 cups fresh spinach, torn in
  bite sized pieces
½ cup sliced water chestnuts
½ cup sliced mushrooms
½ cup bean sprouts

Blend first 6 ingredients in
blender until smooth. Add peanut
oil and blend again. Toss with
spinach salad and serve.
12 servings

**Roswell Public House**
*Roswell, Georgia*

# Bean Sprout Salad
An authentic Chinese recipe

1 pound fresh raw bean
  sprouts
4 ounces fresh snow peas
  (Chinese pea pods), thinly
  sliced (can be omitted if
  not available)
2 Tablespoons good quality
  soy sauce
1 teaspoon sesame seed oil
¼ teaspoon MSG
EGG GARNISH: (optional)
2 eggs
½ teaspoon salt
½ teaspoon dry sherry
¼ teaspoon MSG
2 teaspoons peanut oil

Add bean sprouts to 10 cups boiling water in a large saucepan over high heat. Before water boils again, remove pan from heat and drain sprouts in a colander. Soak sprouts in cold water until thoroughly cold; drain well. Remove strings from snow peas; parboil peas in salted water 2-3 minutes; remove and drain. Cut into thin strips, lengthwise. Mix soy sauce, sesame oil and MSG; set aside. 6 servings

Egg Garnish: Beat eggs with salt, sherry and MSG. Put 1 teaspoon oil in hot non-stick skillet over medium heat; remove excess oil with paper towel. Pour in half of beaten egg and tilt to cover bottom of pan. Cook until edge is lightly brown and lifts out easily; remove to cutting board and cut into 4 even strips. Stack strips and cut into fine slivers. Repeat with other half of egg mixture. Place snow peas, bean sprouts and egg garnish in large salad bowl; chill thoroughly. Add soy sauce mixture immediately before serving and toss well.

**Cookbook Committee**

# Hot Bean Salad
Good for a "cook out"

½ pound bacon
1 medium onion, diced
1 can green beans, drained
1 can wax beans, drained
1 can red kidney beans,
  drained
1 can pork and beans
1 cup brown sugar
1 teaspoon salt

Fry bacon until crisp; drain and crumble. Sauté onion in hot bacon drippings. Add drained green beans, wax beans and kidney beans. Add pork and beans (do not drain), brown sugar and salt. Heat through. Sprinkle with crumbled bacon. May be served immediately or may be frozen. 12 servings

**Barbara M. Hett (Mrs. Richard E.)**

# Bean and Avocado Boats

¼ cup salad oil
2 Tablespoons vinegar
2 Tablespoons lemon juice
1 Tablespoon sugar
½ teaspoon chili powder
¼ teaspoon salt
Dash garlic salt
Dash pepper
1 (15 ounce) can garbanzo
  beans, drained
1 (8 ounce) can kidney beans,
  drained
2 Tablespoons sliced green
  onions
2 avocados, halved lengthwise
  and seeded

Combine first 8 ingredients and pour over garbanzo beans, kidney beans and sliced green onion. Chill thoroughly, stirring occasionally. At serving time, spoon beans into avocados.
4 servings   Serve with Rio Grande Pork Roast. (see Index)

**June L. Wagner (Mrs. James R.)**

# Darvish Salad
"Darvish"is a Persian word for gypsy

4 medium cucumbers
Salt to taste
1 clove garlic, split
1 Tablespoon white vinegar
1 cup plain yogurt
1 teaspoon chopped fresh dill
2 Tablespoons olive oil
1 Tablespoon chopped fresh
  mint (optional)

Peel cucumbers. Cut into halves lengthwise and remove seeds; then cut into ¼ inch slices. Sprinkle with salt, set aside. Rub a salad bowl with garlic. Sprinkle white vinegar on salad bowl and roll around in bowl to collect garlic flavor. Add yogurt and fresh dill and mix well. Drain cucumbers, sprinkle with olive oil, and add to bowl. Garnish with fresh mint. May be prepared in advance. This Middle Eastern dish complements any heavily flavored meat dish or strong fish such as salmon.
6-8 servings

# Broccoli Salad

1 large bunch broccoli (Use
  only the florets)
1 pint cherry tomatoes, cut
  into halves
4 green onions, chopped
½ pound bacon, fried and
  crumbled
DRESSING:
1 bottle Green Goddess
  dressing
Juice of half a lemon
Garlic powder to taste

Pour dressing over salad
ingredients and toss.
4-6 servings

Nancy H. Kelley (Mrs. James E.)

# Cauliflower Salad

1 head cauliflower, broken into
  florets
1 Tablespoon minced onion
½ cup sliced black olives
4 Tablespoons mayonnaise
1 teaspoon salt

Soak cauliflower in salted
water in the refrigerator for 1 hour.
Rinse cauliflower and pat or spin
dry. In bowl combine with onion,
olives, mayonnaise and salt. Chill
well before serving. Amounts of
ingredients may vary according to
size of cauliflower. The crunchy
texture of this sald makes it a
good accompaniment for many
main dishes. 6 servings

Molly L. Ahlquist (Mrs. Ernest, Jr.)

# Cheese Dressed Tomatoes
Good on baked potatoes with bacon bits and chives

8 ounces small curd cottage
  cheese
½ medium onion, grated
2 shakes Tabasco sauce
2-3 teaspoons mayonnaise
½ teaspoon salt
Juice of 2 lemons

Mix all ingredients in blender
or food processor. Chill. Serve on
½ tomato or on tomato slices for
salad. Serves 4-6

Mrs. Grace C. Griffin
*Scott, Georgia*

# Home Garden Marinade

¾ cup fresh lime juice*
6 Tablespoons good quality
  olive oil or salad oil
1 clove garlic, crushed
1 Tablespoon sugar
1½ teaspoons salt
½ teaspoon pepper
1 teaspoon Angostura Bitters*
*These 2 ingredients are
  essential. Although ½ part
  fresh lemon juice may be
  used, lime is better.
Sliced vegetables

Combine ingredients in a jar and shake well. Arrange on a platter, a selection of sliced vegetables: garden lettuce, tomatoes, mild onions, cucumbers, radishes, green pepper, avocado, etc. Pour marinade over and marinate for 1 hour before serving. Baste occasionally. Pour off excess before serving. Marinade may be saved and used again.
6 servings

**Phyllis K. Kennedy**

# Cucumber Salad
### Serve with pork or as a relish with any type meal

3 large cucumbers, peeled and
  thinly sliced
1 cup white vinegar
¾ cup water
¾ cup sugar
1 teaspoon salt
Dash red hot pepper
Dash dried parsley
Dash black pepper
Dash basil

Combine all ingredients except cucumbers and heat until sugar melts. Pour over cucumbers. Store in refrigerator in an airtight container. Keeps well for several days. 6-8 servings

**Winnie R. Goodman (Mrs. James E.)**

# Lemon Marinated Mushrooms

1 pound fresh mushrooms
½ cup salad or olive oil
3 Tablespoons lemon juice
1 Tablespoon Dijon mustard
½ teaspoon salt
¼ teaspoon freshly ground
  pepper

Cut mushrooms in ⅛ inch slices. In screwtop jar combine oil, lemon juice, mustard, salt and pepper. Cover jar and shake well. Pour mixture over mushrooms tossing gently to coat. Let mixture stand at room temperature 1 hour, stirring occasionally. Serve mushrooms on lettuce leaves.
3-4 servings

**Joan M. Adams (Mrs. John P., Jr.)**

# Hot Mushroom Salad

1 green pepper, cut in thin
strips
1 small onion, thinly sliced
1 pound fresh mushrooms,
sliced
1 Tablespoon margarine or
butter, melted
1-1½ Tablespoons soy sauce
1-1½ Tablespoons Teriyaki
sauce
Lettuce
3 slices bacon, cooked
and crumbled

Combine all ingredients except
lettuce and bacon in a skillet.
Cook, stirring frequently, until
mushrooms and onions are tender.
Spoon onto lettuce; garnish with
bacon. Serve immediately.
Vegetables may be sliced ahead
and refrigerated. 3-4 servings

Joan M. Adams (Mrs. John P., Jr.)

# Chilled Lima Bean Salad
Great salad for picnics and large parties

3 cups cooked lima beans (tiny
green limas), drained
1 cup diced celery
¼ cup minced parsley
¼ cup chives
2 teaspoons dill seed
½ cup mayonnaise
½ cup sour cream
1 teaspoon lemon juice
Salt, pepper and paprika to
taste

Combine lima beans, celery,
parsley, chives and dill seed.
Make a dressing with mayonnaise,
sour cream and lemon juice.
Carefully fold in lima bean mixture.
Add salt and pepper. Sprinkle with
paprika. May be prepared the
night before serving. 6-8 servings

Diane D. Mahaffey (Mrs. Randy)
Nancy D. Mahaffey (Mrs. G.T.)

## HINT

To prepare lettuce and spinach for salads, rinse thoroughly and
place in a dish towel or large piece of cheesecloth. Hold cloth by the 4
corners, take outside and, holding cloth in one hand, sling off moisture
by swinging cloth in a circular motion.

## Crunchy Pea Salad

1 (10 ounce) package frozen
   green peas
1 can water chestnuts, drained
   and sliced
1 cup shredded carrots
2-3 stalks celery, sliced
3-4 green onions, sliced
2 Tablespoons salad oil
2 Tablespoons wine vinegar
1 Tablespoon soy sauce
1 teaspoon sugar
1 teaspoon paprika
2-3 teaspoons dry mustard
½ teaspoon salt
1 small clove garlic, crushed

Put frozen green peas in a strainer and run hot water over to thaw. Drain. Combine in a bowl with water chestnuts, shredded carrots, celery and green onions. Mix the marinade by combining salad oil, vinegar, soy sauce, sugar, paprika, dry mustard, salt and garlic. Pour marinade over vegetables. Chill at least 1 hour before serving. Note: This should not be prepared more than 1 day in advance since the water chestnuts change color.
8 servings

**Elise Nardone Yates**
*Haleiwa, Hawaii*

## Dublin Potato Salad
An interesting combination of potato salad and slaw

2 Tablespoons cider or wine
   vinegar
1 teaspoon celery seed
1 teaspoon mustard seed
3 pounds potatoes
2 teaspoons sugar
½ teaspoon salt
2 cups cabbage, shredded
¼ cup chopped dill pickle
¼ cup chopped green onions
1 cup mayonnaise
¼ cup milk
½ teaspoon salt
1 (12 ounce) can corned beef,
   cubed (optional)

Combine first 3 ingredients; set aside. Peel and cook potatoes until barely done; don't overcook. Drain, cube and drizzle with vinegar mixture. Add sugar and salt. Combine remaining ingredients and toss with potato mixture. Chill until serving time.
8-10 servings

**Marcia Scroggs (Mrs. Joe D.)**

## Pepperoni Potato Salad
This unusual salad is good for picnics and casual dinners

10 medium potatoes (red preferred)
4 slices bacon, cooked and crumbled
1 stick pepperoni sausage, sliced and cubed
1 large onion, chopped
3 hard boiled eggs, sliced (optional)
1 Tablespoon dill pickle cubes
½-¾ cup mayonnaise
1 Tablespoon mustard
Salt, pepper, garlic salt to taste
½ green pepper, sliced (optional)
¼ cup sliced green olives (optional)

Boil and slice potatoes while hot. Leave peelings on potatoes if desired. Sauté chopped pepperoni and onion in bacon drippings over medium heat for 2-3 minutes or until onion is softened. Pour hot pepperoni, onion and drippings over potatoes. Toss gently. Add remaining ingredients. Serve immediately or refrigerate until thoroughly chilled and serve. 8 servings

Lachlan M. Fiveash (Mrs. Charlie B.)

## Italian Rice Salad

2 cups long grain rice
2 hard boiled eggs, chopped
½ cup olives, black, green or mixture of both
2 Tablespoons capers
1 (6½ ounce) can tuna
⅓-½ cup olive oil
Juice of 2 lemons
Salt
Black pepper, freshly ground
OPTIONAL:
2 stalks celery, finely chopped
1 small onion, finely chopped
½ green pepper, finely chopped
Radishes, finely chopped
Small jar pimiento, chopped
Cucumber, finely chopped
1 small jar marinated artichoke hearts, drained
1 (8½) ounce can tiny green peas, drained

Cook rice in boiling, salted water until just done. Do not overcook. Grains must not stick together. Add eggs, olives, capers and tuna to cooked, cooled rice, and choose from optional ingredients to suit your taste: any or all of them. Add olive oil, lemon juice, salt and pepper to taste. Chill before serving. 6-8 servings

Barrie C. Aycock (Mrs. Robert R.)

# Scandinavian Salad

1 (16 ounce) can French green
   beans, drained
1 small can pitted black
   olives, drained
1 (16 ounce) can tiny green
   peas, drained
1 (2 ounce) jar pimiento,
   drained and chopped
1 medium onion, sliced and
   separated into rings
1½ cups chopped celery
1 (8 ounce) can water
   chestnuts, drained and
   sliced
1 (16 ounce) can bean sprouts,
   drained
DRESSING:
1 teaspoon salt
1 cup vinegar
⅓ cup vegetable oil
1⅓ cups sugar
Dash paprika

Mix dressing and pour over vegetables. Refrigerate for at least 24 hours. Will keep in refrigerator covered 1 week. 10-12 servings

Carolyn Hoose (Mrs. Kenneth A., Jr.)

# Bleu Cheese Slaw
Change of pace in slaws

¾ cup corn oil
⅓ cup vinegar
¼ cup sugar
1 Tablespoon grated onion
1½ teaspoons salt
½ teaspoon celery seed
2 quarts (1 head) white
   cabbage, prepared for slaw
1 quart (½ head) red cabbage,
   prepared for slaw
2 (4 ounce) packages bleu
   cheese, crumbled

Mix oil, vinegar, sugar, onion, salt and celery seed. Chill several hours (up to 24 hours). Toss with cabbage and bleu cheese at serving time. 8 servings

Beverly Bibent (Mrs. Maury J.)

## Marinated Tomatoes and Green Peppers
Maggi seasoning makes this garden fresh salad different

2 large ripe tomatoes, thinly
   sliced
1-2 green peppers, sliced
MARINADE:
4 Tablespoons red wine
   vinegar
½ teaspoon Dijon mustard
½ teaspoon salt
½ teaspoon chopped frozen
   chives
4-5 dashes Maggi (liquid)
   seasoning
Ground pepper to taste
3 Tablespoons salad oil

Alternate tomatoes and peppers in a shallow dish. Mix marinade ingredients well, adding oil last. Pour over tomatoes and peppers and refrigerate 1-2 hours.
4-6 servings

**Dunja S. Awbrey (Mrs. James J.)**

## Insalata Marinata

1 cup diagonally sliced raw
   carrots
1 cup cauliflower broken into
   small pieces
1 medium green pepper, cut
   in bite-sized pieces
1 package frozen artichoke
   hearts, cooked and drained
1 cup thickly sliced fresh
   mushrooms
½ cup ripe olives
4 slices (2 ounces) proscuitto,
   cut in quarters
6 slices (2 ounces) hard salami,
   cut in quarters
¾ cup prepared Italian dressing

In saucepan cook carrots, cauliflower and green pepper in boiling water until just tender, approximately 5 minutes. Drain. Combine with remaining ingredients. Chill for 6 hours or more, stirring occasionally. Makes about 6 cups. Keeps well for several days. Serve with a cup of light soup and bread sticks.
4 servings

**Cookbook Committee**

## Marinated Vegetable Salad

½ pound mushrooms
1 (14 ounce) can artichoke
 hearts, drained and cut
1 (7 ounce) can baby carrots,
 drained
¼ cup pimientos, chopped
1 cup pitted black olives
DRESSING:
⅔ cup white vinegar
⅔ cup olive oil
¼ cup chopped onions
2 cloves garlic, crushed
1 teaspoon salt
1 teaspoon sugar
1 teaspoon dried oregano
1 teaspoon basil
¼ teaspoon pepper

In salad bowl layer all ingredients starting with mushrooms and ending with olives. Combine dressing ingredients; bring to boil. Remove from heat and cool for 10 minutes. Pour cooked dressing over vegetables. Refrigerate several hours. Toss before serving. Serve on a bed of lettuce. 6-8 servings

**Nancy H. Kelley (Mrs. James E.)**

## Marinated Slaw

1 medium cabbage, prepared
 for slaw
2 large onions, thinly sliced
 and separated into rings
⅞ cup sugar
1 cup vinegar
¾ cup cooking oil
2 Tablespoons sugar
1 teaspoon salt
1 teaspoon celery seed

In a bowl place cabbage alternating with onions. Top with ⅞ cup sugar. Do not stir. Heat vinegar, oil, 2 Tablespoons sugar, salt and celery seed. Let boil. Pour over cabbage and onions. Refrigerate at least 12 hours before serving. Drain before serving. May be prepared 2 days in advance. Nice to serve with fish or barbeque. 6 servings

**Nancy W. Jones (Mrs. Edmund W.)**

# Cobb Salad
A summer meal

**DRESSING:**
¼ cup water
¼ cup red wine vinegar
¼ teaspoon sugar
Dash lemon juice
2 teaspoons salt
¾ teaspoon black pepper
1 scant teaspoon
    Worcestershire sauce
1 scant teaspoon Dijon
    mustard
½ clove garlic, crushed
¼ cup olive oil
¾ cup salad oil
**SALAD:**
Greens—mixture of lettuce,
    watercress, chicory,
    Romaine
2 tomatoes, cut in wedges
2 chicken breasts, cooked
    and chopped
6 strips crisp bacon
1 avocado, sliced
3 hard cooked eggs, chopped
2 Tablespoons chopped chives
½ cup crumbled Roquefort
    cheese

Dressing: Blend all ingredients except oil. Add oil slowly to blender. Chill. Shake before serving.

Salad: Arrange tomatoes, chicken, bacon and avocado decoratively on greens. Sprinkle chopped eggs, cheese and chives on top. Pour dressing and toss just before serving. 6-8 servings

Marty D. Halyburton (Mrs. Porter)

# Chicken Salad Supreme

2½ cups diced, cooked
    chicken
1 cup finely chopped celery
1 cup halved seedless grapes
½ cup slivered toasted
    almonds
2 Tablespoons minced parsley
1 teaspoon salt
1 cup mayonnaise
½ cup heavy cream, whipped

Gently combine all ingredients. Serve on crisp lettuce. Garnish with thin slices of chicken over top and either sliced ripe or stuffed green olives around the salad. Serve this at a luncheon with a tomato aspic, Asparagus Vinaigrette, and Herbed Potato Rolls (see Index). 8 servings

## Curried Turkey Salad

8 cups cooked, diced turkey
(2½-3 pound size)
20 ounces water chestnuts,
drained and sliced
2 pounds seedless grapes
2 cups sliced celery
2-3 cups slivered almonds,
toasted
3 cups mayonnaise
1 Tablespoon curry powder
2 Tablespoons soy sauce
2 Tablespoons lemon juice
1 pound pineapple chunks or
2 (11 ounce) cans lychee
nuts, drained
Boston-Bibb lettuce

Combine all but lettuce and chill for several hours. Serve on bed of fresh lettuce. 12 servings

**Cookbook Committee**

## Crab Aspic

1 pound frozen Alaskan King
crab
1¼ cups boiling water
1 envelope unflavored gelatin,
softened in ¼ cup water
1 (3 ounce) package lemon
flavored gelatin
2 cups tomato juice
1 Tablespoon vinegar
1 Tablespoon Worcestershire
sauce
½ teaspoon salt
1 teaspoon grated onion
4 drops Tabasco
¾ cup chopped celery
⅔ cup chopped cucumber
¼ cup chopped green pepper

Drain thawed crab meat. Reserve some large pieces for garnish. Finely slice the rest. Add boiling water to gelatins, stirring until dissolved. Add tomato juice, vinegar, Worcestershire sauce, salt, onion and Tabasco. Chill until mixture is consistency of egg whites. Add vegetables and crab meat. Pour into greased mold and chill. Garnish with crab pieces and deviled eggs.

**Mrs. John Hellriegel**

## Tuna Salad Surprise

2 large cans tuna, drained
1 cup minced celery
1 medium onion, minced
1 teaspoon lemon juice
1 teaspoon curry powder
1 package small frozen peas
    or canned peas, drained
1 teaspoon soy sauce (or more
    if desired)
¾ cup mayonnaise
1 can chow mein noodles

Combine all ingredients except noodles the night before serving. Add noodles and toss just before serving. Serve on lettuce cups with tomato wedges. 8 servings

**Maureen T. Vandiver (Mrs. Roy W.)**

## Salmon Sour Cream Mold

1 envelope unflavored gelatin
½ cup cold water
1 envelope sour cream sauce
    mix
½ cup mayonnaise or salad
    dressing
2 teaspoons lemon juice
¼ teaspoon dried dill weed or
    ½ teaspoon dill seed
1 (16 ounce) can red salmon
½ cup diced celery
4 green onions including
    green tops, diced
2-3 drops red food coloring
    (optional)
Carrot curls to garnish, if
    if desired

Soften gelatin in cold water. Stir over boiling water until gelatin dissolves. Cool. Prepare sour cream sauce mix according to package directions. Blend in mayonnaise, lemon juice and dill weed. Gradually stir into gelatin. Drain salmon, discarding skin and large bones; flake. Fold salmon, celery, and onions into sour cream mixture; blend in red food coloring, if desired. Turn into greased 3 cup mold. Chill until set 4-5 hours; unmold and garnish with carrot curls, if desired. May be prepared a day in advance. 6 servings

**Carol Ann Neal (Mrs. Michael M.)**

# Shrimp and Rice Salad
A good light supper or luncheon dish

¾ pound fresh mushrooms,
　coarsely chopped
2 Tablespoons salad oil
2 Tablespoons lemon juice
1 teaspoon salt
3¼ cups cooked rice (half
　white, half wild)
2 hard cooked eggs, coarsely
　chopped
1 green pepper, coarsely
　chopped
1½ pounds shrimp, cleaned
　and cooked
GARLIC MAYONNAISE:
1 clove garlic
¼ teaspoon paprika
½ teaspoon dry mustard
⅛ teaspoon pepper
1 teaspoon warm water
¾ cup mayonnaise

Sauté mushrooms in oil. Add lemon juice and salt, and cook until tender (about 10 minutes). Mix rice, eggs, green pepper, mushrooms and shrimp together. Refrigerate overnight. Toss with Garlic Mayonnaise before serving. 10 servings

Garlic Mayonnaise: Blend all ingredients together well.

**Sandra R. Pritchett (Mrs. Edwin P.)**

# Shrimp and Cabbage Collage
Good with buttered pumpernickel

½ cup sour cream or plain
　yogurt
½ cup mayonnaise
4 teaspoons prepared mustard
1 Tablespoon white vinegar
½ teaspoon salt
¼ teaspoon pepper
1 Tablespoon sugar
12 ounces shrimp, cooked
　and chopped
1 small head green cabbage,
　coarsely shredded
2 green onions, thinly sliced

Combine sour cream, mayonnaise, mustard and spices. Fold in the shrimp. Arrange cabbage in salad bowl, mound shrimp in center and sprinkle with green onions. 4 servings

**Susan M. Morley**

# Taco Salad

1 pound lean ground beef
½ bell pepper, chopped
1 cup chopped onion
1 Tablespoon chili powder
¼-½ teaspoons cumin
Salt and pepper to taste
1 head iceberg lettuce,
　shredded
2 medium tomatoes, chopped
6-8 ounces tortilla chips,
　coarsely crushed
1 small purple onion, chopped
1 avocado, sliced
6-8 ounces Cheddar cheese,
　grated

Brown beef with onions and pepper. Drain off fat. Season with chili powder, cumin, salt and pepper. Keep warm. Mix all other ingredients except cheese. Add warm meat mixture and cover with cheese. Let stand a few minutes to melt cheese slightly. Toss and serve immediately.
6-8 servings

**Jerry P. Connor (Mrs. Paul)**

# Winter Salad

Delicious with baked ham, ham sandwiches or hot dogs

½ cup vinegar
½ cup sugar
¼ cup oil
1 Tablespoon salt
½ teaspoon pepper
1 (16 ounce) can sauerkraut
1 medium onion, chopped
1 green pepper, chopped
2 pimientos, chopped
½ teaspoon garlic salt
1 teaspoon celery seed

Combine vinegar, sugar, salt, oil, and pepper and boil, stirring to dissolve sugar. Rinse and drain sauerkraut. Pour sauce over sauerkraut and add remaining ingredients. Mix and allow to cool slightly. Cover and chill at least 4 hours. Best when chilled for 24 hours. 8 servings

**Alicia LaRocco**

---

HINT

To dry large quantities of lettuce or spinach, put in pillow case, tie with twistie, place in washing machine and spin dry.

# Cole Slaw Dressing

2 eggs
½ cup sugar
¼ cup vinegar
½ Tablespoon butter
1 teaspoon mustard
¼ teaspoon salt
¼ teaspoon pepper

Beat eggs well with sugar. Add remaining ingredients. Cook in a double boiler until thick, stirring constantly. Store in refrigerator. Thin with cream if too thick.

Prepare ahead and toss with shredded cabbage before serving. 1 cup

**Dorothy M. Martens (Mrs. G.H.)**

# Creamy Fruit Topping

1 cup heavy cream
1 teaspoon unflavored gelatin
¼ cup sugar
1 cup sour cream
1 teaspoon vanilla

Combine heavy cream, unflavored gelatin and sugar in a saucepan. Heat gently until gelatin and sugar are dissolved. Chill. Fold in sour cream and vanilla, chill and serve over fresh fruit. 8-12 servings

**Dannie Martin (Mrs. H. Fielder)**

# Tarragon Dressing
Especially good on a salad containing Bleu or Roquefort cheese

1½ cups salad oil
⅓ cup tarragon vinegar
1 teaspoon lemon juice
½ teaspoon soy sauce
½ teaspoon sugar
1 teaspoon garlic powder
2 teaspoons salt
2 teaspoons coarsely ground
    black pepper
1 teaspoon dry mustard

Mix all ingredients in order listed and store in the refrigerator in a covered container. 2 cups

**Julia W. Ray (Mrs. Frederick C., Jr.)**

## Danish Feta Cheese Dressing

1 cup finely crumbled Feta
   cheese
½ cup mayonnaise
½ cup sour cream
3 Tablespoons buttermilk
1 Tablespoon fresh lemon
   juice
1 clove garlic, pressed
1 teaspoon grated onion
1 teaspoon Worcestershire
   sauce
½ teaspoon dried mixed salad
   herbs
Freshly ground black pepper
   to taste
Black olives for garnish
Chopped green onion for
   garnish

Combine all ingredients except black olives and green onion, blending well. Cover and chill at least 1 hour to allow flavors to blend. Serve over crisp greens. 1½ cups

**Joan M. Adams (Mrs. John P., Jr.)**

## Famous Mustard Vinaigrette

⅓ cup red wine vinegar or
   tarragon vinegar
2 Tablespoons Dijon mustard
1 cup olive oil (or ½ vegetable
   oil and ½ olive oil)
1½ teaspoons dried thyme
1½ teaspoons dried tarragon
   or less
½ teaspoon salt
¼ teaspoon freshly ground
   black pepper
½ teaspoon sugar

Mix wine vinegar and mustard in medium bowl. Add oil in a very slow stream using a small whisk to incorporate oil as it is added. This step should take several minutes and will result in a dressing that does not separate later. Add other ingredients and chill. Do not use a food processor as it will change the consistency. Serve over green salads, and in potato salads. 1½ cups

**Elise M. Griffin**

# Italian Salad Dressing, Il Giardino

4 egg yolks
1 cup olive oil
½ cup freshly grated Romano
or Parmesan cheese
1 Tablespoon vinegar
1 teaspoon crushed garlic
Juice of 1 lemon
2 teaspoons fresh basil or
1 teaspoon dried
1 teaspoon coarsely ground
black pepper

Beat yolks with fork or whisk. Gradually add oil until yolks will hold no more. Blend in remaining ingredients. Store covered and chilled. Do not use blender or food processor; it changes the consistency. 1½ cups

**Il Giardino**
*Charleston, South Carolina*

# Special French Dressing

1 cup powdered sugar
½ cup cider vinegar
Juice of 1 lemon
8 Tablespoons catsup
½ cup salad oil
Salt and pepper to taste
1 Tablespoon finely minced
onion
1 garlic clove, pressed or
finely minced

In blender, or with mixer, blend powdered sugar, vinegar and lemon juice. Add catsup and blend well. Add oil and blend; add onion and spices and blend thoroughly. Cover tightly and refrigerate for at least 24 hours before use. This dressing will keep 3-4 weeks under refrigeration. 1½ cups

**Ruth Hardy (Mrs. Wallace E.)**

# Roquefort Dressing
Very mild—vary by adding more or less cheese

1 (2-3 ounce) wedge Roquefort
cheese
1 package Cheese Garlic Salad
Dressing mix
1 pint good quality mayonnaise
2 cups buttermilk
(approximately)
Juice of ½ lemon

Crumble cheese into a 1 quart container; add dressing mix and mayonnaise; add buttermilk to equal 1 quart. Season with lemon juice. Shake well. This dressing will keep for 2-3 weeks in the refrigerator. 1 quart

**Nancy Wactor (Mrs. W. Ray)**

# Poppy Seed Dressing
A very versatile dressing

⅔ cup vinegar
¼ cup lemon juice
1½ cups sugar
2 teaspoons salt
3 Tablespoons poppy seed
2 teaspoons dry mustard
1 teaspoon paprika
1 small onion, cut in quarters
2 cups vegetable oil

Heat vinegar, lemon juice, sugar and salt until sugar dissolves. Blend poppy seed, mustard, paprika, onion and hot liquids 30 seconds on high. Turn to low speed. Slowly add oil to the rest of the mixture in the blender and blend on low 10 more seconds. Can be stored at least 4 weeks in refrigerator in a covered container. Use over fresh fruit or over spinach salad as a dressing. Marinate chicken in dressing before grilling. Add to barbecue sauce for a sweet and sour taste. Mix with mayonnaise, half and half, and use on cole slaw. 1 quart

**Sandy L. Carley (Mrs. George H.)**

# Mayfair Dressing
From the Mayfair Hotel in St. Louis

1 cup mayonnaise
½ cup sour cream
1 (2 ounce) can anchovy fillets
¼ cup minced parsley
3 Tablespoons chopped green
    onion
2 Tablespoon tarragon vinegar
2 Tablespoons lemon juice
¼ clove garlic
½ teaspoon salt

Combine ingredients and process in blender or food processor. Store in a covered container.

**Pamela T. Marcus**

# Honey Dressing for Fruit
Good on any frozen or fresh fruit salad

½ cup wine vinegar
¼ cup sugar
¼ cup honey
1 teaspoon dry mustard
1 teaspoon paprika
1 teaspoon celery seed
1 teaspoon celery salt
1 teaspoon grated onion
1 cup vegetable oil

Mix vinegar, sugar, honey, mustard, and paprika; boil for 3 minutes and cool. Add celery seed, salt, onion and oil; pour into 1 pint container and shake vigorously. Store in refrigerator but let come to room temperature before serving. Keeps indefinitely. 1 pint

**Barrie C. Aycock (Mrs. Robert R.)**

# Sour Cream Dressing

½ small onion
4 heaping Tablespoons sour cream
6 Tablespoons oil
1 Tablespoon vinegar
1½ Tablespoons milk
1½ Tablespoons sugar
Salt and pepper to taste

Grate onion or chop fine. Add sour cream, oil, vinegar and milk. Stir until smooth and creamy. Mix in the sugar, salt and pepper. Let stand in the refrigerator at least ½ hour before serving. Best served over Boston or Bibb lettuce, plain, or with tomato. 1 cup

**Melva Jansen (Mrs. Klaus)**

# Tropical Fruit Topping
Good on fruit crêpes too!

1 cup sugar
2 Tablespoons flour
¼ teaspoon salt
2 eggs, well beaten
Juice of 1 lemon
1 cup pineapple juice
1 heaping teaspoon butter
1 cup heavy cream

Mix dry ingredients. Add eggs, then juice. Cook slowly until thick. Add butter. Let mixture cool. Whip cream and fold into cooled mixture. Will keep in the refrigerator for a week. Serve on a fresh fruit salad, or on a fruit crêpe. 2½ cups

# Sauces for Meats and Vegetables

# Flavored Butters for Meats

**GREEN PEPPERCORN BUTTER:**
1½ Tablespoons green peppercorns, drained (found in gourmet shops)
1 stick soft butter
⅛ cup dry white wine
½ Tablespoon tarragon
Juice of ¼ lemon or to taste
⅛ teaspoon salt or to taste

Green Peppercorn Butter: Blend all ingredients by hand. Store covered in refrigerator. Serve with chicken, duck or broiled meats.

**MUSTARD BUTTER:**
1 stick soft butter
1-2 Tablespoons Dijon mustard
2 Tablespoons minced fresh parsley or mixed herbs

Mustard Butter: Blend all ingredients by hand, blender or food processor. Store in refrigerator. Serve with kidneys, liver, steaks, broiled fish or use to enrich sauces or soups.

**TARRAGON BUTTER:**
1 stick soft butter
1 Tablespoon lemon juice
2-3 Tablespoons fresh tarragon (dry if fresh is not available)

Tarragon Butter: Blend all ingredients by hand, blender or food processor. Store in refrigerator. Serve with broiled meats and fish or use to enrich sauces or soups.

**Cookbook Committee**

# Marchand de Vin Sauce

¾ cup butter
⅓ cup sliced mushrooms
½ cup minced ham
⅓ cup chopped green onions
½ cup finely chopped white onion
2 Tablespoons garlic, mashed with ½ teaspoon salt
2 Tablespoons flour
⅛ teaspoon pepper
Dash of cayenne
¾ cup beef stock
½ cup red wine

Melt butter and lightly sauté mushrooms, ham, green onions, white onion and garlic/salt paste. When onion is clear, add flour, pepper and cayenne, continually stirring. Brown flour well over medium heat. This should take 10 minutes or so. Remove from heat and add stock all at once. Add wine and return to heat, blending well. Simmer 35-45 minutes. If not for immediate use, place pan in a pan of water and leave on low heat. 2 cups

**Terry Morris (Mrs. Douglas)**

## Madeira Sauce

1½ Tablespoons butter
1½ Tablespoons flour
2 cups dark beef stock
⅓ cup Madeira wine

Melt butter in heavy saucepan, add flour and stir and cook until brown in color. Add beef stock, simmer for 30 minutes. Add wine and bring to boil. Serve hot over steak, standing rib roast or Beef Wellington. 2 cups

## Mustard Sauce for Ham

1 Tablespoon salad oil
1 Tablespoon prepared mustard
¼ cup granulated sugar
5 Tablespoons catsup
3 Tablespoons vinegar

Mix all ingredients and simmer until well blended. May be prepared 1-2 days in advance. Excellent on sliced ham. 1½ cups

**Myrick L. King (Mrs. David L.G., Jr.)**

## Orange Sauce for Pork

1¼ cups sugar
2 Tablespoons cornstarch
¾ teaspoon salt
1 teaspoon cinnamon
1 Tablespoon whole cloves
3 Tablespoons grated orange
   rind
1 cup fresh orange juice

Mix ingredients and cook until thick and clear. Serve with pork roast or chops. 2 cups

**Decie Nygaard (Mrs. W.F.)**

---

HINT

Always use a dry wine, never a sweet one for cooking, unless specifically requested in the recipe. Dry vermouth is a good substitute for white wine. Dry sherry or Mirin (Japanese rice wine) is best for Oriental dishes.

# Famous Barbecue Sauce
An original family recipe worked out after years of testing

1 pint tomato juice
1 bottle Heinz meat sauce
½ bottle Worcestershire sauce
Juice of 2 lemons
¾ stick butter
3-4 bay leaves
½ jar horseradish
20 peppercorns
½ can chili powder
1 cup water
Salt and pepper

Simmer all ingredients for 20 minutes. This makes a thin old-fashioned barbecue sauce which is delicious on chicken or ribs. The ingredients may vary depending upon individual tastes. Sauce may be frozen.

Elsie B. Manry
*Tampa, Florida*

# Sauce for Duckling

4 Tablespoons lemon juice
3 Tablespoons honey
2 Tablespoons soy sauce
2 Tablespoons melted butter
1 Tablespoon sherry
1 crushed garlic clove

Blend all ingredients together and let stand 1 hour before using. Roast quartered duckling in shallow pan at 325° for 1 hour, piercing skin frequently. Baste with sauce frequently. Brown under broiler, basting, for 5 minutes on each side. Brush with honey for one minute.

# Marinade for Beef or Chicken

2 cups salad oil
¾ cup soy sauce
¼ cup Worcestershire sauce
2 Tablespoons dry mustard
2½ Tablespoons salt
1 Tablespoon pepper
½ cup wine vinegar
1½ teaspoons parsley
⅓ cup lemon juice
½ cup sherry or Burgundy

Mix ingredients together in a quart jar with a tight lid. Store in refrigerator. This can be used over and over, if used only on beef. It will keep in refrigerator for 4 months and will marinate 5 pounds of meat. Note: If used for chicken, discard after using.
1 quart

Linda Chambliss (Mrs. Harold W.)

## Barbeque Sauce for Chicken

1 pint vinegar
½ pint vegetable oil
5 teaspoons black pepper
5 teaspoons poultry seasoning
5 Tablespoons salt
½ stick butter

Mix ingredients in a saucepan and heat to blend flavors. Use to baste chicken while cooking on grill. This recipe makes enough sauce for 5 chickens. Refrigerate in an airtight container.

**Claire W. Johnson (Mrs. A. Sidney)**

## Tartare Sauce

1 cup mayonnaise
1 teaspoon Dijon mustard
1 Tablespoon minced dill pickle
¼ cup chopped green onion
1 teaspoon minced parsley
1 Tablespoon capers

Combine ingredients and chill. Serve with broiled or fried seafood. 1¼ cups

**Florence M. Werden**

## Jezebel Sauce

1 (10 ounce) jar pineapple
    preserves
1 (10 ounce) jar apple jelly
1 (4 ounce) jar Coleman's
    mustard
6 Tablespoons horseradish

At least 24 hours before using, mix all ingredients together with a spoon. Refrigerate. Will keep in refrigerator for 2 weeks. Serve with platters of cold turkey or roast beef; use in place of mayonnaise or mustard. Also fantastic as a topping for cream cheese, served with crackers. 3 cups

**Virginia S. Corley (Mrs. Charles C., Jr.)**

## Shrimp Romanoff Sauce

1 cup mayonnaise
¼ cup catsup
4 teaspoons white wine
¾ teaspoon Maggi Seasoning

Place all ingredients in bowl and blend until smooth. Refrigerate. When ready to serve, arrange boiled shrimp (which have been shelled and refrigerated) on lettuce on individual plates and spoon sauce liberally over shrimp. Serves 8

**Mrs. Earle B. May, Jr.**

## Sauce for Artichokes
Serve with hot or cold artichokes as an appetizer or a vegetable

1 package Good Seasons
    Garlic salad dressing
3 ounces blue cheese
Vinegar
Oil

Note: Deviate from package instructions slightly. Add mix first; then fill to vinegar line on Good Seasons' bottle. Add water and oil as shown on bottle. Put in blender. Add blue cheese and blend; add more or less cheese for personal taste. Chill before serving. Sauce should cling to artichoke leaf when dipped. Will keep several weeks in the refrigerator.
8 servings

**Anne M. Shearer (Mrs. William B.)**

## Hot Sauce for Avocado

3 Tablespoons butter
3 Tablespoons brown sugar
3 Tablespoons vinegar
3 Tablespoons Worcestershire
3 Tablespoons ketchup
⅓ teaspoon salt

Combine all ingredients and cook for 20 minutes in double boiler. Cut avocado in half, remove pit, and fill with hot sauce. Delicious served with chicken salad or barbequed chicken.

**Josephine Fleming (Mrs. Tom)**

## F & W's Basic Mayonnaise with Mustard

3 egg yolks
½ teaspoon Dijon mustard
½ teaspoon salt
¼ teaspoon white pepper
1 Tablespoon lemon juice
1 cup oil (½ olive; ½ vegetable)
Cayenne pepper
Variation: summer mayonnaise;
    add chopped cucumbers,
    lots of freshly chopped
    dillweed and chopped red
    pepper.

Using electric mixer (or blender, food processor or hand whisk) beat first 4 ingredients and 1 teaspoon lemon juice until light and fluffy. Drop by drop add oil beating after each addition until the oil is absorbed. When the mayonnaise begins to thicken, add the oil in spoonfuls as you beat, and then pour very slowly until the entire cup has been incorporated. This should take at least 3 minutes, beating steadily. Add the rest of the lemon juice and Cayenne pepper to taste. Correct the seasoning with more salt, pepper and additional mayonnaise and lemon juice. 1¼ cups

**The Editors**
*The International Review of Food and Wine*

## Blender Mayonnaise

1 egg
1 teaspoon salt
1 teaspoon sugar
1 teaspoon dry mustard
½ teaspoon paprika
3 Tablespoons lemon juice
1½ cups salad oil

Combine egg, salt, sugar, dry mustard, paprika, lemon juice and ¼ cup salad oil in blender or food processor (use steel blade). Cover and blend a few seconds. With cover on and motor still running, gradually add 1¼ cups salad oil. Blend until thick and smooth. Yield: 1 pint

## Flawless Hollandaise

4 egg yolks
½ teaspoon salt
1 Tablespoon lemon juice
Dash tabasco
¼ pound butter, melted

Place egg yolks in blender or food processor with salt, lemon juice and tabasco. Blend briefly. Have melted butter ready, heated to a bubbling stage. Turn blender or food processor on and pour butter in a steady stream until mixture is completely emulsified. Yield: ¾ cup.

# White Sauces

**THIN WHITE SAUCE:**
**1½ Tablespoons butter**
**1½ Tablespoons flour**
**½ teaspoon salt**
**Dash white pepper**
**Dash nutmeg**
**1 cup milk**

**MEDIUM WHITE SAUCE:**
**2½ Tablespoons butter**
**2½ Tablespoons flour**
**Repeat ingredients above**
    **starting with salt**

**THICK WHITE SAUCE:**
**4 Tablespoons butter**
**4 Tablespoons flour**
**Repeat ingredients above**
    **starting with salt**

Melt butter in a saucepan over low heat. Stir in the flour and use a whisk to blend thoroughly. Add milk and seasonings and cook, stirring constantly until sauce is thick and smooth. 1 cup

**Decie Nygaard (Mrs. W.F.)**

# Mustard Sauce for Vegetables

**3 egg yolks**
**1 Tablespoon lemon juice**
**2 teaspoons Dijon mustard**
**¼ teaspoon salt**
**½ cup butter**

In blender or food processor, combine egg yolks, lemon juice, mustard and salt. Cover and blend. In small saucepan heat butter over low heat until it begins to bubble. With blender on high, slowly add bubbling butter. Blend or process until smooth. Serve at once with hot fresh asparagus or broccoli. 1 cup

**Jeanine C. Andrews (Mrs. Edward B.)**

# Fourteen Day Pickles

1 gallon water
Salt to float an egg
    (3 Tablespoons to 1 box)
16 pounds whole pickling
    cucumbers
1 gallon water
½ box alum
1 gallon white vinegar
1 box pickling spice
10 pounds sugar

Make brine with 1 gallon water and enough salt to make an egg float in the water. Place brine and whole cucumbers in a large stone crock and let soak 14 days. Remove cucumbers, discard brine, wash cucumbers well and slice. Soak slices overnight in 1 gallon water mixed with ½ box alum. The next morning rinse and cover with 1 gallon vinegar and soak for 6 hours. Drain and discard vinegar. Place cucumbers, sugar and spices in layers in stone jar. Cover 2-3 days until syrup forms. May be stored in a gallon jar or in refrigerator indefinitely. Serve chilled. Excellent appetizer with a sharp cheese and crackers.

**Mrs. Meredith Bass**
*Hazlehurst, Miss.*

# Dill Beans

4 pounds fresh round string
    beans (blue lake if possible)
Boiling water
6 cloves garlic
12 heads and stems of fresh
    dill
3 teaspoons crushed red
    pepper
2 quarts water
½ cup white vinegar
⅔ cup coarse salt (regular
    salt may be used)

Cook beans in boiling water 5-7 minutes until half cooked. Drain. Place as many beans as possible in six 1-pint jars. Place 1 clove garlic, 2 heads and stems of fresh dill and ½ teaspoon crushed red pepper in each of the pint jars. Bring water, vinegar and coarse salt to a boil. Cool slightly. Remove foam. Cover beans in each jar with this brine. Cover jars loosely, do not screw tight and store in cool place. Beans are ready to eat in 2-3 weeks. 6 pints

**Sue Bufkin (Mrs. Homer)**
*Hazlehurst, Miss.*

## Delicatessen Dill Pickles

**BRINE PROPORTIONS:**
**2 Tablespoons plain table**
**salt per 2 cups water (One**
**gallon container requires**
**2-3 quarts of brine.)**
**Fresh cucumbers (no wax**
**coating)**
**Garlic cloves, peeled (6 cloves**
**per gallon)**
**Fresh dill or 2 Tablespoons**
**dill seed per gallon**
**1 slice rye bread**

Make a brine of salt and water. Bring to boil. Cool to lukewarm. Place cucumbers into crock or glass container. Place peeled garlic cloves and dill (stem as well as top) in layers as cucumbers are added. Cover cucumbers with lukewarm brine. Place slice of rye bread on top and allow brine to soak bread. Place a plate with a weight on top to submerge pickles. Place crock in warm place for 4-5 days. Don't let crock get cold as the yeast from the bread prefers lukewarm temperature. The liquid will become cloudy and there will be a deposit on pickles. Rinse off and chill pickles before serving.

Note: Garlic and dill can be varied according to individual taste as can the amount of time in solution. Brine must be made according to directions. These pickles are like those served in a delicatessen. They must be stored in refrigerator when completed.

**Emy E. Blair (Mrs. H. Duane)**

## Kosher Dill Pickles

**8 quarts medium size fresh**
**pickling cucumbers**
**8 fresh dill heads**
**24-32 cloves garlic**
**8 teaspoons crushed red**
**pepper**
**15 cups water**
**1 cup white vinegar**
**1 cup salt**
**1 teaspoon alum**

Clean cucumbers and place as many cucumbers as will fit into eight 1-quart jars. Add to each jar: 1 fresh dill head, 3-4 cloves garlic and 1 teaspoon crushed red pepper. Bring water, white vinegar, salt and alum to a boil and pour into jars of cucumbers; seal. Let cure for 3-4 weeks.
8 quarts

**Grace Allred (Mrs. Cecil)**
*Hazlehurst, Miss.*

## Bread and Butter Pickles

4 quarts sliced medium-size
  cucumbers
6 medium white onions, thinly
  sliced
⅓ cup coarse-medium salt
  (such as kosher salt)
5 cups granulated sugar
1½ teaspoons tumeric
1½ teaspoons celery seed
2 Tablespoons mustard seed
3 cups cider vinegar
½ teaspoon ground cloves

Do not pare cucumbers; thinly slice and add onions. Add salt; cover with cracked ice; mix thoroughly. Let stand 3 hours; drain thoroughly. Combine remaining ingredients; pour mixture over cucumbers and onions. Heat just to a boil (slowly, take 15-20 minutes if necessary to reach boil). Seal in hot, sterilized jars. Will keep for 1 year. 8 pints

**Maryann B. Chapman (Mrs. James P.)**

## Pickled Okra

Okra
32 cloves garlic
16 teaspoons crushed red
  pepper
16 teaspoons dill weed
3 quarts white vinegar
1 cup coarse salt (regular salt
  may be used)
1 cup water

Wash and dry okra. Remove stem end and pack tightly in jar. To each pint add 2 cloves garlic, ½ teaspoon crushed red pepper, and ½ teaspoon dill weed. Bring wine vinegar, coarse salt and water to boil and cover okra in jars. Seal. Will be ready to eat in 3-4 weeks. Note: Recipe may be adjusted to pickle the amount of okra you might have. 16 pints

**Sue Bufkin (Mrs. Homer)**
*Hazlehurst, Miss.*

## Peach Pickle

6 pounds peaches
Whole cloves
3 pounds sugar
1 pint vinegar
1 pint water
Stick cinnamon (optional)
Ginger (optional)

Select firm peaches and peel. Stick 2 or 3 cloves in each peach. Make a syrup of sugar, vinegar and water and bring to a boil. Drop peaches in syrup and cook until they are clear and tender. Pack into hot jars, cover with syrup and seal. Stick cinnamon and ginger may be added to syrup mixture if desired. 4 quarts

**Virginia Kelly (Mrs. R.L.)**
*Wrens, Georgia*

# Green Pepper Relish

4 cups ground onions
1 medium cabbage
10 green tomatoes
12 green peppers
1 small can pimiento
½ cup salt
6 cups sugar
1 Tablespoon celery seed
2 Tablespoons mustard seed
1½ teaspoons tumeric
4 cups vinegar
2 cups water

Grind vegetables or chop in food processor and put in large bowl or pan. Sprinkle with salt and let stand overnight. Mix sugar, celery seed, mustard seed, tumeric, vinegar and water and pour over vegetables. Heat to boiling and simmer 30 minutes. Put in jars and seal. This relish is very good on fresh vegetables, in tuna, egg or potato salad, or on hot dogs and hamburgers.
8 pints

**Myrick L. King (Mrs. David L.G., Jr.)**

# Creamy Pepper Relish
An unusual relish, great for Christmas giving

5 onions, chopped
5 or 6 cups peppers (sweet
   banana, bell and sweet
   red for color)
1 cup sugar
2 Tablespoons flour
2 Tablespoons butter or
   margarine
2 Tablespoons dry mustard
1 Tablespoon pickling salt
1 cup cider vinegar

Chop peppers and onions coarsely and combine with other ingredients in heavy saucepan. Cook until thick. Seal hot in sterilized jars.

**Decie Nygaard (Mrs. W.F.)**

# Peach-Tomato Relish

6 large fresh peaches (4 cups, chopped)
6 ripe tomatoes (4 cups, chopped)
1 cup ground onions
1 cup diced green pepper
1 small hot red pepper
1 cup cider vinegar
¾ teaspoon salt
2 Tablespoons pickling spices, tied in small cloth bag
2 cups light brown sugar, packed

Peel and pit peaches; cut into small pieces to equal 4 cups. Peel and cut tomatoes in ½-inch pieces. Combine with all other ingredients in kettle. Bring to a boil and cook on medium heat, uncovered, 1-1½ hours or until thick, stirring frequently. Fill 6 hot, sterilized ½ pint jars and seal. A good accompaniment for meats. Wonderful as an appetizer served with cream cheese and crackers. 3 pints

**Maddy S. Kligora (Mrs. John)**

# Lime Marmalade
A good gift item

1 can beef consomme
3¾ cups sugar
½ cup fresh lime juice
¼ cup lime rind, cut in thin strips approximately ½ inch long
¼ cup lemon rind, cut in thin strips approximately ½ inch long
3 ounces fruit pectin
Green food coloring (optional)

In a large heavy saucepan, combine all ingredients except pectin. Place over high heat and bring to a boil, stirring constantly. Cook 3-5 minutes. Stir in pectin. Heat to 220° F. on candy thermometer. Boil hard for 1 minute, stirring constantly. Remove from heat, skim off foam with a metal spoon. Stir and skim to cool and to prevent rind from floating to top, approximately 15-20 minutes. Add food coloring if desired. Pour into jelly glasses; cover with ⅛ inch hot paraffin. Serve over cream cheese and crackers or on hot rolls. Especially tasty on Herbed Potato Rolls (see Index) 3 cups

**Phyllis K. Kennedy**

# Strawberry Preserves

An unusual recipe which produces whole strawberries in a light syrup. Wonderful over ice cream or pancakes, or with biscuits and muffins.

**2 quarts strawberries, caps removed**
**6 cups sugar**

Place berries in a colander or piece of cheesecloth and hold under boiling water for two minutes. Drain; place in a large saucepan and add 4 cups sugar. Boil slowly for three minutes. Remove from heat and add last 2 cups of sugar. Shake the mixture, do not stir. Cool for 5 minutes. Return to heat and boil for 8 to 10 minutes, shaking the pan continuously (reduce heat if needed to keep from cooking too quickly). Cover the pan and let stand overnight. Every time you pass by the pan, shake it. The next morning, process in hot water bath for 15 minutes. Read instructions on your jar lid box to be sure you prepare them correctly to be sure they will seal. 2½ pints

**Mrs. R.B. Barnett**
*Dunwoody, Georgia*

# Apple-Peach Conserve

**1 can (1 pound, 6 ounces) apple-pie filling**
**1 package (12 ounces) frozen sliced peaches, thawed**
**½ cup cranberry-apple juice**
**Grated rind of 1 lemon**

Mix all ingredients in saucepan. Bring to boil and simmer 6 to 8 minutes. Cool and serve as accompaniment for meat or as sauce for pancakes. Yield: 4 cups

## Spring Conserve

1 quart strawberries, free of
  blemishes, caps removed
2 cups fresh pineapple, cubed
1 small orange, halved, seeded
  and thinly sliced (cut end
  slices into small slivers)
4 cups sugar

Combine fruit and sugar; let start overnight. The next morning, bring mixture to a boil and cook until it reaches the thickness you desire, testing by dropping small amounts onto a cold saucer. Cooking time will vary from 45 minutes to 2 hours, depending on ripeness of fruit. 1½-2 pints

**Emy Blair (Mrs. H. Duane)**

## Pear Honey

12 cups grated firm cooking
  pears, peeled and cored
12 cups sugar
1 (1 pound 4 ounce) can
  crushed pineapple
1 lemon, thinly sliced

Put pears through coarse blade of food chopper or grate or thinly slice in food processor. Add sugar and cook on low heat, stirring occasionally until clear. Add pineapple and lemon and cook 5-10 minutes longer. Pour into hot sterilized jars and seal. 6-8 pints

**Mrs. Meredith Bass**
*Hazlehurst, Miss.*

## Pineapple Chutney

1 (1 pound 4 ounce) can sliced
  pineapple, chipped
½ cup vinegar
1 cup brown sugar
½ teaspoon salt
1 or less clove garlic, pressed
¼ cup slivered blanched
  almonds
½ cup golden raisins
½ green pepper, finely chopped
2 Tablespoons crystallized
  ginger, finely chopped
Cornstarch

Cook pineapple, sugar, salt and vinegar slowly about 10 minutes. Stir in remaining ingredients; cook 10 minutes more. Thicken slightly with cornstarch.

**Lou Bothwell (Mrs. Eugene)**

# Breads

# Bread Basics

To make a loaf of bread worthy of a jug of wine and thou, it is important to use the right ingredients and the right technique.

Successful bread begins with the proper choice of flour. Most recipes in this book specify all purpose flour and are tested with nationally marketed white enriched flour which is usually a hard wheat blend. Unbleached, whole wheat, rye, and oatmeal flour may be substituted for all or part of the flour in most recipes, although substitution may require a variation in the amount of liquid needed and the length of time required for the dough to rise. Experiment with combinations of whole grain flours for improved nutrition and interesting taste and texture!

Regional brands of flour sold in the South and some states in the West are usually blends of soft wheat.

Generally, hard wheat flour is best for yeast breads; soft wheat flour makes better biscuits and muffins. The real hard wheat flour found in health food stores produces a bread that is more bakery-like in texture and volume, but is never to be used for cakes or pastries or any product where tenderness is desired. Hard and soft wheat flour blends may be used interchangeably, but remember that hard wheat flour absorbs more moisture, requires more mixing and withstands more yeast fermentation than soft wheat flour.

Bread made with milk has a finer texture, more nutritive value, and stays fresh longer than bread made with water.

Kneading doesn't mean mashing and squeezing! To knead properly, turn the dough a quarter turn with every pushing motion. Keep your fingers curved and fold the dough from the far side toward you. Push away from you with the heel of your palm, maintaining a gentle rhythm as you knead. Dough that is sufficiently kneaded looks satiny smooth, has small blisters showing under the surface and is not sticky.

Adequate rising or fermentation time is necessary for good flavor and texture. The second rising may be omitted in some instances where the first rising has been exceptionally lengthy, but is not generally recommended. Punching down the dough for a second or even third rising is recommended for high altitudes where the dough rises to double its bulk in shorter time, making additional risings necessary for superior flavor and texture. When rising time is a problem, the quantity of yeast may be doubled without changing the taste and quality, but good bread is best unhurried.

The secret of good biscuits and muffins often rests with a gentle hand in the mixing process. Remember that muffins should be lightly mixed and lumpy. A few extra strokes can ruin your muffins.

Biscuit dough should be kneaded until just light and soft, but not sticky. Overmixing the dough makes for a tough biscuit. Keep your touch soft and your biscuits will reward you!

Southern recipes with cornmeal as the primary ingredient anticipate the use of white cornmeal which gives an uneven texture, a more interesting crust and, according to any Southerner, a superior flavor. Yellow cornmeal is used when a smoother, cake-like texture is desired.

When a crisp, hard glaze is needed use an egg white slightly beaten with a small amount of water. When a richer, browner glaze is preferred beat the whole egg with a small amount of water and brush on the loaf.

# Southern Biscuits

Feather light and delicious, this recipe may
make you famous for your biscuits!

**Solid shortening**
**4 cups self-rising Southern**
**soft wheat flour, such as**
**White Lily or Martha White**
**2 heaping Tablespoons**
**baking powder**
**1 cup solid shortening**
**1½ cups buttermilk**

Grease baking sheet with shortening. Prepare a counter space for rolling out dough by generously sprinkling flour on it. Flour a rolling pin. Sift flour and baking powder into medium size mixing bowl. Using a pastry blender, cut in shortening. Add buttermilk and mix thoroughly with wooden spoon. Dough should be light and slightly sticky. If too dry, add more buttermilk. Pick up dough from bowl and place on floured surface. Knead lightly, folding dough inwards and sprinkling flour as needed over dough. Add enough flour so that you can handle dough easily, but maintain light consistency. Using floured rolling pin, roll out dough to ½ inch thickness. Cut with glass or biscuit cutter with diameter of 1½ inches, flouring cutting edge as needed to prevent sticking. Place biscuits on baking sheet. Cook in preheated oven at 450° for about 12 minutes or until lightly browned on top. (Place on baking sheet with sides touching for a soft sided biscuit; ½ inch apart if an all over crust is desired.) Cooked biscuits may be frozen or dough may be refrigerated for 2 days.

Cut biscuits smaller and use with ham for a cocktail party favorite. 48 biscuits

**JoAnne T. Neal (Mrs. George P.)**

# Food Processor Biscuits

2 cups all-purpose Southern
  flour
2 teaspoons baking powder
1 teaspoon salt
¼ teaspoon baking soda
3-4 Tablespoons chilled lard or
  shortening
1 cup buttermilk

Place metal blade in bowl of food processor and add flour, baking powder, salt and soda. Whirl a few seconds to mix. Add lard or shortening. Process until mixture resembles coarse crumbs, about 10 seconds. Add buttermilk and process until just combined. Turn dough out onto a floured surface. Turn over a few times until surface of dough is no longer sticky. Do not knead; use as little flour as possible. Roll or pat into ½ inch thickness. Cut biscuits with a floured cutter. Bake in a 475° oven for 10 minutes or until browned. 14 biscuits

**Barrie C. Aycock (Mrs. Robert R.)**

# Herbed Potato Rolls
### A different, versatile soft roll

5½-6 cups sifted all-purpose
  flour
1 package active dry yeast
¾ cup milk
4 Tablespoons butter
¼ cup sugar
1 teaspoon salt
1 can Cream of Potato Soup
1 egg
2 Tablespoons dried parsley
  flakes, crushed
1 teaspoon ground sage
½ teaspoon celery seed

In large bowl of electric mixer combine 2 cups flour and yeast. In saucepan, heat milk, butter, sugar and salt to lukewarm; add to dry ingredients. Add soup and egg; beat with mixer at low speed 30 seconds, scraping sides of bowl. Beat at high speed 3 min-utes. Stir in seasonings and enough flour to make soft dough. Knead on lightly floured board until smooth, 5-8 minutes. Place in greased bowl; turn once to grease top. Cover and let rise in a warm place until doubled, 50-60 minutes. Punch down. Shape into small balls. Place on greased baking sheet. Let rise until doubled, 25-30 minutes. Bake at 400° for 12 minutes or until lightly browned. May be frozen. 36 large rolls

**Phyllis K. Kennedy (Mrs. Crawford)**

## Mrs. Smith's Refrigerator Rolls

1½ cups buttermilk
½ cup melted shortening
1 teaspoon salt
⅓ cup sugar
2 packages dry yeast
¼ cup warm water
4½ cups all purpose flour
½ teaspoon baking soda
Small amount of melted
    shortening
¼ pound butter, melted

Heat buttermilk until lukewarm (do not overheat or it will separate). Pour over melted shortening, salt and sugar. Cool. Dissolve yeast in warm water, add to buttermilk mixture and mix well. Sift together flour and soda. Add to buttermilk mixture to make a stiff dough (may need to add a little more flour). Knead slightly and place dough in a large greased bowl. Brush top with melted shortening. Cover tightly with waxed paper or foil, then a towel. Refrigerate for at least several hours. (Dough keeps for 2-3 days when refrigerated.) When ready to use, cut off desired amount, roll out to about ½ inch thick and cut with biscuit cutter dipped in flour. Dip in melted butter, fold in half and place in baking pan. Cover with waxed paper or foil and towel* and allow to rise 1 hour or until doubled in bulk. *(At this point the rolls could be refrigerated until 1 hour before desired baking time.) Bake at 425° 10-15 minutes or until golden brown. To freeze, bake only 8-10 minutes, cool and store in plastic bag in freezer. When ready to serve, warm in 250° oven for about 10 minutes. 3 dozen

**Connie R. Smith (Mrs. James T., III)**

## Sour Cream Rolls

So easy to make at the last minute, but avoid the temptation if you're counting calories. They're addictive!

1 cup sour cream
1 stick butter or margarine,
    melted
1 cup self-rising flour

Combine all ingredients in bowl. Stir until well mixed. Bake in tiny, lightly greased muffin tins at 450° for 15 minutes. Leftovers, if any, may be reheated or eaten cold. Great with soup or drinks. 24 tiny rolls

**Lee Shelnutt (Mrs. M.T.)**

# Baps
A French type roll
with a hard crust and a soft inside

**4 cups all purpose flour**
**1 teaspoon salt**
**¾ cup milk**
**¾ cup water**
**¼ cup butter or shortening**
**1 package dry yeast**
**1 teaspoon sugar**

Sift flour and salt into a large bowl. Dissolve yeast in ¼ cup warm water (100°); set aside. Combine milk and ½ cup water and heat; add butter and stir until melted. Add dissolved yeast to *lukewarm* liquid. Add sugar and stir. Make a well in the center of flour and pour in liquid mixture to form a soft dough. Add more flour if necessary. Turn out onto a floured board and knead 8-10 minutes until smooth and elastic. Put dough in a greased bowl, cover with a damp cloth and let rise 1½ hours, or until doubled in bulk. Set oven at 425°, knead dough lightly and shape into 6 loaves or 18 rolls. Sprinkle with flour and let rise again 5-10 minutes. Bake at 425° for five minutes or until pale golden. For loaves or large rolls, lower heat to 400° and bake 5-10 minutes longer. Note: These may also be shaped to form hamburger buns. May be prepared in advance and warmed in a 300° oven, or frozen. 6 small loaves or 18 dinner rolls

**Nathalie Dupree**
*Rich's Cooking School*

To re-heat rolls put them in a wet brown paper bag and then in oven.

# Chili Bread
Especially good with quail, dove or any fowl

2 eggs, beaten
1 cup cream style corn
1 cup buttermilk
1½ teaspoons salt
3 teaspoons baking powder
1 cup water ground corn meal
½ cup high quality vegetable oil
1 small onion, chopped
2 (4 ounce) cans chopped green chili peppers
1 cup grated cheese

Mix eggs, corn, buttermilk, salt, baking powder and corn meal. Add the oil. Pour one half of batter into a greased 9 x 13-inch casserole dish and cover with onion, chili peppers and ½ cup cheese. Carefully pour on rest of batter and top with remaining ½ cup cheese. Bake at 325° for 1 hour. To freeze: mix, freeze and bake later. 6 servings

Carolyn S. Brooks (Mrs. John L.)

# Sally Lunn

1 package active dry yeast
½ cup lukewarm milk
⅓ cup sugar
½ cup solid shortening
3 eggs
4 cups all-purpose Southern flour (White Lily)
1 teaspoon salt

Sprinkle yeast in warm milk. Set aside. Cream sugar and shortening. Add eggs and mix well. Combine salt with flour and add to mixture, alternating with milk and yeast mixture. Mix well after each addition. Cover and let rise in a warm spot for 1½ hours. Beat well again with electric mixer or by hand. Place batter in a well greased Bundt pan. Cover and let rise again for 1½ hours. Bake in preheated oven for 45 minutes at 350° Best when served hot. 12 servings

Mrs. Guy W. Rutland, Sr.

# Beer Bread
An easy bread, suitable for informal dinners

3 cups self-rising flour
3 Tablespoons sugar
1 (12 ounce) can cold beer
½ cup melted butter

Preheat oven to 350°. Mix flour, sugar and beer well. Pour into greased 9 x 5 inch loaf pan or casserole dish. Bake at 350° for 30 minutes. Pour butter over top and cook 10 minutes more or until brown. Best when eaten warm.

Laura G. Ward (Mrs. Peter C.)

# African Honey Bread

1 package dry yeast
¼ cup lukewarm water
1 egg
½ cup honey
1 Tablespoon ground coriander
½ teaspoon ground cinnamon
¼ teaspoon ground cloves
1½ teaspoons salt
1 cup lukewarm milk
6 Tablespoons melted butter
4-4½ cups all-purpose flour

Sprinkle yeast into lukewarm water. Stir to dissolve and set aside until mixture foams. Combine egg, honey, spices and salt in a deep bowl and mix well. Add yeast mixture, milk and 4 Tablespoons butter and beat until blended. Stir in flour, ½ cup at a time. When dough becomes too stiff to stir, work in remaining flour with fingers. Turn onto lightly floured surface and knead until smooth and elastic, using a small amount of melted butter on fingers to make dough more manageable. Place dough in a large, lightly buttered bowl, turning to butter all surfaces. Cover and place in a warm spot to rise until doubled in bulk. Butter the bottom and sides of a 3-quart souffle dish or two smaller ones. Punch down dough and knead lightly for 2 minutes. Shape dough into a ball and place in dish, pressing down in corners so that it covers bottom completely. Cover and let rise until double in bulk. Bake at 300° for 50-60 minutes until crust is light golden brown. Turn out on rack to cool. Loaf will peak in the center to resemble an African hut. Eat with butter and honey. 1 loaf, approximately 16 servings

# Alpine Cheese Bread

1 loaf French bread
½ pound Swiss cheese
1 medium purple onion,
    chopped
3 eggs, slightly beaten
½ cup milk

Cut top off loaf and scoop out inside. Cut cheese in chunks and put into center of loaf with onion. Beat eggs and milk. Pour liquid over loaf. Bake at 375° for 30 minutes. Slice and serve hot. 12 servings

**Martha H. Whitehead (Mrs. Richard)**

## Moroccan Bread

1 package dry yeast
¼ cup lukewarm water
1 teaspoon sugar
3½ cups unbleached flour
1 cup whole wheat flour
2 teaspoons salt
½ cup warm milk
1 teaspoon sesame seed
1 Tablespoon anise seed
Cornmeal

Soften yeast with ¼ cup sugared water. Let stand 2 minutes. Blend flours and salt. Stir yeast into flours. Add milk and lukewarm water to form a stiff dough. Knead 10-15 minutes adding more flour or water if needed to make workable. Add spices at the end of kneading. Form into 2 balls; let rest 5 minutes. Grease and flatten into 2-inch thick circles. Place on baking sheet sprinkled with corn meal. Cover with damp cloth. Let rise 2 hours. Preheat oven to 400°. Prick sides of bread with fork in 4 places. Bake 12 minutes. Lower oven to 300° and complete baking, 30 minutes. Loaves will be somewhat flat and heavy textured. Serve with any meal with a Middle-Eastern flavor. Toast leftover slices with butter; spread with honey. 2 loaves

**Susan M. Morley**

## Southern Spoon Bread

Hot Spoon Bread, traditionally served with lots of butter, salt and pepper is also delightful with butter and peach preserves for brunch, or dinner with ham. Serve from the casserole dish.

1 cup corn meal
1 teaspoon salt
1 Tablespoon shortening
2 cups boiling water
1 cup milk
2 eggs, separated and beaten

Combine corn meal, salt and shortening; add boiling water, stir and cool. Add milk and beaten egg yolks; mix well. Fold in stiffly beaten egg whites. Pour into greased baking dish* and bake in hot oven at 400° for 30-40 minutes. Serve directly from oven as this dish falls easily.
6-8 servings

*Can be held at this point for a short time before baking.

**Agnes S. McLendon**

# Clark Harrison's Loaf Bread

1 cup water
2 Tablespoons active dry yeast
2 Tablespoons sugar
2 eggs
1 cup shortening
3⅔ cups water
½ cup sugar
4-5 teaspoons salt
5 pounds all-purpose flour

Heat water to 105—115°. *In a small bowl combine:*
1 cup water
2 Tablespoons yeast
2 Tablespoons sugar
Stir and let sit 4-5 minutes.
*In a small bowl:*
2 eggs
Stir.
*In a small skillet:*
1 cup shortening
Melt to warm touch.
*In a large dish pan:*
3⅔ cups water
½ cup sugar
4-5 teaspoons salt
Combine all ingredients; stir with a large spoon. Next stir in half of the 5 pound bag of flour. Now dump in remainder of flour and knead for ten minutes. Place dough in the large greased pan and roll it around until the dough is greased. Cover with a cloth or paper towels and let rise for 1½ to 2 hours. Divide into 5 lumps. Mash each lump into a rectangle, roll rectangle up and mash again and put in a greased baking pan. Cover with a cloth or paper towel and let rise for 1½ to 2 hours. Put in a cold oven and bake 15 minutes at 400°; then reduce heat to 375° and bake 30 minutes or until browned, top and bottom. Turn out on cooling rack, paint top with butter and cover with a wet paper towel.
HINTS: For best results room temperature should be 85°; leave to rise longer in cooler room. Put aluminum foil over loaves on top rack of oven and remove for few minutes to brown. 5 loaves

**Clark Harrison**

## Low Sugar and Low Salt White Bread
Great for those on special diets

2 cups warm water
1 package plus 1 teaspoon
   active dry yeast
1 Tablespoon margarine
3 grains saccharin
5½-6½ cups all-purpose flour
   (hard wheat if possible)
1 Tablespoon sugar
1 teaspoon salt

In mixer bowl put 2 cups warm water; sprinkle yeast over water; add saccharin; stir to mix; add margarine. To this liquid mixture add 2 cups flour, sugar and salt; beat 2 minutes with electric mixer on medium speed, scraping bowl occasionally. Add ¾ cup flour or enough to make a thick batter. Beat at high speed 2 minutes, scraping bowl occasionally. Stir in enough remaining flour with spoon to make a soft dough. Turn out onto lightly floured board and knead until smooth and elastic, 8-10 minutes. (Set timer and knead.) Place in greased airtight bowl; turn dough to grease top. Cover and let rise in warm place free from draft until double, about 1 hour. Punch down dough, divide into 2 balls, cover and let rest 10 minutes. Shape into loaves and place into 2 greased 8½ x 4½ x 2½-inch loaf pans. Cover and let rise in warm place free from draft until double, about 1 hour. Bake in 400° oven 25-30 minutes or until done. Remove from pan and cool on wire racks. 2 loaves

**Marceil Joyner (Mrs. John C.)**

## Sesame Seed Bread

1 loaf bread, thinly sliced
2 sticks butter
3 Tablespoons sesame seeds

Cut each slice bread in half. Melt butter; dip 1 side of bread in butter and place buttered side up on a cookie sheet. Will take 2 or 3 cookie sheets depending on size. Sprinkle with sesame seeds. Place in a 250° oven for 4 hours, or until completely dried out. Store in tin when completely cooled. Serve as an accompaniment to salads. 8-12 servings

**Ann Smith (Mrs. George Benton)**

# Earth Bread

2¼ cups boiling water
2 cups rolled oats
½ cup cracked wheat
¼ cup wheat germ
¾ cup blackstrap molasses
2 Tablespoons melted butter
1½ Tablespoons salt
2 packages dry yeast
1 cup warm milk
1 teaspoon sugar
3 cups stone ground whole
    wheat flour
2-3 cups unbleached flour
1 egg white
1 teaspoon water

Preheat oven to 375°. Pour boiling water over rolled oats, cracked wheat and wheat germ. Add molasses, butter and salt; mix well and let cool until mixture is slightly warm to touch. Meanwhile dissolve yeast in warm milk, add sugar and set aside to let mixture bubble. Combine yeast mixture with whole wheat flour and 1 cup unbleached flour; add oat mixture and mix well. Turn out onto a floured surface. Let rest for a few minutes; then knead, adding some of the remaining flour to achieve a firm, pliable consistency; it will be sticky so do not knead too much at this time. Butter a large bowl and place dough in it; cover and let rise in warm place until double in bulk. Turn out on floured surface and knead 8-10 minutes, adding more flour as necessary. Divide into halves and form 2 loaves; place in buttered 9 x 5 x 3-inch bread tins; dough should fill tins about two-thirds. Let rise again until almost doubled; dough should rise to tops of tins. Brush with egg white mixed with 1 teaspoon water. Bake for 15 minutes, then reduce heat to 350° and continue baking for 40-45 minutes until bread sounds hollow when tapped. Remove loaves from pans and return them to oven. Turn off heat and let bread cool in oven. Remove and place on racks. May be frozen. 2 loaves

**Malinda M. Steed (Mrs. Richard)**

# Rapid-Mix Whole Wheat Bread
Loaves have full, rich, wheat flavor

4½ cups whole wheat flour
2¾ cups all-purpose flour
3 Tablespoons sugar
4 teaspoons salt
2 packages active dry yeast
1½ cups water
¾ cup milk
⅓ cup molasses
⅓ cup margarine

Combine flours. In a large bowl thoroughly mix 2½ cups of the combined flour mixture with sugar, salt and undissolved yeast. Combine water, milk, molasses and margarine in a saucepan. Heat over low heat until the liquids are warm (margarine does not need to melt). Gradually add to dry ingredients and beat 2 minutes with electric mixer at medium speed, scraping sides of bowl occasionally. Add ½ cup of remaining flour mixture, or enough to make a thick batter. Beat 2 minutes at high speed, scraping bowl occasionally. Stir in enough remaining flour mixture to make a soft dough. (If necessary add additional all-purpose flour to obtain desired consistency.) Turn dough onto lightly floured board. Knead until smooth and elastic, about 8-10 minutes. Place in greased bowl; turn dough over to grease top. Cover; let rise in warm place free from draft until doubled, about 1 hour. Punch down; turn onto lightly floured board. Divide in half. Shape into loaves. Place in 2 greased 8½ x 4½ x 2½-inch loaf pans. Cover; let rise in warm place free from draft until doubled, about 1 hour. Bake in preheated 400° oven about 25-30 minutes, or until done. Remove from pans and cool on wire racks. 2 loaves

**Marceil Joyner (Mrs. John C.)**

# Cracked Wheat Bread
A nice nutty flavor!

1 cup milk
1½ Tablespoons shortening
1½ teaspoons salt
1½ Tablespoons molasses
1 package active dry yeast
1¼ cups warm water
1 cup rye flour
1 cup cracked wheat
4-4½ cups all-purpose flour
　　(hard wheat if possible)

Scald milk; add shortening, salt and molasses. Cool to lukewarm. Sprinkle yeast on warm water in large mixing bowl; stir to dissolve. Stir in rye flour, cracked wheat, 1½ cups all-purpose flour and milk mixture. Beat with electric mixer at medium speed for 2 minutes, scraping bowl occasionally. This beating process activates the yeast. Stir in remaining flour, a little at a time, to make dough that leaves the sides of the bowl. Turn onto lightly floured board and knead until satiny and elastic, about 10 minutes. Place in lightly greased bowl; turn dough over to grease top. Cover and let rise in warm place until double, 1-1½ hours. (Use an airtight bowl if available.) Punch down, cover and let rise again until double, about 45 minutes. Turn dough onto board; divide in half. Shape into balls, cover and let rest 10 minutes. Shape into loaves by beating with fist to flatten out bubbles; then roll as a jelly roll, tucking ends under at seam. Place into 2 greased 9 x 5 x 3-inch loaf pans. Cover and let rise again until double, about 1 hour. Bake at 375° for 45 minutes; cover with foil last 10 minutes to prevent excessive browning. Turn from pans to wire rack to cool.
2 loaves

**Marceil Joyner (Mrs. John C.)**

# Pita
## (Lebanese Flat Bread)
Makes enough to eat now and freeze some, too

2 packages yeast
Warm water
2 teaspoons sugar
3 pounds all-purpose flour
2 Tablespoons salt

Dissolve yeast in ¼ cup water with sugar. Combine all dry ingredients in large mixing bowl. Add yeast mixture and enough warm water to make a stiff dough. Knead until dough is stiff enough to roll. Place in bowl, cover with cloth, and let rise 2-4 hours in a warm place. When dough has doubled in size, form into orange size balls and roll in flour. (Orange size balls make loaves approximately 10-12 inches in diameter. Use an egg-size ball for sandwich size loaves.) Lay on flat surface and cover; let stand 30 minutes. Pat and roll with rolling pin until about 10-12 inches in size. Place on lower rack in oven which has been pre-heated to 450°, for 3 minutes; then under broiler for 2 minutes until speckled brown. Remove and cool. Keeps frozen for 4 months. 6 large loaves

**Mrs. William Cowles**


# Williamsburg Orange Muffins

2 cups all-purpose flour
1 teaspoon baking soda
1 stick butter
1 cup sugar
2 eggs, beaten slightly
¾ cup buttermilk
1 cup golden raisins
1 cup nuts (pecans)
Sauce:
1 cup sugar
Juice and rind of 2 oranges
    and 1 lemon

Sift flour and soda. Cream butter and sugar; add eggs. Add sifted flour mixture and buttermilk, alternately in thirds. Add raisins and pecans. Pour into paper lined muffin tins, ½ full. Bake at 375° for 15-20 minutes.

Combine sauce ingredients and pour over muffins while they are warm. This recipe may be prepared completely in most food processors. Yield: 24 muffins or 48 petite size

**Sherril Williams (Mrs. Wheat, Jr.)**

# Onion Cheese Bread
For a change of pace try this for sandwiches

2 packages active dry yeast
½ cup warm water
1½ cups milk, scalded
⅓ cup sugar
¼ cup butter or margarine
1 teaspoon salt
½ pound sharp Cheddar
　cheese, shredded
6-7 cups all-purpose flour
1 egg, beaten
1 envelope onion soup mix

In small bowl, soften yeast in water. In large bowl, combine milk, sugar, butter and salt; stir until butter melts. Cool to lukewarm. Stir in cheese and 2½ cups flour; blend in yeast mixture, egg and onion soup mix. Add enough flour to make a soft dough. Knead on a floured board 10 minutes, or until smooth. Place in greased bowl and grease top of dough; cover and let rise in warm place 1½ hours, or until doubled in bulk. Punch down, cut in half and shape into 2 loaves. Place in 2 greased 9 x 5 x 3-inch pans; cover and let rise 1 hour, or until doubled in bulk. Preheat oven to 375°. Bake about 30 minutes. May be frozen. 2 loaves

Lucia H. Sizemore (Mrs. Thomas A., III)

# Tomato-Cheese Batter Bread

1 can condensed tomato soup
½ cup processed cheese
　spread or cheese food
2 Tablespoons butter or
　margarine
¼ cup water
¼ teaspoon baking soda
3-3¼ cups all-purpose flour
2 Tablespoons sugar
1 teaspoon salt
1 Tablespoon dill weed
2 packages active dry yeast
1 egg
12 cup fluted tube or
　Bundt pan

In medium saucepan, heat first 5 ingredients until very warm (120-130°). Lightly spoon flour into measuring cup; level off. In large bowl, combine 2 cups flour, sugar, salt, dill weed and yeast. Add warm liquid and egg to flour mixture. Blend with electric mixer at low speed until moistened; beat 2 minutes at medium speed. By hand, stir in remaining 1-1¼ cups flour to make a stiff batter. Cover and let rise in warm place until light and doubled in size, about 30 minutes. Grease pan with shortening, stir down batter and spoon evenly into pan. Cover; let rise again, approximately 30 minutes. Bake in preheated 350° oven 20-30 minutes until loaf is deep golden brown and sounds hollow when tapped lightly. Remove from pan and cool on wire rack. 25 slices

# Popovers
A breeze in the food processor!

⅞ **cup all purpose flour**
½ **teaspoon salt**
½ **cup milk**
**2 eggs**
½ **cup water**

Sift into bowl flour and salt. Make well in center and add milk. Stir. Beat eggs until fluffy. Add beaten eggs to milk and flour; beat again. Add water. Beat until bubbles surface. (Batter may be left for 1 hour; beat again before baking.) Heat 1 teaspoon of oil in each cup of muffin tin. Pour batter in and bake 20 minutes at 400°; then 10-15 minutes at 350°.

FOOD PROCESSOR: With metal blade in place, beat eggs until fluffy; set aside. Place flour and salt in bowl and mix with on/off motion several times. Add milk, mix again. Add beaten eggs and mix for 3-4 seconds, or until bubbly.

Butter and spun honey are the perfect accompaniment
12 popovers

**Marty D. Halyburton (Mrs. Porter A.)**

# German Oven Pancake
More like a soufflé than a pancake, it is a great innovation for breakfast!

½ **cup sifted all-purpose flour**
**3 eggs, slightly beaten**
½ **cup milk**
**2 Tablespoons melted butter**
¼ **teaspoon salt**

Gradually add flour to beaten eggs, beating with rotary beater. Stir in milk, butter and salt. Pour batter into greased 9-10 inch oven-safe skillet. Bake at 450° for 20 minutes. Serve hot. Cut into wedges. Sprinkle generously with powdered sugar, fresh lemon juice and melted butter, or make a syrup by stirring fresh lemon juice into powdered sugar, adding melted butter. Use approximately ¼ cup of each; adjust to taste. This makes a marvelous breakfast with bacon and fresh fruit. It is easy to make, fun to serve, but plan to get it directly from the oven to the table. 6 servings

**Marty D. Halyburton (Mrs. Porter A.)**

# Bran Muffins

1 cup bran cereal (All Bran)
1 cup buttermilk or sour milk
1 cup all-purpose flour
1 teaspoon salt
½ teaspoon baking powder
¾ teaspoon baking soda
⅓ cup sugar
¼ cup nuts, chopped
1 Tablespoon margarine,
  melted
2 Tablespoons molasses
¼ cup honey
1 egg, slightly beaten

Mix cereal and milk and set aside for 5 minutes. Meanwhile, in food processor or by hand, mix all other ingredients in order as listed and add bran mixture last. Spoon into greased muffin tins, filling cups ⅔ full and bake at 425° for 15-20 minutes. Muffins keep well in an air-tight container.
Serves 12

**Jeneal Benton (Mrs. Gene R.)**

# Wheat Germ Muffins
Great! Even the kids like them!

1 cup whole wheat flour*
½ cup all-purpose flour*
1 cup wheat germ
¼ cup brown sugar
1 teaspoon salt
1 teaspoon baking powder
½ teaspoon soda
½ cup milk
½ cup honey
¼ cup cooking oil
1 egg, slightly beaten
*1½ cups white flour may
  be used.

Combine flours, wheat germ, brown sugar, salt, baking powder and soda. Add milk, honey, oil and egg to dry ingredients, and stir just to moisten. Do not over-mix. Fill well greased muffin cups two-thirds full. Bake at 400° for 15 minutes. Serve with butter.
12 muffins

**JoAnn P. Whitehead (Mrs. Harry C.)**

# Date Muffins
A good luncheon companion for chicken or shrimp salad

½ cup butter, creamed
¾ cup brown sugar
½ teaspoon ground cloves
½ teaspoon nutmeg
1 teaspoon cinnamon
¼ cup water
2 eggs
1½ cups all-purpose flour
½ cup broken pecans
1 cup chopped dates

Place all ingredients except pecans and dates in a mixing bowl. Mix well with electric mixer. Fold in pecans and dates. Grease muffin tins and fill ½-¾ full. Bake 25-30 minutes at 350°. May be frozen. 12 muffins

**Vonnie Powell (Mrs. J. Montgomery)**

## Cranberry Nut Muffins

1⅓ cups all-purpose flour
1 teaspoon baking soda
1¼ teaspoons baking powder
½ teaspoon salt
¾ cup sugar
Peel of 1 medium orange
6 Tablespoons butter
1 teaspoon lemon juice
2 eggs
¼ cup orange juice
1¼ cups fresh cranberries
1 cup chopped pecans

Mix together flour, baking soda, baking powder and salt; set aside. Place sugar and orange peel in bowl of food processor and process with metal blade until peel is finely chopped. Add butter and lemon juice and with off/on motion combine until well mixed. Add eggs and orange juice and process until smooth. Add cranberries and nuts; combine with off/on motion. Add flour mixture and combine just until flour disappears. Spoon into well greased tiny muffin tins. Bake in preheated 350° oven until golden brown, approximately 20 minutes. Remove from tins to cool. May be frozen. Serve with Cream Cheese and Marmalade Spread. Muffins may be made just as successfully with electric mixer, using grated orange peel and finely chopped cranberries.
36 tiny muffins

## Hobo Bread
Great for Christmas gifts and campers

3 one pound coffee cans
1 cup white raisins
1 cup dark raisins
2 cups boiling water
4 teaspoons baking soda
2 cups sugar
¼ cup oil
½ teaspoon salt
4 cups all purpose flour
½ cup chopped nuts (optional)

*Night before baking:* Soak raisins in boiling water. Add baking soda and cover container tightly.
*Next day:* Add sugar, oil, salt, flour and nuts to raisin mixture. Mix well with wooden spoon. Grease and flour coffee cans and fill each ½ full. Bake at 350° for one hour. Take out of oven and let set for five minutes. Remove bread from cans and let cool. Return bread to cans and cover with plastic lids. Store in refrigerator. Will keep up to 6 months. Serve with butter or cream cheese. Yield: 3 loaves, 12 slices per loaf

**Mrs. Jack Mielke**

# Banana Nut Bread
A better banana bread!
Very moist and flavorful

4 ripe bananas
2 large eggs
1 teaspoon lemon juice
Grated rind of ½ lemon
½ cup bran cereal
1½ cups sifted all-purpose
   flour
¾ cup sugar
1 teaspoon salt
1 teaspoon baking soda
¼ cup wheat germ
½ cup chopped walnuts or
   pecans

Beat together in large mixing bowl, bananas, eggs, lemon juice and rind. Add bran and allow to soften for 5 minutes. Beat. Sift together flour, sugar, salt and baking soda. Add to banana mixture and beat. Stir in wheat germ and nuts. Grease and flour one 9 x 5-inch loaf pan or three 5¾ x 3¼-inch miniature loaf pans. Pour batter into pan(s) and bake at 350° for 50-60 minutes. Test with a toothpick. May be frozen.
1 large loaf

**Barbara R. Schuyler (Mrs. Lambert, Jr.)**

# German Butterkuchen
Rich, tasty and worth the effort

1 cup milk
½ cup sugar
1 teaspoon salt
¼ cup butter
1½ packages active dry yeast
1 teaspoon sugar
¼ warm water
2 eggs
3¼ cups unsifted all-purpose
   flour
⅓ cup chopped almonds
Butter Topping:
1 cup sugar
½ cup butter
½ teaspoon cinnamon

Scald milk. Add ½ cup sugar, salt and shortening. Dissolve yeast and 1 teaspoon sugar in warm water; stir into cooled milk mixture. Beat eggs with 1 cup flour. Add the remaining flour alternately with milk and yeast mixture. Mix well after each addition. Add almonds. Dough will be very soft and sticky. Pour into greased 9 x 13-inch pan, spreading evenly. Set in a warm place to rise. Let rise at least one hour. Cut ingredients for topping together to form fine crumb mixture. Sprinkle topping over dough and bake at 375° for 30 minutes. Delicious for breakfast or dessert.

**Maddy S. Kligora (Mrs. John)**

## "Squiggles"

Try these for breakfast in place of pancakes or French toast.
Invite the children to help and plan on a mess!

2 eggs, beaten
1½ cups milk
2 cups all-purpose flour
1 teaspoon baking powder
½ teaspoon salt
2 cups oil
powdered sugar

Combine eggs and milk. Sift together flour, baking powder and salt. Add to egg mixture. Beat until smooth with rotary mixer. In an 8-inch skillet heat oil to 360°. Pour batter in funnel and release from spout or pour from measuring cup in a narrow stream to form spiral shapes or circles. (Cakes may be formed in any shape, including alphabet letters for initials of the children assisting. Shapes should be kept 3-4 inches in circumference for ease in handling.) Fry until golden (3 minutes); turn carefully and brown other side. Drain on paper towel and sprinkle with powdered sugar. Serve hot with syrup. 8 servings

**Kimpy Edge (Mrs. J. Dexter, Jr.)**

## Dutch Pannekoek

Served in Holland with fried bacon or thinly sliced apples
as a filling, this is a brunch or supper dish. Although
basically a crêpe recipe, the pancake is
thicker and larger in size.

1 cup cold water
1 cup cold milk
5 eggs
¼ teaspoon salt
2 cups sifted all-purpose flour
5 Tablespoons butter, melted
Thinly sliced apples or cooked
    bacon for filling

In blender or food processor, mix ingredients to form batter. Let stand overnight in refrigerator for best results, but it is not absolutely necessary. Oil and heat an 8 or 10-inch skillet. Pour enough batter to cover bottom well. Add apple or cooked bacon over top; cover with a little more batter. When bubbles appear and pancake lifts easily, turn it and brown slightly on other side. Serve immediately with lots of powdered sugar on top or stack pancakes on plate, cover with a damp tea towel and keep warm in oven for as long as needed.

**Joan Roes (Mrs. Hans)**

## Sour Cream Pecan Coffee Cake

1 cup margarine or butter
2 cups sugar
2 eggs
2 cups flour, sifted
1 teaspoon baking powder
¼ teaspoon salt
½ teaspoon vanilla
1 cup sour cream
TOPPING AND FILLING:
3 Tablespoons brown sugar
½ teaspoon cinnamon
½ cup pecans, chopped

Cream margarine or butter and sugar; add eggs and beat. Sift dry ingredients and add to creamed mixture. Add vanilla, fold in sour cream and mix carefully. Spoon ½ topping mixture into a greased and floured Bundt or tube pan. Cover with ½ of batter. Spoon on rest of topping and cover with batter. Bake at 350° for 55-60 minutes. (Do not overbake.) Toothpick will come out clean. Let sit for 10 minutes. Run sharp knife around edge. Invert on plate. Sprinkle with powdered sugar when cool. Hint: This cake keeps well several days when wrapped in plastic wrap. 12-15 servings

**Carolyn Hoose (Mrs. Kenneth A., Jr.)**

## Puffy French Toast with Orange Sauce
This recipe was served on trains back in the
days of first class pullman travel

Batter:
1 cup all-purpose flour
1½ teaspoon sugar
1½ teaspoon baking powder
½ teaspoon salt
¼ teaspoon cinnamon
1 cup milk
1 egg, beaten
8 slices white bread
Oil for frying

Mix dry ingredients. Blend milk and egg; combine with flour mixture and beat until smooth. Dip bread slices into batter. Fry in deep fat 375° until golden brown (about 2 minutes on each side). Drain on paper towels. Serve hot with orange sauce. 8 servings

Orange sauce:
1 Tablespoon cornstarch
½ cup sugar
½ teaspoon salt
1 cup orange juice
2 teaspoons grated orange rind
⅛ teaspoon nutmeg
1 Tablespoon butter
1 orange, sectioned

Mix together cornstarch, sugar and salt in saucepan. Gradually stir in juice; add rind. Cook over medium heat until mixture comes to a boil, stirring constantly. Add nutmeg, butter and orange sections. Beat until well mixed. Yield: 1¼ cups

**Southern Plantation Cookbook**
**Corinne Carlton Geer**

# Danish Pastry Puff

1 cup sifted all-purpose flour
½ cup margarine
2 Tablespoons water
½ cup margarine
1 cup water
1 teaspoon almond extract
1 cup sifted flour
3 eggs
1½ cups powdered sugar
Almond extract
Sliced Almonds
Maraschino Cherries

Cut ½ cup margarine into 1 cup sifted flour. Sprinkle with 2 Tablespoons water and mix with fork. Round into ball and divide in half. Pat each half into a strip 12 x 3 inches and place strips 3 inches apart on an ungreased baking sheet. Mix second ½ cup margarine and 1 cup water in saucepan. Bring to a boil and add almond extract. Remove from heat. Stir in 1 cup flour immediately. (Must be stirred in while liquid is very hot to prevent lumping.) When smooth and thick, add 1 egg at a time, beating until smooth after each. Divide mixture in half and spread over strips of pastry. Bake at 350° for 45-60 minutes until crisp and light brown. Cool. Add to powdered sugar enough almond extract to make spreadable consistency. Frost pastry and sprinkle with almonds and cherries. May be frozen. 2 loaves

**Karen DeFazio (Mrs. Richard)**

# Wales Kringle
A not-too-sweet to serve with coffee

1 cup all-purpose flour
¼ teaspoon salt
½ cup margarine
1 cup water
4 eggs
Glaze:
Confectioners sugar mixed
    with water, almond and rum
    flavorings to taste

Sift flour and salt. Heat water to a boil and add margarine, stir until melted. Add flour and salt at once. Stir until combined. Remove from heat and add eggs, one at a time, stirring after each until smooth. Drop mixture by spoonfuls onto a cookie sheet forming two 12-inch circles or a Kringle (figure 8) shape. Bake at 425° for about 30 minutes or until puffed and brown. Cool slightly and glaze. 4-6 servings

**Winnie R. Goodman (Mrs. James E.)**

# Wine and Cheese Spread
Have your wine, cheese and bread all in one!
This recipe is designed for cooks who like to taste and adjust!

**Dehydrated minced onion**
**Dry wine (red or white)**
**8 ounce package cream**
  **cheese, softened**

Pour wine over dried onion to soften (start with approximately equal amounts of each). When soft, blend with cream cheese in food processor, blender or mixer. Taste and adjust! Spread over warm French or Italian bread or spoon over spaghetti, lasagna or ravioli.

# Cream Cheese and Marmalade Spread

**1 (8 ounce) package cream**
  **cheese, softened**
**½ cup marmalade (orange,**
  **grapefruit—your choice)**

Blend cream cheese and marmalade in food processor or mixer until well mixed. Adds an extra spark to almost any fruit bread or muffins. Also very good on a warmed slice of pound cake.

# Orange Butter

**Juice of 2 oranges or**
  **2 Tablespoons undiluted**
  **frozen orange juice**
**Rind of 2 oranges**
**1 cup plus 2 Tablespoons**
  **powdered sugar**
**1 cup butter**

Mix all ingredients in blender or food processor. Put in small mold and chill before serving. Excellent on blueberry muffins. Serve for dinner with any bread that is compatible with a fruit spread.

**Elise M. Griffin**

# Desserts and Sweets

## Sweetened Condensed Milk
A new old standby for your recipe file

1 cup instant dry milk
⅔ cup sugar
⅓ cup boiling water
3 Tablespoons melted butter

Combine ingredients. Makes same amount as 1 (15-ounce) can condensed milk.

## Basic Crêpe Batter

1 cup flour
1 egg plus 1 yolk
1 cup milk
¼ cup water
Cooking oil

Mix flour, egg plus yolk and milk lightly. Let mixture sit at least ½ hour (overnight if possible). Add water. Season crêpe pan with 1 Tablespoon oil; pour excess into batter. Into a hot pan, pour just enough batter to barely cover bottom of pan (tilt pan to cover with batter; pour remainder back into bowl) and cook until edges begin to turn brown. Turn crêpe and cook a few seconds more. Cool on a wire rack. Crêpes may be frozen between sheets of wax paper. Fill with desired filling. 16 crêpes

**Nathalie Dupree**
*Rich's Cooking School*

## Dessert Crêpe Filling

1 (8-ounce) package cream cheese
1 egg, slightly beaten
¼ cup sugar (or more to taste)
1 teaspoon vanilla
1 pint strawberries, or blueberries, sweetened if desired

In food processor or by hand, blend cream cheese, egg, sugar and vanilla. Spoon about 1½ Tablespoons mixture down the center of each crêpe. Fold and place, seam side down, on a serving plate. Top with fruit.

# Lemon Filling For Crêpes

½ cup sugar
¼ cup butter, softened
1 Tablespoon lemon juice
    (or more to taste)
grated rind of 1-2 lemons

Cream butter and sugar; add rind and juice to taste. Place a tablespoon of mixture in the center of each crêpe. Roll up and place in a baking dish. Heat at 300° until heated through. Spoon excess sauce from dish over crepes. Crêpes may be frozen after filling. Put frozen crêpes in oven until heated through.

**Nathalie Dupree**
*Rich's Cooking School*

# Lemon Curd
### Versatile and delicious

1 stick butter, softened
1½ cups sugar
4 eggs
Grated rind and juice of 4
    lemons

Cream butter and sugar. Add eggs 1 at a time. Add rind and lemon juice. Cook in heavy saucepan over very low heat until thick and shiny. You must stir at all times. If egg whites cook, strain to remove. Store in pint jar in refrigerator up to 2 weeks. Serve in pastry tart shells, over ice cream or on a toasted English muffin. Does not freeze. 1 pint

**Mrs. Meredith Bass**
*Hazlehurst, Miss.*

# Sabayon à la Creole

1 cup sugar
6 egg yolks
½ teaspoon vanilla
1 cup sweet or dry white wine
1 Tablespoon orange peel
5 Tablespoons Grand Marnier
1 cup heavy cream, whipped

Beat eggs and sugar until ribbon forms. Add vanilla, wine and orange peel. Cook in double boiler over low heat. Whisk until frothy. Cool by placing bowl of double boiler into larger bowl of cold water, continuing to whisk. Add Grand Marnier and whipped cream. Mix rapidly and chill. Serve with lace cookies or over pound cake, fruit, or cooked custards.

# Citrus Soufflé

10 egg yolks
1 cup sugar
Zest of 2 lemons
Zest of 2 limes
½ **cup lemon juice**
½ **cup lime juice**
¼ **teaspoon salt**
2 envelopes unflavored gelatin
½ **cup rum or Grand Marnier**
10 egg whites
1 cup sugar
2 cups heavy cream
1 cup heavy cream
2 Tablespoons sugar
Candied violets (optional)

Beat egg yolks until light and fluffy. Gradually add 1 cup sugar. Beat until mixture forms ribbon. Add zests, juices and salt. Beat thoroughly . Pour into heavy pan and cook over low heat, stirring until thick and coats spoon. Pour into bowl and cool. Sprinkle gelatin over rum or Grand Marnier. Set aside until mixture solidifies. Beat egg whites until foamy. Gradually add 1 cup sugar and beat until like marshmallow. Set aside. Beat 2 cups cream until it mounds (not stiff). Dissolve solidified gelatin over low heat and add yolk mixture. Fold in egg whites and 2 cups whipped cream. Pour into 2-quart soufflé dish with an oiled collar. Chill 3 or more hours. Remove collar. Whip 1 cup cream and 2 Tablespoons sugar. Pour on top of soufflé. Decorate with candied violets. Spoon into iced stemmed sherbet glasses. Do not freeze. 12 servings

**Mrs. Carl Welch**

---

**HINT** ■■■

Before peeling oranges, cover with boiling water and let stand 5 minutes. The bitter white membrane can be removed more easily.

# Chilled Peach Soufflé
Very light and refreshing

½ cup sugar
1 envelope unflavored gelatin
¼ teaspoon ground nutmeg
⅛ teaspoon salt
½ cup water
4 beaten egg yolks
1 Tablespoon lemon juice
½ teaspoon vanilla
4-5 drops almond extract
4 large peaches
4 stiffly beaten egg whites
½ cup heavy cream

In a 2-quart saucepan, combine sugar, gelatin, nutmeg, and salt. Stir in water. Stir over low heat until gelatin dissolves. Gradually stir hot mixture into beaten egg yolks. Return to saucepan and add lemon juice. Cook and stir until thickened. Remove from heat. Stir in vanilla and almond extracts. Peel, pit, and slice 2 of the peaches (should have 1½ cups). Place sliced peaches in blender and blend until finely chopped. Stir into gelatin mixture. Chill until partially set. Peel, pit and chop remaining peaches; fold into gelatin mixture. Fold in stiffly beaten egg whites. Whip cream; fold into gelatin. Chill until mixture mounds when dropped from a spoon. Turn into a 1½-quart soufflé dish. Chill until firm. Garnish with toasted almonds and peach slices if desired. May be prepared the day before serving. 8 servings

**Joan M. Adams (Mrs. John P., Jr.)**

---

**MICROWAVE HINT**

Heat brandy for flaming desserts in a glass cup for 10-15 seconds.

**MICROWAVE HINT**

To soften "overly dried" dried fruits, sprinkle with ½ to 1 teaspoon water, cover tightly and heat in microwave oven 15 to 45 seconds.

## Cold Lemon Soufflé with Wine Sauce
Elegant summertime treat

1 package unflavored gelatin
¼ cup cold water
5 eggs, separated
1½ cups sugar
¾ cup fresh lemon juice
2 teaspoons grated lemon rind
1 cup heavy cream
WINE SAUCE:
½ cup sugar
1 Tablespoon cornstarch
¼ cup water
1 Tablespoon lemon juice
1 teaspoon grated lemon rind
2 Tablespoons butter
½ cup dry white wine

Sprinkle gelatin over water to soften. Mix 5 egg yolks with lemon juice and rind and ¾ cup of sugar. Place in top of double boiler, cook stirring constantly until lemon mixture is slightly thickened—about 8 minutes. Remove from heat and stir in gelatin until dissolved. Chill 30-40 minutes until mixture mounds slightly when dropped from spoon. Beat egg whites until stiff, gradually adding the remaining ¾ cup sugar. Beat cream until stiff. Fold egg whites and cream into yolk mixture until no white streaks remain. Pour into a 2-quart soufflé dish and chill 4 hours or more.
6-8 servings
WINE SAUCE:
In small saucepan, mix sugar and cornstarch. Stir in water, lemon juice and rind until smooth. Add butter. Bring to boil, lower heat and cook until thickened. Add wine, chill, stirring occasionally.

## Frozen Lemon Mousse

2-3 cups graham cracker crumbs
1 cup sugar
3 egg yolks
Juice of 2 lemons
1 Tablespoon water
Grated lemon rind
1 large can evaporated milk, chilled
3 egg whites, stiffly beaten

Sprinkle two-thirds of crumbs into a buttered 2 quart oblong casserole. Cook sugar, egg yolks, lemon juice and water in top of double boiler until mixture coats spoon. Cool. Add grated lemon rind. Whip chilled milk until stiff. Fold in egg whites and add cooked, cooled mixture. Pour over top of crumbs and sprinkle with remaining crumbs. Freeze. Remove from freezer several minutes before serving to soften.
8 servings

**Eleanor R. McCormack (Mrs. Wayne)**

## Frozen Soufflé with Hot Strawberry Sauce

½ gallon vanilla ice cream,
   softened
12 almond macaroons,
   crumbled
5 Tablespoons Grand Marnier
2 cups heavy cream
½ cup chopped toasted
   almonds
Confectioners sugar
HOT STRAWBERRY SAUCE:
1 quart fresh strawberries,
   cleaned and halved
   or 3 (10-ounce) packages
   frozen sliced strawberries
Sugar
5 Tablespoons Grand Marnier

Soften ice cream slightly. Stir in crumbled macaroons and Grand Marnier. Whip cream until thick and shiny. Fold into ice cream mixture. Spoon into an angel food cake pan. Sprinkle surface lightly with almonds and confectioners sugar. Cover with plastic wrap. Freeze until firm, about 4-5 hours or overnight. Unmold onto cold platter. Return to freezer until serving time. 12 servings
SAUCE:
Just before serving, put berries in a saucepan with sugar (about ½ cup for fresh berries; less for frozen); simmer until soft, but not mushy. Remove from heat; stir in Grand Marnier. Serve frozen soufflé and top with sauce.

**Joan M. Adams (Mrs. John P., Jr.)**

## Mousse à L'Orange

3 egg yolks
⅓ cup sugar
1 Tablespoon unflavored
   gelatin
¼ cup cold water
1 cup fresh orange juice
1 Tablespoon cornstarch
1 Tablespoon grated orange
   peel
3 egg whites
¼ cup heavy cream, whipped
Orange shells
Whipped cream flavored with
   Grand Marnier or Cointreau

Beat egg yolks and sugar until light and fluffy. Sprinkle gelatin over cold water to soften. Then combine gelatin with orange juice, cornstarch and orange peel. Heat this mixture in a saucepan just to the boiling point. Add it gradually to the egg yolks, beating briskly as you do until thickened. Let cool. Fold in beaten egg whites and whipped cream. Pour into orange shells or individual glasses. Top with whipped cream flavored with liqueur. 4-6 servings

**Fran Scott (Mrs. Romney E.)**

# Vanilla Soufflé with Cold Raspberry Sauce
Make the sauce first and serve very cold over the hot soufflé

## Soufflé

2 Tablespoons butter
2 Tablespoons flour
1 cup milk, heated
½ cup sugar
¼ teaspoon vanilla
5 egg yolks, beaten
6 egg whites

Preheat oven to 350°
Melt butter in top of double boiler; stir in flour, cook one minute; add hot milk and sugar. Stir until thick and smooth. Remove from heat, add vanilla. Add beaten yolks and let cool until you can comfortably hold the bowl in palm of hand. Beat whites until stiff but not dry. Add a large spoonful to yolks to lighten the sauce, folding until mixture is slightly foamy. Pour over remaining whites and fold in carefully until thoroughly mixed. Slide into a buttered and sugared 2-quart soufflé dish. Bake 20 minutes or until top of soufflé jiggles only slightly when dish is pushed.
4 servings

## Raspberry Sauce

2 Tablespoons cornstarch
½ cup water
¼ cup currant jelly
1 (10-ounce) package frozen
raspberries, partially thawed

Over medium heat, blend cornstarch, water and jelly until thick. Stir in raspberries, chill until serving.

**Cookbook Committee**

# Carnival Cream

8 eggs, separated
1 cup sugar
¾ cup rum or brandy
2 envelopes unflavored gelatin
½ cup cold water
½ cup hot water
1 teaspoon vanilla
Lady fingers
1 cup heavy cream, whipped
½ cup chopped almonds
½ cup almond macaroon
crumbs

Beat egg whites until stiff; gradually add sugar. Beat egg yolks until thick and yellow; add rum or brandy and fold into whites. Soften gelatin in cold water, dissolve in hot water. Cool and fold into egg mixture. Add vanilla. Line ring mold with lady fingers and pour in mixture. Chill until set. Unmold and fill center with whipped cream mixed with nuts and macaroon crumbs. 10 servings

**Susan N. Barton (Mrs. David L.)**

## Orange Charlotte
A scrumptious orange cloud for dessert!

1⅓ Tablespoons unflavored
  gelatin
⅓ cup cold water
⅓ cup boiling water
1 cup sugar
3 Tablespoons fresh lemon
  juice
1 cup fresh orange juice
1 cup heavy cream
2 teaspoons vanilla flavoring
3 egg whites
Cherries and nuts if desired
  for garnish

Soften gelatin in cold water. Dissolve in boiling water. Add sugar and stir until dissolved over low heat if necessary. Add lemon juice and orange juice to mixture. Chill in refrigerator until mixture begins to congeal slightly. Whip cream, flavor with vanilla and fold into juice mixture. Fold in beaten egg whites. Return to refrigerator until firm. Garnish with cherries and nuts. May be served in individual dishes or crystal bowl. Note: Use a sweet and juicy orange for the best taste. Hint: Frozen concentrate may be used in place of fresh orange juice. 6-8 servings

**Mrs. Walter P. McCurdy, Sr.**

## Peach Crème Brulée
Crème de la Crème

3 cups heavy cream
6 egg yolks
6 Tablespoons sugar
Dash salt
1 teaspoon vanilla
¾ cup light brown sugar
raspberry jam—1 teaspoon
  per peach half
10-12 canned peach halves,
  drained well

Heat cream in top of double boiler. Beat egg yolks, sugar, salt in bowl until light and fluffy. Add warm cream gradually to egg mixture. Pour mix back into double boiler and cook, stirring constantly, until custard coats spoon (do not have water boiling). Cool. Arrange peach halves in shallow baking dish and spoon 1 teaspoon jam in each peach center. Pour the cooled cream mix over peaches and chill overnight. Next day, cover custard with sifted brown sugar about ¼ inch thick. Broil 6-9 inches away from heat until sugar melts and bubbles. Be very careful that sugar does not burn. Refrigerate until ready to serve. 8-10 servings

# Almond Custard
Very rich with florentine quality
Well worth the expensive ingredients

**3 cups heavy cream**
**⅔ cup sugar**
**Dash salt**
**½ cup almond paste**
**8 egg yolks**
**1 teaspoon vanilla**
**½ cup slivered toasted**
**almonds (or sliced)**

8 servings

Heat first four ingredients carefully until almond paste melts. Do not boil. Remove from heat and add the beaten egg yolks, vanilla, and almonds. Pour into custard cups and place in hot water bath. Bake at 350° for 20-25 minutes until a knife inserted near rim of cup comes out clean. Serve at room temperature. Hint: Pour a small amount of the hot mixture into the egg yolk mixture stirring all the while. Then pour the yolks into the remaining hot mixture, again stirring all the while so you do not get scrambled eggs.

# Classic Flan

**½ cup sugar**
**2 cups heavy cream**
**¼ cup sugar**
**3 eggs**
**1 teaspoon vanilla**

The day before serving, melt ½ cup sugar until brown but not too dark. Pour immediately into 1 quart casserole. Scald cream. Beat eggs with ¼ cup sugar and add to cream. Add vanilla. Stir until sugar dissolves. Pour into casserole. Bake inside another dish, pour boiling water in to reach halfway up inside dish. Bake at 325° until knife inserted near center comes out clean, about 1 hour. Chill in form overnight. Turn out upside down to serve. May also be made in individual custard cups lined with the caramelized sugar. Note: Milk may be substituted for cream but flan will not be as creamy.

**Beth Koenig (Mrs. William)**

Before scalding milk, rinse pan in cold water to avoid coating.

# Flan De Queso
A flan with a flair

**CARAMEL:**
**1½ cups sugar**
**⅓ cup water**
**CUSTARD:**
**1 (8-ounce) package cream
  cheese**
**4 eggs**
**1 can sweetened condensed
  milk plus 1 can water**
**3 slices white bread**
**Almond slivers (optional)**

Caramel: Heat sugar and water in a heavy saucepan stirring constantly until sugar melts and turns light amber. Pour immediately into an 8-inch square pan tipping until bottom is coated with caramel. Cool while making custard.

Custard: Heat oven to 350°. Put all ingredients except almonds into blender. Cover and process at "stir" until well mixed. Pour into caramel-coated pan. Add almonds. Cover and place in larger pan containing hot water. Bake 1 hour and 15 minutes, or until a silver knife inserted at center comes out clean. Cool about 2 hours then remove custard from mold. 10-12 servings

**Susan M. Morley**

# President's Pudding

**½ cup vanilla wafer or graham
  cracker crumbs**
**1 envelope Dream Whip**
**6 ounces cream cheese**
**1½ cups confectioners sugar**
**½ cup smooth peanut butter**
**1 teaspoon vanilla**
**¾ cup sweet milk**
**¾ cup crushed salted peanuts**

At least 4 hours before serving, prepare 8-10 custard cups placing 2 teaspoons crumbs in each. Whip Dream Whip as directed on package and set aside. Cream together cream cheese, sugar and peanut butter. Add milk and vanilla. Fold in prepared Dream Whip and spoon into custard cups. Top with crushed salted peanuts. Freeze for at least 4 hours. Will keep indefinitely. Note: The size of custard cups determines the number of servings obtained. 8-10 servings

**Mrs. Lupo**
*Mary Mac's Tea Room*
*Atlanta, Georgia*

# Devonshire Cream
This is also lovely served in
miniature pastry shells with coffee after dinner

1 (8-ounce) package cream
   cheese, softened
½ cup confectioners sugar,
   sifted
¼ cup heavy cream
1 egg yolk
2 Tablespoons brandy
Fresh fruit of your choice
TO SEAL FRUIT:
2 Tablespoons apricot
   preserves
2 teaspoons kirsch

In bowl of mixer or food processor beat cream cheese, sugar, cream and egg yolk until light. Stir in brandy. Divide into 4 stemmed champagne glasses. Refrigerate at least 2 hours before serving. Decorate with any fresh fruit combination—mandarin oranges and blueberries are pretty. Seal fruit with apricot preserves and kirsch. Heat and paint on. This will seal and keep colors true. 4 servings

**Fran Scott (Mrs. Romney E.)**

# Strawberry Bread Pudding

1 (10-ounce) package frozen
   strawberries, thawed
2 Tablespoons cornstarch
Few drops red food coloring
2 eggs, slightly beaten
2½ cups milk
½ cup sugar
2 Tablespoons butter, melted
½ teaspoon vanilla extract
¼ teaspoon salt
4 slices bread, cut in ½ inch
   cubes (about 4 cups)

In a small saucepan combine undrained strawberries and cornstarch. Cook and stir over medium heat until mixture thickens and bubbles. Stir in food coloring. Spread mixture evenly over bottom of a 6 x 10 x 2-inch baking dish. In a mixing bowl, combine eggs, milk, sugar, butter, vanilla and salt. Add bread cubes; stir to moisten. Carefully pour custard mixture over berries. Bake at 350° for 50-55 minutes. Serve warm. 6-8 servings

**Linda D. Bobo (Mrs. W. Earl)**

# Boston Cream Pie

A very old New England recipe from a nineteenth
century "gourmet" cook

**CAKE:**
**1 cup flour**
**1 cup sugar**
**2 teaspoons baking powder**
**Dash salt**
**½ cup milk**
**1 Tablespoon butter**
**2 eggs, separated**
**FILLING:**
**2 cups milk**
**½ cup flour**
**½ cup sugar**
**2 eggs, beaten**
**Dash salt**
**1 Tablespoon butter**
**1 teaspoon vanilla**
**1 cup heavy cream, whipped**
**FROSTING:**
**3 squares unsweetened**
  **chocolate**
**¾ cup sugar**
**6 Tablespoons milk**
**1½ Tablespoons butter**
**½ teaspoon vanilla**

Cake: Sift dry ingredients together. Scald milk and butter; add dry ingredients. Add beaten yolk. Whip egg whites stiff. Fold into mixture. Bake in 2 round cake pans at 375° for approximately 20 minutes.

Filling: Scald milk. Mix flour and sugar and add to beaten eggs in double boiler. Add milk gradually and cook until thick. Remove from heat and add salt, butter and vanilla. Cool and add whipped cream.

Frosting: Melt chocolate, sugar and milk*. Boil 2 minutes. Remove from heat and add butter and vanilla. Beat well.

*A little more milk may be needed to achieve a smooth consistency.

Split both layers of cake. Put filling between layers. Frost top with chocolate. Makes 2-two layer cakes or 1-four layer cake. Refrigerate. 8 servings

**Mrs. Alfred J. Westcott**
*Norfolk, Virginia*

## Chocolate Pastry Cake

8 ounces sweet chocolate
½ cup sugar
½ cup water
1½ teaspoons instant coffee
2 teaspoons vanilla
2 cups heavy cream
CRUST:
1 (9 or 10-ounce) package pie
  crust mix or make your
  own pastry: 1 teaspoon
  salt, 2 cups flour, ⅔ cup
  shortening. Add no liquid.
  Blend.

At least 8 hours before serving, in saucepan combine chocolate, sugar, water and coffee. Cook over low heat stirring constantly until smooth. Add vanilla. Cool to room temperature or pastry will melt. Blend ¾ cup chocolate sauce into pastry mixture. Divide pastry mixture into 6 equal parts. Press each part over bottom of an inverted 8-inch round cake pan to ½ inch from edge. Do in relays as to how many pans you have. Bake at 425° for 5 minutes until done. Cool. Then run tip of knife under edges to loosen. Lift off carefully. Whip cream until it just begins to hold soft peaks. Fold in remaining chocolate sauce. Stack baked pastries spreading chocolate cream between layers and over top. Chill at least 8 hours or overnight. 1 cake

**Patricia H. Adams (Mrs. P.H.)**

## Layered Chocolate Cream
A make ahead success

½ cup margarine
1½ cups graham cracker
  crumbs
½ cup chopped nuts
8 ounces cream cheese,
  softened
1 cup sugar
1½ cups whipped topping
2 small packages instant
  chocolate pudding
3 cups milk
Additional whipped topping

Melt margarine in oblong baking dish (11¾ x 7½ x 1¾-inch) in oven; add crumbs and nuts. Press in pan to form crust. Bake at 350° for about 5 minutes. Blend cream cheese and sugar well; fold in whipped topping. Put this on top of crust in mounds and spread. Prepare pudding following package directions except use 3 cups milk. Blend 2 minutes. Layer chocolate on top of cream cheese layer. Top with additional whipped topping and sprinkle with nuts. For a bit of a difference try whipped cream in place of whipped topping. Chill.

**Mrs. Richard A. Smith**

# Boccone Dolce
A favorite all around

4 egg whites
Dash salt
¼ teaspoon cream of tartar
1 cup sugar
1 (6-ounce) package chocolate
  chips
3 Tablespoons water
3 cups heavy cream, whipped
⅓ cup sugar
1 pint fresh strawberries,
  sliced (Save a few whole
  ones for garnish.)

Preheat oven to 250°. Beat egg whites, with salt and cream of tartar until stiff. Gradually add sugar and beat until meringue is stiff and glossy. Line three 8-inch pans with waxed paper, or trace three 8-inch circles on waxed paper and bake on cookie sheet. Spread meringues on circles ¼ inch thick and bake 20-25 minutes until pale gold and still pliable. Remove from oven and peel waxed paper from bottom and allow to dry on racks. Melt chocolate and water in double boiler over boiling water. Whip cream until stiff. Gradually add sugar and beat until very stiff. Place 1 meringue on serving plate, spread with a thin layer of chocolate, ¾-inch layer of cream, and layer of strawberries. Repeat. Top third layer with only cream. Frost sides with remaining cream. Decorate top with whole strawberries. Refrigerate until ready to serve. Hint: Meringue layers may be made ahead and kept in an airtight container.
8 servings

**Barbara Johnson (Mrs. Larry)**

HINT

When melting chocolate in your double boiler, line the top with wax paper to save chocolate and dishwashing.

HINT

Sift powdered sugar to prevent lumping.

# Chocolate Roulade

This elegant and easy dessert recipe may be doubled or frozen

**6 ounces semi-sweet**
  **chocolate**
**3-4 Tablespoons water**
**5 eggs, separated**
**1 cup sugar**
**½ cup chopped pecans**
  **(optional)**
**Confectioners sugar**
**FILLING:**
**2 cups heavy cream, whipped**
**¼ cup sugar**
**Flavoring, if desired (rum,**
  **brandy, vanilla extract, etc.)**

Oil a 10 x 15-inch jelly roll pan. Line with wax paper extending paper over sides of pan. Oil paper. Place chocolate and water in a saucepan over low heat to melt; set aside to cool. Beat egg yolks until thick and lemon colored. Add sugar. Beat egg whites until stiff. Stir cooled chocolate into egg yolk mixture. Fold in pecans if desired. Fold in a large spoonful of egg whites to soften mixture; then fold in remaining whites as lightly as possible. Spread mixture in prepared pan and bake at 350° for 25-30 minutes. Remove from oven and cool to room temperature. Cover with a lightweight dish towel which is only slightly damp. Refrigerate overnight, if possible. To assemble: Remove cloth and turn roulade out on wax paper which has been dusted with confectioners sugar. Carefully remove all paper from top of cake. trim rough edges. Spread cake with 1½ cups whipped cream to which sugar and any desired flavoring has been added. Roll up like a jelly roll, sprinkle generously with confectioners sugar and decorate with remaining whipped cream. Serve within 2-3 hours or freeze. If frozen, defrost in refrigerator or serve partially frozen.
6 servings

**Nathalie Dupree**
*Rich's Cooking School*

# Almond Butter Cream Roll
Serve with tart strawberries for a wonderful combination

3 eggs, separated
1 teaspoon cider vinegar
½ cup sugar
½ teaspoon almond extract
½ cup flour, sifted
⅛ teaspoon salt
ALMOND BUTTER CREAM:
⅓ cup butter, softened
3 cups powdered sugar, sifted
Few drops almond extract
About 2 Tablespoons milk or
   cream
1 egg yolk

Oil a jelly roll pan well—also oil brown paper well (cut to fit pan). Beat yolks until they form a ribbon. Beat whites with vinegar until they form soft peaks, gradually adding sugar and extract, beat until stiff. Fold in beaten yolks. Sift flour and salt over top and fold in. Spread batter in pan. Bake at 400° for 12-15 minutes. Turn out on dish towel which has been sprinkled with powdered sugar. Strip off paper and roll up in towel. Let cool. Unroll. Mix all ingredients together for Almond Butter Cream and spread on baked cake. Reroll. Sprinkle with powdered sugar. May be frozen.

**Sylvia Dorough (Mrs. Don)**

# Blitz Torte

½ cup butter, softened
¾ cup confectioners sugar
4 egg yolks, beaten
1 cup flour
1 teaspoon baking powder
½ teaspoon salt
3 Tablespoons milk
4 egg whites
½ cup confectioners sugar
½ cup granulated sugar
1 cup sliced almonds
4 Tablespoons sugar
2 cups milk
½ cup sugar
2 eggs
1 teaspoon vanilla
3 Tablespoons cornstarch
large package Cool Whip
¼ cup almonds, sliced and
   toasted

Mix butter and sugar; beat in yolks. Sift together flour, salt and baking powder and stir into creamed mixture. Stir in milk. Spread batter in 2 greased and floured 8-inch round cake pans.
   Make meringue by beating egg whites and adding sugar. Spread on batter in pans and sprinkle with ½ cup sliced almonds and 2 Tablespoons sugar over each layer. Bake at 325° for 40 minutes.
   While layers bake, cook milk, sugar, eggs, vanilla and cornstarch in top of double boiler to make custard filling. Cool. Spread custard between cooled layers and frost with Cool Whip leaving a round opening on top. Fill opening with toasted sliced almonds.

**Sandy Ford (Mrs. Harold)**

# Pineapple Torte
Very festive and pretty for a party or spring fling

**MERINGUE:**
**8 egg whites**
**2 cups sugar**
**1½ teaspoons vinegar**
**2 teaspoons vanilla**
**½ teaspoon cream of tartar**
**TOPPING:**
**½ pint heavy cream**
**1 cup crushed pineapple,**
  **well drained**
**½ cup chopped maraschino**
  **cherries**

Prepare several hours in advance of serving.

Meringue: Preheat oven to 450° Allow egg whites to warm to room temperature. Line 2 round cake pans with waxed paper. Beat egg whites until stiff and add sugar, cream of tartar, vinegar, and vanilla. Pour into cake pans, place in pre-heated oven, turn off heat and let stand in oven several hours or overnight. Do not open oven door. (May bake at 300° for 1 hour and 15 minutes.) Carefully remove meringues from pan and allow to cool. 8-10 servings

Topping: Whip cream until stiff. Drain pineapple thoroughly. Drain cherries and chop coarsely. Fold pineapple and cherries into whipped cream and spread a thin layer on top of first meringue. Place second meringue on top. Spread mixture over top and sides. Place in refrigerator for several hours before serving.

**Judy L. O'Shea (Mrs. Timothy)**

---

**HINT** ▬▬▬▬▬▬▬▬▬▬▬

When mailing cookies, pack them in popcorn to keep them from crumbling.

---

**HINT** ▬▬▬▬▬▬▬▬▬▬▬

Keep a brand new powder puff in flour canister for dusting greased cake pan.

# Chocolate Mousse Torte
A working person's dream; looks difficult but isn't

1 (8-ounce) package semi-
  sweet chocolate squares
6 eggs, at room temperature,
  separated
2 teaspoons vanilla extract
1 (8½ ounce) package
  chocolate wafers
¼ cup orange juice
½ cup heavy cream

In double boiler, over hot (not boiling) water, melt 7 chocolate squares; remove from heat and cool slightly. Stir in egg yolks until well mixed; then stir in vanilla. Beat egg whites until stiff peaks form. Fold beaten egg whites into chocolate mixture; set aside. Dip half of chocolate wafers in orange juice. Arrange wafers, in bottom of 9 x 2-inch springform pan, overlapping slightly, in one layer. Spoon half of chocolate mixture evenly over wafers. Repeat process. Cover pan with plastic wrap or foil; refrigerate at least 5 hours. Dip knife in warm water, loosen cake from side of spring-form pan, and carefully remove side of pan. Coarsely grate remaining chocolate square; press chocolate on side of torte with hand. Whip cream until stiff peaks form, and spoon into pastry tube with medium rosette tip. Decorate top of torte. Refrigerate. To serve: With sharp knife dipped in hot water, cut into thin wedges.
10 servings

**Debbie McCurdy**

# Sherman Strikes Again

4 large peaches (peeled and
  sliced)
½ cup white wine
2 ounces of peach or apricot
  brandy
1 quart peach ice cream

Put peaches in pan, add wine; heat just before servng, add brandy and heat. Ignite and serve flaming over ice cream
4 servings

## Pears with Apricot Sauce

6 Bartlett pears
⅓ cup almond paste
1 Tablespoon kirsch
1 cup sugar
3 cups water
2 Tablespoons kirsch
1½ teaspoons vanilla
1 cup dried apricot halves
Kirsch to taste
Toasted slivered almonds

Peel and core pears from bottom making deep cavity. Mix almond paste and 1 Tablespoon kirsch and stuff each cavity three-fourths full. Seal cavity with foil. Dissolve sugar and water in sauce-pan just large enough to hold pears. Add 2 Tablespoons kirsch and vanilla and simmer 5 minutes. Add pears; barely simmer 4-6 minutes on each side. Remove pears and chill covered. Add apri-cots to syrup. Cook covered 30 minutes. Drain apricots reserving syrup. Thin purée with enough syrup so that purée will coat pears. Add kirsch to taste. Chill purée. Remove foil from pears; stand them upright. Pour purée over them; thin with more kirsch if necessary. Sprinkle with almonds. 6 servings

## Ginger Fruit
A lovely dessert for an Oriental dinner

1 (1-pound) can sliced
   peaches, drained
1 cup orange juice
2 teaspoons candied ginger,
   finely chopped
2 bananas
¼ cup sherry or ⅛ cup fruit
   brandy or cordial (optional)
Mint leaves for garnish
   (optional)

Combine peaches, juice and candied ginger. Chill several hours to blend flavors. Just before serv-ing peel bananas and run fork tines down sides to flute. Slice on the bias and add to peach mixture. Add sherry, brandy or liqueur if desired. Serve immediately, garnishing with mint leaves.

**Judy George (Mrs. Graham W., Jr.)**

## Chilled Peaches in Chablis
An elegant dessert after a heavy meal

6 small ripe peaches
1 cup sugar
1 cup water
Peel of 1 orange
1 cinnamon stick
1 cup Chablis
Whipped cream

Wash peaches and put in saucepan with sugar, water, orange peel and cinnamon stick, broken in half. Cover saucepan and simmer peaches for 15 minutes. Add Chablis and cook uncovered for 15 minutes or until tender. Hold each peach (using a clean kitchen towel to protect your fingers) and gently rub off skin. Transfer to a deep serving dish, cover and allow to cool. Carefully slice to remove pits. Cook the liquid until reduced to the consistency of light syrup. Pour over peaches and chill in the refrigerator. Serve very cold with whipped cream. Hint: Serve without whipped cream as an accompaniment to chicken. 6 servings

**Elise M. Griffin**

## Strawberries Romanoff
Try this with blueberries too

1 cup heavy cream
4 Tablespoons confectioners
    sugar
1 pint vanilla ice cream,
    slightly softened
Juice of 1 lemon
2 ounces Cointreau
1 ounce white rum
1 quart strawberries

In a 2-quart bowl whip heavy cream with confectioners sugar until stiff. Add vanilla ice cream, lemon juice, Cointreau and rum. Blend the mixture lightly until smooth. Stem strawberries, wash, clean and thoroughly chill. Fill champagne glasses with the fruit. Spoon 3-4 Tablespoons ice cream mixture over the berries.
8 servings

**Gale B. Probst (Mrs. William R.)**

# Brandied Peaches

A wonderful Christmas gift, these peaches are an elegant
finale to your most sophisticated dinner party.

**Ripe fresh freestone peaches**
**1½ cups sugar**
**1¼ cups water**
**Brandy**
**Sweetened whipped cream**

Skin peaches and prick all over with a needle. Mix water and sugar in large pan, bring to boil. Halve peaches and simmer in syrup mixture for 5 minutes. Put peaches in sterilized hot quart jars (about 10 peaches fill a quart jar) filling a bit more than half full with syrup. Cool slightly and fill with brandy to cover. Seal immediately. Keep several months turning jars upside down for some of the time. Chill and serve in crystal goblets over whipped cream with a crisp cookie on the side. Hint: If doing a large number of peaches, the peeled and halved fruit will not discolor if placed in a bowl of water. The peaches release some of their juice into the syrup which eventually changes color and sugar content of syrup. If doing many quarts, it may be best to remake syrup halfway through. makes several quart jars

**Vivian de Kok (Mrs. Peter)**

# Fresh Strawberries with Raspberry Sauce

**2 (10-ounce) packages frozen**
  **raspberries**
**2 pints fresh nicely shaped**
  **strawberries**
**¼ cup confectioners sugar**
**2-3 Tablespoons kirsh, Grand**
  **Marnier or Cointreau**
  **(optional)**

Thaw raspberries, purée and strain out seeds. Rinse strawberries; remove stems. Sprinkle sugar over still wet berries. Refrigerate berries and sauce until ready to serve. Before serving, add liqueur to sauce and pour over strawberries. 6 servings

**Sharon Herrli (Mrs. John)**

# Fruit and Cheese Combinations

Blue—apples, pears (especially
  Anjou or Bosc pears)
Brick—Tokay grapes
Camembert—apples, pears and
  plums
Cheddar—Tart apples and
  melon slices
Edam or Gouda—apples, orange
  sections, fresh pineapple
  spears
Muenster or Swiss—apples,
  seedless grapes, orange
  sections
Provolone—sweet Bartlett pears

# Orange Cheese Dessert Spread

2 cups (8-ounces) shredded
  Cheddar cheese
1 (3-ounce) package cream
  cheese, softened
2 Tablespoons butter, softened
3 Tablespoons orange liqueur
½ teaspoon dry mustard
Dash cayenne

Blend in mixer or food processor. Pack into lightly oiled 2 cup mold. Cover and chill until firm. Unmold and let stand at room temperature one hour before serving. Serve with an assortment of sliced fresh fruits and crackers.

---

**HINT** ████████

For its most distinct flavor, cheese should be served at room temperature. Cream, cottage, and Neufchatel cheese should be chilled when served.

# Gin's Ice Cream

4 eggs
1½ cups sugar
1 can sweetened condensed
   milk
1½ quarts milk
1½ teaspoons vanilla
4 cups very ripe
   mashed fruit, peaches,
   strawberries, etc.

Beat eggs until very light and fluffy, gradually add sugar. Add condensed milk, fruit, milk and vanilla. Pour into churn and freeze. Makes about 1 gallon

**Virginia Kelley (Mrs. R.L.)**
*Wrens, Georgia*

# Peach Ice Cream

1 (15-ounce) can sweetened
   condensed milk
1 (15-ounce) can evaporated
   milk
2 cups half and half
2-3 cups crushed ripe peaches
   (more if you like)
1 (13-ounce) container Cool
   Whip
1½ cups sugar
Pinch salt
1 teaspoon vanilla

Mix condensed milk, evaporated milk, and half and half together; add mashed peaches; fold in Cool Whip, add sugar, salt and vanilla. Pour into an ice cream freezer for the freezing process or pour into plastic containers and place in freezer. Remove from freezer and let sit for a few minutes before serving to soften. 10 servings

**Mrs. Earle B. May, Jr.**

# Frozen Peanut Butter Mousse

⅔ cup sweetened condensed
   milk
½ cup crunchy peanut butter
½ cup coffee
1 teaspoon vanilla
1 cup heavy cream

Mix condensed milk with peanut butter. Add coffee and vanilla. Whip heavy cream until thick but not stiff; fold into peanut butter mixture. Freeze in bowl stirring after 30 minutes to keep creamy.

**Jane Nardone (Mrs. A. Joseph, Jr.)**

# Butterscotch Sauce

2 cups light brown sugar,
   packed
½ cup evaporated milk
¼ teaspoon salt
⅓ cup light corn syrup
⅓ cup butter

Combine all ingredients in saucepan. Bring to boil and cook rapidly for 3 minutes. Serve hot or cold.

**Agnes Siebert (Mrs. Sam)**

# Cherry Rum Sauce

1 cup dark cherry preserves
½ cup coarsely chopped nuts
   (almonds, walnuts, pecans)
¼ cup dark rum

Combine all ingredients and stir to blend. Store in jar in refrigerator putting plastic wrap right on sauce. Serve over ice cream, cake or baked custard. Note: Use dark rum only.

# Georgia Peanut Butter Sauce
### Divine on French vanilla ice cream
### (no one ever suspects peanut butter)

1 cup sugar
1 Tablespoon white Karo syrup
¼ teaspoon salt
¾ cup milk
6 Tablespoons peanut butter
½ teaspoon vanilla extract

Mix sugar, Karo, salt and milk. Cook over low heat, stirring constantly until thickened. Add peanut butter and mix well. Remove from heat, let cool, add vanilla.

**HINT**

To cut marshmallows or sticky fruit, rub butter or oil on scissors.

# Heavenly Hot Fudge Sauce
### The name says it all

4 squares unsweetened
   chocolate
½ cup butter or margarine
Dash salt
3 cups granulated sugar
1 tall can (1⅔ cups)
   evaporated milk, heated
1 teaspoon vanilla

Melt chocolate and butter in top of double boiler. Add salt; then start adding sugar slowly. Add evaporated milk a little at a time. Remove from heat and add vanilla. 1 quart

**Merrilee F. Martin (Mrs. J.S.)**

# Vanilla Sauce

1 cup sugar
4 Tablespoons butter
½ cup cream
¼ cup light Karo syrup
2 teaspoons vanilla

Mix sugar, butter, cream and syrup and boil for 2 minutes, stirring constantly until sauce thickens. Remove from heat and add vanilla.

**Agnes Siebert (Mrs. Sam)**

# Peach Sorbet

1 cup water
2 cups sugar
4 cups peaches
Juice of 2 lemons
Juice of 1 orange

Boil water and sugar 5 minutes. Cool. Purée peaches in processor with steel blade. Add lemon, orange juice and peaches to cool syrup. Pour into shallow metal pan and freeze. As mixture freezes at edges, stir with fork to make smooth two or three times. When almost solid, beat in processor or mixer until smooth. Pour back into pan or individual glasses and freeze 3-4 hours. Serve with lace cookies. Hint: This dessert may be prepared with blueberries, apricots or strawberries.

**Jean Schmidt (Mrs. James C.)**

## Lemon Cream Sherbet

1 cup sugar
2 cups milk
Juice of 2 lemons
Rind of 1 lemon
2 egg whites, beaten
2 Tablespoons sugar
1 cup heavy cream

Add sugar to milk and stir to dissolve. When thoroughly dissolved, stir in lemon rind and juice. Turn into freezer tray and freeze 45-60 minutes. Beat egg whites, adding sugar. Whip cream to a thick custard consistency. Combine with beaten egg whites. Add to frozen mixture and mix lightly. Return to freezer and freeze 2-2½ hours. Do not stir. Garnish with sprig of mint. 6 servings

**Margaret S. Westbrook (Mrs. William)**

## Pineapple Sherbet

2 cups milk, chilled
½ cup pineapple juice
1 Tablespoon grated lemon
    rind
2 teaspoons sugar
1 small can crushed pineapple,
    drained

After milk is chilled, add remaining ingredients. Freeze until hard. Remove and turn into bowl and beat. Return to freezer until ready to serve. 4-6 servings

**Margaret S. Westbrook (Mrs. William)**

## Butterscotch Crumb Squares
Rich, delicious and unusual!

1 cup all-purpose flour
¼ cup rolled oats
¼ cup brown sugar
½ cup butter
½ cup pecans, chopped
1 (12 ounce) jar caramel
    topping
1 quart vanilla ice cream,
    softened

Combine flour, oats and sugar. Cut in butter until mixture resembles coarse crumbs. Stir in pecans. Pat mixture into a 9 x 13-inch pan. Bake at 400° for 15 minutes. Stir, while still warm, to crumble. Cool; then spread half of mixture in a 9-inch square pan. Drizzle half the the topping over this. Spoon ice cream carefully into pan. Drizzle remaining topping over ice cream. Sprinkle with remaining crumbs. Freeze. Cut in squares to serve. 8 servings

# Frozen Chocolate Velvet

1½ cups finely crushed
   chocolate wafers
⅓ cup margarine, melted
1 (8-ounce) package cream
   cheese, softened
½ cup sugar, divided
1 teaspoon vanilla
2 eggs, separated
1 (6-ounce) package semi-
   sweet chocolate chips,
   melted
1 cup heavy cream, whipped
¾ cup chopped pecans

To make crust, combine chocolate wafers with margarine. Press into bottom of a 9-inch springform pan and bake at 325° for 10 minutes. Combine cream cheese, ¼ cup sugar and vanilla, mixing until well blended. Stir in well-beaten egg yolks and chocolate. Beat egg whites until peaks form, gradually beat in ¼ cup sugar and fold into chocolate mixture. Fold in whipped cream and nuts. Pour over crumb crust and freeze. Decorate with additional whipped cream or wafer crumbs, if desired. 10 servings.

**Lib Tuck (Mrs. Bennett F., Jr.)**

# Italian Cassata

1 quart chocolate ice cream
1 egg white
1 Tablespoon sugar
1 cup cake crumbs, sponge,
   yellow or white
Small carton chopped fruits for
   fruit cake, soaked in 3
   Tablespoons sherry
½ teaspoon almond extract
½ pint heavy cream, whipped
1 quart vanilla ice cream
1 ounce slivered toasted
   almonds
Stemmed cherries or sliced
   pineapple for decoration

Line a loaf pan smoothly with foil leaving long ends to cover loaf. Soften chocolate ice cream and smooth into pan. Freeze. Beat egg white until stiff, adding sugar. Fold in cake crumbs, fruit, almond extract and ½ of the whipped cream. Freeze. Soften vanilla ice cream, smooth over whipped cream. Freeze. Remove whole loaf from pan, place on cold tray. Remove foil and ice loaf with remaining whipped cream and almonds. Decorate with stemmed cherries or pineapple as desired. Place on serving tray, wrap whole loaf in foil and refreeze. To serve, do not thaw; slice and serve. 10 servings

**Judy George (Mrs. Graham)**

# Lulabell

This recipe is 40 years old and still a favorite!

½ box vanilla wafers (about 50), crushed
6 Tablespoons butter, melted
2 eggs separated
3 Tablespoons bourbon or brandy
1 (8-ounce) bottle cherries, drained and chopped
1 cup pecans, coarsely chopped
2-3 Tablespoons sugar
1 cup heavy cream, whipped

Mix vanilla wafer crumbs with butter, reserving 2 Tablespoons crumbs for top. Press into 8-inch square pan. Beat egg yolks with bourbon or brandy; add cherries and pecans. Beat egg whites with sugar. Fold egg whites and whipped cream into cherry-nut mixture. Pour over crumbs in pan; sprinkle with reserved crumbs on top; cover with plastic wrap. Freeze. To serve, cut into squares.
8-10 servings

**Hazel R. Rutland (Mrs. Calvin)**

# Chocolate Mousse

6 egg whites at room temperature
1 teaspoon cream of tartar
⅔ cup sugar
1 teaspoon vanilla
2 cups heavy cream, stiffly beaten
4 ounces semi-sweet chocolate
½ cup rum (dark or light)
Whipped cream for garnish
Shaved chocolate for garnish

Add cream of tartar to egg whites and beat until stiff. Gradually beat in sugar and vanilla. Continue to beat stiffly as for a meringue. Fold in whipped cream and egg whites together with a wide rubber spatula. Refrigerate. In saucepan, carefully melt, then cool chocolate and rum. Fold COOLED chocolate into meringue. Note: If mixture is too warm, meringue will collapse. Place in bowl or individual serving dishes. Garnish with whipped cream and grated chocolate. Refrigerate.
8 servings

**Jean Schmidt (Mrs. James C.)**

# Food Processor Cheese Cake

**CRUST:**
**1½ cups zwieback crumbs**
**1 teaspoon cinnamon**
**½ cup melted butter**
**½ cup sugar**
**FILLING:**
**3 (8-ounce) packages cream
    cheese**
**1 cup sugar**
**3 eggs**
**½ cup melted butter, cooled**
**½ teaspoon orange extract**
**GARNISH:**
**1 pint strawberries or blue-
    berries, cleaned and
    trimmed**
**2 Tablespoons apricot jam**
**1 Tablespoon kirsch**

Combine crust ingredients and press into a 9-inch springform pan. Preheat oven to 425°. Process cream cheese and sugar. Add eggs one at a time beating well after each. Pour in butter and orange extract and blend. Pour into prepared crust. Bake 35-40 minutes. Cool and place berries on top. Glaze with heated mixture of 2 Tablespoons apricot jam and 1 Tablespoon kirsch.

# New York Deli Cheese Cake
True New York style cheese cake

**1 small box graham crackers**
**¾ cup sugar**
**4 Tablespoons melted butter**
**1 teaspoon cinnamon**
**1½ pounds cream cheese**
**1 pint sour cream**
**1 cup sugar**
**5 eggs, separated**
**1 Tablespoon flour**
**1 Tablespoon cornstarch**
**1 Tablespoon vanilla**

Crush crackers. Mix crumbs with ¾ cup sugar, melted butter and cinnamon. Reserve ¾ cup and use the remaining to line a greased springform pan. Mix cream cheese and sour cream; add beaten egg yolks, sugar, flour, cornstarch and vanilla. Beat egg whites until stiff and fold into cheese mixture. Pour into pan. Sprinkle reserved crumb mixture on top. Bake at 325° for 1 hour. Turn off heat, open oven door and let rest for several hours or overnight. May be served with a glazed strawberry or cherry sauce. 10 servings

# Pumpkin Cheesecake
A very special cheesecake

**CRUST:**
1½ cups graham cracker crumbs
⅓ cup ground almonds
½ teaspoon ginger
½ teaspoon cinnamon
⅓ cup butter, melted

**FILLING:**
4 (8-ounce) packages cream cheese
1¼ cups sugar
3 Tablespoons maple syrup
3 Tablespoons cognac or brandy
1 teaspoon ginger
1 teaspoon cinnamon
½ teaspoon nutmeg
4 eggs (room temperature)
¼ cup heavy cream
1 cup cooked or canned pumpkin

**TOPPING:**
2 cups sour cream
¼ cup sugar
1 Tablespoon maple syrup
1 Tablespoon cognac or brandy
¼ cup almonds, sautéed in butter

Crust: Preheat oven to 425°. Combine crust ingredients and press into the bottom of a 10-inch springform pan. Bake 10 minutes. Remove pan from oven and reduce temperature to 325°.

Filling: Beat cream cheese until smooth. Gradually add sugar, beating until fluffy. and light. Add maple syrup, cognac, ginger, cinnamon and nutmeg. Blend well. Add eggs, one at a time, beating well after each addition. Add cream and pumpkin and mix well. Pour filling into prepared crust. Bake for 45 minutes. Turn off oven. Do not open door during baking time or for 1 hour after oven is turned off. Remove cake.

Topping: Preheat oven to 425°. Blend sour cream, sugar, maple syrup and cognac. Spread over cake and bake for 10 minutes. Allow to cool at room temperature for about 1 hour. Arrange almonds in a ring around the perimeter of cake. Chill at least 3 hours before removing sides of pan. May be frozen. 12 servings

**Cookbook Committee**

---

**MICROWAVE HINT**

Soften lumpy brown sugar by placing in a dish with a slice of apple. Cook for 15 seconds or until soft.

# Brown Sugar Pound Cake

1 cup Crisco
½ cup butter
1 box light brown sugar
½ cup white sugar
5 eggs
3 cups cake flour
½ teaspoon salt
½ teaspoon baking powder
1 cup milk
1 teaspoon maple flavoring
1 teaspoon vanilla flavoring
1 cup chopped nuts
ICING:
½ stick margarine
½ cup dark brown sugar
2 Tablespoons milk
1½ cups confectioners sugar

Cream Crisco, butter and sugars together; add eggs one at a time and beat well after each. Sift dry ingredients together and add alternately with milk. Stir in flavorings and nuts. Bake in a greased and floured tube pan at 325° for 1 hour and 15 minutes.

Icing: Bring first 3 ingredients to a boil in saucepan. Remove from heat and add confectioners sugar.

**Jeneal Benton (Mrs. Gene R.)**

# Mother's Cream Cheese Cake
A fine textured moist cake

3 cups sugar
1½ cups butter, softened
6 eggs
1 (8-ounce) package cream
    cheese, softened
3 cups flour
1 teaspoon vanilla
1 teaspoon butter flavoring

Cream butter and sugar. Add eggs one at a time. Blend in cream cheese. Add flour and mix well. Add vanilla and butter flavoring. Bake in a tube pan at 325° for 1½ hours. Check for doneness after 1 hour. Do not overbake.

**Ann Benton**

# Fresh Apple Cake

*Crunchy and Different*

2 cups sugar
3 cups flour
1 teaspoon soda
1 teaspoon salt
1 teaspoon cinnamon
1½ cups Wesson oil
3 eggs
1 teaspoon vanilla
3 cups chopped red apples
  (do not peel)
1 cup chopped nuts

Sift together dry ingredients; add oil, eggs and vanilla. Stir in the apples and nuts. Grease, but do not flour a tube pan. Bake at 350° for 1 hour. Cool 10 minutes in pan and turn out on plate. Serve with sweetened whipped cream.

**Melva Jansen (Mrs. Klaus)**

# Carrot Cake

1 package good quality spice
  cake mix
1 package (4 serving size)
  vanilla instant pudding mix
¼ cup water
½ cup cooking oil
1 cup sour cream
4 eggs
1 cup chopped walnuts or
  pecans
3 cups grated carrots (can be
  grated in blender)

Preheat oven to 350°. Combine all ingredients except nuts and carrots. Mix on low speed briefly, just to blend. Beat at medium speed 1 minute. Stop and scrape down sides of bowl, then beat for 1 minute more. Fold in carrots and nuts. Pour batter into well greased and floured Bundt or tube pan. Bake at 350° for 40-60 minutes, or until the cake springs back when touched lightly with finger, towards the center. Let cool on rack in pan for 15 minutes. Turn out onto serving plate. Glaze if desired.

**Susan L. Kreitzman**
*The Nutrition Cookbook*
*Harcourt, Brace, Jovanovitch*

# Pineapple Cake

**CAKE:**
2 cups sugar
3 eggs
1 20-ounce can crushed pineapple (sweet, in syrup) with juice
2 cups all-purpose flour
1 cup chopped nuts (pecans)
Dash salt
1 teaspoon vanilla
2 teaspoons baking soda (add last)
**FROSTING:**
1½ cups confectioners sugar
1 (8 ounce) package cream cheese, softened
½ cup butter, softened
1 teaspoon vanilla

Cake: Beat or mix ingredients by hand. Spread into greased 9 x 13-inch pan. Bake at 350° for 40-45 minutes.

Frosting: Mix with electric beater. Frost cake while warm. Refrigerate before cutting.

**Dannie Martin (Mrs. Fielder)**

# Tia Maria Pecan Cake

Aunt Mary's Favorite Pecan Cake

9 large eggs separated (7 yolks 2 yolks, 9 whites)
1½ cups sugar
⅓ cup orange juice
2½ cups pecan meal (finely ground pecans)
⅓ cup flour
**CREAM FILLING:**
¾ cup sweet butter
2 squares bitter chocolate
2 egg yolks
1½ cups confectioners sugar
⅓ cup Tia Maria (any coffee liqueur)
Pecans (optional)

Beat egg whites until stiff and add ½ cup sugar. Beat 7 yolks with 1 cup sugar until thick. Add orange juice to yolks and beat until thick again. Fold yolk mixture slowly into whites; then fold in pecan meal. Sift flour over mixture and fold in. Pour into three well greased and slightly floured 9-inch cake pans. Bake 375° for 15-18 minutes till edges loosen.

Cream Filling: Melt chocolate slowly, put in small bowl. Add butter, yolks, sugar. Beat and add the liqueur slowly until light and fluffy. When layers are cold, frost cake. Cover with pecan pieces or whole pecans.

**Susan Barton (Mrs. David L.)**

# Napoleon Cake

*Napoleon may even have enjoyed Waterloo if he'd had this*

1 frozen loaf pound cake (store bought)
1 (6-ounce) package chocolate chips
⅛ cup boiling water
⅛ cup brandy
4 egg yolks
1 teaspoon vanilla
½ cup butter, softened

Slice pound cake horizontally into 5 or 6 slices. Frost layers with following mixture: In blender or food processor place chocolate chips, water and brandy. Blend 20 seconds on high. Add egg yolks, vanilla and butter. Blend. Frost cake. Store in refrigerator. May be frozen.

**Pat Barton (Mrs. William L.)**

# Kim's Poppy Seed Cake

*The sherry makes the difference*

1 package good quality yellow cake mix
1 package (4 serving size) vanilla instant pudding mix
2 ounces poppy seeds
4 eggs
1 cup cooking oil
1 cup cream sherry
2 teaspoons vanilla extract

Combine all ingredients in bowl of electric mixer. Mix on low speed briefly to blend ingredients. Beat at medium speed for 1 minute. Stop and scrape down sides of bowl; then beat for 1 minute more. Pour batter in well greased and floured bundt or tube pan. Bake at 350° for 40 minutes to an hour, until cake springs back when pressed with finger near the center. Let cool in pan on rack for 15 minutes. Turn on serving plate. Glaze if desired.

**Susan L. Krietzman**
*The Nutrition Cookbook*
*Harcourt Brace Jovanivitch, Inc.*

# Pumpkin Spice Cake

1 package spice cake mix
1 cup canned pumpkin
½ cup salad oil
1 small package vanilla instant pudding
3 eggs
1 teaspoon cinnamon
½ cup water

Mix ingredients. Pour into greased and floured Bundt pan. Bake 45 minutes at 350°. Let sit in pan 15 minutes before removing.

**Cookbook Committee**

## Chocolate Town Cupcakes
So chocolatey, you need not even frost them!

½ cup butter
1 cup granulated sugar
1 teaspoon vanilla
4 eggs
1¼ cups all-purpose flour
¾ teaspoon baking soda
1½ cups (1-pound can) Hershey's chocolate flavored syrup

Cream the butter, sugar and vanilla until light and fluffy. Add the eggs, one at a time, beating well after each addition. Combine the flour and baking soda. Add alternately with the chocolate syrup to the creamed mixture. Pour the batter into paper-lined muffin cups filling each ½ full. Bake at 375° for 20 to 25 minutes. Frost with your favorite icing. 30 servings

**Peggy M. Youngblood (Mrs. Robert M.)**

## Shawneetown Chocolate Cake

1 pound box dark brown sugar
3 eggs
2 squares unsweetened chocolate
½ cup butter
2 cups flour
1 teaspoon soda
½ cup buttermilk
1 cup boiling water

Mix sugar and eggs. Melt chocolate and butter in double boiler. Combine sugar-egg mixture with chocolate-butter mixture. Sift flour and soda and add to mixture. Add buttermilk and boiling water. Mix until well blended (batter will be thin). Pour into 2 greased and floured 8-inch square pans. Bake at 350° for 20-25 minutes or until firm. Frost with a white butter icing. Chill 1 cake and put the other in the freezer for next week.

**Edna Snider (Mrs. George E.)**

HINT ■■■■■■■■■■■■■■■■■■■■■■■■

Improve the taste of raisins by soaking them overnight in orange juice or sherry. Drain before using. They will be plump and delicious.

# Hummell Futter
"Heavenly Food"
Sinfully rich, simple and divine

2 eggs, beaten
1 cup sugar
1 teaspoon baking powder
1 Tablespoon flour
1 (8-ounce) package whole
   pitted dates, chopped
2 cups pecans, coarsely
   chopped
Sliced bananas
Sliced oranges
1 cup heavy cream, whipped

Gradually add sugar to well beaten eggs. Blend in flour and baking powder. Stir in dates and nuts. Spread in a greased 9-inch pan and bake at 350° for 30 minutes. When cool, crumble on a small tray or in individual dishes. To serve, cover with sliced bananas and oranges. Top with whipped cream. 8-10 servings

Judy H. Lewis (Mrs. William)

# Gingerbread with Maple Cream
An old-fashioned favorite with a new-fashioned topping

GINGERBREAD:
½ cup sugar
½ cup butter
1 egg, beaten
1 cup molasses
1 cup hot water
2½ cups sifted flour
1½ teaspoons soda
1 teaspoon cinnamon
1 teaspoon ginger
½ teaspoon powdered cloves
½ teaspoon salt
1½ cups raisins
MAPLE CREAM TOPPING:
1 cup sour cream
¼ cup pure maple syrup

Cream butter and sugar; add beaten egg and molasses. Sift all dry ingredients together and add to creamed mixture. Add hot water and beat until smooth. Fold in raisins. Pour in well buttered 9 x 13-inch baking pan and bake in preheated 350° oven until tests done. Cut and serve while warm (good cold, too) and top with maple-sour cream mixture.

Barbara R. Johnson (Mrs. Larry)

# Lemon Pecan Cake
A delicious light fruit cake!

1 pound margarine
2 cups sugar
6 eggs, separated
2 ounces pure lemon extract
4 cups all-purpose flour
1 box white raisins
½ pound candied cherries
½ pound candied pineapple
1 teaspoon baking powder
1 quart chopped pecans
　(or more)
Dash salt

Cream margarine and sugar. Add beaten egg yolks, then extract. Add baking powder to flour. Then add fruit and pecans to flour and mix well. Beat egg whites until stiff. Add butter and sugar mixture to flour mixture and mix well. Add beaten egg whites and fold in thoroughly by hand. Bake at 250° for 2 hours or until done. Bake in generously greased large tube pan or 2 smaller pans. Other fruits may be added, or for a moister cake add 1 cup of orange marmalade or applesauce.

**Maureen T. Vandiver (Mrs. Roy W.)**

# Million Dollar Bourbon Cake
A favorite of a French chef we know, from his wife's collection

2 teaspoons nutmeg (Freshly
　grated is best)
1 cup bourbon
4 cups pecans, coarsely
　chopped
2 cups raisins
3 cups flour, sifted
2 teaspoons baking powder
1 cup butter, softened
2 cups plus 4 teaspoons sugar
6-7 eggs (depending on size),
　separated
Dash salt

Soak nutmeg in bourbon at least 15 minutes. Put pecans and raisins in a bowl with 1 cup sifted flour. Combine remaining 2 cups flour with baking powder and sift twice more. Cream butter and sugar; add egg yolks 1 at a time and beat until smooth. Add flour and bourbon alternately; blend well. Fold in raisin-nut-flour mixture. Beat egg whites and salt until stiff. Gently fold in egg whites. Put batter in a 9-inch tube pan which has been greased and lined with wax paper. Bake at 325° for 1 hour and 15 minutes. Let stand 30 minutes before removing.

**Rainey Vivier (Mrs. Pierre)**

# Fruit Cake
A rich moist cake; almost like a confection

½ pound figs
1 pound candied cherries (half red, half green)
1 pound candied pineapple
1 pound freshly grated or frozen coconut
1 pound white raisins
3 pounds pecans (3 quarts)
1 package dates
1 pound butter
2 pounds sugar (4 cups)
1 dozen eggs
2 pounds (8 cups) plain flour
1 Tablespoon baking powder
1 teaspoon salt
2 Tablespoons nutmeg
2 Tablespoons cinnamon
2 Tablespoons vanilla

Butter mixing pan well (choose a large utensil that cake can be baked in, such as a deep roasting pan). Finely chop fruit and nuts by hand or in food processor. Cream butter and sugar until fluffy. Add 1 egg at a time, beating well after each addition. Add spices to flour. Add half of flour-spice mixture to creamed mixture and blend well. Use remaining flour-spice mixture over fruit and nuts, mixing to coat well. Add fruit and nuts to batter and mix. Bake for 1½ hours at 325° in same pan as mixed in. Remove from oven at 15 minute intervals and stir well with long handled spoon, counting stirring time as part of cooking time. When batter has been cooked and stirred for 1½ hours, pack in shallow pans lined with foil and seal. Do not overcook. Mixture will not be firm. Cake keeps indefinitely, always stays moist. 6 loaves

**Virginia Kelly (Mrs. R. L.)**
*Wrens, Georgia*

# White Fruit Cake
Make in fall; serve in winter

2 quarts chopped pecans
1 pound candied cherries
1 pound candied pineapple
1 pound coconut
1 box white raisins
2 cans condensed milk

Cut and mix fruit and nuts with 1 can condensed milk; stir. Pack firmly in oiled and floured tube pan. Pour other can of condensed milk over mixture in pan. Bake at 350° for 1 hour. Make this cake in early fall, wrap in cheese cloth and store in cool dark place. Pour ¼ cup bourbon or rum over cake once a month. By December the cake is really delicious.

**Mrs. Ivy Lee Snipes**

# Food Processor Pastry

2 cups all-purpose flour
1 teaspoon salt
2/3 cup unsalted butter
1 egg yolk in 1/4 cup water
1 teaspoon sugar

Put all ingredients in bowl of processor. Process on and off to mix, then turn on until a ball forms, about 40 seconds. Refrigerate 2-3 hours or freeze 30-45 minutes before working dough.
1 (10-inch) shell

# Coconut Cream Pie

1 (10-inch) baked pie shell
2/3 cup sugar
1/4 cup cornstarch
1/2 teaspoon salt
3 cups milk
4 egg yolks beaten
2 Tablespoons butter
4 teaspoons vanilla
1 (10-ounce) flaked coconut
1/2 cup heavy cream, whipped

In saucepan, stir together sugar, cornstarch and salt. Blend milk and egg yolks and gradually stir into sugar mixture. Cook over medium heat, stirring constantly until mixture thickens and comes to boil. Boil and stir one minute. Remove from heat and blend in butter and vanilla. Add 3/4 can of coconut. Pour into pie shell. Refrigerate. Before serving, top with whipped cream (you may sweeten this to taste) and sprinkle with the rest of the coconut.

**Rosamond Buckler (Mrs. Robert)**

# Cottage Coconut Pie

3 eggs
1 cup sugar
1/2 cup butter, melted
1/2 cup cottage cheese
1 small can coconut
1 teaspoon vanilla
1 unbaked pie shell

In mixer or food processor, beat eggs; add sugar, butter, cottage cheese, coconut and vanilla. Mix well and pour into unbaked pie shell. Bake 1 hour at 300° until golden brown.
8 servings

**Jane H. Nardone (Mrs. A. Joseph, Jr.)**

## Peach Custard Pie

1 unbaked (9-inch) pie shell
6-8 large peaches
3 eggs
1 cup sugar
pinch salt

Peel peaches and cut into large slices; place in pie shell. Beat eggs, sugar and salt together and pour over peaches. Bake at 400° for 15 minutes. Reduce heat to 325° and continue baking for another 45 minutes. Serve warm or cool. 6 servings

**Jeanine Andrews (Mrs. Edward B.)**

## Pumpkin Praline Chiffon Pie
This could become a new tradition at your Thanksgiving table

1 (10-inch) pie shell, unbaked
6 Tablespoons butter
⅓ cup light brown sugar
½ cup chopped walnuts
1½ cups canned eggnog
¾ cup sugar
2 envelopes unflavored gelatin
1 teaspoon cinnamon
½ teaspoon ginger
¼ teaspoon nutmeg
3 eggs, separated
1 (16 ounce) can pumpkin
¼ teaspoon cream of tartar
1 cup heavy cream, whipped

Several hours before serving, while your pie shell partially bakes, cream butter and brown sugar. Stir in walnuts and spread on bottom of partially baked pie shell. Bake 5 minutes longer until shell is golden brown. Combine ½ cup sugar, gelatin, cinnamon, ginger and nutmeg in medium saucepan. Beat in egg yolks and eggnog. Heat, stirring constantly, over low heat until gelatin is dissolved. Stir in pumpkin. Pour in large bowl. Chill stirring often until mixture mounds on spoon. Beat egg whites with cream of tartar until they hold peaks. Fold into pumpkin mixture; also fold in whipped cream. Spoon into crust. Chill several hours until firm. Garnish with walnuts and cream if desired. 6-8 servings

# Holiday Pie
Even those who don't care for mince pie
will love this creamy combination

1 cup Non-Such mincemeat
1 large tart unpeeled apple,
  diced fine
3 Tablespoons sherry, brandy
  or rum
1 cup sugar
3 eggs, beaten
2 cups canned pumpkin
1 teaspoon cinnamon
¼ teaspoon ginger
1 Tablespoon melted butter
½ teaspoon salt
1 teaspoon allspice
1 cup milk
1 (9 or 10-inch) pie shell,
  unbaked

Mix in a bowl mincemeat, apple and sherry, brandy or rum. Combine in a separate bowl sugar, eggs, pumpkin, cinnamon, ginger, butter, salt, allspice and milk. Place mincemeat mixture in bottom of pie shell. Pour pumpkin mixture over mincemeat mixture. Bake at 350° for 45 minutes until firm. Serve plain or with dollop of whipped cream flavored with brandy, sherry or rum. 8 servings

**Mrs. Charles A. Neubauer**

# Apple Cream Pie
An old standby with a new twist

⅔ cup sugar
2 Tablespoons flour
⅛ teaspoon salt
1 cup sour cream
1 egg, slightly beaten
1 teaspoon vanilla
3-4 cups chopped tart apples
1 (9-inch) pie shell, unbaked
TOPPING:
½ cup sugar
¾ cup flour
⅓ cup butter
1 teaspoon cinnamon (optional)

Combine sugar, flour and salt. Add sour cream, egg and vanilla and beat until smooth. Fold in apples and pour into unbaked pie shell.
Topping: Combine flour and sugar and cut in the butter. Sprinkle over pie and bake at 425° for 25-30 minutes.
6-8 servings

**Mrs. Charles A. Neubauer**

## Pecan Pie

1 cup sugar
½ cup melted butter (no
    substitutions)
1 cup light corn syrup
4 eggs, beaten
1 teaspoon vanilla extract
¼ teaspoon salt
1 (9-inch) unbaked pie shell
1-1½ cups pecan halves

Combine sugar, butter and corn syrup. Stirring constantly, cook over low heat until sugar is dissolved, about 20 minutes. This is a slow process. Cool. Add eggs, salt and vanilla. Mix well. Pour filling into pie shell and arrange pecan halves in a pin wheel design; start at outer edge and work to the center. Bake at 325° for 50-55 minutes. 8 servings

**Dunja S. Awbrey (Mrs. James J.)**

## Amelia Island Mud Pie

CRUST:
21 Oreo cookies, crushed
6 Tablespoons butter, melted
FILLING:
1 quart chocolate ice cream,
    softened
2 Tablespoons instant Sanka
    coffee
2 Tablespoons ground coffee
2 Tablespoons brandy
2 Tablespoons coffee liqueur
1 cup heavy cream, whipped
1 (12-ounce) jar fudge sauce
    (or your favorite homemade)
Toasted almonds and cherries
    to garnish

Mix cookie crumbs with butter. Press into 9 or 10-inch pie pan. Freeze.
Filling: Whip ice cream with coffee, brandy and liqueur. Whip cream, add 4 Tablespoons whipped cream to ice cream mixture and continue to whip. Spread in frozen pie shell. Freeze until very hard. Dip knife in hot water, spread fudge sauce on top of frozen pie working quickly. Cover with whipped cream. Garnish with toasted almonds and cherries. Freeze. 8 servings

**Sharon Hooten (Mrs. James)**

# "The" Strawberry Pie

1 (9-inch) pastry shell, baked
2 cups strawberries
3 Tablespoons cornstarch
¾ cup sugar
2 Tablespoons lemon juice
2 cups whole or halved
    strawberries

In saucepan crush 2 cups strawberries, cornstarch and sugar. Cook, stirring constantly, until mixture boils. Boil 2 minutes. Cool slightly and fold in lemon juice and halved strawberries. Pour into crust. Chill. Serve topped with whipped cream. 6 servings

**Hazel Mattingley**

# Toffee Ice Cream Pie

18 vanilla or brown edge
    wafers
½ gallon vanilla ice cream,
    slightly softened
1 cup chopped toffee bar
    (Heath Bar)
1½ cups sugar
1 cup evaporated milk
¼ cup butter or margarine
¼ cup light corn syrup
Dash salt

Line bottom and sides of 9-inch buttered pie plate with wafers. Spoon half of ice cream into shell. Sprinkle ½ cup of chopped toffee candy over ice cream. Spoon remainder of ice cream over toffee layer. Store in freezer until serving time.

Sauce: Prepare toffee sauce by combining sugar, milk, butter, corn syrup and salt in a saucepan. Bring to a boil over low heat; boil 1 minute. Remove from heat and stir in remaining toffee candy; cool, stirring occasionally. Serve pie topped with cool or warm sauce. 8 servings

**Joan M. Adams (Mrs. John P., Jr.)**

# French Apple Cobbler
A delicious change from the standard apple pie

**FILLING:**
5 cups peeled, sliced tart
   apples
¾ cup sugar
2 Tablespoons flour
½ teaspoon cinnamon
¼ teaspoon salt
1 teaspoon vanilla extract
¼ cup water
1 Tablespoon margarine,
   softened
**BATTER:**
½ cup sifted plain flour
½ cup sugar
½ teaspoon baking powder
¼ teaspoon salt
2 Tablespoons soft margarine
1 egg, slightly beaten

Filling: In medium bowl, combine apples, sugar, flour, cinnamon, salt, vanilla and water. Turn into a 9-inch square pan. Dot apples with margarine.

Batter: Combine all batter ingredients. Beat with wooden spoon until smooth. Drop batter in 9 portions on apples, spacing evenly. Batter will spread during baking. Bake 35-40 minutes at 375° or until apples are fork tender, and crust is golden brown. Serve warm with cream.
6-8 servings

**Mrs. William Schley Howard**

# Chocolate Chess Pie
Everyone's favorite

½ cup butter
1½ ounces unsweetened
   chocolate
1 cup light brown sugar, firmly
   packed
½ cup granulated sugar
1 Tablespoon flour
2 eggs, well beaten
2 Tablespoons milk
1 teaspoon vanilla
1 (8-inch) unbaked pie shell

In saucepan melt butter and chocolate over moderate heat. Remove pan from heat and add brown sugar and granulated sugar mixed with flour. Beat in eggs, milk and vanilla. Prick bottom of pie shell with fork and bake at 400° for 10 minutes or until it is lightly colored. Cool. Pour mixture into shell and bake at 325° for 35-40 minutes or until filling is set. Hint: Pie may be prepared the day before using. Serve topped with whipped cream or ice cream sprinkled with chocolate shavings for a lovely dessert. 6-8 servings

**Nancy Kirby (Mrs. Jeff D., III)**

# Almond Macaroons
Hard to find, but easy to make

1 (8-ounce) can almond paste
¾ cup sugar
2 egg whites, unbeaten
¼ cup all-purpose flour, sifted
Dash salt

Beat paste to soften. Beat in sugar and unbeaten egg whites gradually. Mix thoroughly. Add flour and salt and mix well. Drop by teaspoonfuls onto lightly greased cookie sheet. Bake at 300° for 25-30 minutes. Remove onto racks immediately or these will stick. These freeze well.
3 dozen

# Butter Pecan Turtles
Chew these turtles slowly to make them last!

CRUST:
2 cups all-purpose flour
1 cup firmly packed brown
   sugar
½ cup softened butter
1 cup pecan pieces
CARAMEL LAYER:
⅔ cup butter
½ cup brown sugar
TOPPING:
1 (6-ounce) package chocolate
   chips

Mix crust ingredients with electric mixer until particles are fine. Line pan with foil before putting crust into it to make removal easier. Pat into 9 x 13 x 2-inch pan. Sprinkle pecans over crust. Combine caramel layer ingredients in saucepan and cook, stirring until entire surface boils. Boil ½-1 minute until ingredients combine, stirring constantly. Pour over crust. Bake at 350° for 18-20 minutes. Remove from oven and sprinkle with chocolate chips, spreading slightly by swirling. Cool completely. Cut into bars.

**Mrs. James P. McMahan**

## Ardy's Blonde Brownies

⅔ cup butter
2 cups brown sugar
2 teaspoons vanilla
3 eggs
1 teaspoon baking powder
1 teaspoon salt
2 cups flour
1 cup chopped nuts
1 (6-ounce) package chocolate
   chips

Melt butter in saucepan and remove from heat. Add remaining ingredients one at a time. Pour into a 9 x 13-inch pan. Bake at 350° for 35-40 minutes.

**Barbara R. Johnson (Mrs. Larry)**

## Christmas Spritz
Make these the first week in December;
by Christmas they will be buttery delicious

1½ cups unsalted butter
1 cup sugar
1 egg
1 Tablespoon milk
1 teaspoon vanilla
½ teaspoon almond extract
4 cups all purpose flour, sifted
1 teaspoon baking powder
½ teaspoon grated lemon peel

Cream butter and sugar; add egg, milk, vanilla and almond extract, beat well. Sift together flour and baking powder and add to creamed mixture; add lemon peel. Force dough through a cookie press onto ungreased cookie sheet in the shape of an "S". Bake at 400° for 8-10 minutes until light golden brown. About 9 dozen

**Melva Jansen (Mrs. Klaus)**

## London Tea Cakes

¾ cup butter
¼ cup sugar
3 egg yolks
¼ cup water
1½ cups flour
½ teaspoon soda
½ teaspoon salt
½ teaspoon vanilla
1 (12-ounce) jar raspberry jam
2 egg whites
½ cup sugar
Sliced almonds or ground
   pecans

Cream butter and sugar; add egg yolks and water. Combine flour, soda and salt; add to mixture. Add vanilla. Spread thin on jelly roll pan. Bake 10 minutes at 350°. Spread raspberry jam over. Make meringue with egg whites and sugar and spread over jam. Sprinkle with nuts; return to oven to brown. Cool and cut in squares.

# Oatmeal Lace Cookies
These are a nice accompaniment for a sorbet

½ cup flour
¼ teaspoon baking powder
½ cup sugar
¼ teaspoon nutmeg (optional)
½ cup quick cooking oats
2 Tablespoons heavy cream
⅓ cup melted butter
1 Tablespoon vanilla
2 Tablespoons white corn
   syrup

Sift together flour, baking powder and sugar. Add oats, cream, butter, vanilla and corn syrup. Mix until well blended. Drop by ¼ teaspoons onto ungreased cookie sheet allowing 3-4 inches between as these cookies spread. Bake at 375° for 4-6 minutes until lightly browned. Remove from oven and let stand 30 seconds before removing from pan. If cookies become too hard to remove, return to oven for a few seconds to soften. 4 dozen

**Jean Schmidt (Mrs. James C.)**

# Chocolate Macaroons

2½ Tablespoons margarine
4 squares unsweetened
   chocolate
2 cups sugar
4 eggs
2 teaspoons vanilla
2¾ cups all-purpose flour
3½ teaspoons baking powder
1 cup confectioners sugar

In a saucepan over low heat, melt: margarine, sugar and chocolate and mix to a smooth paste. Transfer to a large bowl and add eggs one at a time stirring well after each addition. Add vanilla. Sift flour and baking powder and add to mixture. Put confectioners sugar in a pie plate. Drop cookie mixture by teaspoonfuls into sugar and roll to form 1-inch balls (If mixture is too soft to form balls, add a little more flour.) Place balls 1 inch apart on a greased cookie sheet and bake for 8 minutes at 350°. Do not overcook. Cookies will still be soft. Allow to cool completely and remove from sheet with a spatula. 4 dozen

**Peggy P. Weitnauer (Mrs. John H., Jr.)**

# Cowboy Cookies

1 cup shortening
1 cup brown sugar
1 cup white sugar
2 eggs
2½ cups flour
1 teaspoon soda
½ teaspoon baking powder
½ teaspoon salt
2 teaspoons vanilla
1 (12 ounce) package
    chocolate chips
2 cups oats
1 cup chopped nuts

Cream shortening and sugar. Add eggs. Sift dry ingredients and add to shortening mixture. Mix well and add other ingredients. Stir until evenly mixed. Drop by teaspoonfuls onto greased cookie sheet. Bake at 350° for 12 minutes. May be frozen. 7 dozen

**Elizabeth Crotwell (Mrs. Wm. V.)**
*Birmingham, Alabama*

# Smackeroos

½ cup shortening
1 cup brown sugar
1 egg
1 cup flour
¼ teaspoon salt
1 teaspoon vanilla
24 maraschino cherries

Blend shortening and sugar until smooth. Add egg and blend. Add flour, salt and vanilla; blend well. Fill small muffin tins two-thirds full. Put cherry in center of each. Bake at 375° for 12-15 minutes. Variation: Substitute date or nut if desired. May be frozen. 24 small muffins

**Karen DeFazio (Mrs. Richard A.)**

# Drop Sugar Cookies

1 cup butter
1½ cups confectioners sugar,
    sifted
1 egg
1 teaspoon vanilla
¼ teaspoon salt
2½ cups flour
1 teaspoon baking soda
1 teaspoon cream of tartar
1 cup pecans, chopped
    (optional)

Cream butter and confectioners sugar well. Add egg and vanilla. Sift dry ingredients and add to creamed mixture. (Add nuts if desired.) Chill dough overnight. Drop by teaspoonfuls onto greased cookie sheet and bake at 350° for 8-10 minutes. Remove from oven and sprinkle sugar on still warm cookies. 6-7 dozen

**Kaye Waters (Mrs. Allan)**

# Old Fashioned Raisin Squares

1 cup water
1 cup seedless raisins
½ cup salad oil
1 egg beaten
1 cup sugar
1¾ cups all-purpose flour
¼ teaspoon salt
1 teaspoon ground allspice
1 teaspoon ground nutmeg
½ teaspoon ground cloves
½ cup chopped walnuts or
    pecans
Powdered sugar (optional)

Combine water and raisins; bring to a boil. Add salad oil; cool to lukewarm. Add remaining ingredients except powdered sugar, blending well. Spoon batter into a greased 9 x 13 x 2-inch pan. Bake at 375° for 25 minutes. Sprinkle with powdered sugar, if desired. Cut into 2 inch squares. 2 dozen

Lucia H. Sizemore (Mrs. Thomas H., III)

# Pecan Tassies

CHEESE PASTRY:
1 (3-ounce) package cream
    cheese, softened
½ cup butter, softened
1 cup sifted all-purpose flour
PECAN FILLING:
1 egg
¾ cup brown sugar
1 teaspoon vanilla
2 teaspoons butter
Dash salt
⅓ cup coarsely broken pecans
24 pecan halves

Cheese Pastry: Blend cream cheese and butter; stir in flour. Chill slightly about 1 hour. Shape in 2 dozen 1 inch balls. Place in tiny ungreased 1¾ inch muffin cups. Press dough against bottoms and sides of cups.

Pecan Filling: Beat together egg, sugar, butter, vanilla and salt, just until smooth. Sprinkle broken pecans in pastry lined cups; add egg mixture over pecans and top with pecan halves. Bake at 325° for 25 minutes or until filling is set and crust is golden. Remove from oven; run sharp knife around edges to loosen any filling which has stuck to tin. Cool and remove from tins. Hint: These may be frozen. 6-8 servings

Jean Schmidt (Mrs. James C.)

## Cheese Cake Tarts
Beautiful sweet for a coffee

1 box vanilla wafers, crushed
2 pounds cream cheese,
    softened
⅓ teaspoon salt
1 cup granulated sugar
4 eggs, well beaten
1 teaspoon lemon juice or
    vanilla extract
1 can fruit pie filling

Use miniature muffin tins and paper liners. Place 1 teaspoon vanilla wafer crumbs in the bottom of each tin. Beat cream cheese, salt, sugar, eggs and flavoring together. Fill cups ¾ full. Bake at 350° for 12-15 minutes. Allow to cool. Decorate tops with pie filling of your choice using small amount of fruit on each one. Hint: Tarts may be frozen before adding toppings. 75 tarts

**Nancy Kirby (Mrs. Jefferson D., III)**
**Ann McCrory (Mrs. Charles O.)**

## Toffee Bars
These are wonderful served with fresh fruit

2 cups plain flour
1 cup brown sugar (packed)
½ cup butter
⅔ cup butter
½ cup brown sugar
1-2 cups whole pecans
2 cups chocolate chips

At least 8 hours before serving, mix together flour, brown sugar and butter with fingers. Press this crust mixture into an ungreased 9 x 13-inch pan. Combine butter and brown sugar in saucepan and bring to rolling boil; pour this hot mixture over crust. Sprinkle pecans over all this and bake at 350° for 20 minutes or until brown and bubbling. Remove from oven and sprinkle with chocolate chips. Let melt about 10 minutes; then spread with spatula. Do not put back in oven. After mixture cools, if chocolate is still sticky, put in refrigerator for about 15 minutes and chocolate will set up. 20 bars

**Margaret D. Stent (Mrs. F. Terry)**

# Hawaiian Bars
Excellent for a coffee or a buffet

¼ pound butter or margarine
2 cups white sugar
4 large eggs
1½ cups all-purpose flour
½ teaspoon salt
½ teaspoon baking soda
1 (20-ounce) can crushed
  pineapple, well drained
1 cup chopped nuts

Melt butter in pan; cool slightly. Add sugar. Beat eggs until thick and creamy. Add butter and sugar. Beat well. Sift dry ingredients; add to above mixture. Add pineapple and nuts. Bake on greased 15 x 11-inch cookie sheet with sides at 350° for 30-45 minutes until done. Makes 36 large bars about ½ inch thick. Store in airtight container. 36 bars

**Alice I. Noble (Mrs. David A.)**

# Buckeyes
These taste exactly like chocolate covered peanut butter cups

1½ cups creamy peanut butter
½ cup softened butter
1 pound confectioners sugar
1 teaspoon vanilla
1 (12-ounce) package semi-
  sweet chocolate chips
¼-½ block parrafin

In food processor or by hand, combine peanut butter, butter and sugar. Mix thoroughly. Transfer mixture to a large bowl and continue mixing until mixture can be shaped to form balls. Add ¼ cup water if needed. Melt chocolate and parrafin over low heat. Shape peanut butter mixture into 1 inch balls. Pierce each ball with a toothpick and dip into chocolate mixture to partially cover. Set aside on wax paper until hardened.

**Barbara Ender (Mrs. Steven)**
*Watkinsville, Georgia*

# Congo Squares

1 cup butter
1 box brown sugar
3 eggs
2¾ cups flour
1 cup nuts
1 (6 ounce) package chocolate
  chips

Melt butter and add brown sugar. Add eggs one at a time beating well. Add flour. Mix well and add nuts and chocolate chips. Bake in a greased and floured 9 x 13-inch pan at 350° for 30-45 minutes. Cool and cut into squares.

**Mrs. Edna Peacock**

# Cheese Cake Cookies
Cheese cake lovers love cheese cake cookies!

⅓ cup butter
⅓ cup brown sugar, packed
1 cup flour
½ cup walnuts
¼ cup sugar
1 (8-ounce) package cream
   cheese, softened
1 egg
2 Tablespoons milk
1 Tablespoon lemon juice
½ teaspoon vanilla

Heat oven to 350°. Cream butter with brown sugar. Add flour and walnuts; mix to make crumbs. Reserve 1 cup for topping. Press remainder into bottom of an 8-inch square pan. Bake at 350° for 12-15 minutes until lightly browned. Blend sugar with cream cheese until smooth. Add eggs, milk, lemon juice and vanilla. Beat well. Spread over baked crust. Sprinkle with remaining crumb mixture. Bake at 350° for 25 minutes. Cool. Cut into 2-inch squares. Store in the refrigerator.
16 squares

**Maddy Kligora (Mrs. H. John)**

# Ranger Cookies

1 cup margarine
1 cup brown sugar
1 cup white sugar
2 eggs
1 teaspoon vanilla
2 cups sifted flour
1 teaspoon soda
½ teaspoon baking powder
½ teaspoon salt
2 cups oatmeal
2 cups corn flakes
1 cup coconut

Cream margarine and sugars. Beat in eggs and vanilla. Mix flour, soda, baking powder and salt. Stir into creamed mixture. Combine oatmeal, corn flakes and coconut; mix well and add to first mixture. Roll in small balls; press down on ungreased cookie sheet with a fork. Bake at 350° for 10-12 minutes. May be frozen.
75-85 cookies

**Jane O. Duckworth (Mrs. E. J.)**

# Lemon Squares

1 cup butter
2 cups flour
½ cup powdered sugar
¼ teaspoon salt
4 eggs
2 cups sugar
4 Tablespoons flour
5 Tablespoons lemon juice

Blend first four ingredients and press into a 9 x 13-inch pan. Bake 15 minutes at 350°. Do not let top brown. Cool 5 minutes. Beat together remaining ingredients and pour over pastry. Bake at 350° for 25 minutes. Remove from oven and while warm, sprinkle with powdered sugar. When cool cut into squares.

**Joy Butler**

# Amaretto Kisses
Almond lovers delight

1 (6-ounce) package chocolate
  chips
½ cup sugar
3 Tablespoons light corn syrup
½ cup chocolate amaretto
  liqueur (or regular amaretto)
2½ cups finely crushed vanilla
  wafers
1 cup finely chopped pecans

Melt chocolate in bowl of double boiler over hot, not boiling, water, stirring until chocolate is melted. Remove from heat; stir in sugar and corn syrup. Add liqueur and blend well. Combine nuts and vanilla wafer crumbs in bowl and stir in chocolate mixture. Mix well. Form into 1 inch balls; roll in granulated sugar. Store in airtight container several days before serving.

# Birds Nest Cookies

½ cup butter, creamed
¼ cup brown sugar
1 egg yolk
1 cup flour
1 egg white
1 cup pecan meal or ground
  pecans
Jam—strawberry, blackberry,
  blueberry—your choice

Beat butter, brown sugar and egg yolk together. Add flour. Form balls and push flat. Beat egg white lightly. Roll cookie in egg white; then roll in ground nuts. Bake for 8 minutes at 350°. Make a dent with a thimble in center of each cookie and fill with dot of jam or jelly. Return to oven and bake 10 more minutes. Store in an air-tight container. 2 dozen

**Susan Barton (Mrs. David L.)**

# Granny Squares
Especially pretty at Christmas

32 single graham crackers,
  crushed
2 Tablespoons sugar
⅔ cup butter, softened
1 (15-ounce) can condensed
  milk
1 cup coconut
1 teaspoon vanilla
1 cup mixed candied fruit
½ cup walnuts or pecans

Mix crumbs, sugar and butter as for a pie crust. Pack in an 8-inch square pan reserving ⅓ of crumbs for topping. Bake at 350° for 10 minutes. Mix remaining ingredients and pour on top of crumbs. Sprinkle reserved crumbs on top. Bake at 350° for 20 minutes. This can be made in a food processor.

**Mrs. Charles A. Neubauer**

# Easy Chocolates
Those who don't like coconut don't even know it's in these!

**1 box confectioners sugar**
**½ cup melted butter**
**1 can condensed milk**
**2 cups flaked coconut**
**2 cups chopped pecans**
**12 ounces chocolate chips**
**½ block paraffin**

Combine sugar, butter, milk, coconut and pecans and chill 1 hour. Melt chocolate pieces and paraffin in double boiler over hot, not boiling, water. Roll candy mixture in 1-inch balls; insert toothpick in each. Return to refrigerator for 30 minutes. Dip in chocolate mixture. Remove toothpick. Spoon small amount of chocolate mixture over toothpick hole. Chill and store in refrigerator. Variation: Add an 8-ounce jar of chopped, drained maraschino cherries.

**Linda P. Hightower (Mrs. Charles R.)**

# Divinity Fudge
Constant beating is the secret that makes this Divinity divine

**2 cups sugar**
**½ cup light corn syrup**
**½ cup cold water**
**2 egg whites**
**1 teaspoon vanilla**
**1 cup chopped pecans (more**
    **if you like)**

Mix sugar, syrup and water in saucepan over low heat. Stir only until sugar dissolves, then cook to soft ball stage. Beat egg whites stiff, continue beating and pour half the syrup slowly over the beaten egg whites. While continuing to beat this mixture, cook the rest of the syrup to the hard ball stage. Add this gradually to the syrup and egg white mixture. Add vanilla and continue beating until the candy is thick enough to drop from a spoon. Add the chopped pecans and place by spoonful on a buttered cookie sheet. 3 dozen servings

**Virginia Carson (Mrs. Francis)**

# Caramelized Almonds
For a special touch
sprinkle over ice cream, pumpkin pie or chocolate mousse

**1 cup slivered blanched
   almonds
½ cup sugar**

In a heavy skillet over medium heat, stir sugar and almonds constantly until a light caramel color. Spread on a greased cookie sheet. Break apart when cool. Store in an airtight container.

# Georgia Pralines

**1 cup brown sugar
2 cups granulated sugar
1 cup water
1 Tablespoon butter
¼ teaspoon salt
1 teaspoon vanilla
3 cups pecan halves**

Line baking sheets with waxed paper. In saucepan combine sugars and water. Stir over medium heat until sugars are melted. Bring to boil; boil to soft ball stage (236°F.). Remove from heat; stir in butter, salt and vanilla. Beat until syrup starts to become creamy. Stir in pecans. Drop by teaspoon onto baking sheets. If candy becomes too hard to drop from spoon, place pan over hot water; stir a few drops hot water into mixture to soften. 24 pralines

**JoAnn P. Whitehead (Mrs. Harry C.)**

# Swedish Nuts
This is a lovely Christmas present

**1 pound pecans or combination
   pecans and almonds,
   shelled
3 egg whites
Dash salt
1 cup sugar
½ cup butter**

Toast pecans at 325° until light brown. Beat egg whites with salt until frothy. Add sugar and beat until stiff. Fold in nuts. Melt butter in a 10 x 15 x 1-inch jelly roll pan. Spread nut mixture over butter and bake at 325° for 30 minutes. Stir carefully every 10 minutes until light brown. Cool on paper towels and break into pieces.

# Chinese Party
## MENU

Egg Drop Soup
Boiled Rice
Chicken Wings in Red Sauce
Barbecued Spareribs
Steamed Fish
Cabbage in Cream Sauce with Peanuts
Pears in Ginger Sauce
Almond Cakes
Chinese Tea

Most of this dinner can be prepared in advance. The following schedule will help you have everything ready at the same time and still not be in the kitchen a long time just before serving.

Early in the day or the day before the dinner:
1. Make chicken soup
2. Bake almond cakes.
3. Barbecue spareribs, refrigerate.
4. Make Sweet and Sour Sauce, refrigerate.
5. Buy fish, select serving dish to steam and serve in.
6. Buy pears and fresh ginger root (powdered ginger no substitute).
7. Cook chicken wings and refrigerate.
8. Cut scallions for garnish and refrigerate.
9. Select all serving dishes and utensils.

1 hour before dinner:
1. Wash rice and cook.
2. Clean and cut cabbage into 1 inch pieces.
3. Fry peanuts, set aside with cabbage. Open soup can.
4. Peel and slice pears and pour hot syrup over them.
5. Make cornstarch thickener.
6. Warm chicken wings.
7. Warm ribs and sauce slowly.

15 minutes before serving:
1. Steam fish.

Just before serving:
1. Reheat soup. When boiling add reconstituted cornstarch, egg and transfer to serving tureen. Garnish with chopped scallions.
2. Transfer wings to serving dish.
3. Transfer ribs to platter, mask with sauce; serve extra sauce.
4. Cook cabbage, transfer to serving dish, garnish with peanuts.
5. Rice may be served in casserole it was cooked in or transferred to appropriate serving dish.
6. Put water on for tea, warm tea pot.

Bon Appetit!

# Chicken Egg-Drop Soup

4 cups chicken broth
½ cup finely diced water
   chestnuts
2½ Tablespoons cornstarch
2½ Tablespoons cold water
½ cup green part of scallions,
   cut in ¼ inch pieces
1 egg, slightly beaten

Add water chestnuts to the broth in pan and simmer 1 minute. Mix cornstarch and water together until smooth and stir into soup. Continue stirring until soup thickens. Add scallions. Turn off heat. Slowly pour in beaten egg, stirring gently with chopsticks or fork. Serve at once. This part may be done after soup has been transferred to tureen if service is to occur at dining room table.

It is important to not waste meat, bones, skin and vegetable peelings...a plastic bag in the freezer to "catch" each scrap is practical and this corresponds to the "stock pot" of former years. When a sizeable amount is collected, a very good broth may be made as follows:

Thaw contents of freezer bag and with about 1 quart add 2 quarts water and a slice of ginger root and 2 teaspoons salt. Bring to boil. Cover pan and turn heat to simmer for 15 minutes. Turn off heat and cool in broth...discard "solids", strain broth and refrigerate for future use. Will keep in refrigerator a few days.

# Boiled Rice

1 cup long grain rice, rinsed
1¾ cups cold water

Place rice in a 2 quart saucepan that has a tight lid. Add water. Turn heat to high and bring to hard boil; watch carefully as this probably will take 3-4 minutes. Cover; turn heat to low and simmer for 20 minutes. Remove from heat. Without uncovering pan, let rice relax for another 20 minutes. Stir briskly with chop sticks or fork to loosen rice before serving. 3 cups cooked rice

FOR LARGER QUANTITIES OF RICE: Follow table below. Note that as quantity of rice is increased, proportionately less water is used. Cooking time: Once the rice is brought to a rolling boil, the simmering and the relaxing time is the same, regardless of the amount cooked. Rice triples in volume when cooked.

| Rice | Cold Water | Pan Size |
|------|-----------|----------|
| 2 cups | 3¼ cups | 2 quart |
| 3 cups | 4 cups | 4 quart |
| 4 cups | 5 cups | 4 quart |

Four cups raw rice is about the maximum amount to cook well. If more is needed, use additional pan with desired amount.

# Chicken Wings in Red Sauce

3 or 4 wings per serving,
separated at joints, washed
and dried
2 Tablespoons dry cocktail
sherry
3 Tablespoons soy sauce
(imported)
1 Tablespoon honey
4 slices fresh ginger root
3 scallions or 2 small onions,
cut into 1 inch pieces
4 star anise seeds

Heat 2½ quart saucepan with small amount of cooking oil until very hot. Add chicken wings and coat well with hot oil. Add other ingredients, cover, bring to a boil, reduce heat and simmer for about 1 hour. Stir often. This dish is better made ahead and reheated. Also freezes well.

# Barbecued Spareribs

1 slab (about 2 pounds) fresh,
young spareribs. Have
butcher cut slab in half
lengthwise so ribs are
about 2 inches long
MARINADE:
4 Tablespoons imported soy
sauce
4 Tablespoons hoisin sauce
2 Tablespoons dry sherry
½ teaspoon 5 spice powder
5 Tablespoons honey
1 clove garlic, minced or
pressed

Preparation time: 10 minutes
Marinating time: 2-3 hours (or overnight in refrigerator)
Cooking time: 1 hour 20 minutes (more or less)

Marinade: Mix all ingredients, brush on spareribs on all sides. Place ribs in a large pan and pour over remaining marinade. Set aside 2 or 3 hours at room temperature (or overnight) in the refrigerator.

To cook: Set oven at 375°. Pour water to cover bottom of roasting pan. Place ribs on roasting rack and set over water. Do not let ribs touch water. Place pan on mid rack in oven. After 30 minutes or so, baste with remaining marinade. After 1 hour or so total cooking time, remove from oven and pour off water. Raise temperature to 450°F. Return ribs for 8-10 minutes or until nicely crisp and brown.

To serve: Cut into individual ribs to be eaten with fingers. Pile on serving plate. Serve with Hot Mustard Sauce or Sweet and Sour Sauce.

Note: Once cooked, ribs may be frozen and reheated.

## Steamed Fish

1½ pounds fresh fish, whole,
  fillets or chunks
½ teaspoon shredded fresh
  ginger root
1 scallion, cut in 2 inch pieces
½ teaspoon fermented black
  beans
1 Tablespoon soy sauce
1 Tablespoon dry sherry
1 Tablespoon peanut or corn
  oil

If using a whole fish, clean, wash and dry inside and outside. Put whole fish into a heatproof dish that fits into your steamer. Mix remaining ingredients and pour all over fish and rub some inside. Heat water until boiling and steam for 30 minutes or until done. Do not peek into steamer during steaming process; large, thick pieces may require 5 additional minutes while thin pieces may require less; decide first. Note: Regular salt may be substituted for fermented black beans although some flavor will be lost.

## Cabbage in Cream Sauce with Fresh Peanuts

½ cup fresh, raw peanuts
Oil
1 head cabbage, cut in half
  and then sliced into 1 inch
  square pieces, rinsed and
  drained
Salt and pepper to taste
½ cup chicken broth or water
1 Tablespoon dry cocktail
  sherry
½ can cream of chicken soup

Fry peanuts in a little oil. Drain on paper. In a wok, large skillet or stew pot, measure 2 Tablespoons oil and heat very hot. When oil "ripples" add cabbage all at once and stir to coat with oil. Add salt and pepper. Stir well and add broth or water to make vegetable steam. Cover with lid for 5 seconds. Uncover and stir again. Recover for another 5 seconds. Add sherry and recover for 5 seconds. At this point, cabbage should be crisp-tender. If not, recover for another 5 seconds or so. When crisp-tender, make well in center and add chicken soup mixing well with liquid in pan. Transfer to serving dish and garnish with peanuts.

# Chinese Almond Cakes

¾ cup sugar
1 teaspoon baking powder
½ teaspoon salt
¾ cup softened margarine
1 egg
2 Tablespoons water
2 teaspoons almond extract
2½ cups unbleached flour
42 whole almonds

In a large bowl blend sugar, baking powder, salt, margarine, egg, water and almond extract well. Gently measure flour and gradually add to above mixture. Shape dough into 1 inch balls; place on greased cookie sheet about 2 inches apart. Flatten balls slightly with glass dipped in granulated sugar. Press a whole almond firmly into center of each cookie. Bake at 350° for 8-12 minutes until firm but not brown. Do not overbake. These freeze well.

# Pears in Ginger Sauce

1 cup sugar
2 cups boiling water
5-6 pieces fresh ginger root
4 firm pears

Make syrup using sugar, boiling water and ginger root. Dissolve sugar and let steep for ½ hour. Peel and core pears and slice into glass serving bowl. Discard ginger and pour syrup over pears. Let stand at room temperature until ready to serve. A beautiful garnish is a peeled and sliced Chinese gooseberry (Kiwi Fruit) which may be added just after the syrup.

# Sweet and Sour Sauce

½ scallion, cut in 1-inch pieces
2 green peppers, cut in 1-inch pieces
4 slices canned pineapple, cut into 8 pieces each
12 maraschino cherries
1 carrot, parboiled and cut into 1 inch cubes (optional)
6 Tablespoons catsup
5 Tablespoons vinegar
5 Tablesoons sugar
2 Tablespoons cornstarch
1 cup water

Heat small amount of oil in wok and quickly stir-fry fruit and vegetables; remove from wok and set aside. In a small bowl, mix catsup, vinegar, sugar, cornstarch and water. Heat 4 Tablespoons oil in wok and when hot pour catsup mixture all at once into wok. Stir until sauce thickens. Add fried fruit and vegetables and stir quickly. Transfer to serving bowl or pour over meat that has specially been prepared for Sweet and Sour recipes. Note: If you have leftover jam, preserves or jelly in the refrigerator, try using it in place of sugar in this recipe; also substitute honey or add a few slivers of fresh ginger root and stir-fry along with the other vegetables and fruit.

# Hot Chinese Mustard

2 Tablespoons water
¼ teaspoon vinegar
¼ teaspoon peanut oil
Dry Coleman's mustard

In a very small bowl add water, vinegar and peanut oil. Into this mixture, fold in dry Coleman's mustard until a thin paste forms. The mustard swells, so add a teaspoon at a time; you can always add a drop or two of water if you have too much mustard powder; this keeps sealed in a small jar in refrigerator or add small amounts to your regular mustard to "jazz it up".

**Deen Terry**
*The Chinese Cooking School*
*Atlanta, Georgia*

## Danish Christmas Dinner
# MENU

Pork Roast
Gravy
Brown Potatoes
Red Cabbage
Sweet and Sour Pickles
Danish Rice Pudding

Glaedelig Jul!

Merry Christmas from Denmark!

This is a traditional dinner that has been served on Christmas Eve in my Danish family for generations. It is a Christmas tradition that I now share yearly with my Atlanta friends.

## Pork Roast

**1 (10-15 pound) pork ham with skin left on**

Slice the pork skin with sharp knife in thin slices through the fat. Salt all sides of pork. Cook at 325° for 40 minutes per pound. During cooking pour cold water over roast several times. When finished cooking, before removing from oven, turn temperature up to 400° to brown the rind; this will also make it crisp. Save all the juice and drippings for the gravy.

## Gravy

**4 Tablespoons margarine**
**4 Tablespoons flour**
**Drippings and juice from roast**

Melt butter in saucepan, stir in flour and mix to a paste. Gradually add drippings and juice from roast stirring until smooth. Will require 4 cups of juice at least; if more liquid is needed use cold water. Add salt and pepper if needed, also Kitchen Bouquet for color.

# Brown Potatoes

2 sticks margarine
1 cup sugar
4 cans small white potatoes, drained (1 can per two people)

Melt butter in large frying pan, add sugar, stir and heat until melted and light brown. Add potatoes; simmer for 15-20 minutes turning potatoes as necessary to brown them on all sides with a slight sugar coating.

# Red Cabbage

2 medium heads red cabbage
2 large apples, shredded
1 cup vinegar
2 Tablespoons butter
1 cup sugar
2 cups cranberry juice
2 teaspoons salt

Cut cabbage very fine; mix with shredded apples. Cook cabbage and apples in vinegar and butter for 1½ hours. Add sugar, cranberry juice and salt, adding more sugar or salt if needed. Cook another 30 minutes or until cabbage is done.

This freezes well. Serve as a vegetable with pork roast, Danish meatballs, pork chops, etc. Also excellent cold on an open face sandwich.

# Danish Rice Pudding
### (Christmas Dessert)

1 cup rice
4 cups milk
½ pint heavy cream, whipped
Vanilla
Chopped or sliced almonds
Blueberry sauce or syrup

Cook rice in milk over very low heat until all milk has been absorbed, 20-30 minutes. Cool. This can be prepared ahead of time and stored in the refrigerator. Before serving add the whipped cream, vanilla and almonds. It should be a smooth pudding; if too thick, add a little more milk. Serve with blueberry sauce or syrup. At Christmas we serve it with 1 whole almond in one dessert. The person who finds the almond then receives a prize.

**Winnie R. Goodman (Mrs. James E.)**

# Cold French Buffet

# MENU
Tomates Farcis
Potage Crème d'Asperges
Filet de Boeuf
Legumes pour le Grand Aioli
Peches à la Franz Josef

An elegant buffet, suitable for a luncheon or dinner. Everything may be prepared beforehand, and no rewarming is necessary.

Tomatoes Farcis (stuffed tomatoes)
Potage Creme d'Asperges (cream of asparagus soup)
Filet de Boeuf (fillet of beef)
Legumes, Sauce Aioli (vegetables, garlic mayonnaise)
Peches a la Franz Josef (peaches stuffed with buttercream)

# Tomates Farcis
(Stuffed Tomatoes)
Serve these little hors d'oeuvres with cocktails.
In France, something that can be eaten in a single bite is
called an amuse-gueule, something to "amuse your mouth".

**1 basket cherry tomatoes**
**Herbed cheese, such as**
 **Boursin**
**3 Tablespoons finely chopped**
 **parsley**

Cut a slice from the smooth end of each tomato. With your fingertip, scoop out the seeds. Dip the cut edge into the parsley to make a green rim. Beat the cheese until smooth. Place in a pastry bag fitted with a medium star tip and pipe a rosette of cheese into each tomato. Chill until serving time.

# Potage Crème D'Aspèrges
(Cream of Asparagus Soup)

2 Tablespoons butter
3 Tablespoons flour
1 cup milk
1 small onion, sliced
2 cups chicken stock
1 generous pound fresh
 asparagus
1 cup heavy cream

Add flour to hot melted butter. Cook over low heat 3 minutes. Whisk in the milk and stock. Add the onion. Let this simmer while cooking the asparagus. Wash asparagus. Snap off butt ends. Cut into 2-inch pieces. Place tips loosely in a cheesecloth bag. Place all asparagus in 4 cups salted water that has just come to a rolling boil. Remove tips as soon as they are tender, about 8 minutes. Boil the other pieces about 5 more minutes. Reserve the tips to use as a garnish. Place asparagus stem pieces in the simmering sauce. The asparagus cooking water should now be reduced to about 1¾ cup. Stir this liquid into the sauce. If necessary, continue boiling water until it is reduced enough. Simmer the soup, partially covered, 45 minutes or until asparagus pieces are very soft. Sieve soup through a food mill or a strainer, pressing through all of the tender pulp. This is necessary to eliminate the unpleasant texture of the tougher peels. If you want to purée the soup in a food processor, the asparagus should be peeled below the tips with a vegetable peeler before cooking. Chill soup. Stir in the cream and season to taste before serving. Garnish each serving with a few asparagus tips. 6-7 servings

# Filet De Boeuf
### (Filet of Beef)

**1 beef fillet**
**3 Tablespoons butter**

Trim the beef of all sinews, tough membranes and excess fat. The "chain", the long, thin piece of meat along the side, should be removed. (It may be ground for steak tartare or cut in bits and quickly sautéed.) If desired, lard the fillet using a larding needle and thin strips of pork fat. Tuck the tail end of the fillet under so that the piece of meat is approximately the same thickness along the entire length. This prevents the tail, or thin end, from overcooking. Tie the fillet in several places with kitchen string to insure juiciness and a compact shape. Heat butter in a skillet or shallow roasting pan. Quickly brown the fillet over a fairly high burner heat, turning the fillet to brown on all sides. Place pan in a 475° oven. Cook 20 minutes, turning it occasionally. Cook to an internal temperature of 135° for medium rare. Seven minutes per pound will give you an estimate of time required, but the thermometer is much more accurate. Remove from pan and let rest at least 15 minutes before serving. Season slices with salt and freshly ground pepper. This may be served warm or cool, with or without the aioli sauce.

## Légumes Pour Le Grand Aioli
### (Vegetables, garlic mayonnaise)

**1 bunch broccoli**
**1 head cauliflower**
**1 bunch carrots**

Cut broccoli and cauliflower into flowerets. Peel carrots. If using miniature carrots, leave them whole. Otherwise, cut into julienne strips ½ inch wide and 3-4 inches long. Bring 3 large pots of water to a boil. For every 4 quarts water, add 2 teaspoons salt. Gently boil each vegetable until just tender enough to be pierced with the point of a knife, about 5 minutes for broccoli and 10 minutes for carrots and cauliflower. Drain vegetables and quickly refresh by pouring cold water over them until they are cool to the touch. This locks in the color and stops the cooking. Drain on a towel. Arrange the vegetables on lettuce leaves and serve with the aioli. 6 servings

## Aioli Mayonnaise

This sauce is served with practically anything in the South of France: grilled fish or chicken, fish soup, vegetables. It's easily made in a food processor or blender.

**1 slice bread, crust removed**
**2 Tablespoons white wine**
**vinegar**
**3 large garlic cloves, skinned**
**and crushed well**
**2 egg yolks**
**½ cup olive oil**
**½ cup vegetable oil**
**½ teaspoon salt**

Soak the bread in the vinegar. Chop the crushed garlic in processor bowl. Blend in the bread. Add the egg yolks, 3 Tablespoons of the oil and the salt. Blend 4 seconds. Pour in the remaining oil in a slow steady stream. Taste for seasoning.

# Pêches à la Franz Josef
### (Peaches stuffed with buttercream)

4 peaches
3 egg yolks
Rounded ½ cup sifted
   confectioners sugar
Quick dash of salt
9 Tablespoons soft unsalted
   butter
3 Tablespoons very finely
   chopped almonds (or
   praline powder)
Scant Tablespoon rum,
   Cognac or B & B
GARNISH:
Mint leaves

Drop peaches in pot of boiling water for 15 seconds. Immediately refresh with cold water. Peel and rub all over with lemon or fruit fresh to prevent discoloration. Beat together the yolks, salt, and sugar until light and thick. Beat in half of the butter. Then beat in the remaining butter Tablespoon by Tablespoon. Beat in the nuts, and liqueur to taste. Cut peaches in half. Top with buttercream. Chill if made ahead of time. Take peaches from refrigerator 20 minutes before serving to resoften the buttercream. Top peaches with a mint leaf. 4 servings

**Diane Wilkinson**
*School of Cooking*
*Atlanta, Georgia*

## French Nouvelle Cuisine
## A DINNER MENU FOR 4

Rack of Lamb Provençale
Sweated Vegetables
Onion Soup in the French Manner, Gratineéd
Orange and Onion Salad
Crêpes Normande

A typical Nouvelle Cuisine menu, with fine, fresh ingredients, fast cooking time, without the use of flour, and little preparation time.

## Rack of Lamb Provençale
### (2-3 pound racks are needed to serve 4)

**1 (2½-3 pound) rack of lamb**
**2 cloves garlic, peeled and cut in slivers**
**1 teaspoon rosemary**
**1 teaspoon thyme**
**2-3 Tablespoons olive oil**
**Salt and pepper**
**½ cup white wine**
**½ cup chicken stock**
**SWEATED VEGETABLES:**
**Onions**
**Celery**
**Carrots**
**Salt, pepper, butter**

Scrape bones. Make incisions in lamb with point of knife and insert slivers of garlic. Heat oil in roasting pan, put in lamb, baste and sprinkle with herbs and salt and pepper. Roast, basting often in 375° oven for 1¼ hours or until meat registers 140°F (or rare)

To serve: Tranfer the lamb to platter, decorate chop bones with paper chop frills and keep warm. Lamb may be carved into individual portions in the kitchen before serving. Discard any fat from roasting pan and deglaze pan juices with wine and stock. Bring to boil, simmer 1-2 minutes, strain, taste for seasoning and serve sauce separately.

Sweated Vegetables: Slice vegetables, place in pan with seasoning and butter with wax paper over them. On low heat, cook until tender.

# Onion Soup in the French Manner, Gratinéed

4 Tablespoons butter
2 pounds onion (preferably
Bermuda onion), peeled and
thinly sliced (about 7 cups)
1 teaspoon salt
1 Tablespoon flour
2 quarts brown beef stock,
freshly made or canned; if
you use concentrated
canned type, dilute it with
equal amount of water
Freshly ground black pepper
6-8 one inch slices of French
bread
About 4 ounces Swiss and
imported Parmesan cheese,
freshly grated, mixed.
Should equal 1 cup.

Melt butter over moderate heat in a heavy 5-6 quart casserole. When foaming, add onions and salt. Stirring occasionally, fry them 20-30 minutes, letting onions become a deep rich brown. This will give the soup color and flavor. Don't hurry this, or onions will char and have a particularly unpleasant flavor. Now stir in flour, off heat; return to heat, stirring constantly for a minute or two, then pour in the stock. Bring stock to a boil, stirring until it boils, and reduce heat to a simmer; partially cover casserole, and simmer for 20-30 minutes. Taste for seasoning. You may add considerably more salt than indicated to give the soup more body and flavor. Nothing's worse than undersalted soup, especially onion—this soup is dictated by its stock so if your stock is poor, so will be your soup. Make the croûtes. Preheat oven to 325°. Arrange slices of bread side by side on a baking sheet, then slide it into the upper third of the oven and toast them for about 15 minutes. If you brush them with a good oil or butter, they will add more flavor to the soup.

Variation: Soupe a l'Oignon Soufflé
For 1 quart, make a soufflé mixture with 1 teaspoon butter, 1 teaspoon flour, ¼ cup milk, 1 Tablespoon grated Swiss cheese, salt and white pepper to taste, 2 egg yolks and 2 beaten egg whites. Float this mixture on top of soup in which you have already placed slices of toasted bread. Put in 375° oven for 10 minutes or until soufflé rises and is golden brown.

When you are ready to serve the soup, preheat the oven to 375°. Arrange the croûtes side-by-side on top of the soup, and sprinkle them evenly with cheese. (You may ladle the soup into individual bowls before adding a croûte to each, and sprinkle it with cheese.) Bake soup in middle of oven for 10-15 minutes, or until cheese has melted and formed a light brown crust. If it is not brown enough for your taste, slide casserole or individual bowls under broiler for a few seconds or so to brown tops further. Serve at once.

## Orange and Onion Salad

Boston lettuce, red leaf
    lettuce or Romaine
Naval oranges, peeled and
    sectioned
Red onions, thinly sliced
VINAIGRETTE DRESSING:
¼ cup white wine vinegar with
    tarragon
¾ cup salad oil
Pinch sugar
1 teaspoon salt
Freshly ground pepper

Whisk dressing ingredients to combine, and taste. If too oily, add more salt. Combine lettuce, oranges and onions; toss with dressing. If desired add toasted slivered almonds.

## Crêpes Normandes

8 cooked crêpes
3 tart apples, pared, cored
    and thinly sliced
2 Tablespoons melted butter
½ cup heavy cream
½ cup sugar

Lay 4 crêpes in bottom of 4 heatproof plates. Brush crêpes with melted butter, lay another crêpe on each one and brush again with butter. Put apple slices on top and pour over the cream. Sprinkle generously with sugar and broil for 6-8 minutes or until sugar has caramelized and apples are tender.

**Nathalie Dupree**
*Rich's Cooking School*
*Atlanta, Georgia*

## French Nouvelle Cuisine
# A LUNCHEON MENU FOR 4

Stuffed Tomato Salad with Flounder Goujonnettes
Wholemeal Soda Bread
Profiteroles with Ginger Ice Cream and Raspberry Puree

Some of the elements of Nouvelle Cuisine represented here are the shorter cooking time for the fish and vegetables, the fresh ingredients, the ginger in the ice cream and the overall lightness of the meal. The soda bread, although English, complements the salad nicely.

## Wheatmeal Soda Bread

**2 pounds whole wheat flour**
**(Hodgson Mill)**
**2 teaspoons\* baking soda**
**4 teaspoons\* cream of tartar**
**2 teaspoons\* sugar**
**3 Tablespoons\* butter**
**2 teacups\* (approximately) milk**
**All purpose flour**

**\*when measuring, use**
**tableware instead of**
**regulation measuring spoons**

Mix dry ingredients in a large bowl. Rub in butter with fingers. Add milk to make a soft dough that is firm but sticky. Turn dough onto board that has been sprinkled with enough all-purpose flour to make dough easy to handle. Knead 8-10 times. Shape into a large round. Flour the handle of a wooden spoon and make a deep cross in the dough. Place on a greased baking sheet and bake 25-35 minutes or until done. Serve this moist bread warm with lots of butter.

## Stuffed Tomato Salad with Flounder Goujonnettes

4 medium size, firm tomatoes,
   peeled
12 large shrimp, cooked and
   peeled
2 flounder fillets, cut in
   diagonal strips
16-20 lettuce leaves
2 teaspoons fresh mixed herbs
   (parsley, mint, tarragon),
   chopped
**HERB MAYONNAISE:**
1 egg yolk
Salt and pepper
1 Tablespoon vinegar
½ Tablespoon mustard
⅓ cup vegetable oil
⅓ cup olive oil
1 Tablespoon lemon juice
2 Tablespoons grapefruit juice
1 Tablespoon catsup
2 teaspoons fresh mixed herbs
   (parsley, mint, tarragon),
   chopped

½ pound small snap beans,
   split in half lengthwise
**VINAIGRETTE:**
½ Tablespoon Dijon mustard
1 Tablespoon vinegar
3 Tablespoons oil
Salt and pepper

Tomato Shells: Cut off the top of each tomato, scalloping the edges, to make a cup. With a teaspoon carefully remove the seeds. Sprinkle with salt, turn upside down and leave to drain.

Flounder: Poach the flounder fillets in boiling salted water for 2-3 minutes or until tender but still quite firm to avoid their being broken up when mixed with the mayonnaise. Drain thoroughly and dry on a towel. Cool and mix carefully with herb mayonnaise.

Herb Mayonnaise: Using blender, food processor or mixer, mix yolk, salt and pepper and mustard. Add oil slowly, drop by drop, to incorporate it well. Then mix in other ingredients and taste for herbs and seasonings.

Green Bean Salad: Cook the green beans in a large pan of boiling salted water for about 5-7 minutes or until barely tender. Drain, refresh under cold running water and drain thoroughly. Mix the green beans with enough vinaigrette to moisten.

To assemble: Place the strips of flounder inside the tomatoes, standing up. Decorate with the shrimp by placing them, facing each other, inside the tomato also. On each plate arrange a bed of lettuce leaves. Place the stuffed tomato in the center. Arrange the green bean salad in a wreath around the tomato. Sprinkle the fresh herbs on the flounder.

# Ginger Ice Cream

4 cups milk
10 egg yolks
1½ cups sugar
5 Tablespoons chopped
   candied ginger (can be
   done in food processor)
1-1½ cups heavy cream,
   whipped until it holds a
   soft shape

Bring the milk to a full rolling boil. In another saucepan, beat the egg yolks with the sugar until thick and light. Whisk in all the hot milk slowly—don't whisk too hard or you will get too much foam—and return to heat. Heat gently, stirring constantly with a wooden spoon, until the custard thickens slightly; if you draw your finger across the back of the spoon, it will leave a clear trail. The foam should subside by the time the custard is done. Do not overcook or boil the custard or it will curdle. Remove the custard at once from the heat, strain it into a bowl, and stir in the chopped candied ginger. Let cool and pour into a churn. After about 5 minutes of churning or when the ice cream is partly set, add the lightly whipped cream to the mixture and continue freezing the mixture until set. Remove dasher, taste, and either stir in ginger from bottom of freezer or throw away if ice cream is flavored enough. Serve immediately or replace lid covered with aluminum foil, wrap churn in towels or a blanket, and let ice cream cure. Serve in cream puffs with raspberry or strawberry purée (use blender or food processor to purée fresh berries, sweeten lightly, if necessary).

**Sarah Rhodes**
**Martha Summerour**
*Rich's Cooking School*
*Atlanta, Georgia*

## Hungarian Cookery—A Collection of Recipes

Classic French cookery is believed to have its roots in the famous marriage between the young Italian Catherine De'Medici and a French youth who was to become King Henry II. This sixteenth century nuptial happening has had far reaching culinary reverberations, and historically inclined gourmets tend to agree that Italy, not France is the true cradle of gastronomy. But about 100 years earlier, another country had received the enriching civilized Italian touch, a touch that would begin the development of one of the most exciting and savory cuisines in the world. In 1475, King Matthias of Hungary married an Italian noblewoman, Beatrice, daughter of the King of Naples. Beatrice brought with her, as a sort of culinary dowry, an array of chefs, fine china, cookware, cookery books and exotic ingredients. The wedding feast of Beatrice and Matthias was a study in ultra-sophisticated gastronomic excess. From that day on King Matthias became obsessed with fine food and drink. During the time of his reign Hungary became one of the world's richest and most powerful nations. All the arts were of the utmost importance in the royal court, but the art of cookery provided the greatest pleasures.

During the next century, after the death of the great king, Hungary entered a dark period...the country suffered a long Turkish occupation. This occupational influence brought changes and new dimensions to Hungarian food. The famous Hungarian strudel is a direct descendant of Turkish filo; the Turks eventually introduced two gifts of the new world—paprika and tomatoes—to Hungarian cooks; and Turkish pita bread became Hungarian Langos. The strong Turkish cultural impact on the Hungary of Matthias, which in turn was built on a strong foundation of Magyar cookery techniques, has produced a cuisine of great subtlety and delicacy; a combination of peasant and aristocratic tastes that is unmatched anywhere in the world.

The soul of modern Hungarian cookery is paprika, not the tasteless red dust often used for coloring the top of egg salad, but lovely full flavored Hungarian rose paprika. I buy it several pounds at once from a shop in New York called, appropriately enough, Paprikas Weiss, but it is available in the "gourmet" section of local super markets in little red cans.

The following is a collection of my favorites to share with you in good taste...

## Blueberry Soup*

**2 (10 ounce) packages frozen
  blueberries**
**2 cups water**
**1 lemon, sliced**
**1 cinnamon stick**
**⅓ cup granulated sugar**
**1 cup half and half**
**Fresh blueberries (optional)**

Combine first 5 ingredients in a saucepan. Bring to a boil. Reduce heat and simmer for 10 minutes. Remove lemon and cinnamon stick, and purée soup in the blender. This soup should be very smooth and velvety. Cool, then chill thoroughly in the refrigerator. Just before serving, stir in half and half. If fresh blueberries are in season, garnish each bowlful with a few. 6 servings

## Cold Hungarian Tomato Soup

4 pounds vine ripened tomatoes
2 onions, chopped
½ cup fresh parsley
Slivered zest of ½ lemon
1 Tablespoon sweet Hungarian
   paprika
1 Tablespoon sugar
Salt and freshly ground
   pepper to taste
Juice of 1 lemon
Sour cream

Peel, seed and juice the tomatoes. Chop them coarsely into a large, non metallic pot. Add the onions, parsley, lemon zest, paprika, sugar, salt and pepper. Bring to a simmer and simmer for 5-7 minutes. Stir in the lemon juice. Put the soup into the blender in batches and flick the blender on and off. This soup should be lumpy; not a puree. Pour into a glass bowl and chill. Serve with a dollop of sour cream on top of each bowlful. 6-8 servings

## Stiriai Metelt
(Noodle Pudding)

½ pound wide egg noodles
4 eggs
⅔ cup sugar
1 cup sour cream
Grated rind of 1 lemon
¾ cup yellow raisins
4 Tablespoons butter

Preheat oven to 375°. Cook noodles according to package directions. Meanwhile, beat eggs with sugar. Beat in sour cream. Stir in lemon rind and raisins. Drain noodles. Rinse under hot running water. Place in large bowl and toss with butter. Stir in egg, sour cream mixture. The noodles should be well coated with the mixture. Pour the noodles into an oblong buttered 1½ quart baking dish. Spread them evenly in the dish. Bake for 30-40 minutes, until the top is lightly browned and crispy and the pudding is set. (A knife inserted near the center will emerge clean.) Serve warm.
6 servings

# Bogracs Gulyas
### (Kettle Goulash)

4 Tablespoons bacon fat
5 large onions, chopped coarsely
2 large green peppers,
    chopped coarsely
3 cloves garlic, minced
1½ Tablespoons Hungarian
    Paprika
3 pounds well trimmed stewing
    beef, cut into 1 inch cubes
Salt and freshly ground pepper
    to taste
1 (6 ounce) can tomato paste
Sour cream at room
    temperature

Preheat oven to 325°. Heat fat in a deep heavy pot. Cook the onions, peppers, and garlic until the onions are limp and transparent. Add paprika. Stir over very low heat until vegetables are well coated and paprika has lost its raw taste. Add beef and remaining ingredients except sour cream. Stir well to combine. Simmer in preheated oven for 1½-2 hours or until the meat is tender. Adjust oven temperature during cooking time so contents of pot remain at a simmer. Serve in shallow soup bowls with a tablespoon of sour cream atop each serving.
6 servings

# Erdelyi Zsivanypecsenye
### (Bandit's Meat)

2 pounds well trimmed flank
    steak
Paprika
Salt and freshly ground pepper
½ pound bacon, each slice
    cut in half
1 Tablespoon bacon fat

Slice the flank steak, against the grain, about ¼ inch thick. Spread wax paper over your work surface. Place the beef slices on the paper. Cover with another sheet of wax paper. With a kitchen mallet or the flat side of a wide knife, gently pound the pieces until they are about ⅛ inch thick. Remove top sheet of paper. Sprinkle upper side of each slice with paprika, salt and pepper. Roll each slice into a sausage like shape. Wrap with a bacon slice and secure with a toothpick. Melt bacon fat in a wide, heavy skillet. When sizzling, add the beef rolls and brown quickly on all sides. When browned, pour into a colander over a bowl to drain away all fat. Return rolls to skillet. Cover and cook over very low heat for 10 minutes, shaking pan frequently. Serve at once.
6 servings

# Pork Paprikash*

1 Tablespoon butter
1 Tablespoon corn oil
1 pound mushrooms, trimmed
   and sliced
1 Tablespoon butter
2 Tablespoons corn oil
2 pounds well trimmed pork
   tenderloin, sliced ¼ inch
   thick
Salt and pepper
1 large onion, chopped
1 small clove garlic, minced
1 teaspoon sweet paprika
½ cup dry, white wine
½ cup chicken stock
1 teaspoon Dijon mustard
¼ cup sour cream at room
   temperature
¼ cup half and half at room
   temperature
½ cup fresh, chopped parsley

Heat butter and oil. Sauté the mushrooms in a heavy skillet until just limp. Scrape into a bowl and set aside. Heat remaining butter and oil in the skillet. Sprinkle the pork slices with salt and pepper and add to the skillet. Cook over high heat, turning the slices in the hot oil until browned, about 2 minutes. Add the pork slices to the mushrooms. Add the onions and garlic to the fat remaining in the skillet. Sauté them until the onions are limp and transparent. Add the paprika and stir over low heat until the onions are well coated. Transfer the onions to the bowl with the pork. Add the wine and stock to the skillet and cook over high heat for 3 minutes. Use a wooden spatula or spoon to scrape up any brown bits adhering to the pan. Stir in the mustard. Return the onions, mushrooms and pork to the skillet. Simmer for 5 minutes. Combine the half and half and sour cream. Blend some of the liquid in the pan into the cream. Then stir the mixture back into the pork and mushrooms. Simmer over very low heat for 3-5 minutes, or until tender. Do not boil. Sprinkle with parsley and serve at once.
6 servings

## Green Beans in Sour Cream

2 pounds fresh green beans, trimmed
4 Tablespoons butter
1 large onion, cut in half and thinly sliced info half moons
1 green pepper, cut in half and thinly sliced
1 can plum tomatoes, well drained and chopped
½ cup chopped parsley
½ teaspoon dried basil
Salt and freshly ground pepper to taste
1 Tablespoon flour
1 cup sour cream at room temperature

Steam the beans over boiling water until crisp tender, 7-10 minutes. Rinse under cold water and drain well. Melt butter in a heavy skillet. In it, saute the onion and green pepper until tender. Add tomatoes and cook until they begin to render their juices. Add beans, parsley, basil, salt and pepper. Cook until it is all piping hot. Whisk flour into sour cream. Stir some hot liquid from the skillet into the sour cream, then stir cream mixture into the vegetables in the skillet. Simmer for 5 minutes. Taste and adjust seasonings. Serve at once.
6 servings

## Squash with Sour Cream and Dill*

2 pounds yellow squash, peeled, seeded and cut lengthwise into long thin strips (to seed squash, after peeling, cut in half lengthwise and remove seeds with a teaspoon)
Salt
2 Tablespoons corn oil
2 Tablespoons enriched flour
1 cup sour cream at room temperature
1½ teaspoons white wine vinegar
1 Tablespoon dried dill or 2 Tablespoons fresh snipped dill
Salt and pepper

Sprinkle squash with a generous amount of salt in a glass or enameled bowl. Let stand for 20-30 minutes. Rinse, drain and pat dry. Heat oil, toss squash in oil for about 5 minutes. Squash should still be crisp. With a wire whisk, stir flour into sour cream. Pour over squash and stir. Simmer gently about 5 minutes. Stir in vinegar, dill, salt and pepper. Serve hot. 6 servings

**Susan L. Krietzman**
*Courtesy **The Nutrition Cookbook**
*Harcourt Brace Jovanovitch*

all other recipes
**Susan L. Krietzman**
*In Good Taste School of Cookery
Atlanta, Georgia*

# Ron Cohn's Palacsinta
## (Hungarian Crêpe Dessert)
The carbonated water makes an unusually light crêpe

**CREPES:**
**3 eggs**
**1¼ cups flour**
**1 cup milk**
**1 teaspoon sugar**
**Pinch of salt**
**1 cup carbonated water or**
    **1 cup combination**
    **carbonated water and**
    **cherry liqueur**
**Clarified butter for cooking**
**APRICOT JELLY:**
**12 ounces dried apricots**
**½ cup sugar**
**Brandy or cherry liqueur to**
    **taste**
**TOPPING:**
**½ pound sugar**
**3 egg whites**
**1 cup walnuts, finely ground**

Crepes: Mix flour, milk, sugar and salt to make a smooth pancake like dough. Let rest for 1 or 2 hours. Stir in carbonated water at last minute, just before cooking. Heat 8-inch crêpe pan. When hot, add ¼ teaspoon butter. Pour ladle full of dough into pan, twist to cover entire pan. When top of the batter bubbles turn over and cook 4 or 5 seconds longer. Add more butter for each Palacsinta. Keep warm covered with wax paper. Fill with apricot jelly.

Apricot Jelly: Put dried apricots in saucepan with water to cover, cook over low heat until apricots disintegrate into a jelly. Add liqueur and sugar to taste. Place some jelly across one end of pancake and roll.

Topping: Top with powdered sugar which has been standing with a vanilla bean, or mix topping ingredients until fluffy. Put 2 Tablespoons of this mixture on top of filled Palacsinta and place in broiler until lightly browned.
12-14 crepes

**Ron Cohn**
*Hal's Restaurant*
*Atlanta, Georgia*

## A Family Italian Dinner for Eight
# MENU
Spinach Soup
Baked Fish and Potatoes
Zucchini Frittata
Green Salad
Zuccotto

Italian cooking seeks to procure the best fresh ingredients and preserve their identity. The traditional Italian recipes are mainly derived from homespun creations, rather than from chef and restaurant recipes.

## Spinach Soup

**2 pounds spinach—before
cooking or 2 packages
frozen spinach, thawed
and drained
4 Tablespoons olive oil
2 cloves garlic, crushed
4 Tablespoons flour
8 cups chicken stock (or
canned chicken broth)**

Cook and purée spinach. Heat oil in heavy pan, add crushed garlic and when brown remove. (Watch carefully. The garlic will burn very easily.) Blend in the flour, add puréed spinach and stock; bring to a boil and cook gently for half an hour. Serve with croûtons of toast and grated Parmesan cheese.

# Baked Fish and Potatoes

2 pounds boiling potatoes
¾ cup olive oil (or half salad
  oil and half olive oil)
1 heaping Tablespoon finely
  chopped garlic
⅓ cup chopped parsley
Salt and pepper to taste
8 fish fillets, with skin on
  (Blue fish is superb, but
  any firm-fleshed fish will
  work.) If frozen, thaw before
  using, and dry as much
  as possible

Preheat oven to 450°. Peel potatoes and slice thinly. Wash in cold water and pat dry. (If they are not dry, they have a tendency to "steam-cook".) Mix oil, garlic, parsley, salt and pepper together. Put potatoes into 16 x 10-inch baking dish, pour half of the oil mixture over and mix well. Place the dish in the upper third of the oven. Bake until the potatoes are half-cooked, about 15 minutes. Place fish fillets, skin side down, over the potatoes. Pour remaining oil mixture over the fish, add a sprinkle of salt, and continue baking. After 10 minutes, baste and cook for another 5 minutes. Serve hot, using all of the cooking juices.

# Zucchini Frittata
### (Italian Egg Pancake with Zucchini)

2½ Tablespoons olive oil
1 clove garlic, peeled and
  crushed, but left whole
4 zucchini, sliced ¼ inch thick
Flour
3 Tablespoons minced parsley
½ - ¾ teaspoon salt
⅛ teaspoon pepper
3 Tablespoons butter
10 eggs, lightly beaten
1 teaspoon salt
⅛ teaspoon pepper

Heat oil in large skillet, add garlic and saute 1-2 minutes. Remove. Lightly coat zucchini with flour and stir fry over medium heat until golden, about 8 minutes. Remove oil from skillet and add parsley and salt and pepper. Remove from heat. In 10-12 inch skillet melt butter over high heat. Add eggs and remaining salt and pepper as soon as butter foams. Reduce heat to low and add zucchini mixture. Fry over direct heat, slowly, loosening edges and allowing uncooked portion to run underneath. Also prick with fork to allow uncooked portion to seep to bottom. When all but top is softly set, run under broiler 10-15 seconds. Cut into wedges or cool to room temperature before serving (as is frequently done in Italy). Grated cheese may be added before broiling.

# Zuccotto
(Dome-shaped Florentine Dessert)

1 (12-16 ounce) sponge cake
3 Tablespoons brandy or
    cognac
2 Tablespoons sweet liqueur
3 Tablespoons cointreau
5 ounces semi-sweet chocolate
3 cups cold heavy cream,
    whipped
¾ cup confectioners sugar
¾ cup fruit (Any combination
    of candied and fresh; must
    use some candied. Frozen
    strawberries, crushed and
    drained, may be used for
    some of the fresh fruit.)
4 ounces shelled nuts,
    preferably ½ of which are
    unskinned almonds

Line a 3-quart round bottomed bowl such as Tupperware with damp cheese cloth or spray with Pam. Cut cake into ⅜ inch thick slices. Cut each of these slices on the diagonal, to form 2 triangular sections. Mix all cordials and moisten each cake section and place cake against insides of bowl with narrowest end of sections at bottom. Continue until inside of bowl is completely lined with cake, filling any gaps. Press edges together to completely seal bowl. There will be some cake left; it is to be used later. Whip cream in chilled bowl, adding powdered sugar. Grate chocolate and add to whipped cream; divide into three parts. Assemble by placing a layer of ½ of the fruit, and then ⅓ of the cream; all of the nuts, and the ⅓ of the cream; ½ of the fruit and ⅓ of the cream. This should completely fill the bowl. Trim edges of cake around rim of bowl. Cover and seal top of bowl completely with moistened cake sections. Be sure this is even since this will become the bottom of the finished dessert. Cover with plastic wrap; refrigerate overnight and/or up to two days. May be frozen. To serve: Loosen edges, cover with flat plate, turn over and serve. Do this before serving dinner, if using frozen. Slice as you would any cake.

**Rosellen Amisano**

# Japanese Tempura Dinner

Make dinner a Far Eastern adventure with a crisp Japanese delicacy—tempura. Cover a low table with a bamboo mat and bring in plenty of soft floor pillows. (Plan on no more than six to eight people.) Cooking at the table while guests watch is the heart of the fun: you batter-dip the shrimp and vegetables, then deep-fry in an electric skillet. Serve drained and piping hot in individual baskets. Guests use chopsticks to dunk the tidbits in a trio of condiments.

# Shrimp Tempura
Ice cubes keep the batter well chilled without diluting

**Raw shrimp, peeled and deveined**
**Assorted fresh vegetables: asparagus spears, spinach, green beans, mushrooms, sweet potatoes, parsley**
**Cooking oil**
**1 cup sifted all-purpose flour**
**1 cup ice water**
**1 slightly beaten egg**
**2 Tablespoons cooking oil**
**½ teaspoon salt**
**½ teaspoon sugar**
**TEMPURA CONDIMENTS:**
**Grated fresh gingeroot**
**Equal parts of grated turnip and grated horseradish, mixed**
**½ cup prepared mustard mixed with 3 Tablespoons soy sauce**

Wash and dry shrimp and vegetables thoroughly; slice or cut into strips or bite size pieces, if necessary. Fill electric skillet half full with cooking oil; heat to 360° on deep fat thermometer. To prepare the batter: Combine flour, ice water, egg, the 2 Tablespoons cooking oil, the salt and sugar. Beat just until ingredients are moistened, a few lumps should remain. Stir in 1 or 2 ice cubes. Use immediately. Dip shrimp and vegetables, a few at a time, in cold batter. Fry in hot oil until browned; drain on paper toweling. Serve in individual paper lined baskets.

**Cookbook Committee**

## Jr. League of DeKalb Publications

P.O. Box 183 • Decatur, GA 30031 • 404-377-2973

Please send me_____copies of **PUTTIN' ON THE PEACHTREE**
@ $16.95/copy (Georgia residents add $1.18 sales tax per book).

Please send me_____copies of **PEACHTREE BOUQUET**
@ $14.95/copy (Georgia residents add $1.05 sales tax per book).

Please add $3.00 shipping and handling per book.
Gift wrap available for an additional $2.00 per book.

Enclosed is my check for $_____payable to "JLD Publications"

Ship to: Name:_____

Address:_____

City:_____ State:____ Zip Code:_____

All proceeds from cookbook sales will be returned to the community
through volunteer projects of the Jr. League of DeKalb County. Many thanks!

- - - - - - - - - - - - - - - - - - - - - - - - - - - - - - - - - - - - - - - - - - - - - - - - - -

## Jr. League of DeKalb Publications

P.O. Box 183 • Decatur, GA 30031 • 404-377-2973

Please send me_____copies of **PUTTIN' ON THE PEACHTREE**
@ $16.95/copy (Georgia residents add $1.18 sales tax per book).

Please send me_____copies of **PEACHTREE BOUQUET**
@ $14.95/copy (Georgia residents add $1.05 sales tax per book).

Please add $3.00 shipping and handling per book.
Gift wrap available for an additional $2.00 per book.

Enclosed is my check for $_____payable to "JLD Publications"

Ship to: Name:_____

Address:_____

City:_____ State:____ Zip Code:_____

All proceeds from cookbook sales will be returned to the community
through volunteer projects of the Jr. League of DeKalb County. Many thanks!

Re-Order Additional Copies

I would like to see **PUTTIN' ON THE PEACHTREE** and
**PEACHTREE BOUQUET** in the following stores:

Store: _____

Address: _____

Store: _____

Address: _____

Store _____

Address: _____

Store _____

Address: _____

- - - - - - - - - - - - - - - - - - - - - - - - - - - - - - - - - - - - - - - - - - - - - - - - - - - - - - - - - - - - - - - - - - - - -

I would like to see **PUTTIN' ON THE PEACHTREE** and
**PEACHTREE BOUQUET** in the following stores:

Store: _____

Address: _____

Store: _____

Address: _____

Store _____

Address: _____

Store _____

Address: _____